VOLUME

Willmington's Notes on
NEW TESTAMENT:
Acts to Revelation

Liberty Bible Institute
Accelerated Learning Program

Dr. Harold Willmington

LBI Press
An Imprint of Publishers Solution

ISBN: 978-1-937925-14-7

© 2008, 2011, 2012, 2013 by Harold L. Willmington and Internet Marketing Communications, LLC. All rights reserved.

Scriptures, unless otherwise noted, are from the King James Version of the Bible.

Scriptures quotations marked NIV are from the Holy Bible, New International Version®. Copyright ©1973, 1978, 1984 International Bible Society. Used by permission of Zondervan Bible Publishers. NIV and New International Version trademarks are registered in the United States Patent and Trademark Office by International Bible Society.

Scripture quotations marked TLB are taken from The Living Bible, copyright © 1971 owned by assignment by KNT Charitable Trust. All rights reserved.

Scripture quotations marked NASB are from the New American Standard Bible, copyright ©1960, 1962, 1963, 1968, 1971, 1972, 1973, 1975, 1977 by The Lockman Foundation. Used by permission.

Scripture quotations marked NLT are taken from the Holy Bible, New Living Translation, copyright 1996. Used by permission of Tyndale House Publishers, Inc., Wheaton, Illinois 60189. All rights reserved.

LBI PRESS
AN IMPRINT OF PUBLISHERS SOLUTION

www.PublishersSolution.com

14805 Forest Rd., Suite 205
Forest, VA 24551
www.LHBIonline.com/press

Cover & Interior Design by the Publishers Solution Design Team

The Bible

The Bible is a beautiful palace built up out of sixty-six blocks of solid marble—the sixty-six books. In the first chapter of **Genesis** we enter the vestibule, which is filled with the mighty acts of creation. The vestibule gives access to the law courts—**the five books of Moses**—passing through which we come to the picture gallery of the **historical** books. Here we find hung upon the walls scenes of battlefields, representations of heroic deeds, and portraits of eminent men belonging to the early days of the world's history.

Beyond the picture gallery we find the philosophy's chamber—book of **Job**—passing thru which we enter the music room—the book of **Psalms**—where we listen to the grandest strains that ever fell on human ears. Then we come to the business office—the book of **Proverbs**—where right in the center of the room, stands facing us the motto, "Righteousness exalteth a nation, but sin is a reproach to any people." From the business office we pass into the chapel—**Ecclesiastes**, and the **Song of Solomon** with the Rose of Sharon and the Lily of the Valley, and all manner of fine perfume and fruit and flowers and singing birds.

Finally we reach the observatory—the **Prophets**, with their telescopes fixed on near and distant stars, and all directed toward "the Bright and Morning Star," that was soon to arise. Crossing the court we come to the audience chamber of the King—the **Gospels**—where we find four vivid life-like portraits of the King Himself. Next we enter the work-room of the Holy Spirit—the **Acts** of the Apostles—and beyond that the correspondence-room—the **Epistles**—where we see Paul and Peter and James and John and Jude busy at their desks, and if you would know what they are writing about, their epistles are open for all to study. Before leaving we stand a moment in the outside gallery—the **Revelation**—where we look upon some striking pictures of the judgments to come, and the glories to be revealed, concluding with an awe-inspiring picture of the New Jerusalem when the kingdoms of this world shall have become the kingdoms of our God and of His Christ!

Contents

One: HISTORY 1
- **Lesson 16**: *Acts—Part 1* 3
- **Lesson 17**: *Acts—Part 2* 19
- **Lesson 18**: *Acts—Part 3* 29
- **Lesson 19**: *Acts—Part 4* 37
- **Lesson 20**: *Acts—Part 5* 45

Two: LETTERS BY PAUL TO THE CHURCHES 53
- **Lesson 21**: *Romans—Part 1* 55
- **Lesson 22**: *Romans—Part 2* 73
- **Lesson 23**: *Romans—Part 3* 83
- **Lesson 24**: *First Corinthians—Part 1* 93
- **Lesson 25**: *First Corinthians—Part 2* 109
- **Lesson 26**: *First Corinthians—Part 3* 117
- **Lesson 27**: *Second Corinthians* 131
- **Lesson 28**: *Galatians* 147
- **Lesson 29**: *Ephesians* 159
- **Lesson 30**: *Philippians* 173
- **Lesson 31**: *Colossians* 185
- **Lesson 32**: *First Thessalonians* 195
- **Lesson 33**: *Second Thessalonians* 207

Three: LETTERS BY PAUL TO INDIVIDUALS 217
- **Lesson 34**: *First Timothy—Part 1* 219
- **Lesson 35**: *First Timothy—Part 2, Second Timothy, and Titus* ... 231
- **Lesson 36**: *Philemon and GENERAL LETTERS: Hebrews—Part 1* ... 247

Four: GENERAL LETTERS 253
- **Lesson 37**: *Hebrews—Part 2* 267
- **Lesson 38**: *James* 279
- **Lesson 39**: *First Peter* 289
- **Lesson 40**: *Second Peter* 303

- **Lesson 41**: *First, Second, and Third John* 313
- **Lesson 42**: *Jude* 335

Five: PROPHECY 345

- **Lesson 43**: *Revelation—Part 1* 347
- **Lesson 44**: *Revelation—Part 2* 365
- **Lesson 45**: *Revelation—Part 3* 379

One: HISTORY

An examination of the history of the early Church:

> Acts

LESSON 16
INTRODUCTION TO ACTS

THE BIRTH OF THE BRIDE
A TREMENDOUS TALE OF GROWING, GLOWING, AND GOING FOR GOD

Preface:

The Book of Acts is in reality a letter written by Luke.

The person to whom Luke wrote—*"The former treatise have I made, O Theophilus..."* (1:1a). Luke writes his second letter to Theophilus. His first one (the Gospel of Luke) was written to tell what Christ did while on earth through his physical body (see Luke 1:1-4). His second letter (the Book of Acts) was written to tell what Christ was doing while in heaven through his spiritual body, the church. He begins by reminding Theophilus *"of all that Jesus began both to do and teach"* (1:1). This, of course, was in stark contrast to the wicked Pharisees, who, according to the Savior, *"say, and do not"* (Matt. 23:3). Luke speaks of the *"many infallible proofs"* which surrounded the resurrection ministry. During that time our Lord appeared at least 10 different times to his followers.

The person of whom Luke wrote—*"Of all that Jesus began both to do and teach, until the day in which he was taken up, after that he through the Holy Ghost had given commandments unto the apostles whom he had chosen: To whom also he shewed himself alive after his passion by many infallible proofs, being seen of them forty days, and speaking of the things pertaining to the kingdom of God: And, being assembled together with them, commanded them that they should not depart from Jerusalem, but wait for the promise of the Father, which, saith he, ye have heard of me. For John truly baptized with water; but ye shall be baptized with the Holy Ghost not many days hence"* (Acts 1:1b-5).

  A. Interesting Facts About the Book
   1. The book of Acts is the true story relating the first 30 years of the early church. In many ways it is the highmark of Christian witness.
   2. The action centers around two great "crusades," the Greater Jerusalem Crusade (Acts 1-12) headed up by Peter, and the Global Crusade (Acts 13-28), led by Paul.
   3. The associates involved in their campaigns were John the apostle, Stephen, Philip, Barnabas, Silas, Timothy, and Luke. The record tells us of the first:
      a. Deacons—Philip, Stephen, et al (6:1-5)
      b. Martyrs—Stephen, James (7:60; 12:2)
      c. Missionaries—Paul, Barnabas, Silas (13:1-3; 15:40)
      d. Evangelists—Philip, Apollos (8:5,26; 18:24-28)
   4. The book of Acts is in reality a fulfillment of John 15:26-27. *"But when the Comforter is come, whom I will send unto you from the Father, even the Spirit of truth, which proceedeth from the Father, he shall testify of me: And ye also shall bear witness, because ye have been with me from the beginning."*
   5. Believers were first called Christians during this time (11:26).
   6. The preaching of the gospel is viciously attacked by the devil when he attempted to:
      a. Ban it—The Jewish religious leaders (4:18; 5:28)

  b. Buy it—Simon the sorcerer (8:9-11, 18-19)
  c. Bury it—Saul of Tarsus (9:1-2)
  d. Bridle it—The legalists (15:1)
  e. Blur it—The demon-possessed girl (16:16-18)
  f. Belittle it—The Stoics and Epicureans (17:18-21, 32)
  g. Blaspheme it—Demetrius the silversmith (19:24-34)
7. Both angels and demons are seen in action. An angel protects an apostle (Peter, 12:7-8) and plagues a king (Herod, 12:23). Demons possess sorcerers (8:9; 13:6-10), damsels (16:16-18), and vagabonds (19:13-16).
8. Both revivals (19:18-20) and riots break out (19:28-34).
9. The book of Acts lists three significant conversions.
  a. The eunuch (8:36-38), a descendant of Ham (Gen. 10:6-20)
  b. Saul (9:1-6), a descendant of Shem (Gen. 10:21-31)
  c. Cornelius (10:44-48), a descendant of Japheth (Gen. 10:2-5). The convert number jumps from 120 (1:15) to 3,120 (2:41), to 8,120 (4:4), to untold multitudes (5:14).
10. Acts provides for us the final two of five of the most famous New Testament sermons.
  a. The Sermon on the Mount (Matt. 5-7)
  b. The sermon on the kingdom of heaven (Matt. 13)
  c. The sermon on the second coming (Matt. 24-25)
  d. The sermon at Pentecost (Acts 2)
  e. The sermon on Mars Hill (Acts 17)
11. In fact, an outstanding feature of the book of Acts is the number of speeches and sermons. No less than 24 messages are found in its 28 chapters.
12. The book opens with Peter preaching in Jerusalem, the Jewish religious capital, and ends with Paul preaching in Rome, the Gentile political capital (2:14; 28:31).
13. Paul preached before prison keepers (16:25-34), philosophers (17:16-31), Pharisees (23:6), and potentates (24:24-25; 26:24-28).
14. The ministry of prayer plays an all-important role in Acts.
  a. The prayers of the apostles
    (1) In the Upper Room (1:14, 24)
    (2) Following Pentecost (2:42)
    (3) In the hour of persecution (4:23-30)
    (4) Upon ordaining the deacons (6:6)
  b. The prayers of Peter and John
    (1) In the temple (3:1)
    (2) At Samaria (8:15)
  c. The prayers of Peter
    (1) At Joppa, at the raising of Dorcas (9:40)
    (2) At Joppa, resulting in his vessel vision (10:9)
  d. The prayer of Cornelius at Caesarea (10:4)
  e. The prayer of the Jerusalem church for Peter (12:12)
  f. The prayer of the Antioch church upon ordaining Saul and Barnabas (13:3)
  g. The prayers of Paul and Barnabas for the churches founded during their missionary journey (14:23)
  h. The prayers of Paul and Silas
    (1) At Philippi, by a riverside (16:13)
    (2) At Philippi, inside a prison (16:25)
  i. The prayers of Paul
    (1) In Damascus following his conversion (9:11)

        (2) In Jerusalem (22:17)
        (3) In Miletus (20:36)
        (4) In Tyre (21:5)
        (5) On the Isle of Melita (28:8)
  15. The books of Luke and Acts may be favorably compared.
     a. Both were written by the same author, Luke.
     b. Both were written to the same individual, Theophilus.
     c. Luke is the longest New Testament book.
     d. Acts is the second longest New Testament book.
     e. Luke records the birth of the Son of God.
     f. Acts records the birth of the Church of God.
     g. Luke tells us what the Father began to do through the body of his Son (the Savior).
     h. Acts tells us what the Father continued to do through the body of his Spirit (the saints).
  16. Acts 2 and Genesis 11 may be instructively compared.
     a. In Genesis 11 human language was confused by God.
     b. In Acts 2 human language was clarified by God.
     c. In Genesis 11 the builders are seen working for human glory.
     d. In Acts 2 the believers are seen waiting for God's glory.
  17. Acts lists two of nine famous biblical teams.
     a. Moses and Aaron (Exod. 5:1)
     b. Joshua and Caleb (Num. 14:6-9)
     c. Elijah and Elisha (1 Kings 19:19-21)
     d. Zerubbabel and Joshua (Ezra 3:2)
     e. Haggai and Zechariah (Ezra 5:1)
     f. Ezra and Nehemiah (Neh. 8:9)
     g. Peter and John (Luke 22:7; Acts 3:1)
     h. Paul and Barnabas/Silas (Acts 13:2; 15:40)
     i. Elijah and possibly Moses (Rev. 11:3-12)

B. Acts—A Book of Firsts and Lasts
  1. In essence, the following may be said about the book of Acts.
     a. It is a bridge book, which leads across the gap between the Gospel accounts and the epistles.
     b. We read of several "firsts" and "finals" in Acts.
        (1) First (in the Bible)
           (a) First example of tongue speaking (2:1-4)
           (b) First official religious and political persecution of believers (4:3, 18; 5:17-18, 40)
           (c) First practice of communism (2:44-47). Note: This is a far cry from communism. The first says, *"What is mine is thine,"* while the second says, *"What is thine is mine."*
           (d) First example of sin unto death (5:1-11)
           (e) First church election of deacons (6:5-6)
           (f) First Christian martyr—Stephen (7:59)
           (g) First apostolic martyr—James (12:2)
           (h) First view of the ascended Savior (7:55-56)
           (i) First missionary journey (13:2-4)
        (2) Finals (in the Bible)

(a) Final appearance of God's glory cloud (1:9)
(b) Final mention of Mary (1:14)
(c) Final listing of the 12 apostles (1:13)
(d) Final casting of lots (1:26). Other instances include: to choose the scapegoat (Lev. 16:8); to divide the land (Josh. 18:10); to obtain Christ's garment (Matt. 27:35).

2. Three of the greatest evangelistic meetings in the New Testament were conducted in Acts.
   a. The meeting at Pentecost (2:41)
   b. The meeting in Samaria (8:5-8)
   c. The meeting in Ephesus (19:18-20)
3. Acts 10 is the greatest example showing how God arranges those circumstances to bring together a seeking sinner and a soul winner.
4. Acts 12 gives us the most dramatic New Testament account of an angel ministering to a believer.
5. Acts 15 describes the most important church council ever held.
6. Acts 16 records the most important New Testament vision (vv. 9-10).
7. Acts 16 presents the most dramatic conversion of a Gentile in the Bible (vv. 22-34).
8. Acts 20 records for us the most touching farewell address in the New Testament.
9. Acts 24:25 records one of the saddest responses to the gospel message in the Bible. Compare with Luke 18:23.
10. Acts 27 describes possibly the most severe ocean storm since the great flood.
11. There are quotations or allusions in Acts from 25 Old Testament books. Acts is the second longest New Testament book and 14th longest biblical book, with 28 chapters, 1,007 verses, and 24,250 words.
12. Great passages would include:
    a. 1:8
    b. 1:11
    c. 2:17-21
    d. 2:37-38
    e. 2:41-47
    f. 3:6
    g. 4:11-12
    h. 4:33
    i. 5:29
    j. 7:54-55
    k. 9:3-6
    l. 10:34-35
    m. 15:15-18
    n. 16:30-31
    o. 17:31
    p. 20:35
    q. 24:24-25
    r. 26:28

Overview of the Book of Acts

Part One: The Holy Land, Greater Jerusalem Crusade
Headed by Peter the fisherman; assisted by John, Stephen, and Philip (Acts 1-12)

I. The Activities of Peter
  A. Peter and the 120
   1. On the Mount of Olives
   2. In the Upper Room
  B. Peter and the crowd at Pentecost
   1. The cloven tongues
   2. The congregation
   3. The confusion
   4. The clarification
   5. The comparison
   6. The condemnation
   7. The conclusion
   8. The conviction
   9. The command
   10. The challenge
   11. The conversions
   12. The communion
  C. Peter and the lame man
   1. The miracle
   2. The message
  D. Peter and the high priest Annas
   1. The reason for the arrest
   2. The evidence supporting the arrest
   3. The dialogue in the arrest
   4. The conference during the arrest
   5. The warning accompanying the arrest
   6. The praise service following the arrest
   7. The blessings resulting from the arrest
  E. Peter and Ananias and Sapphira
   1. The couple's deception
   2. Their discovery
   3. Their deaths
  F. Peter and the sick
  G. Peter and the lawyer Gamaliel
   1. The anger of the Sadducees

        2. The appearance of the Lord
        3. The astonishment of the jailors
        4. The accusation of the council
        5. The address of the apostles
        6. The advice of Gamaliel
        7. The attitude of the apostles
    H. Peter and Simon the Sorcerer
        1. The pride of Simon
        2. The popularity of Simon
        3. The pretense of Simon
        4. The perversion of Simon
        5. The problem of Simon
        6. The plea of Simon
    I. Peter and Aeneas
        1. The misery
        2. The miracle
    J. Peter and Dorcas
        1. The deeds of Dorcas
        2. The death of Dorcas
        3. The deliverance of Dorcas
    K. Peter and Cornelius
        1. Cornelius, a religious sinner in Caesarea
        2. Peter, a reluctant soul winner in Joppa
        3. Peter and Cornelius, redeemed saints in Christ
    L. Peter and the Jewish believers at Jerusalem
        1. The accusation
        2. The argumentation
        3. The acceptance
    M. Peter and the angel of the Lord
        1. The angel in a prison
        2. The angel in a palace
    N. Peter and the Jerusalem Council
        1. His comments
        2. His caution
        3. His conclusion

II. The Activities of Stephen
    A. The complaint of the leaders
    B. The conference of the leaders
        1. Their dilemma
        2. Their decision
        3. Their dedication
    C. The choice of the laborers
        1. The individuals
        2. The installation
        3. The increase

D. The champion of the Lord
   1. The maturity of Stephen
   2. The miracles of Stephen
   3. The maligning of Stephen
   4. The meekness of Stephen
   5. The message of Stephen
   6. The martyrdom of Stephen

III. The Activities of Philip
   A. The deacon in Jerusalem
   B. The evangelist in Samaria
      1. His message
      2. His miracles
   C. The soul winner in Gaza
      1. His message from an angel
      2. His ministry to a eunuch
   D. The family man in Caesarea
      1. The visitors to Philip's home
      2. The virgins in Philip's home

Part Two: The Whole Earth, Global Crusade

Headed up by Paul, the tentmaker; assisted by Barnabas, Silas, Timothy, Mark, and Luke

I. The Conversion of Paul
   A. His vendetta against the saints of God
      1. Luke's official account of this vendetta
      2. Paul's personal account of the vendetta
   B. His vision of the Son of God
      1. What he saw
      2. What he heard
   C. His visitation by a servant of God
      1. Ananias and God
      2. Ananias and Saul

II. The early Ministry of Paul
   A. Preaching in the Damascus synagogues
      1. The message
      2. The marvel
   B. Retiring to the Arabian desert for a period of several years
   C. Returning to Damascus with greater knowledge and preaching power
   D. Escaping from Damascus
      1. Why he escaped
      2. How he escaped
   E. Visiting Jerusalem for the first time since his conversion
      1. The duration of this visit

2. The difficulties during this visit
F. Escaping from Jerusalem and settling in Tarsus
 1. The plot to destroy Paul
 2. The plan to deliver Paul
G. Joining Barnabas in the work at Antioch
 1. The origin of the Antioch church
 2. The overseers in the Antioch church
H. Visiting Jerusalem for the second time carrying a love offering for the needy there
 1. The messages from the Spirit of God directing the visit
 2. The meeting with the saints of God during the visit
I. Returning to Antioch to preach and teach the word

III. The First Missionary Journey of Paul
A. First stop, Cyprus
 1. Preaching at Salamis, the island's eastern city
 2. Preaching at Paphos, the island's western city
B. Second stop, Perga
C. Third stop, Antioch in Pisidia
 1. His first sermon
 2. His second sermon
D. Fourth stop, Iconium
 1. The revival
 2. The riot
E. Fifth stop, Lystra
 1. The cripple
 2. The cure
 3. The commotion
 4. The confusion
 5. The corruption
 6. The consternation
 7. The correction
 8. The condemnation
 9. The confirmation
F. Sixth stop, back to Antioch in Syria

IV. The Jerusalem Council, attended by Paul
A. The reason for the council
B. The reports given in the council
 1. Peter's report
 2. Paul's report
 3. James' report
C. The recommendation of the council
 1. Concerning the messengers who carried their recommendation
 2. Concerning the message contained in their recommendation
D. The return following the council

V. The Disagreement between Paul and Barnabas
   A. The background of the disagreement
   B. The blessing from the disagreement

VI. The Second Missionary Journey of Paul
   A. First stop, Lystra
      1. The choosing of Timothy
      2. The circumcising of Timothy
   B. Second stop, Troas
      1. Forbidden by the Holy Spirit to go north or south
      2. Bidden by the Holy Spirit to go west
   C. Third stop, Philippi
      1. The salvation of a business woman
      2. The salvation of a demoniac girl
      3. The salvation of a prison keeper
   D. Fourth stop, Thessalonica
      1. The faithfulness of Paul
      2. The fruits of Paul
      3. The foes of Paul
   E. Fifth stop, Berea
      1. The openness to God's Word
      2. The opposition to God's Word
   F. Sixth stop, Athens
      1. The need for this sermon
      2. The audience of this sermon
      3. The introduction to this sermon
      4. The text of this sermon
      5. The points in this sermon
      6. The reaction to this sermon
   G. Seventh stop, Corinth
      1. Paul's friends in this city
      2. Paul's foes in this city
      3. Paul's fruits in this city
      4. Paul's heavenly Father in this city
   H. Eighth stop, Ephesus
      1. He is accompanied by his friends Aquilla and Priscilla
      2. He is asked by his converts to dwell in Ephesus
   I. Final stop, back to Antioch

VII. The Third Missionary Journey of Paul
   A. First stop, Asia Minor
   B. Second stop, Ephesus
      1. The forerunner of Paul in Ephesus
      2. The fruits of Paul in Ephesus

  C. Third stop, Greece
  D. Fourth stop, Troas
    1. The midnight address
    2. The midmorning accident
    3. The miraculous awakening
  E. Fifth stop, Miletus
    1. He reviews the past
    2. He views the present
    3. He previews the future
  F. Sixth stop, Tyre
    1. A message from the Spirit
    2. A meeting on the sand
  G. Seventh stop, Ptolemais
  H. Eighth stop, Caesarea
    1. The warrior of God
    2. The women of God
    3. The warning from God
    4. The will of God

VIII. The Final Visit to Jerusalem by Paul
  A. The rumors against Paul
    1. That he had denounced the Law of Moses
    2. That he had desecrated the temple of God
  B. The reaction by Paul
  C. The rescue of Paul
  D. The replies by Paul
    1. His replies to the chief captain
    2. His reply to the Jewish mob
    3. His reply to the Sanhedrin
  E. The revelation to Paul
  F. The revenge against Paul
  G. The relative of Paul
    1. Overhearing the plot against his uncle
    2. Overturning the plot against his uncle
  H. The removal of Paul
    1. The soldiers
    2. The salutation

IX. The Imprisonment of Paul in Caesarea
  A. Paul before Felix
    1. Felix reviews a lawsuit against Paul
    2. Felix refuses a lecture delivered by Paul
    3. Felix requests some lucre (money) from Paul
  B. Paul before Festus
    1. Festus and the plotters

        2. Festus and the prisoner
    C. Paul before Agrippa
        1. Learning about Paul
        2. Listening to Paul

X. The Voyage of Paul to Rome
    A. Phase one—From Caesarea to Fair Havens
        1. Julius' kindness to Paul
        2. Paul's caution to Julius
    B. Phase two—From Fair Havens to Melita
        1. The fearful storm
        2. The cheerful saint
    C. Phase three—At Melita
        1. Paul and the people
        2. Paul and Publius
    D. Phase four—From Melita to Rome
    E. Phase five—At Rome
        1. The two meetings
        2. The two years

THE BOOK OF ACTS

PART ONE: The Holy Land, Greater Jerusalem Crusade
Headed by Peter the fisherman; assisted by John, Stephen, and Philip (Acts 1-12)

> **I. The Activities of Peter**
>   A. Peter and the 120 (Acts 1:1-26)
>   1. On the Mount of Olives (Acts 1:1-12)
>   a. Receiving the assurance from Christ
>   (1) The confusion *(Read Acts 1:6)*

✷ **1:6** The disciples' question here was in direct response to Jesus' prophecy in 1:5 that they would soon be baptized with the Holy Spirit. Stanley Toussaint writes: "In the disciples' minds the outpouring of the Holy Spirit and the coming of the promised kingdom were closely associated. And well they should be, because the Old Testament frequently joined the two (cf. Isa. 32:15-20; 44:3-5; Ezek. 39:28-29; Joel 2:28-3:1; Zech. 12:8-10). When Christ told the disciples of the soon-coming Spirit baptism, they immediately concluded that the resurrection of Israel's kingdom was near in time" (*Bible Knowledge Commentary*, New Testament edition, p. 354).

>   (2) The commission *(Read Acts 1:7-8)*

✷ **1:8**
- We note that they were to be witnesses—not potentates, or psychologists, or promoters—but witnesses.
- This verse is actually a table of contents and divine outline for the entire book of Acts. Note:
    - Witnessing in Jerusalem (Acts 1-7)
    - Witnessing in Judea and Samaria (Acts 8-12)
    - Witnessing unto the uttermost part of the earth (Acts 13-28)

>   b. Witnessing the ascension of Christ
>   (1) The action involved *(Read Acts 1:9)*

✷ **1:9** When he had spoken these words, our Lord was taken up by God's shekinah glory cloud. This marks the seventh of at least nine appearances of this dazzling and divine cloud. Note that it appeared:
- To Israel en route to Palestine (Exod. 13:21; 14:19-20)
- Over the tabernacle holy of holies (Lev. 16:2)
- Over the temple holy of holies (2 Chron. 5:13-14)
- In Ezekiel's time (Ezek. 10)
- At the birth of Christ (Luke 2:9-11)
- At his transfiguration (Matt. 17:5)
- Here at this ascension (Acts 1:9)
- It will appear next at the Rapture (1 Thess. 4:17)
- It will appear again during his second coming (Matt. 24:30).

>   (2) The attendants involved *(Read Acts 1:10)*

(3) The announcement involved *(Read Acts 1:11)*

✶ **1:11** These two individuals may have been heavenly men (like Moses and Elijah; see Matt. 17:3) or angels (see Luke 24:4; John 20:12). At any rate, we are told several things concerning his return:

- ■ The going was personal, and so shall the return be (1 Thess. 4:16).
- ■ The going was visible, and so shall the return be (Phil. 3:21).
- ■ The going was from the Mount of Olives, and so shall the return be (Zech. 14:4).

2. In the Upper Room (Acts 1:13-26)

a. The prayer meeting *(Read Acts 1:13-14)*

✶ **1:14**

- ■ The 11 apostles return to Jerusalem where they join an assembly of believers totaling 120 in a large upper room. This was probably the same upper room where the Last Supper was held (Luke 22:12); and where Jesus appeared to them after his resurrection (John 20:19, 26). It may have been the home of John Mark's mother. (See Acts 12:12.) We are not to believe, however, that the number of disciples was limited at that time to 120 (see 1 Cor. 15:6).
- ■ We are told that *"these* [120] *all continued with one accord in prayer and supplication"* (1:14). The words "with one accord" come from a single Greek word, homothumadon, meaning "like mindedness." It is used 12 times in the Greek New Testament, and 11 instances are found in the book of Acts. This word was a favorite with both the people of God and people of Satan.
  - ● As used by God's people (2:1; 2:46; 4:24; 5:12; 15:25)
  - ● As used by Satan's people (7:57; 12:20; 18:12; 19:29)
- ■ We note, then, that the early believers acted with one accord in matters of:
  - ● Supplication (1:14)
  - ● Expectation (2:1)
  - ● Communication (2:46)
  - ● Consecration (4:24)
  - ● Separation (5:12)
  - ● Cooperation (15:25)
- ■ Among the 120 were *"the women, and Mary, the mother of Jesus, and ... his brethren"* (1:14). Note:
  - ● The women—A reference to those godly women who had followed Jesus from Galilee. These would include (among many others):
    - ✦ Joanna, the wife of Herod's steward (Luke 8:3)
    - ✦ Mary and Martha (John 11)
    - ✦ Mary, the mother of James the Less (Mark 15:40)
    - ✦ Mary Magdalene (Mark 16:9)
    - ✦ Salome (Mark 15:40)
    - ✦ Susanna (Luke 8:3)
  - ● Mary, the mother of Jesus (Acts 1:14)—This is the final mention of Mary in the Bible.
  - ● His brethren—These were Jesus' half brothers (Matt. 13:55; Mark 6:3), who had been unbelievers during his earthly ministry (John 7:3-5) but were now believers. Two of these are thought to have written the New Testament epistles of James and Jude, which bear their names.

b. The business meeting (Acts 1:15-26)

(1) Concerning the defection of Judas *(Read Acts 1:15-20)*

✶ **1:20**
- During the prayer meeting Simon Peter discusses the defection and death of Judas, which required the election of a new apostle to take his place (1:15-26).
  - Peter quotes two Old Testament passages to show that the apostasy of Judas demands his replacement. Psalm 69:25 predicted his removal, and 109:8 his replacement. Jesus had already related Judas to Psalm 41:9 (John 13:18-19).
  - It should be noted, however, that it was the defection of Judas and not his death that caused the replacement. No effort was made later to replace the martyred apostle James (see Acts 12:2).
- The account of Judas's violent end in 1:18— *"He burst asunder in the midst and all his bowels gushed out,"* seems to contradict Matthew 27:5, which starkly says he "hanged himself." Stanley Toussaint observes: "One explanation is that Judas' intestines quickly became swollen and distended after he hanged himself, so he burst open. Another explanation, more probable, is that Judas hanged himself over a cliff and the rope or branch of the tree he was using broke. When he fell to the rocks below, he burst open" (Bible Knowledge Commentary, New Testament edition, p. 356).

> (2) Concerning the election of Matthias *(Read Acts 1:21-26)*

✶ **1:26**
- There were two requirements concerning the replacement.
  - Peter The man had to have been a follower of Christ throughout his ministry, and not a recent convert (see John 15:27).
  - He had to have been a witness to the resurrection.
- At this point, two questions have been asked:
  - Was the method of the election appropriate? We are told the disciples *"gave forth their lots"* (1:26). How was this carried out? Dr. Charles Ryrie writes: "The two names were put on lots, placed in an urn, and then the one which first fell from the urn was taken to be the Lord's choice" (The Acts of the Apostles, p. 16). This method was in perfect harmony with Old Testament practice. The high priest used this method to choose the scapegoat (Lev. 16:8); and, later, to divide the land of Palestine among the tribes (Num. 26:55).
  - Was the election itself correct? There are those who would say it was in error, that God apparently intended for Paul and not Matthias to become the 12th apostle. However, there is no proof whatsoever of this. The title of apostle was not limited to the 12, for Barnabas (Acts 14:14), James (Gal. 1:19; 1 Cor. 15:7), and Apollos (1 Cor. 4:6-9) were all called apostles also. Apparently it will be Matthias who will be included in the fulfillment of such promises as Matt. 19:28 and Rev. 21:14.

LESSON 17

> B. Peter and the crowd at Pentecost (Acts 2:1-47)
> 1. The cloven tongues *(Read Acts 2:1-4)*

✱ **2:1-4**
- This is the first of but four instances of tongue speaking in the entire Bible.
  - The apostles in Jerusalem (Acts 2:4)
  - The Gentiles (Cornelius and his household in Caesarea) (Acts 10:46)
  - The disciples of John the Baptist in Ephesus (Acts 19:6)
  - The church members in Corinth (1 Cor. 14)
- Luke begins by saying, *"When the day of Pentecost was fully come"* (Acts 2:1). Here is a summary of that historical day.
  - The chronology of Pentecost. Pentecost (a Greek word which simply means 50) was the third of six great Israelite feasts mentioned in Leviticus 23:
    - The Passover, unleavened bread feast (Lev. 23:4-8, a reference to Calvary)
    - The sheaf of firstfruits (Lev. 23:9-14, a reference to the resurrection)
    - The feast of seven weeks (Lev. 23:15-21, a prophetical reference to Pentecost)
    - The feast of trumpets (Lev. 23:23-35, a reference to the Rapture and second coming of Christ)
    - The feast of atonement (Lev. 16; 23:26-32, a reference to the coming tribulation)
    - The feast of tabernacles (Lev. 23:33-43, a reference to the millennium)
  - The comparison of Pentecost
    - New Testament Pentecost may be compared with Old Testament Pentecost. Old Testament Pentecost occurred 50 days after Israel left Egypt. Note: the Passover lamb was slain on April 14, 1491 B.C., and Israel left Egypt the next night (Exod. 12:1-2, 6, 12, 31). Exactly 50 days later they arrived at Mt. Sinai during the first week of June (Exod. 19:1).
      New Testament Pentecost occurred 50 days after Christ rose from the dead. Note: Our Lord was, of course, crucified during the Passover week in April (John 19:14). He then spent 40 days with his disciples after the resurrection (Acts 1:3). Then, some 10 days later (Acts 1:5; 2:1) New Testament Pentecost occurred.
      Old Testament Pentecost celebrated a birthday, that of the nation Israel (Exod. 19:5).
      New Testament Pentecost celebrated a birthday, that of the church (Acts 2:41-47).
      Old Testament Pentecost witnessed the slaying of some 3,000 souls (Exod. 32:28).
      New Testament Pentecost witnessed the saving of some 3,000 souls (Acts 2:41).
      Old Testament Pentecost was introduced in a mighty way (Exod. 19) *(Read Exod. 19:16, 18)*.
      New Testament Pentecost was also introduced in a mighty way *(Read Acts 2:1-4)*.
    - New Testament Pentecost may be compared to Bethlehem. At Bethlehem, God the Father was preparing a body for his Son to work through *(Read Heb. 10:5)*. At Pentecost God the Father was preparing a body for his Spirit to work through *(Read 1 Cor. 6:19)*.
    - New Testament Pentecost may be compared to Old Testament Babel. At Babel we see sinful people working for their own glory (Gen. 11:4). At Pentecost we see saved people waiting for God's glory (Acts 1:14). At Babel, God confounded human language (Gen. 11:9). At Pentecost God clarified human language (Acts 2:8). At Babel, God scattered people throughout the world (Gen. 11:9). At Pentecost God gathered people within the Church (Eph. 1:10).

> 2. The congregation *(Read Acts 2:5-11)*
> 3. The confusion *(Read Acts 2:12-13)*

★ **2:13** Peter quickly denies this. However, a comparison can be made between being filled with wine and being filled with the Holy Spirit. (See Eph. 5:18.) Note:
- Both are the result of a crushing process (see John 7:37-39).
- Both give a new boldness to the one under their control.
- Both produce a longing for more.

> 4. The clarification *(Read Acts 2:14-15)*
> 5. The comparison (Acts 2:16-21)
>   a. The Old Testament prophet *(Read Acts 2:16)*
>   b. The Old Testament prophecy *(Read Acts 2:17-21)*

★ **2:21** Peter compares what has just happened with Joel's Old Testament prophecy concerning the visitation of God's Spirit upon all flesh (Joel 2:28-32; cf. Acts 2:16-21). It should, however, be noted that the ultimate fulfillment of Joel's prophecy will occur during the tribulation (Acts 2:19-20; cf. Isa. 13:10; Ezek. 32:7; Matt. 24:29; Rev. 6:12).

> 6. The condemnation (Acts 2:22-28)
>   a. The Messiah had been crucified by his foes *(Read Acts 2:22-24)*

★ **2:23** This is but the first of at least eight occasions in which the Jewish leaders are accused of crucifying their own Messiah.
- Peter accuses them (2:23, 36; 3:15; 4:10; 5:30;10:39).
- Stephen accuses them (7:52).
- Paul accuses them (13:28).

> b. The Messiah had been resurrected by his Father *(Read Acts 2:24)*

★ **2:24** Both Peter and Paul repeatedly stress that all-important doctrine of Christ's resurrection in the book of Acts.
- The references of Peter (2:24, 32; 3:15, 26; 4:10; 5:30; 10:40)
- The references of Paul (13:30, 33-34, 37; 17:31; 26:23)

> 7. The conclusion *(Read Acts 2:29-36)*
>   a. As predicted by the prophet *(Read Acts 2:29-31)*
>   b. As performed by the Father *(Read Acts 2:32-33)*.
> 8. The conviction *(Read Acts 2:37)*

★ **2:37** Here is the first instance of the convicting ministry of the Holy Spirit as promised by Jesus in John 16:8-9. For other instances, see:
- The Samaritans (8:12)
- Saul (9:18; 22:16)
- Cornelius (10:47-48)
- Lydia (16:15)
- The Philippian jailor (16:33)

> 9. The command *(Read Acts 2:38-39)*

★ **2:39** What did Peter mean by his command to be baptized "for the remission of sins"?
- It must be remembered that the book of Acts is a dispensational, and therefore, transitional book. This was a message to Israel concerning their national crime of murdering their own Messiah.

- The preposition eis, here translated "for," can also be rendered "because of," as it is in Luke 14:35; Matthew 3:11; 12:41.
- Whatever Peter meant here, it must be understood that nowhere do the Scriptures teach us that salvation is dependent upon water baptism (1 Cor.1:27; cf.15:1-4). Here Paul clearly states what the gospel is, and baptism is definitely not included. Thus, those who insist upon baptismal regeneration literally "rob Paul to pay Peter" (see also 2 Pet. 3:15-16).

> 10. The challenge *(Read Acts 2:40)*
> 11. The conversions *(Read Acts 2:41)*
> 12. The communion *(Read Acts 2:42, 44)*

★ **2:44** This early system of mutual ownership was commonism, but definitely not communism. Observe the difference:
- Commonism says, "What is mine is thine."
- Communism says, "What is thine is mine."
- It should be noted that: This system was temporary. It had its problems (Acts 5:1; 6:10). It soon failed (2 Thess. 3:7-10).

> C. Peter and the lame man (Acts 3:1-26)
>   1. The miracle (Acts 3:1-11)
>   a. The need for the healing *(Read Acts 3:2)*
>   b. The name in the healing *(Read Acts 3:6)*

★ **3:6** In A.D. 1260, St. Thomas Aquinas visited the Roman Pope Innocent IV, who showed him all the fabulous wealth of the papacy. After the tour, Innocent said, "So you see, good Thomas, unlike the first pope, I cannot say, 'Silver and gold have I none.'" "Aquinas nodded in quiet agreement, and then said softly: 'And neither can you say, 'In the name of Jesus Christ of Nazareth, rise up and walk.'"

>   c. The new convert after the healing *(Read Acts 3:8)*

★ **3:8** This verse is a reminder of Israel's future golden age, as described by Isaiah *(Read Isa. 35:6)*.

>   2. The message (Acts 3:12-26)—Peter now delivers a powerful sermon on the cross.
>   a. The promoters of the cross—The Jews *(Read Acts 3:13-15)*
>   b. The prophecies about the cross—The Old Testament scriptures *(Read Acts 3:18)*
>   c. The power of the cross
>   (1) It had healed the body of a man *(Read Acts 3:16)*
>   (2) It could heal the souls of all men *(Read Acts 3:26)*
>   d. The program of the cross (Acts 3:15, 18, 21)
>   (1) Christ would suffer and die (Acts 3:18)
>   (2) God would raise him from the dead (Acts 3:15)
>   (3) He would be taken up for awhile *(Acts 3:21)*
>   (4) He will come again *(Read Acts 3:19-20)*
>   e. The plea of the cross *(Read Acts 3:19, 26)*
> D. Peter and the high priest Annas (Acts 4:1-37)—Annas the high priest has Peter and John arrested.
>   1. The reason for the arrest *(Read Acts 4:2)*
>   2. The evidence supporting the arrest *(Read Acts 4:4)*

★ **4:4** The numerical growth as experienced by the early church was nothing less than supernatural.
- It began with 120 (1:15).
- Then 3,000 were added (2:41).
- And 5,000 men were added (4:4).

LESSON 17: THE BOOK OF ACTS—PART 2

- Multitudes of men and women were added (5:14).
- A great number of Jewish priests were added (6:7).

> 3. The dialogue in the arrest
>   a. The demand *(Read Acts 4:7)*

✱ **4:7** The Sanhedrin was, here (however impure the motives were), acting within its jurisdiction, for the Mosaic Law specified that whenever someone performed a miracle and used it for the basis of teaching, he was to be examined and stoned, if the teaching was false (Deut. 13:1-5).

>   b. The declaration *(Read Acts 4:10,12)*

✱ **4:12** Peter, filled with the Holy Spirit, tells the assembly that the miracle was performed through the name of the Messiah, whom they had crucified. (Note: Peter's defense here was the first direct fulfillment of Jesus' promise in Matt. 10:16-20. See also Peter's later testimony and advice in 1 Pet. 3:15.) He then associates Jesus with the Old Testament prophecy by showing that Christ is the cornerstone spoken of in Psa. 118:22. Jesus had previously applied this passage to himself (Mark 12:10; 1 Pet. 2:4-8).

> 4. The conference during the arrest (Acts 4:13-18)
>   a. The astonishment *(Read Acts 4:13)*
>   b. The acknowledgment *(Read Acts 4:14-16)*

✱ **4:16** There is little doubt that they would have denied it if they could have (Matt. 28:11-15). Not only could they not deny the miracle; neither could they deny Peter's message concerning the resurrection of Christ. There is no record that here or at any other time the Sanhedrin ever attempted to deny the historical fact of Christ's resurrection. It may be said in passing that, concerning the healed cripple, there is no argument against the evidence of a transformed life.

>   c. The agreement *(Read Acts 4:17)*
> 5. The warning accompanying the arrest (Acts 4:18-22)
>   a. You can't continue *(Read Acts 4:18)*
>   b. We must continue *(Read Acts 4:19-20)*
> 6. The praise service following the arrest *(Read Acts 4:23-30)*
> 7. The blessings resulting from the arrest (Acts 4:31-37)
>   a. The believers were filled by the Spirit of God *(Read Acts 4:31)*
>   b. The brotherhood was supplied by the grace of God *(Read Acts 4:32,34-35)*
> E. Peter and Ananias and Sapphira (Acts 5:1-11)
>   1. The couple's deception *(Read Acts 5:1-2)*

✱ **5:2** The account here is reminiscent of that of Achan in Joshua 7.
- Satan used both Achan and Ananias to attack God's people from within the camp.
- The sin of both involved greed and lying.
- Each was confronted and condemned by God's chief leader.
  - Joshua dealt with Achan.
  - Peter dealt with Ananias.
- Both men, along with their wives, were killed for their sin.
- Both served as an example (Acts 5:11; 1 Cor. 10:6).

>   2. Their discovery *(Read Acts 5:3-4)*

✶ **5:4** The two "whys" used here by Peter strongly support the position that Ananias was a saved man. One does not ask an unsaved person why he commits sin.

> 3. Their deaths *(Read Acts 5:5, 10)*

✶ **5:5** These two thus become the first recorded believers to commit the sin unto death (see 1 Cor. 11:30-32; 1 John 5:16). Peter perhaps had Ananias and his wife in mind when he later wrote: *"For the time is come that judgment must begin at the house of God: and if it first begin at us, what shall the end be of them that obey not the gospel of God?" (1 Pet. 4:17).*

> F. Peter and the sick *(Read Acts 5:12-16)*
> G. Peter and the lawyer Gamaliel *(Acts 5:17-42)* — For the second time Peter is arrested for preaching Christ.
>   1. The anger of the Sadducees *(Read Acts 5:17-18)*
>   2. The appearance of the Lord *(Read Acts 5:19-20)*

✶ **5:20**
- This is the first of three miracles involving individuals being released from prison in Acts.
  - The apostles are released (5:19-20).
  - Peter is released (12:6-10).
  - Paul and Silas are released (16:26-27).
- It also marks the first of six angelic appearances in Acts.
  - An angel frees the apostles from prison (5:19).
  - An angel directs Philip to the Gaza desert (8:26).
  - An angel instructs Cornelius to send for Peter (10:3, 22).
  - An angel frees Peter from death row (12:7).
  - An angel judges Herod Agrippa I (12:23).
  - An angel encourages Paul during an ocean storm (27:23).

>   3. The astonishment of the jailors *(Read Acts 5:22-23, 25)*
>   4. The accusation of the council *(Read Acts 5:27-28)*
>   5. The address of the apostles
>   a. The witness involved *(Read Acts 5:29-32)*

✶ **5:32** Note the expression, *"We ought to obey God rather than men" (5:29)*. Peter believed in law and order (1 Pet. 2:13-14), but on this occasion had to submit to God's higher law.

>   b. The wrath involved *(Read Acts 5:33)*
>   6. The advice of Gamaliel *(Read Acts 5:34)*
>   a. His warning *(Read Acts 5:35)*
>   (1) The first illustration *(Read Acts 5:36)*
>   (2) The second illustration *(Read Acts 5:37)*
>   b. His wisdom *(Read Acts 5:38-39)*

✶ **5:39** A Persian wife once gave similar advice to her wicked husband: *"And Haman told Zeresh his wife and all his friends every thing that had befallen him. Then said his wise men and Zeresh his wife unto him, 'If Mordecai be of the seed of the Jews, before whom thou hast begun to fall, thou shalt not prevail against him, but shalt surely fall before him'" (Esther 6:13).*

>   7. The attitude of the apostles *(Acts 5:40-42)*
>   a. Their pain *(Read Acts 5:40)*

> b. Their praise *(Read Acts 5:41)*
> c. Their persistence *(Read Acts 5:42)*
> H. Peter and Simon the Sorcerer (Acts 8:9-25)
> 1. The pride of Simon *(Read Acts 8:9)*
> 2. The popularity of Simon *(Read Acts 8:10-11)*
> 3. The pretense of Simon *(Read Acts 8:12-13)*
> 4. The perversion of Simon
> a. The bribe *(Read Acts 8:18)*
> b. The blasphemy *(Read Acts 8:19)*

✱ **8:19** His action has given to the vocabulary of church history the word "Simony," which denotes the buying and selling of ecclesiastical rights and offices. He was not saved. Jesus himself had previously discounted this kind of false faith (John 2:23-25; 6:26, 66).

> 5. The problem of Simon
> a. Peter tells Simon what he was doing *(Read Acts 8:20-22)*

✱ **8:20** In the 1880s the American circus showman and promoter P. T. Barnum attempted to entice the great London Baptist preacher Charles H. Spurgeon to "join his act." Spurgeon would be furnished with a huge tent, guaranteed a full house, and paid $1,000 per "preaching performance." All Barnum wanted in return was to pocket the ticket take. Upon receiving this brazen offer, Spurgeon answered as follows:

"Dear Mr. Barnum:
I have before me your offer to come to America. You will find my answer in the book of Acts, Chapter 8 and verse 20.
Very sincerely,
C. H. Spurgeon."

Had the materialistic promoter turned to Acts, he would have read: *"Thy money perish with thee, because thou hast thought that the gift of God may be purchased with money."*

> b. Peter tells Simon why he was doing it *(Read Acts 8:23)*
> 6. The plea of Simon *(Read Acts 8:24)*
> I. Peter and Aeneas (Acts 9:32-35)
> 1. The misery *(Read Acts 9:32-33)*
> 2. The miracle
> a. In the physical realm *(Read Acts 9:34)*
> b. In the spiritual realm *(Read Acts 9:35)*
> J. Peter and Dorcas (Acts 9:36-42)
> 1. The deeds of Dorcas *(Read Acts 9:36)*
> 2. The death of Dorcas *(Read Acts 9:37)*
> 3. The deliverance of Dorcas *(Read Acts 9:38)*
> a. The grief of the widows *(Read Acts 9:39)*
> b. The gladness of the widows *(Read Acts 9:40-42)*

✱ **9:42** After raising Dorcas, Peter remains for a while in Joppa at the house of a tanner named Simon. Apparently Peter's attitude toward the restrictions of Judaism was already widening (even though he would still need the sheet vision from God); for here he was, staying with a skin tanner. This was an unclean trade in the eyes of the Jews, for it involved the handling of dead bodies (9:43).

K. Peter and Cornelius (Acts 9:43-10:48)
   1. Cornelius, a religious sinner in Caesarea (Acts 10:1-8)
      a. His veneration for God *(Read Acts 10:1-2)*

✱ **10:2** We are immediately told three things about this man:
- He was a centurion—This would make him commander of 100 Roman soldiers. The various centurions in the New Testament are usually pictured in a good light. (See Matt. 8:5-10; 27:54; Acts 22:25-26; 27:1, 3, 42-44.)
- He was devout—He desired to know about God. Jesus had once said: "If any man will to do his will, he shall know of the doctrine ... of God" (John 7:17).
- He was nevertheless lost (cf. Nicodemus, John 3).

      b. His visitation from God (Acts 10:3-8)
         (1) The messenger involved *(Read Acts 10:3-4)*
         (2) The message involved *(Read Acts 10:5-6)*

✱ **10:6** It can be said that there are three factors necessary for the salvation of a sinner:
- The Spirit of God (John 16:8)
- The Word of God (Rom. 10:17)
- The soul winner of God (Rom. 1:14)

   2. Peter, a reluctant soul winner in Joppa (Acts 10:9-23)
      a. The message of the trance *(Read Acts 10:11-14)*

✱ **10:14** Peter's reply here was in the form of a great contradiction. If he is Lord, one cannot say "Not so"; and if one says, "Not so," he cannot be Lord.

      b. The meaning of the trance *(Read Acts 10:15-23)*

✱ **10:20** It is thrilling to note that God prepares both sinner and soul winner, for whenever he is at work, God leads at both ends of the line. The Lord always prepares us for what he is preparing for us (10:17-21). We note that this marks the second time in history that God sent a Jewish missionary from Joppa to reach some Gentiles. (See also Jonah 1:3.)

   3. Peter and Cornelius, redeemed saints in Christ (Acts 10:24-48)
      a. The conversation with Cornelius (Acts 10:24-35)
         (1) The reception *(Read Acts 10:25-26)*

✱ **10:26** This is the first of at least four occasions in the New Testament in which a man was forbidden to fall down before anyone (human or angel) other than God.
- Paul rebukes the people at Lystra for this *(Read Acts 14:13-15)*
- An angel rebukes John the apostle on Patmos for this.
  - First occasion *(Read Rev. 19:10)*
  - Second occasion *(Read Rev. 22:8-9)*

         (2) The perception *(Read Acts 10:28, 34-35)*
      b. The clarification to Cornelius (Acts 10:36-43)—Peter's sermon:
         (1) He talked about the Word of God *(Read Acts 10:36-37)*
         (2) He talked about the work of God *(Read Acts 10:38)*
         (3) He talked about the witnesses of God *(Read Acts 10:39-41)*

LESSON 17: THE BOOK OF ACTS—PART 2

> (4) He talked about the will of God *(Read Acts 10:42-43)*
>   c. The conversion of Cornelius (Acts 10:44-48)
>   (1) The divine baptizer *(Read Acts 10:44-45)*
>   (2) The human baptizer *(Read Acts 10:46-48)*
> L. Peter and the Jewish believers at Jerusalem (Acts 11:1-18)
>   1. The accusation *(Read Acts 11:1-3)*
>   2. The argumentation (Acts 11:4-17)
>   a. Peter presents his case *(Read Acts 11:4, 15-16)*
>   b. Peter presents his conclusion *(Read Acts 11:17)*
>   3. The acceptance *(Read Acts 11:18)*

★ **11:18** Stanley Toussaint writes: "With Peter the saints recognized that the conversion of Gentiles was initiated by God and that they should not stand in His way. This response had two ensuing and significant results. First, it preserved the unity of the body of Christ, the church. Second, it drove a huge wedge between church-age believers and temple worshippers in Jerusalem. Before this the common Jewish people looked on Christians with favor (cf. 2:47; 5:13, 26), but soon thereafter the Jews opposed the church. This antagonism is attested by Israel's response to the execution of James (12:2-3; cf. 12:11). Perhaps this concourse with Gentiles was a starting point of the Jewish opposition" (*Bible Knowledge Commentary*, New Testament edition, p. 382).

> M. Peter and the angel of the Lord (Acts 12:1-24)
>   1. The angel in a prison (Acts 12:1-18)
>   a. The martyrdom of James *(Read Acts 12:1-2)*

★ **12:2** King Herod Agrippa I, the murderer of John the Baptist and the ruler who questioned Jesus (Matt. 14:1-12; Luke 23:6-12), suddenly and viciously orders the murder of James the apostle, and puts Peter on death row. James thus becomes the first apostle to die a martyr's death. His death is the only recorded one (with the exception of Judas) among the 12. This execution was no doubt a fulfillment of Matthew 20:23; Mark 10:39. It is believed that James' brother, John, was the last of the 12 to die.

>   b. The freedom of Peter (Acts 12:3-18)
>   (1) His success in escaping a prison house *(Read Acts 12:5-7, 10)*

★ **12:6** On the eve of his scheduled execution Peter is sound asleep in prison. He no doubt had full confidence in Jesus' promise that he would live to be an old man (John 21:18).

>   (2) His struggle in entering a prayer house *(Read Acts 12:12-16)*

★ **12:12** "This verse introduces the reader to John Mark, who figures prominently in Paul's first missionary journey. Evidently his mother, Mary, was a woman of prominence and means. Probably her house was a principal meeting place of the church, so it must have been spacious. Because John Mark's father is not named, Mary may have been a widow. This same Mark is considered to be the writer of the Gospel bearing his name" (cf. Mark 14:51-52; 1 Pet. 5:13) (Ibid., p. 385).

With some amusement we note that it was far easier for Peter to escape the prison house than to enter this house of prayer! It is ironic but true that often the most surprised people of all, when God performs a miracle, are the very ones who prayed the hardest for it.

>   2. The angel in a palace (Acts 12:19-24)
>   a. The particulars *(Read Acts 12:20-21)*
>   b. The pride *(Read Acts 12:22)*
>   c. The punishment *(Read Acts 12:23)*

✶ **12:23** Herod Agrippa I should have learned from the historical account of Nebuchadnezzar how God hates and humbles the proud *(Read Dan. 4:30-32)*.

> N. Peter and the Jerusalem Council (Acts 15)
> 1. His comments *(Read Acts 15:7-9)*
> 2. His caution *(Read Acts 15:10)*
> 3. His conclusion *(Read Acts 15:11)*

LESSON 18

II. The Activities of Stephen (Acts 6:1-7:60)
   A. The complaint of the leaders *(Read Acts 6:2-4)*

✶ **6:1** The Grecian Jews were those who could not speak Aramaic, the native tongue of Jews living in Israel. They may have been born and raised outside of Israel, speaking both Greek and their native tongue. This Grecian group may have also included Gentile proselytes to Judaism who later became Christians.

   B. The conference of the leaders (Acts 6:2-4)
      1. Their dilemma *(Read Acts 6:2)*

✶ **6:2** The word for tables here is *trapezal*, and often denotes banks, for moneylenders sat at tables to conduct their business (Matt. 21:12). Thus the stated need here was to find some qualified superintendents, and not just mere table waiters and cooks.

      2. Their decision *(Read Acts 6:3)*

✶ **6:3**
- Five requirements are listed for this new office.
  - They must be men.
  - They had to be saved.
  - They were to be reputable.
  - They were to be spiritual.
  - They were to possess wisdom.
- We note that there existed no "double standard" between pastors and the deacons and trustees in the early church.
- Stanley Toussaint suggests: "Selecting seven men may go back to the tradition in Jewish communities where seven respected men managed the public business in an official council" (*Bible Knowledge Commentary,* New Testament edition, p. 367).

      3. Their dedication *(Read Acts 6:4)*
   C. The choice of the laborers (Acts 6:5-7)
      1. The individuals *(Read Acts 6:5)*

✶ **6:5** All seven had Greek names and may have all come from the Grecian group. If so, this was a gracious gesture to the complainers.

      2. The installation *(Read Acts 6:6)*

✶ **6:6** The laying on of hands was done in the Bible:
- As an act of benediction (Matt. 19:13, 15; Gen. 48:14-20)
- For the purpose of healing (Mark 5:23; 6:5)
- To impart the Holy Spirit (Acts 8:17, 19; 9:17)
- For the purpose of ordination (Acts 6:6; 13:3; 1 Tim. 4:14; 2 Tim. 1:6; Num. 8:9-10)

3. The increase *(Read Acts 6:7)*

★ **6:7** These Jewish leaders, unlike those described in the Gospel of John, displayed the courage of their convictions. Note the sad account of the former group: *"Nevertheless among the chief rulers also many believed on him; but because of the Pharisees they did not confess him, lest they should be put out of the synagogue: For they loved the praise of men more than the praise of God" (John 12:42-43).*

D. The champion of the Lord
1. The maturity of Stephen
   a. He was a man of faith (Acts 6:5).
   b. He was controlled by the Spirit (Acts 6:5, 10).
   c. He possessed divine wisdom (Acts 6:10).
2. The miracles of Stephen *(Read Acts 6:8)*
3. The maligning of Stephen (Acts 6:9-14)—Stephen was viciously slandered by a group of religious men.
   a. Who they were *(Read Acts 6:9)*

★ **6:9** The preaching ministry of Stephen had offended the synagogue of the Libertines, a group of former slaves who apparently had their own synagogue in Jerusalem.

b. What they said *(Read Acts 6:11-14)*
c. Why they said it *(Read Acts 6:10)*

★ **6:10** This blessed unanswerable wisdom was a fulfillment of Jesus' words in *Luke 21:12-15: "But before all these, they shall lay their hands on you, and persecute you, delivering you up to the synagogues, and into prisons, being brought before kings and rulers for my names sake. And it shall turn to you for a testimony. Settle it therefore in your hearts, not to meditate before what ye shall answer: For I will give you a mouth and wisdom, which all your adversaries shall not be able to gainsay nor resist."*

4. The meekness of Stephen *(Read Acts 6:15)*

★ **6:15** This heavenly glow was experienced by Moses in a physical sense and described by Peter in a spiritual sense.
■ As experienced by Moses *(Read Exod. 34:29)*
■ As described by Peter *(Read 1 Pet. 4:14)*

5. The message of Stephen (Acts 7:1-53)—As has been seen (Acts 7:13-14), the charge against Stephen was that he had predicted the coming destruction of Israel's second (Herodian) temple. In his defense Stephen points out the following:
   a. Israel had been blessed by God even before possession of the first (Solomonic) temple.
      (1) God had led Abraham into Canaan (Acts 7:2-8).
      (2) God had protected his seed while in Egypt (Acts 7:9-17).

★ **7:17** At least two apparent discrepancies occur in these verses (7:6-16) during Stephen's address:
■ Concerning the length of the Egyptian bondage (7:6)—Stephen said it was for 400 years, while Paul gave the time at 430 years (Gal. 3:17). The simplest explanation is that Stephen used round numbers. Stanley Toussaint suggests: "Another explanation is that the 400 years was the actual time of bondage whereas the 430 years described the time from the confirming of the covenant in Genesis 35:9-15 to the Exodus, which occurred in 1446 B.C." (*Bible Knowledge Commentary*, New Testament edition, p. 370).

- Concerning the number in Jacob's family who moved to Egypt (7:14)—Stephen stated the number to be 75, but Moses said it was 70 (Gen. 46:27; Exod. 1:5). One of the most widely accepted solutions is to recognize that Moses includes Jacob, Joseph, and Joseph's two sons, Ephraim and Manasseh (a total of 70); but that Stephen omits Jacob and Joseph but includes Joseph's seven grandchildren (mentioned in 1 Chron. 7:14-15, 20-25).

> (3) God had brought them out of Egypt (Acts 7:18-36)
> (4) God had led them back into Canaan (Acts 7:37-45)
> b. Israel had nevertheless turned from God
> (1) During the days of its first temple *(Read Acts 7:43)*

✷ **7:43**
- Stephen had apparently been teaching that the Jewish temple was no longer necessary for the worship of the true God. Christ, of course, had already said this (John 4:20-24). To prove his assertion, Stephen pointed out the following facts:
  - That God had blessed Abraham and their fathers, even though they had not always lived in Palestine
  - That during much of its history while in the land, Israel did not worship God in the temple
  - That even the possession of its temple did not save Israel from being rebellious and disobedient
- The purpose of his speech, then, seemed to be to show Israel from her own history that the possession of the temple had been neither a necessity for, nor a guarantee of, the true worship of God.

> (2) During the days of her second temple *(Read Acts 7:51-53)*

✷ **7:53** Stephen points out that Israel had rejected Christ (7:52) as that nation had once rejected both Joseph (7:9), and Moses (7:23-29). It is vital to thus observe the following concerning these three persons:
- Both Joseph and Moses, while rejected during their first appearance, were later highly accepted during their second appearance.
- Christ, likewise, was rejected as the Lamb, but will be highly accepted during his second appearance as the Lion.

> 6. The martyrdom of Stephen (Acts 7:54-60)
> a. His persecutors (Acts 7:54, 57-58)
> (1) The wickedness involved *(Read Acts 7:57)*
> (2) The witness involved *(Read Acts 7:58)*

✷ **7:58**
- Here it may be observed that there are three murders in Israel's history that especially mark out her rejection of God's will.
  - The murder of John the Baptist, indicating the rejection of the Father
  - The murder of Christ, showing the rejection of the Son
  - The murder of Stephen, demonstrating the rejection of the Holy Spirit
- This is the first mention of Saul in the Bible.

> b. His preview of glory
> (1) What he saw *(Read Acts 7:55)*

✷ **7:55** Stephen begins his sermon by speaking of the God of glory (7:2); and ends it by seeing the glory of God.

> (2) What he said *(Read Acts 7:56)*

★ **7:56**
- Stephen becomes the first of three men to see Jesus after his ascension. The other two are Paul (Acts 9:3-6) and John (Rev. 1:10, 12-16). Note: Stephen saw Jesus standing at God's right hand. This is the only reference to the Savior standing (after his ascension) until one reaches the book of Revelation. In all other descriptions he is said to be seated (See Matt. 26:64; Acts 2:34; Col. 3:1; Eph.1:20; Heb. 1:3, 13; 8:1; 10:12). Perhaps our Lord rises to welcome his saints home.
- This verse records the final usage of the name, "Son of man." It was by far the most common name used by the Savior in the Gospels to describe himself.

> c. His prayers (Acts 7:59-60)
> (1) For himself *(Read Acts 7:59)*
> (2) For his enemies *(Read Acts 7:60a)*
> d. His passing *(Read Acts 7:60b)*

★ **7:60**
- Stephen dies at the hands of wicked men, as once did his Master.
  - He calls upon God to *"receive my spirit" (7:59)*, as once did Jesus (Luke 23:46).
  - He prays for his enemies, *"Lord, lay not this sin to their charge" (7:60)*, as once did Jesus (Luke 23:34).
- We are told that, *"when he had said this, he fell asleep" (7:60)*. This is God's description of a believer's death (Matt. 27:52; John 11:11; Acts 13:36; 1 Cor. 15:18, 20, 51; 1 Thess. 4:13-15; 2 Pet. 3:4).

> **III. The Activities of Philip (Acts 6:5; 8:5-8, 26-40)**
> A. The deacon in Jerusalem—Philip was one of seven men chosen by the early church to serve in the office of a deacon (Acts 6:5).
> B. The evangelist in Samaria (Acts 8:5-8)
> 1. His message *(Read Acts 8:5)*

★ **8:5** We are told that the church at Jerusalem would soon send Peter and John to help Philip in Samaria. The Holy Spirit had done a great work in John's heart, for both he and his brother James had once asked Jesus to call down fire from heaven upon the Samaritans (Luke 9:54).

> 2. His miracles *(Read Acts 8:6-8)*
> C. The soul winner in Gaza (Acts 8:26-40)
> 1. His message from an angel *(Read Acts 8:26)*
> 2. His ministry to a eunuch
> a. The charge of the eunuch *(Read Acts 8:27)*
> b. The confusion of the eunuch
> (1) The passage involved *(Read Acts 8:28, 32-33)*
> (2) The problem involved *(Read Acts 8:29-30, 34)*

★ **8:31** Philip asked him if he understood what he was reading. The answer of the eunuch reflects the tragic condition of all lost sinners: *"How can I, except some man should guide me?" (8:31)*; see Luke 24:32; 45; Rom.10:13-15, 17).

> c. The clarification to the eunuch *(Read Acts 8:35)*
> d. The conversion of the eunuch *(Read Acts 8:36-37)*
> e. The confession of the eunuch *(Read Acts 8:38-39)*

> D. The family man in Caesarea *(Read Acts 8:40)*
>   1. The visitors to Philip's home *(Read Acts 21:8)*
>   2. The virgins in Philip's home *(Read Acts 21:9)*

PART TWO: The Whole Earth, Global Crusade

Headed up by Paul, the tentmaker; assisted by Barnabas, Silas, Timothy, Mark, and Luke (Acts 13-28)

> **I. The Conversion of Paul (Acts 9:1-19; 22:5-16; 26:12)**
>   A. His vendetta against the saints of God (Acts 9:1-2; 22:4; 26:9-12)
>   1. Luke's official account of this vendetta *(Read Acts 9:1-2)*

★ **9:2** This is the first of several instances when believers were referred to as those of "this way." See Acts 19:9, 23; 22:4; 24:14, 22. It doubtless came from Jesus' statement in *John 14:6: "Jesus saith unto him, I am the way, the truth, and the life: no man cometh unto the Father, but by me."*

>   2. Paul's personal account of the vendetta *(Read Acts 22:4 and Acts 26:9-11)*
>   B. His vision of the Son of God (Acts 9:3-9; 22:6-11; 26:12-18)
>   1. What he saw—A blinding light brighter than the noonday sun (Acts 9:3; 22:6; 26:13)

★ **9:3** He also saw Jesus at this time. (See 9:17, 27; 22:14; 26:16; 1 Cor. 9:1; 15:8.) This marks the first of at least seven instances when Paul saw the ascended Savior. Other occasions were:
- At Troas (16:9-10)
- In Corinth (18:9-10)
- In Jerusalem, during his first visit as a believer (22:17-21)
- In Jerusalem, during his final visit (23:11)
- En route to Rome (27:23-24)
- When he was caught up into the third heaven (2 Cor. 12:1-4)

>   2. What he heard
>   a. He heard the Savior saying, *"I am the One you have been persecuting"* (Acts 9:4-5; 22:7-8; 26:9-15).

★ **9:4** We note here in 9:4 that to persecute Christians is in reality to persecute Christ. Jesus thus identifies with his people. (See also Matt. 25:31-34; 1 Cor. 12:12-27.)

>   b. He heard the Savior saying, "I am the One you shall be proclaiming" (Acts 9:6; 22:10; 26:16-18).
>   (1) The what of the matter *(Read Acts 26:16)*
>   (2) The who of the matter *(Read Acts 26:17)*
>   (3) The why of the matter *(Read Acts 26:18)*
>   C. His visitation by a servant of God (Acts 9:10-18; 22:13-16)
>   1. Ananias and God
>   a. The revelation to Ananias *(Read Acts 9:10-12)*

★ **9:12** These three words, *"Behold, he prayeth"* (9:11), are in themselves a summary of Paul's life. Here he begins his ministry by prayer, and ends it in the same way. (See 2 Tim. 4:16.) Paul literally prayed anywhere and everywhere about anything and everything. He prayed for sinners and saints, or potentates and prison guards, for Jews and Gentiles, for leaders and laymen. (See the following references: Acts 16:25; 20:36; 21:5; 22:17; 28:8; Rom. 1:9; 10:1; Eph. 1:16; Phil. 1:4, 9; Col. 1:3, 9; 1 Thess.1:2; 2 Tim. 13; Philem.1:4.)

> b. The reluctance by Ananias *(Read Acts 9:13-14)*

✴ **9:14** Ananias' concern over "how much evil he hath done to thy saints" was totally justified. Note the extent of Saul's "much evil" in his war against the church (Acts 7:57-58; 8:1-4; 22:4-5, 19-20; 26:9-11; 1 Cor. 15:9; Gal. 1:13, 22-24; Phil. 3:6; 1 Tim. 1:13):
- He "kept the raiment" of those that murdered Stephen, and consented to his death (Acts 7:57-58; 8:1-2; 22:20).
- He made havoc of the church (Acts 8:3). This word describes the act of a wild hog viciously uprooting a vineyard.
- He entered the homes of Christians and dragged them out to prison (Acts 8:3).
- He hounded Christians to their death in various cities (Acts 22:5).
- He beat believers (Acts 22:19).
- He voted to have them put to death (Acts 26:10).
- He attempted through torture to force them into cursing Christ (Acts 26:11).
- He persecuted the church beyond measure and "wasted it" (Gal. 1:13).

> c. The reassurance of Ananias *(Read Acts 9:15-16)*

✴ **9:16** Note two phrases here:
- *"He is a chosen vessel."* He surely was. In addition, God would make Saul:
  - A vessel of mercy (Rom. 9:23)
  - An earthen vessel (2 Cor. 4:7)
  - A vessel of honor (Rom. 9:21)
  - A sanctified and worthy vessel (2 Tim. 2:21)
- *"How great things he must suffer for my name's sake"* — In a nutshell, this statement would aptly summarize Paul's future life of service for Jesus.
  - He was plotted against on at least five occasions.
    - In Damascus (Acts 9:23-25)
    - In Jerusalem during his first visit as a believer (Acts 9:29)
    - In Greece (Acts 20:3)
    - In Jerusalem during his final visit as a believer (Acts 23:10, 12-14)
    - In Caesarea (Acts 25:2-3)
  - He was at first mistrusted by believers (Acts 9:26).
  - He was disliked by some believers (Phil. 1:14-16).
  - His work for God was constantly opposed by his own countrymen. This was experienced:
    - In Antioch (Acts 13:45, 50)
    - In Iconium (Acts 14:2)
    - In Thessalonica (Acts 17:5)
    - In Berea (Acts 17:13)
    - In Corinth (Acts 18:6)
  - He was on one occasion stoned and left for dead (Acts 14:19).
  - He suffered from repeated beatings (2 Cor. 11:24-25; Gal. 6:17).

- He experienced at least three shipwrecks (2 Cor. 11:25; Acts 27).
- He was subjected to intense satanic pressure (Acts 13:8; 16:16-18; 1 Thess. 2:18; 2 Cor. 12:7).
- He was ridiculed (Acts 17:18, 32; 26:24).
- He was falsely accused on numerous occasions (Acts 18:13; 21:21; 24:5-6).
- He probably suffered from eye trouble (Gal. 4:13-14; 6:11).
- He suffered the bite of a poisonous serpent (Acts 28:3-4).
- He was imprisoned.
  - In Philippi (Acts 16:24)
  - In Caesarea (Acts 24:27)
  - In Rome, for the first time (Acts 28:30)
  - In Rome, for the final time (2 Tim. 4:6-9)
- He was acquainted with physical hardships (2 Cor. 6:4-5; 11:27).
- He was in constant danger (2 Cor. 11:26).
- He bore the awful pressure of concerns over his beloved churches (2 Cor. 11:28).
- He was slapped (Acts 23:2).
- He was nearly torn apart by an angry mob (Acts 21:30-32).
- He experienced terrible internal pressure (2 Cor. 1:8; 7:5).
- He was forsaken by his friends in the final hours (2 Tim. 4:10, 16).

2. Ananias and Saul
   a. His message for Saul *(Read Acts 9:17)*
   b. His ministry to Saul
     (1) Pastoring *(Read Acts 9:18)*

★ **9:18**
- The conversion of Saul, the second of three great salvation stories in the first section of Acts, vividly illustrates God's desire to redeem all who will but believe.
- Following the universal flood, God placed all future humanity into three basic groupings, each headed up by one of Noah's three sons, Ham, Shem, and Japheth (Gen. 10:1). Note:
  - In 8:37, the Ethiopian eunuch, a descendant of Ham, is saved.
  - In 9:6, Saul of Tarsus, a descendant of Shem, is saved.
  - In 10:44, Cornelius, a descendant of Japheth, is saved.

     (2) Predicting *(Read Acts 22:14-15)*

LESSON 19

II. The Early Ministry of Paul (Acts 9:19-30; 11:24-30; 12:25-13:3; 22:21; Gal. 1:16; 2:1-10)
   A. Preaching in the Damascus synagogues (Acts 9:19-21)
      1. The message *(Read Acts 9:19-20)*
      2. The marvel *(Read Acts 9:21)*
   B. Retiring to the Arabian desert for a period of several years *(Read Gal. 1:16-17)*
   C. Returning to Damascus with greater knowledge and preaching power *(Read Acts 9:22; Gal. 1:17)*
   D. Escaping from Damascus (Acts 9:23-25)
      1. Why he escaped *(Read Acts 9:23-24)*.
      2. How he escaped *(Read Acts 9:25)*
   E. Visiting Jerusalem for the first time since his conversion (Acts 9:26-29; Gal. 1:18-19).

★ **9:26** This marks the first of at least five trips Paul made to Jerusalem after his conversion. The others are:
- His second (Acts 11:30)
- His third (Acts 15:1-30; Gal. 2:1-10)
- His fourth (Acts 18:21-23)
- His final (Acts 21:17-23:35)

      1. The duration of this visit *(Read Gal. 1:18-19)*
      2. The difficulties during this visit (Acts 9:26-29)
         a. The fears *(Read Acts 9:26)*
         b. The fellowship *(Read Acts 9:27)*
   F. Escaping from Jerusalem and settling in Tarsus (Acts 9:29-30; 22:17-21; Gal. 1:21)
      1. The plot to destroy Paul *(Read Acts 9:29)*
      2. The plan to deliver Paul
         a. The revelation *(Read Acts 22:17-18)*
         b. The regret *(Read Acts 22:19-20)*
         c. The reassurance *(Read Acts 22:21)*
   G. Joining Barnabas in the work at Antioch (Acts 11:22-26)
      1. The origin of the Antioch church
         a. The conflict involved *(Read Acts 11:19-20)*
         b. The converts involved *(Read Acts 11:21)*
      2. The overseers in the Antioch church
         a. Barnabas
            (1) The missionary of God *(Read Acts 11:22-23)*
            (2) The man of God *(Read Acts 11:24)*
         b. Saul *(Read Acts 11:25-26)*

★ **11:26** This is the first of three occasions on which believers are called Christians in the Bible. The other two references are:
- King Agrippa uses the term (Acts 26:28).
- Simon Peter uses the term (1 Pet. 4:16).

LESSON 19: THE BOOK OF ACTS—PART 4

> H. Visiting Jerusalem for the second time carrying a love offering for the needy there (Acts 11:27-30; Gal. 2:1)
>   1. The messages from the Spirit of God directing the visit (Acts 11:28; Gal. 2:2)
>   a. The revelation to Agabus *(Read Acts 11:28)*
>   b. The revelation to Paul (Gal. 2:2)
>   2. The meeting with the saints of God during the visit *(Read Gal. 2:9)*
> I. Returning to Antioch to preach and teach the word *(Read Acts 12:25-13:1)*

✶ **13:1**
- The ministers in Antioch—This church was blessed to have a number of godly prophets and teachers, five of whom are named. Two deserve special consideration:
  - Simeon, called Niger—He may have been the Simon of Cyrene mentioned in Mark 15:21. "Niger" means black, indicating he may have been from North Africa.
  - Manaen—The adjective describing Manaen means foster brother. He and wicked King Herod the Great had apparently once been raised together in the royal court.
- The missionaries from Antioch—Two of these five are sent out to preach the gospel *(Read Acts 13:2-3)*.
  - Note what these men were doing at the time. They were ministering to the Lord. It does not say for, but to the Lord. What is involved here? In essence, to minister to God signifies the worship of God. Two examples can be cited at this point:
    - The example of King David *(Read 1 Chron. 23:25-26, 28, 30)*
    - The example of heaven's angels *(Read Rev. 4:8)*
  - After a hand-laying dedication service, the Antioch church sends forth the world's first Christian foreign missionaries. We note here that the church at Antioch was totally independent of the Jerusalem church and recognized no ecclesiastical hierarchy whatsoever. A beautiful cooperation is seen here between a local church and the Holy Spirit (13:2-4).

> **III. The First Missionary Journey of Paul (Acts 13:2-14:2)**
>   A. First stop, Cyprus (Acts 13:4-12)
>   1. Preaching at Salamis, the island's eastern city *(Read Acts 13:5)*
>   2. Preaching at Paphos, the island's western city (Acts 13:6-12)
>   a. The openness to the Word of God *(Read Acts 13:6-7)*
>   b. The opposition to the Word of God
>   (1) The blasphemy of Elymas *(Read Acts 13:8)*
>   (2) The blindness of Elymas *(Read Acts 13:9-11)*
>   c. The obedience to the Word of God *(Read Acts 13:12)*
>   B. Second stop, Perga (Acts 13:13)—John Mark leaves the team at this point.

✶ **13:13** Stanley Toussaint writes: "What caused Mark to desert is open to speculation: (1) Perhaps he was disillusioned with the change in leadership. After all, Barnabas, the original leader, was John Mark's cousin. (2) The new emphasis on Gentiles may have been too much of an adjustment for a Palestinian Jew like Mark. (3) Possibly he was afraid of the dangerous road over the Taurus Mountains to Antioch which Paul was determined to travel. (4) There is some evidence Paul became quite ill in Perga, possibly with malaria, as the city of Perga was subject to malarial infections. Furthermore, Paul preached to the people of Galatia 'because of an illness' (Gal. 4:13). The missionary party may have gone inland to higher ground to avoid the ravages of malaria and Mark in discouragement over this may have returned home. (5) Some think Mark was homesick. His mother may have been a widow (Acts 12:12); perhaps Mark became lonesome for her and home. Whatever the reason, Paul considered it a defection and a fault (cf. 15:38)" (*Bible Knowledge Commentary*, New Testament edition, p. 388).

C. Third stop, Antioch in Pisidia (Acts 13:14-50)—Paul spends several weeks here and preaches two sermons in the synagogues in Antioch.
  1. His first sermon (Acts 13:14-43)—It was a sermon about a Savior.
     a. The preparation for this Savior
        (1) Historical preparations—He would come from a special nation.
           (a) God chose a nation—Israel (Acts 13:17).
           (b) He led that nation out of Egypt into Canaan (Acts 13:18-19).
           (c) He sent judges to deliver them (Acts 13:20).
           (d) He chose kings to rule over them (Acts 13:21).
        (2) Prophetical preparations—The Psalms had predicted his death and resurrection *(Read Acts 13:33-37)*
        (3) Homiletical preparation—John the Baptist had preached sermons on him *(Read Acts 13:24-25)*
     b. The identity of this Savior
        (1) He came from the seed of David (Acts 13:23).
        (2) His name is Jesus (Acts 13:23).
     c. The rejection of this Savior *(Read Acts 13:27-29)*
     d. The resurrection of this Savior *(Read Acts 13:30-32)*
     e. The salvation from this Savior *(Read Acts 13:38-39)*
  2. His second sermon Acts 13:44-50 *(Read Acts 13:44)*
     a. Rejected by the Jewish listeners (Acts 13:45-46, 50)
        (1) The incrimination against Paul *(Read Acts 13:45)*
        (2) The indictment by Paul *(Read Acts 13:46)*

✷ **13:46** This statement, first uttered in Antioch of Pisidia, would be repeated at Corinth (Acts 18:6), and at Rome (Acts 28:23-28).

     b. Received by the Gentile listeners (Acts 13:47-49)
        (1) They heard God's Word *(Read Acts 13:47)*
        (2) They honored God's Word *(Read Acts 13:48)*
D. Fourth stop, Iconium (Acts 13:51-14:5)
  1. The revival *(Read Acts 14:1, 3)*
  2. The riot *(Read Acts 14:2, 4)*
E. Fifth stop, Lystra (Acts 14:6-23)
  1. The cripple *(Read Acts 14:8)*

✷ **14:8** This marks the final of three occasions in Acts on which a cripple was healed. (See 3:1-10; 9:33-35.)

  2. The cure *(Read Acts 14:9-10)*
  3. The commotion *(Read Acts 14:11)*
  4. The confusion *(Read Acts 14:12)*
  5. The corruption *(Read Acts 14:13)*

✷ **14:13** The Roman poet Ovid (43 B.C.) records the ancient myth concerning a visit of Zeus and Hermes (two Greek gods) to this area once, disguised as mortals. All turned them away except one old couple. Later a flood supposedly came in judgment and drowned all except this couple. Determining not to make the same mistake, the priest of Jupiter in Lystra prepares to worship the team by the sacrifice of animals and flowers.

  6. The consternation *(Read Acts 14:14)*
  7. The correction *(Read Acts 14:15-18)*

LESSON 19: THE BOOK OF ACTS—PART 4

> 8. The condemnation (Acts 14:19-20)
>   a. The murder *(Read Acts 14:19)*
>   b. The miracle *(Read Acts 14:20)*

★ **14:20** Some believe Paul actually died here and was then resurrected by God, experiencing at this time his heavenly visit spoken of in 2 Corinthians 12:1-9. However, there is a time problem here, for the stoning occurred in A.D. 47 or 48 and Paul wrote 2 Corinthians some seven years later in A.D. 55. But in 2 Corinthians he said the event occurred 14 years prior. At any rate, this may have been where he received the scars he bore for Jesus' sake mentioned in Galatians 6:17. Whether he was dead or simply unconscious, a miracle is seen here; and we get the impression that he immediately rose up, and came into the city (14:20).

> 9. The confirmation *(Read Acts 14:21-23)*

★ **14:23** Dr. Homer Kent writes: "In each church they visited the believers were organized by the choosing of elders. The word 'ordained' (14:23) translates a Greek term that originally meant to elect by a vote of raised hands. The word also developed the more general sense of 'choose' or 'appoint,' as the compound verb in Acts 10:41 indicates. Does 14:23 mean that Paul and Barnabas appointed the elders for each church, or does the more restricted meaning prevail with the sense that the missionaries established elders in the churches by arranging for congregational elections? Although there is no question but that the term is capable of either meaning, the following factors favor the interpretation of an election: (1) The choice of the verb cheirotoneo rather than one of the many general words for 'appoint' suggests that the special characteristics of this word should be understood. (2) The only other New Testament use of this exact verb is clearly with the sense of a congregational selection (2 Cor. 8:19). (3) Congregational selection was the apostolic practice in the choice of the Seven (Acts 6:3)" (*Jerusalem to Rome*, pp. 118-119).

> F. Sixth stop, back to Antioch in Syria *(Read Acts 14:24-28)*
> **IV. The Jerusalem Council, attended by Paul (Acts 15:1-35)**
>   A. The reason for the council *(Read Acts 15:1-2, 5-6)*
>   B. The reports given in the council
>   1. Peter's report (Acts 15:7-11)
>   a. His reminder *(Read Acts 15:7)*
>   b. His rebuke *(Read Acts 15:10)*
>   c. His rationale *(Read Acts 15:11)*
>   2. Paul's report *(Read Acts 15:12)*
>   3. James' report (Acts 15:13-21)
>   a. The summary—James summarizes the no-circumcision-for-Gentiles position through two arguments.
>   (1) A practical argument—God had already saved Gentiles without the rite of circumcision *(Read Acts 15:14)*
>   (2) A prophetical argument—Amos the prophet had already predicted this would happen *(Read Acts 15:15-18)*
>   b. The suggestion *(Read Acts 15:19-21)*

★ **15:19** We note that the final decision was announced not by Simon Peter, but by James, the pastor of the Jerusalem church. Nowhere in the history of the early church is Peter seen exercising ecclesiastical authority over the other apostles. This decision (directed by the Holy Spirit, see v. 28) showed great wisdom, in that it avoided undue and unnecessary offending of the unsaved Jew. (See also 1 Cor. 10:32-33.)

> C. The recommendation of the council (Acts 15:22-29)
>   1. Concerning the messengers who carried their recommendation (Acts 15:22-27).
>   a. Who they were *(Read Acts 15:22)*

> b. What they were *(Read Acts 15:26)*
> 2. Concerning the message contained in their recommendation *(Read Acts 15:28-35)*
> D. The return following the council *(Read Acts 15:30, 35)*
> **V. The Disagreement between Paul and Barnabas (Acts 15:36-40)**
> A. The background of the disagreement *(Read Acts 15:36-38)*
> B. The blessing from the disagreement—*"And the contention was so sharp between them, that they departed asunder one from the other: and so Barnabas took Mark, and sailed unto Cyprus; and Paul chose Silas, and departed, being recommended by the brethren unto the grace of God" (Acts 15:39-40)*. Thus, there were now twice as many missionaries on the field. Paul probably wrote Galatians at this time from Antioch.

★ **15:40** Barnabas takes John Mark and leaves for Cyprus. Happily, the New Testament records that Paul was later reconciled to both Barnabas (1 Cor. 9:6) and John Mark (Col. 4:10; Philem. 24; 2 Tim. 4:11). This is the last mention of Barnabas in the book of Acts.

> **VI. The Second Missionary Journey of Paul (Acts 15:41-18:22)**
> A. First stop, Lystra (Acts 16:1-5)
> 1. The choosing of Timothy (Acts 16:1-2)
> 2. The circumcising of Timothy (Acts 16:3)

★ **16:3** He is circumcised by Paul because he was partly Jewish, so he would not give undue offense to the Jews. Later, Paul would refuse to circumcise Titus, a Gentile (Gal. 2:3). This was an application of Paul's stated principle in 1 Corinthians 9:20.

> B. Second stop, Troas (Acts 16:6-10)
> 1. Forbidden by the Holy Spirit to go north or south (Acts 16:6-7)
> 2. Bidden by the Holy Spirit to go west (Acts 16:9-10)
> a. The visitation *(Read Acts 16:9)*
> b. The verification *(Read Acts 16:10)*

★ **16:10**
- We note that the need alone did not by itself constitute the call. It may be also said that they did not attempt to second-guess God. They had just come from the east; they had been forbidden to go south or north; but still they waited. God's perfect will is not always the easiest thing on earth to find; but once found, it becomes the most blessed. (See Matt. 7:7-8; Luke 11:9-10.)
- The gospel team leaves immediately for Macedonia, now being joined by the beloved Greek physician, Luke. Acts 16:10 is the first of several "we" sections in this book. (See also 20:5-6; 21:18; 27:1.)

> C. Third stop, Philippi (Acts 16:11-40)—At Philippi three tremendous conversions took place.
> 1. The salvation of a business woman (Acts 16:13-15)
> a. Her business *(Read Acts 16:14a)*
> b. Her new birth *(Read Acts 16:14b)*
> c. Her baptism *(Read Acts 16:15)*

★ **16:15** There are at least seven New Testament "household salvation" accounts; that is, the conversion of an individual along with his or her entire family. These persons and their households are:
- Cornelius (Acts 10:24, 44)
- Lydia (Acts 16:15)

LESSON 19: THE BOOK OF ACTS—PART 4

- The Philippian jailer (Acts 16:31)
- Crispus (Acts 18:8)
- Aristobulus (Rom. 16:10)
- Narcissus (Rom. 16:11)
- Stephanas (1 Cor. 1:16)

    2. The salvation of a demoniac girl (Acts 16:16-18)
       a. The demon in this girl
         (1) The money it produced through her *(Read Acts 16:16)*
         (2) The message it proclaimed through her *(Read Acts 16:17)*

★ **16:17** Note the cleverness of the demon here who attempted to identify with the message of Paul's true gospel in order to continue deceiving the people with the false gospel propagated through this poor girl.

       b. The deliverance of this girl *(Read Acts 16:18)*
    3. The salvation of a prison keeper (Acts 16:19-40)
       a. The charges *(Read Acts 16:19-21)*
       b. The cruelty *(Read Acts 16:22-23)*
       c. The confinement *(Read Acts 16:24)*
       d. The consternation
         (1) The singing of the prisoners *(Read Acts 16:25)*

★ **16:25** We thus have the first sacred concert ever held in Europe. They sang, as did Christ on the eve of his passion (Matt. 26:30; Mark 14:26).

         (2) The shaking of the prison *(Read Acts 16:26)*
       e. The command *(Read Acts 16:27-28)*
       f. The confusion *(Read Acts 16:30)*
       g. The clarification *(Read Acts 16:31)*
       h. The conversion
         (1) The jailer's belief in Christ *(Read Acts 16:32)*
         (2) The jailer's baptism in Christ *(Read Acts 16:33)*
       i. The celebration *(Read Acts 16:34)*
       j. The conclusion *(Read Acts 16:35, 37-39)*
  D. Fourth stop, Thessalonica (Acts 17:1-9)
    1. The faithfulness of Paul *(Read Acts 17:2-3)*
    2. The fruits of Paul *(Read Acts 17:4)*
    3. The foes of Paul
       a. Their assaults *(Read Acts 17:5)*
       b. Their accusations *(Read Acts 17:6-7)*
  E. Fifth stop, Berea (Acts 17:10-14)
    1. The openness to God's Word
       a. The Bereans researched it *(Read Acts 17:11)*
       b. The Bereans received it *(Read Acts 17:12)*
    2. The opposition to God's Word—"But when the Jews of Thessalonica had knowledge that the word of God was preached of Paul at Berea, they came thither also, and stirred up the people" (Acts 17:13). Timothy and Silas remain in Berea.

F. Sixth stop, Athens (Acts 17:15-34)—Here Paul preached his famous sermon on Mars Hill.
  1. The need for this sermon *(Read Acts 17:16-17)*
  2. The audience of this sermon (Acts 17:18-21)
     a. Who they were *(Read Acts 17:18)*

✱ 17:18
- This first group was named after their founder, Epicurus (341-270 B.C.). They believed that while God existed, he had no interest whatsoever in the welfare of men, and the chief end of life was pleasure. The second group was founded by Zeno (300 B.C.) and believed God was the world's soul which indwelt all things. They held life's goal was to rise above all things and show no emotion whatsoever to either pain or pleasure.
- Both groups took a dim view of Paul's theology, referring to him as a "babbler" (17:18). This word in Greek is *spermologos*, used literally of birds making their nests.

     b. What they did *(Read Acts 17:21)*

✱ 17:21 This may be considered a simplified description of godless, worldly, manmade philosophy. Someone has defined this kind of philosophy as that futile and foolish attempt to learn more and more about less and less until finally one knows everything about nothing.

  3. The introduction to this sermon *(Read Acts 17:22)*
  4. The text of this sermon *(Read Acts 17:23)*
  5. The points in this sermon (Acts 17:24-31)
     a. Regarding the past—God was the Creator of all (Acts 17:24-26, 28-29).
     b. Regarding the present—God desires to be the Savior of all (Acts 17:27, 30).
        (1) Providing they reach out *(Read Acts 17:27)*
        (2) Providing they repent *(Read Acts 17:30)*
     c. Regarding the future—God will judge all people *(Read Acts 17:31)*

✱ 17:31
- Paul presents four great truths about God.
  - He is the Creator (17:24-25).
  - He is the Governor (17:26-29).
  - He is the Savior (17:30).
  - He is the judge (17:31).
- During the course of his sermon (17:28) Paul quotes from one of their own heathen poets (Arotus). (See also Titus 1:12.) If this fact of the appointed judgment day were well known, Easter Sunday morning would become the most dreaded day of all the year for unsaved people (see Rev. 20:11-15).
- Stanley Toussaint observes: "At this point Paul introduced a distinctively Christian viewpoint. His reference to the man clearly looks to Daniel 7:13-14 which speaks of the Son of man. This One, appointed by God the Father, will judge the world with justice (cf. John 5:22). The authentication of Christ's person and work was his resurrection. Here again the resurrection of Jesus was preached. The idea of resurrection (cf. Acts 17:18, 32) was incompatible with Greek philosophy. The Greeks wanted to get rid of their bodies, not take them on again. A personal judgment was also unpalatable to Greeks. The gospel message struck at the center of the Athenians' needs. Paul (vv. 30-31) discussed the topics of sin ('to repent'), righteousness ('justice'), and judgment ('He will judge'), the same areas in which Jesus said the Holy Spirit would convict people (John 16:5-11)" (*Ibid.*, p. 404).

LESSON 19: THE BOOK OF ACTS—PART 4

      6. The reaction to this sermon (Acts 17:32-34)
         a. Some mocked (Acts 17:32).
         b. Some delayed (Acts 17:32).
         c. Some believed (Acts 17:34).
   G. Seventh stop, Corinth (Acts 18:1-18)
      1. Paul's friends in this city (Acts 18:1-5)
         a. The tentmakers (Acts 18:1-3)—He meets a godly couple, Aquila and Priscilla who, like Paul, were tentmakers by trade.

★ **18:3** This remarkable couple is mentioned six times in the New Testament. There are inscriptions in the catacombs which hint that Priscilla was of a distinguished family of high standing in Rome. Later in Ephesus a church met in their home (1 Cor. 16:19). In later years, they apparently moved back to Rome (Rom. 16:3-5).

         b. The team members (Acts 18:5)—Silas and Timothy now catch up with Paul from Macedonia.
      2. Paul's foes in this city (Acts 18:5-6, 12-17)
         a. Their identity *(Read Acts 18:5)*
         b. Their insolence *(Read Acts 18:6)*
         c. Their insurrection (Acts 18:12-17)
            (1) The futility of their efforts (Acts 18:12-16)—They unsuccessfully attempt to indict Paul before Gallio, the Roman deputy.
            (2) The irony of their efforts *(Read Acts 18:17)*
      3. Paul's fruits in this city *(Read Acts 18:8, 11)*
      4. Paul's heavenly Father in this city *(Read Acts 18:9-10)*—Paul wrote 1 and 2 Thessalonians from Corinth.

★ **18:10**
- Every minister and missionary serving in God's perfect will can boldly claim this precious promise concerning their particular field of service.
- A similar promise is later given to the church in the city of Philadelphia: *"I know thy works: behold, I have set before thee an open door, and no man can shut it: for thou hast a little strength, and hast kept my word, and hast not denied my name" (Rev. 3:8).*

   H. Eighth stop, Ephesus (Acts 18:19-21)
      1. He is accompanied by his friends Aquila and Priscilla (Acts 18:18).
      2. He is asked by his converts to dwell in Ephesus *(Read Acts 18:20-21)*

★ **18:21** Paul's last phrase here should condition all our plans (see 21:14; 1 Cor. 4:19; 16:7; Heb. 6:3; James 4:15).

   I. Final stop, back to Antioch (Acts 18:22)

LESSON 20

VII. The Third Missionary Journey of Paul (Acts 18:23-21:14)
  A. First stop, Asia Minor (Acts 18:23)—Paul revisits these churches to exhort and instruct them.
  B. Second stop, Ephesus (Acts 18:24-19:41)
    1. The forerunner of Paul in Ephesus (Acts 18:24-28)— *"And a certain Jew named Apollos, born at Alexandria, an eloquent man, and mighty in the scriptures, came to Ephesus" (Acts 18:24).*
      a. The teaching of Apollos *(Read Acts 18:25)*
      b. The teachers of Apollos *(Read Acts 18:26)*
    2. The fruits of Paul in Ephesus (Acts 19:1-41)
      a. The disciples of John (Acts 19:1-7)—Paul finds 12 disciples of John the Baptist who knew only of the ministry of Christ and nothing of Pentecost. He brings them up to date *(Read Acts 19:5-6)*.

✴ **19:6**
- This is the final of three instances in Acts in which individuals spoke in tongues (see 2:1-4 and 10:44-47 for the first two).
- This is also the only instance in the entire Bible where people were rebaptized.
- Finally, this marks the last of nine occasions on which individuals were baptized in the book of Acts. The first eight were:
  - The 3,000 at Pentecost (2:41)
  - The believers at Samaria (8:12)
  - The Ethiopian eunuch in the desert of Gaza (8:38)
  - Saul at Damascus (9:18)
  - Cornelius at Caesarea (10:48)
  - Lydia and her household at Philippi (16:15)
  - The jailer and his household at Philippi (16:33)
  - Crispus and his household at Corinth (18:8)

      b. The duration with Tyrannus *(Read Acts 19:8-10)*

✴ **19:10** During this time the churches at Colosse, Laodicea, and Hierapolis were founded (Col. 4:13). It is also possible that all seven churches of Revelation 2-3 were started at this time.

      c. The distribution of prayer cloths *(Read Acts 19:11-12)*
      d. The divinations of Sceva (Acts 19:13-17)— *"Then certain of the vagabond Jews, exorcists, took upon them to call over them which had evil spirits the name of the Lord Jesus, saying, We adjure you by Jesus whom Paul preacheth. And there were seven sons of one Sceva, a Jew, and chief of the priests, which did so" (Acts 19:13-14).*
        (1) The hostile answer by the evil spirit *(Read Acts 19:15)*
        (2) The hostile action by the evil spirit *(Read Acts 19:16)*

✴ **19:16** This is the final of at least 11 New Testament instances of demon-possessed individuals. These are:
- Man of Capernaum, healed by Christ in the synagogue on the Sabbath (Mark 1:24; Luke 4:35)
- Maniac of Gadara, possessed by and healed of a legion of demons (Matt. 8:28-32; Mark 5:2-13; Luke 8:33)
- A mute man healed by Christ, causing the multitudes to rejoice (Matt. 9:32-33)

- A girl from Tyre and Sidon, healed at the request of her heartbroken mother (Matt. 15:28; Mark 7:29)
- A boy at the base of Mount Hermon, healed at the request of his heartbroken father (Matt. 17:18; Mark 9:25; Luke 9:42)
- A blind and deaf man whom Christ was accused of healing by the power of Beelzebub (Matt. 12:22; Luke 11:14)
- Woman with an 18-year infirmity, healed by Christ in a synagogue on the Sabbath (Luke 13:10-13)
- Mary Magdalene, healed by Christ of seven demons (Mark 16:9; Luke 8:2)
- Judas Iscariot, possessed by Satan himself (Luke 22:3; John 6:70; 13:27)
- A slave girl with powers of divination, healed by Paul at Philippi (Acts 16:16-18)
- Sceva's sons, renegade Jews at Ephesus (Acts 19:15-16)

> e. The dedication of the converts *(Read Acts 19:18-20)*
> f. The decision of Paul (Acts 19:21-22)—At this time Paul determines to visit Rome someday.
> g. The defenders of Diana (Acts 19:23-41)
> (1) The libel of Demetrius (Acts 19:23-28)—An anti-Paul meeting is conducted by Demetrius, a silversmith who had profited by making silver shrines for the goddess Diana. At the meeting he said: *"Moreover ye see and hear, that not alone at Ephesus, but almost throughout all Asia, this Paul hath persuaded and turned away much people, saying that they be no gods, which are made with hands: so that not only this our craft is in danger to be set at nought; but also that the temple of the great goddess Diana should be despised, and her magnificence should be destroyed, whom all Asia and the world worshippeth"* (Acts 19:26-27).

★ **19:27** The temple of Diana (the Greek name was Artemis) was one of the seven wonders of the ancient world. The image within the temple was of a woman carved with many breasts to signify the fertility of nature. The original stone from which the image had been carved was reported to have fallen from heaven, leading some historians to believe it may have been a meteorite.

> (2) The lunacy of the crowd (Acts 19:29-34)—*"And the whole city was filled with confusion: and ... rushed with one accord into the theater"* (Acts 19:31). *"Some therefore cried one thing, and some another: for the assembly was confused; and the more part knew not wherefore they were come together"* (Acts 19:32). For the next two hours this mob screamed out: *"Great is Diana of the Ephesians!"* (Acts 19:34).
> (3) The logic of the town clerk (Acts 19:35-41)—This intelligent Greek official calms down the mob through four logical arguments:
> (a) The divinity of the statue *(Read Acts 19:35-36)*

★ **19:36** This argument was somewhat similar to one once made by Joash, father of Gideon, concerning the Canaanite god Baal (Judg. 6:31). In essence, both were saying, "These are well-known gods, so let them defend themselves."

> (b) The honesty of the opponents *(Read Acts 19:37)*
> (c) The legality of the matter *(Read Acts 19:38-39)*
> (d) The (possible) hostility of the Romans *(Read Acts 19:40)*. Paul wrote 1 and 2 Corinthians from Ephesus.
> C. Third stop, Greece (Acts 20:1-5)—After a stay of three months he leaves to escape a plot of the Jews to kill him. Paul wrote Romans from Greece.
> D. Fourth stop, Troas (Acts 20:6-12)
> 1. The midnight address *(Read Acts 20:7)*

★ **20:7** Note: Especially significant in this portion of Scripture is the phrase, *"Upon the first day of the week"* (20:7).

The *New Scofield Bible* observes: "Although Paul was in Troas seven days (v. 6), apparently neither he nor the local church met for the breaking of bread until the first day of the week (v. 7).

The fact that Paul and others sometimes attended Sabbath services in Jewish synagogues (17:1-3) does not prove that the apostolic Church kept the seventh day as a special day of worship. It only shows that the early missionaries took the Gospel message wherever and whenever they found people gathered together (5:19-20; 13:5; 16:13, 25-33; 17:17, 19, 17:17, 19, 22; 125:6, 23). This witness was carried on daily (2:47; 17:17; 19:9) in every possible way (1 Cor. 9:19-22).

The early churches were specifically warned against submitting themselves to the bondage of any legalistic observance of Sabbath days (Col. 2:16, cf. Gal. 4:9-11). On the other hand, in the exercise of their Christian liberty (Rom. 14:5-6), these same churches voluntarily chose the first day of the week as an appropriate time for fellowship and worship (Acts 20:7; 1 Cor.16:2), the day on which the Lord arose and repeatedly appeared to his disciples (John 20:19-29). It was a new day for a new people belonging to a new creation (2 Cor. 5:17), a day of commemoration and joy (Matt. 28:9, marg.), service (Matt. 28:10), and spiritual rest (Heb. 4:9-10). This observance of the first day of the week is corroborated by the early fathers: in the writings of Barnabas (c. A.D.100), Ignatius (A.D. 107), Justin Martyr (A.D.145-150), and Irenaeus (A.D. 155-202). The edict of Laodicea (fourth century A.D.) did not change the day of worship from the seventh to the first day of the week, as is sometimes alleged, but rather put the stamp of official approval upon an observance already long established in the early churches." (*The New Scofield Bible*, pp. 1194-1195).

> 2. The midmorning accident *(Read Acts 20:8-9)*
> 3. The miraculous awakening *(Read Acts 20:10-12)*

★ **20:12** This marks the final of eight resurrections in the Bible. This number does not include the resurrection of Christ, nor the ones who arose with him. The eight resurrections are:
- The son of a widow at Zarephath, raised by Elijah (1 Kings 17:22)
- The son of the Shunammite woman, raised by Elisha (2 Kings 4:35)
- A man, raised by Elisha (2 Kings 13:21)
- The son of a widow at Nain, raised by Jesus (Luke 7:14-15)
- The daughter of Jairus, raised by Jesus (Luke 8:54-55)
- Lazarus, at Bethany, raised by Jesus (John 11:44)
- Dorcas, at Joppa, raised by Peter (Acts 9:40)
- Eutychus, at Troas, raised by Paul (Acts 20:12)

> E. Fifth stop, Miletus (Acts 20:13-38)—"*And from Miletus he sent to Ephesus, and called the elders of the church*" *(Acts 20:17)*.
> 1. He reviews the past *(Read Acts 20:31)*
>   a. His role as a servant of Christ *(Read Acts 20:19)*
>   b. His role as a teacher of saints *(Read Acts 20:20, 27)*
>   c. His role as a witness to sinners *(Read Acts 20:21, 26)*

★ **20:26** He had taught "*publickly, and from house to house*" the grace of God to sinners and saints alike (20:20-21). It is significant that the world's most famous theologian was also a great soul winner.

> d. His role as an example to all *(Read Acts 20:33-35)*

★ **20:35** Note: This statement is not found in the four Gospel accounts (although perhaps implied in Luke 14:12). His own life, of course, perfectly exemplified it. (See 2 Cor. 8:9; Eph. 5:2; Phil. 2:5-8; also John 21:25.)

> 2. He views the present.
>   a. Summarizing his situation *(Read Acts 20:22-23, 25)*
>   b. Summarizing their situation (Acts 20:28, 32)
>   (1) What they were to do *(Read Acts 20:28)*
>   (2) How they were to do it *(Read Acts 20:32)*

> 3. He previews the future.
>   a. What his desire was *(Acts 20:24)*
>   b. What their dangers would be *(Read Acts 20:29-30)*

★ **20:30** Paul later writes Timothy, who is in Ephesus, concerning the "grievous wolves" (1 Tim. 1:3-7). His prophecy concerning apostasy from "your own selves" was tragically fulfilled by men like Hymenaeus, Alexander, Philetus, and others. (See 1 Tim. 1:20; 2 Tim. 2:17.)

> F. Sixth stop, Tyre (Acts 21:1-6)
>   1. A message from the Spirit *(Read Acts 21:4)*

★ **21:4**
- It would seem that the apostle missed God's will here. He had already been warned during the beginning of his ministry by the Lord to: *"Make haste, and get thee quickly out of Jerusalem: for they will not receive thy testimony concerning me"* (22:18).
- Paul's motive for going to Jerusalem at this time seems to have been his great love for his people (Rom. 9:1-5) and his hope that the gifts of the Gentile churches, sent by him to the poor saints at Jerusalem (Rom. 15:25-28), would open the hearts of the law-bound Jewish believers to the Gospel of God's grace. At any rate, it is very significant that his Jerusalem stop (even though brief) is one of the very few at which absolutely no fruit is recorded.

>   2. A meeting on the sand *(Read Acts 21:5-6)*
> G. Seventh stop, Ptolemais *(Read Acts 21:7)*
> H. Eighth stop, Caesarea (Acts 21:8-14)
>   1. The warrior of God *(Read Acts 21:8)*
>   2. The women of God *(Read Acts 21:9)*

★ **21:9** He visits the home of Philip the evangelist and his four unmarried daughters, all of whom are prophetesses. These young women are the last mentioned in the Bible who had this gift. Others were:
- Miriam (Exod. 15:20)
- Deborah (Judg. 4:4)
- Isaiah's wife (Isa. 8:3)
- Huldah (2 Kings 22:14)
- Anna (Luke 2:36)

>   3. The warning from God *(Read Acts 21:10-11)*
>   4. The will of God *(Read Acts 21:12-14)*.
> **VIII. The Final Visit to Jerusalem by Paul (Acts 21:15-30)**
>   A. The rumors against Paul (Acts 21:18-22, 27-30)
>   1. That he had denounced the Law of Moses (Acts 21:18-21)—James informs Paul that many Jews were saying this about him *(Read Acts 21:21)*.
>   2. That he had desecrated the temple of God (Acts 21:27-30)—He was incorrectly accused of bringing a Gentile named Trophimus into the temple.
>   B. The reaction by Paul (Acts 21:23-26)—To counteract these false rumors Paul agrees to put himself back under the Law, shaves his head, and takes a seven-day vow.
>   C. The rescue of Paul *(Read Acts 21:20-32)*—In spite of Paul's efforts the rumors persist and he is set upon by a murderous Jewish mob.
>   D. The replies by Paul (Acts 21:33-23:10)
>   1. His replies to the chief captain
>   a. First dialogue (Acts 21:33-39)

                        (1) The captain's confusion *(Read Acts 21:38)*
                        (2) The apostle's correction *(Read Acts 21:39)*
                    b. Second dialogue (Acts 22:24-30)
                        (1) The command of the captain (Acts 22:24)—In an attempt to secure more information, the captain orders Paul to be scourged. The apostle then said: *"And as they bound him with thongs, Paul said unto the centurion that stood by, Is it lawful for you to scourge a man that is a Roman, and uncondemned?" (Acts 22:25)*.
                        (2) The concern of the captain *(Read Acts 22:28-29)*
            2. His reply to the Jewish mob (Acts 21:40-22:23)—*"And when he had given him licence, Paul stood on the stairs, and beckoned with the hand unto the people. And when there was made a great silence, he spake unto them in the Hebrew tongue" (Acts 21:40)*.
                a. The speech (Acts 22:1-21)
                    (1) His conversion (Acts 22:1-16)—*"And it came to pass, that, as I made my journey, and was come nigh unto Damascus about noon, suddenly there shone from heaven a great light round about me. And I fell unto the ground, and heard a voice saying unto me, Saul, Saul, why persecutest thou me? And I answered, Who art thou, Lord? And he said unto me, I am Jesus of Nazareth, whom thou persecutest.... And I said, What shall I do, Lord? And the Lord said unto me, Arise, and go into Damascus; and there it shall be told thee of all things which are appointed for thee to do" (Acts 22:6-8, 10)*.

✶ Paul continues relating his salvation experience and meeting with Ananias, as first recorded in Acts 9:15-17. Here though, before this Jewish mob, Paul includes a comment made by Ananias not found in the original account: *"And now why tarriest thou? arise, and be baptized, and wash away thy sins, calling on the name of the Lord" (Acts 22:16)*.

Stanley Toussaint writes: "Two questions revolve about this verse. First, when was Paul saved on the Damascus Road or at Judas' house? Several factors suggest he was saved on the Damascus Road: (1) The gospel was presented to him directly by Christ (Gal. 1:11-12), not later by Ananias. (2) Already (Acts 22:10) Paul said he had submitted in faith to Christ. (3) Paul was filled with the Spirit before his baptism with water (9:17-18). (4) The Greek aorist participle, epikalesamenos, translated calling on His name refers either to action, which is simultaneous with, or before that of the main verb. Here Paul's calling on Christ's name (for salvation) preceded His water baptism. The participle may be translated, 'having called on His name."

"Second, what then do the words wash your sins away mean? Do they teach that salvation comes by water baptism? Because Paul was already cleansed spiritually [see comments in preceding paragraph], these words must refer to the symbolism of baptism. Baptism is a picture of God's inner work of washing away sin (cf. 1 Cor. 6:11; 1 Pet. 3:21)" *(Ibid.*, p. 418).

                    (2) His call *(Read Acts 22:17-21)*
                b. The screams *(Read Acts 22:22-23)*
            3. His reply to the Sanhedrin (Acts 23:1-10)
                a. The reprisal *(Read Acts 23:1-2)*
                b. The retaliation *(Read Acts 23:3)*

✶ **23:3** The phrase "whited wall" suggested a tottering wall whose precarious position had been disguised by a generous coat of whitewash. The meaning was that, although he held a high position, he would someday fall. In fact, he was assassinated some eight years later.

                c. The regret *(Read Acts 23:4-5)*
                d. The ruse *(Read Acts 23:6-10)*
        E. The revelation to Paul *(Read Acts 23:11)*

✶ **23:11** Paul had often hoped to get to Rome (Rom. 1:13). In Ephesus he had made definite plans to go, but at this point he was not sure he would get away from Jerusalem alive (Rom. 15:31-32). But now, for the first time, God had said it.

LESSON 20: THE BOOK OF ACTS—PART 5

F. The revenge against Paul *(Read Acts 23:12-15)*
G. The relative of Paul (Acts 23:16-22)
    1. Overhearing the plot against his uncle *(Read Acts 23:16)*
    2. Overturning the plot against his uncle *(Read Acts 23:17, 19-20)*
H. The removal of Paul (Acts 23:23-32)
    1. The soldiers *(Read Acts 23:23-24)*
    2. The salutation (Acts 23:25-32)—The chief captain wrote a letter to Felix explaining the circumstances surrounding Paul's arrest.

IX. The Imprisonment of Paul in Caesarea (Acts 23:33-26:32)
A. Paul before Felix (Acts 23:33-24:27)
    1. Felix reviews a lawsuit against Paul *(Read Acts 23:33, 35)*

✶ 23:35
- Both officially and personally, Felix was noted for his evil deeds. Tacitus, the Roman historian, writes: "Felix, indulging in every kind of barbarity and lust, exercised the power of a king in the spirit of a slave." Felix was later guilty of having the Jewish high priest Jonathan (Annas's son) assassinated.
- He is one of three Roman procurators referred to in the New Testament. The others are:
  - Pontius Pilate (Matt. 27:2)
  - Porcius Festus (Acts 24:27)

       a. The defamation by the prosecution *(Read Acts 24:1)*—This articulate Jewish lawyer accused Paul of three things.
          (1) That he was a political rebel *(Read Acts 24:5a)*
          (2) That he was a religious heretic *(Read Acts 24:5b)*
          (3) That he desecrated the temple *(Read Acts 24:6a)*
       b. The defense by the prisoner
          (1) Paul pleads innocent concerning charges 1 and 3 *(Read Acts 24:11-13)*
          (2) Paul pleads guilty concerning charge number 2 *(Read Acts 24:14-16, 20-21)*
       c. The decision by the politician *(Read Acts 24:22-23)*
    2. Felix refuses a lecture delivered by Paul *(Read Acts 24:24-25)*

✶ 24:25
- Both Felix and Drusilla are affected by Paul's preaching. This girl, not yet 20, is the youngest daughter of Herod Agrippa I (murderer of James, Acts 12:1-2), and the sister of Agrippa II and Bernice, mentioned in 25:13. She had left a pagan Syrian king to marry Felix. (Drusilla died 21 years later in the eruption of Mt. Vesuvius.)
- Felix thought he could call upon God in a "convenient season," a time, of course, which never comes. (See Prov. 27:1; Luke 12:16-20; James 4:13-14.)

    3. Felix requests some lucre (money) from Paul *(Read Acts 24:26)*
B. Paul before Festus (Acts 25:1-12)
    1. Festus and the plotters
       a. Their ungodly plan *(Read Acts 25:1-3)*
       b. Their unsuccessful plan *(Read Acts 25:4-6)*
    2. Festus and the prisoner
       a. The accusations *(Read Acts 25:7)*
       b. The answer *(Read Acts 25:8)*
       c. The appeasement *(Read Acts 25:9)*
       d. The appeal *(Read Acts 25:10-11)*

★ **25:11** The Caesar to whom Paul appeals is Nero, who began his reign in A.D. 54. His early years were gentle in nature and gave no hint of the cruelties which would follow.

> e. The agreement *(Read Acts 25:12)*
> C. Paul before Agrippa (Acts 25:13-26:32)
>   1. Learning about Paul *(Read Acts 25:13-15)*

★ **25:13** Stanley Toussaint writes: "The King Agrippa referred to here was Agrippa II, son of Herod Agrippa I (Acts 12:1) and a great-grandson of Herod the Great (Matt. 2:1). At this time he was a young man of about 30 years of age and the ruler of territories northeast of Palestine with the title of King. Because he was a friend of the Roman imperial family he was awarded the privilege of appointing the Jewish high priest and also had been made the custodian of the temple treasury. His background made him eminently qualified to hear Paul; he was well acquainted with the Jews' religion (cf. Acts 25:26-27). Agrippa II and his sister Bernice came to Caesarea to pay their respects to Festus. Though Bernice had a tendency to support the Jews, she lived a profligate life. She had an incestuous relationship with Agrippa, her brother" (*Ibid.*, p. 423).

>   2. Listening to Paul
>   a. The pomp involved *(Read Acts 25:23)*
>   b. The permission involved *(Read Acts 26:1)*
>   c. The preaching involved
>   (1) Paul reviews his life as a religious man *(Read Acts 26:4-5, 9-11)*
>   (2) Paul reviews his life as a redeemed man *(Read Acts 26:12-19)*
>   d. The protest involved *(Read Acts 26:24-25)*
>   e. The persuasion involved *(Read Acts 26:26-29)*

★ **26:29** Note: It cannot be determined from this verse that Agrippa was at the point of accepting Christ. The Greek text reads: "In short, you are trying to persuade me to be a Christian." The king may have meant he could not be convinced in such a brief period of time.

> f. The postscript involved *(Read Acts 26:30-32)*—Paul may have written Hebrews at this time in Caesarea.
> **X. The Voyage of Paul to Rome (Acts 27:1-28:15)**
>   A. Phase one—From Caesarea to Fair Havens (Acts 27:1-12)
>   1. Julius's kindness to Paul *(Read Acts 27:1, 3)*
>   2. Paul's caution to Julius *(Read Acts 27:9-11)*

★ **27:11** At this time it is late autumn. Among the ancients the dangerous season for sailing was from September 14 to November 11. After this date all navigation on the open sea was discontinued. In spite of this knowledge, and over the protests of Paul (who had already been through at least three shipwrecks; see 2 Cor. 11:25), the boat officials set sail for Phoenix, planning to winter there.

>   B. Phase two—From Fair Havens to Melita (Acts 27:13-44)
>   1. The fearful storm *(Read Acts 27:14-20)*

★ **27:20** This is the final, perhaps most furious of four well-known biblical storms. The other three are:
- The storm experienced by Jonah (Jonah 1:4-15)
- The first storm experienced by the disciples (Matt. 8:23-27; Mark 4:35-41; Luke 8:22-25).
- The second storm experienced by the disciples (Matt. 14:22-32; Mark 6:45-52; John 6:15-21)

LESSON 20: THE BOOK OF ACTS—PART 5

       2. The cheerful saint (Acts 27:21-26, 33-37)
           a. The prophetical aspect *(Read Acts 27:23-25)*
               (1) There would be no loss of life (Acts 27:22)
               (2) Only the ship would be lost (Acts 27:22)
               (3) They would be cast on an island (Acts 27:26)
           b. The practical aspect *(Read Acts 27:33-37)*
           c. The political aspect *(Read Acts 27:39-44)*
  C. Phase three—At Melita (Acts 28:1-10)
       1. Paul and the people (Acts 28:1-6)
           a. First viewed as a murderer *(Read Acts 28:2-4)*
           b. Finally viewed as a messiah *(Read Acts 28:5-7)*

✶ **28:6**
- This event was a direct fulfillment of Jesus' prophecy in Mark 16:18 and Luke 10:19.
- This is the second time in Acts when Paul was looked upon as a god (see 14:11-15).

       2. Paul and Publius (Acts 28:7-10)
           a. Healing a father (Acts 28:8)
           b. Healing his friends (Acts 28:9)
  D. Phase four—From Melita to Rome (Acts 28:11-15)

✶ **28:15** Luke informs us that "when the brethren heard of us, they came to meet us." The phrase in 28:15 "to meet us" is the same word found concerning the rapture of all believers in 1 Thessalonians 4:17, where we read, "to meet the Lord in the air." It is a term regularly used of the official welcome tendered by a delegation who went out to meet a visiting official and accompany him into the city.

  E. Phase five—At Rome (Acts 28:16-31)
       1. The two meetings—During which the gospel is explained to the Roman Jews (Acts 28:17-29)
           a. First meeting (Acts 28:17-22)
               (1) The review of the apostle—He gives them the background for his appearing there in chains (Acts 28:17-20).
               (2) The reaction of the audience *(Read Acts 28:21-22)*
           b. Second meeting (Acts 28:12-19)
               (1) The Son of God *(Read Acts 28:23-24)*
               (2) The Scripture of God *(Read Acts 28:25-26)*
               (3) The salvation of God *(Read Acts 28:28)*
       2. The two years—During which the gospel is explained to all. *"And Paul dwelt two whole years in his own hired house, and received all that came in unto him, preaching the kingdom of God, and teaching those things which concern the Lord Jesus Christ, with all confidence, no man forbidding him" (Acts 28:30-31)*. Paul wrote the books of Ephesians, Colossians, Philemon, and Philippians from Rome.

Two: Letters by Paul to the Churches

A study of the epistles of Paul written to the churches:

- Romans
- I Corinthians
- II Corinthians
- Galatians
- Ephesians
- Philippians
- Colossians
- I Thessalonians
- II Thessalonians

LESSON 21
INTRODUCTION TO ROMANS

THE FORT KNOX IN BIBLE DOCTRINE — BASIC THEOLOGY IN ITS PUREST FORM

The most profound discussion about the most profound subject in all of Scripture—God's plan and purpose for saving sinners:

A. These words can only refer to one book in the Bible, and that is Romans.
B. If one were to attempt to determine the worth of this amazing no-nonsense, bottom line summary of God's person, plan, and purpose in matters of doctrine, practical living, and prophecy, and by the untold millions of saints and theologians its pages have produced during the last 20 centuries, then every single one it its 9,447 words would be equal to at least a billion dollars each.
C. This marvelous manuscript is in reality the Declaration of Independence, Constitution, and Bill of Rights of the Christian faith.
D. The founder of the Roman church is unknown.
  1. It was definitely not Paul.
  2. It was probably not Peter (see 15:20-21).
E. Both Peter and Paul, however, were later martyred at Rome (2 Pet. 1:14; 2 Tim. 4:6-8).
F. The church was probably founded by converts at Pentecost (Acts 2:10).
G. The membership consisted of both Jews and Gentiles, but mostly Gentiles (1:13; 11:13; 15:16).
H. Paul was anxious to visit this church (1:8-11).
I. God later assured Paul he would indeed go to Rome (Acts 23:11).
J. Paul knew many believers there in Rome, sending his greeting to 26, calling them by name (Rom. 16).
K. He requests prayer from this church (15:30-32).
L. At least four facts are brought out concerning the internal affairs of this church.
  1. The positive things:
    a. They shared their faith (1:8).
    b. They were obedient to the faith (16:19).
  2. The negative things:
    a. Some were guilty of judging others (14:10).
    b. Some were causing divisions (16:17).
M. Romans provides us with the most detailed indictment of God's hatred for sexual perversion in all the Bible (1:18-32).
N. This book is a book about righteousness. It says, God is righteous, God *demands* righteousness, and God *provides* righteousness. We are told just what righteousness is, what it isn't, who needs it, why it is needed, where one may and may not find it.
O. Romans provides the greatest contrast between Christ and Adam in the Bible (5:12-21).
P. It gives us the most expanded explanation of God's past, present, and future dealings with Israel in all the Bible (9-11).

Q. It includes the most comforting verse in the Scriptures for Christians in distress (8:28).
R. Romans 8 is considered by many as the most profound and precious chapter in the New Testament.
S. This book spells out in great detail the vocabulary of salvation—terms such as: justification, sanctification, glorification, preservation, and transformation. All of them deal directly with the power of the gospel and the person (Christ) of the gospel.
T. Romans is the only New Testament book with no less than five distinct benedictions. (See 11:33-36; 15:13; 15:30-33; 16:20; 16:24-27.)
U. There are quotations or allusions from 23 Old Testament books in Romans. Romans is the eighth longest New Testament book, and 29th longest biblical book, with 16 chapters, 433 verses, and 9,447 words.
V. Great passages would include:
   1. 1:16-17
   2. 3:10-19
   3. 5:1-11
   4. 6:1-5
   5. 8:33-39
   6. 11:33-36
   7. 12:1-2

Overview of the Book of Romans

The Courthouse of Law: God's Wrath (Condemnation and Justification) — Romans 1-5

I. The Court Reporter
   A. The credentials of the reporter — How Paul describes himself
      1. He was a servant
      2. He was an apostle and a separated saint
      3. He was a gospel preacher
      4. He was a missionary to the Gentiles
   B. The Christ of the reporter
      1. As prophesied in the Old Testament
      2. As proclaimed in the New Testament
   C. The concern of the reporter
      1. The identity of this church
      2. The intercession for this church
      3. The interest in this church
      4. The indebtedness to this church
   D. The confidence of the reporter
   E. The conclusion of the reporter

II. The Court Record
   A. The charge
   B. The defendants
      1. A heathen — The pagan
      2. A hypocrite — The moral person
      3. A Hebrew — The religious person
   C. The detailed indictment
      1. First indictment — Ingratitude
      2. Second indictment — Insolence
      3. Third indictment — Idolatry
      4. Fourth indictment — Immorality
      5. Fifth indictment — Incorrigibility
   D. The jury
      1. The conscience of a person
      2. The deeds of a person
      3. The works of God
      4. The Law of God
   E. The defense
      1. The pagan's defense

  2. The moral person's defense
  3. The religious person's defense
 F. The verdict
  1. Man's character is depraved
  2. People's conversation is depraved
  3. People's conduct is depraved
 G. The sentence
 H. The miracle
  1. The nature of this miracle
  2. The persons in this miracle
  3. The source of this miracle
  4. The scope of this miracle
  5. The bestowal of this miracle
  6. The witnesses of this miracle
  7. The legal accomplishments of this miracle
  8. The harmony seen in this miracle
 I. The two spokesmen for the court
  1. Abraham, Israel's racial father
  2. David, Israel's royal father

III. The Court Review
 A. summary of justification
  1. The believer has peace with God
  2. The believer has access to God
  3. The believer receives assurance from God
  4. The believer is indwelled by God
  5. The believer is preserved in God
 B. A summary of condemnation
  1. The work of Adam
  2. The work of Christ

The Power Plant of Grace: God's Way (Sanctification and Preservation) — Romans 6-8

I. The Plan — First Floor of Sanctification
In this chapter Paul lists God's three-fold method leading to sanctification
 A. Know ye
  1. That we have been baptized with Christ into his death
  2. That we have been planted together in the likeness of his resurrection
  3. That because of these two facts, the believer is:
   a. Delivered from his sin
   b. Delivered to his Savior
 B. Reckon ye
 C. Yield ye

1. The rationale for this yielding
2. The rewards of this yielding

II. The Pain — The Second Floor of Frustration
  A. The spiritual man and the Law
    1. His relationship to the Law
    2. His relationship to the Savior
  B. The natural person and the Law
    1. The condemnation usage
    2. The illustration usage
  C. The carnal person and the Law
    1. Any attempt to keep the Law will lead to carnality
    2. No attempt to keep the Law can lead to spirituality

III. The Prize
  A. The believer has a new position
    1. His position in regard to the Son of God
    2. His position in regard to the law of God
  B. The believer has a new guest
  C. The believer has a new adoption
  D. The believer has a new hope
    1. The Christian himself
    2. The creation itself
  E. The believer has a new prayer helper
    1. The identity of this helper
    2. The necessity for this helper
    3. The intensity of this helper
    4. The infallibility of this helper
  F. The believer has a new confidence
  G. The believer has a new destiny
    1. The nature of this goal
    2. The steps involved in this goal
    3. The guarantee of this goal

The Synagogue of Israel: God's Wisdom (Explanation and Vindication) — Romans 9-11

I. The Sovereignty of God and Israel's Selection in the Past
  A. The nine spiritual advantages of this sovereign selection
    1. They were Israelites (a special nation)
    2. They had been adopted by God
    3. They had the glory cloud
    4. They had the covenants
    5. They had the Law

      6. They performed services for God
      7. They had the messianic promise
      8. They had a regenerate ancestry
      9. They were the people from which Christ came
  B. The historical example of this sovereign selection
      1. The example of Ishmael and Isaac
      2. The example of Esau and Jacob
      3. The example of Pharaoh
      4. The example from Hosea
      5. The example from Isaiah
  C. The two conclusions concerning this sovereign selection
      1. Through faith the Gentiles had attained righteousness without even seeking it
      2. Through the Law Israel had not attained righteousness even after seeking it

II. The Righteousness of God and Israel's Rejection at the Present
  A. The prayer for God's righteousness
  B. The source of God's righteousness
  C. The availability of God's righteousness
  D. The method of God's righteousness
  E. The scope of God's righteousness
  F. The presentation of God's righteousness
      1. A sinner must call upon the Lord to be saved
      2. He must believe in order to call
      3. He must hear in order to believe
  G. The rejection of God's righteousness
      1. Isaiah had prophesied this rejection
      2. Moses had prophesied this rejection

III. The Wisdom of God and Israel's Restoration in the Future
  A. This restoration is assured because Israel's rejection was not total
      1. The factions of Israel
      2. The fullness of the Gentiles
  B. This restoration is assured because Israel's rejection was not permanent
      1. The Israel of God
      2. The God of Israel

The Temple of God: God's Will (Transformation & Exhortation) — Romans 12-16

I. Personal Responsibilities for All the Redeemed
  A. The believer and self
      1. What he is to offer: Body dedication
      2. What he is to avoid: Worldly conformation
      3. What he is to achieve: Godly transformation
  B. The believer and service
      1. The tools for Christian service

        2. The techniques of service
    C. The believer and society
        1. The what of the matter
        2. The why of the matter
        3. The who of the matter
    D. The believer and weaker saints
        1. No believer is to be judged by another down here
        2. All believers will be judged up there
    E. The believer and the Savior
        1. It was a sacrificial ministry
        2. It was a suffering ministry
        3. It was a sharing ministry
        4. It was a settling ministry
        5. It was a sure ministry

II. Personal Remarks to the Roman Redeemed
    A. Paul reviews his past
        1. He mentions his specialized ministry
        2. He mentions his miracles
        3. He mentions his mission field
        4. He mentions his modus operandi
    B. Paul previews his future
        1. He determines to visit them at a later time, as he goes to Spain
        2. He desires their prayers at the present time, as he goes to Jerusalem
        3. He delivers greetings to his many Roman friends
        4. He denounces troublemakers
        5. He declares the doom of Satan
        6. He delivers his final benediction

THE BOOK OF ROMANS

The Courthouse of Law: God's Wrath (Condemnation and Justification) — Romans 1-5

> I. The Court Reporter (Rom. 1:1-17)
>   A. The credentials of the reporter—How Paul describes himself
>   1. He was a servant (Rom. 1:1).
>   2. He was an apostle and a separated saint (Rom. 1:1).

✶ **1:1**
- He was a called apostle. Two things were necessary for apostleship:
  - He had to have seen Jesus (1 Cor. 9:1; 15:8-9).
  - His call must have come from God (John 6:70; Acts 9:15)—No man should enter the ministry unless God calls him. (See John 15:16; Matt. 9:38; Heb. 5:14; Jer. 23:21; Ezek. 13:4-6, 10.)
- He was a separated saint—There are three specific separations which took place in Paul's life.
  - At his birth (Gal. 1:15)
  - On the Damascus Road (Acts 9:15-16)—His conversion to Christ
  - At Antioch (Acts 13:1-2)—His call to service. Paul was separated, as were Jeremiah (Jer. 1:5) and John the Baptist (Luke 1:15).

> 3. He was a gospel preacher (Rom. 1:2).
> 4. He was a missionary to the Gentiles (Rom. 1:5,13-14).
>   B. The Christ of the reporter
>   1. As prophesied in the Old Testament *(Read Rom. 1:2)*
>   2. As proclaimed in the New Testament *(Read Rom. 1:3-4)*

✶ **1:5** Paul lists six facts about the glorious gospel in 1:2-5.
- It is not new—Paul said the Old Testament prophets spoke of it. In Romans he quotes from the Old Testament no less than 61 times, from 14 books. This totally refutes any claims of cults to have new and exotic truth concerning the gospel. It is rightly observed that "if something is new, it's probably not true, and if it's true, then it is not new."
- It is about Jesus—The founder and finisher of the gospel is Christ.
- It was manifested through the incarnation—Paul speaks of the virgin birth and humanity of Christ in 1:3. Christ is the seed of David.
- It was declared through the resurrection—The Greek word "declared" in 1:4 is *horizo* (from which comes our word "horizon"), meaning "to mark out by sure signs." Thus, God's clear boundary between earth and heaven is Christ, the Son of God.
  - His humanity is spoken of, as seen by the following:
    - He grew (Luke 2:40, 52).
    - He looked like a man (John 4:9; 20:15).
    - He became hungry (Matt. 4:2).
    - He knew thirst (John 19:28).

- ✦ He grew weary (Mark 4:38; John 4:6).
- ✦ He wept (John 11:35; Luke 19:41).
- ✦ He suffered, bled, and died (1 Pet. 2:21; John 19:34; Matt. 27:50).
- His deity is spoken of, as seen by the following:
  - ✦ He is called God (Titus 2:13).
  - ✦ He is eternal (Rev. 1:8, 18).
  - ✦ He is unchanging (Heb. 13:8).
  - ✦ He is all-powerful (Heb. 1:3).
  - ✦ He is all-knowing (Col. 2:3).
  - ✦ He is ever-present (Matt. 18:20). Both natures are spoken of in Isaiah 9:6; Galatians 4:4; and 1 Timothy 3:16. Note: The phrase *"by the resurrection from the dead" (1:4)* is literally "of the dead ones." Christ's resurrection is always referred to in the plural as it takes in all believers. (See Rom. 6:4; John 5:21; 1 Cor. 15:22.)
- ■ It bestows both salvation and service-Note Paul's testimony here: *"By whom we have received grace and apostleship" (1:5).* We note that grace precedes apostleship. A man must be saved before he can serve. Unsaved ministers are described in 2 Corinthians 11:13-15. Jesus must say, "Come unto me," before he says, "Go ye into all the world." John Wesley was a great example of this.
- ■ It is received by faith (see also Rom. 5:1; Eph. 2:8-9).

> C. The concern of the reporter—Paul addresses his thoughts to a specific local church.
> 1. The identity of this church *(Read Rom. 1:6-7)*

✱ **1:7** We note here that grace precedes peace. There can be no peace apart from grace. (See Isa. 57:21; Jer. 6:14; Luke 7:50; 8:48; Rom. 5:1; 1 Thess. 5:3.) Paul prefaces every single one of his 13 epistles with these words, "Grace and peace." Peter (1 Pet. 1:2; 2 Pet. 1:2) and John (2 John 3) do the same. Grace is "unmerited favor" and is first mentioned in Genesis 6:8. It is perhaps God's second greatest characteristic (after holiness) and may be spelled out and thought of as "God's righteousness at Christ's expense." (See Rom. 5:20; Eph. 2:8-9; 1 Pet. 3:18; 1 Cor. 15:10.)

> 2. The intercession for this church
>   a. His praise for them *(Read Rom. 1:8)*

✱ **1:8** Paul commends them for their universally known faith (1:8). We know that the Emperor Claudius had forced the Jews out of Rome because of one Chrestus, which is thought to be a misspelling for "Christ." (See also 1 Thess. 1:6-8.)

>   b. His prayers for them *(Read Rom. 1:9-10)*

✱ **1:10** God later answered this prayer, but not in the way that Paul might have supposed (Acts 27-28). In Romans 16 Paul refers to 26 Roman saints by name.

> 3. The interest in this church
>   a. Paul desired to see them *(Read Rom. 1:11)*
>   b. Paul desired to serve them *(Read Rom. 1:13)*

✱ **1:13** He desired to come that he might both remit and receive a blessing (1:12). He had planned to come previously, but was hindered concerning his plans, once by Satan (1 Thess. 2:18) and once by God (Acts 16:6-7). Thus, Paul's human plans were no more inspired than those of Christians today (see Rom. 15:22-23). The spiritual gift mentioned in 1:11 was probably doctrine (1 Pet. 2:2).

4. The indebtedness to this church *(Read Rom. 1:14-15)*

✶ **1:15** He felt he owed a great gospel debt to every sinner (1:14; see also 2 Kings 7:9). Because of this, Paul could say: *"So, as much as in me is [literally, my side is ready], I am ready to preach the gospel to you that are at Rome also" (1:15).* Paul preached at Jerusalem (the religious center of the world) and was mobbed (Acts 21:31; 22:22-23). He preached at Athens (the intellectual center) and was mocked (Acts 17:32). He would later preach in Rome (the political center) where he would be martyred (2 Tim. 4:6).

D. The confidence of the reporter *(Read Rom. 1:16)*

✶ **1:16** The gospel is God's power (1:16). There are two standards by which God's power is measured in the Bible. In the Old Testament it was according to that power by which God brought Israel out of Egypt. (See Exod. 14-15; Psa. 78.) In the New Testament the unit of measurement is the resurrection of Jesus (Eph.1:20). The Greek word for "power" is *dunamis*, from which two words come: (1) dynamite—destructive power, and (2) dynamo—constructive power. The gospel of Christ is both. (See 2 Cor. 2:16.)

E. The conclusion of the reporter *(Read Rom.1:17)*

✶ **1:17**
- ■ The gospel produces righteousness (1:17). This word, simply defined, means "right clothing." The Bible teaches that all sinners are naked before God (Gen. 3:10; Heb. 4:13; Rev. 3:17). Some sinners realize this and attempt to make their own suit of spiritual clothes; but God looks upon such clothes as filthy rags (Isa. 64:6). However, the gospel provides new clothes to all repenting sinners. (See 2 Cor. 6:7; Eph. 6:14; Rev. 19:7-8.) This word may be used to summarize the book of Romans in a three-fold manner:
  - ● God is righteous.
  - ● God demands righteousness.
  - ● God provides righteousness.
- ■ The gospel says, *"The just shall live by faith"* (1:17b). These six words started the Protestant Reformation when Martin Luther experienced them. The phrase originates in Habakkuk 2:4 and is quoted three times in the New Testament.
  - ● Here in Romans 1:17, where the emphasis is on "the just."
  - ● In Galatians 3:11, where the emphasis is on "shall live."
  - ● In Hebrews 10:38, where the emphasis is on "by faith."
- ■ Bishop Lightfoot has pointed out the following concerning these six words:
  - ● The whole Law was given to Moses in 613 precepts.
  - ● David reduces them to 11 in Psalm 15.
  - ● Isaiah brings it down to six.
  - ● Micah limits it to three.
  - ● Isaiah in another passage narrows it to two.
  - ● But Habakkuk and Paul here summarize God's plan in a single statement. Faith has been defined as "the hand of the heart."

II. The Court Record (Rom. 1:18- 4:25)
A. The charge—High treason against the King of the universe *(Read Rom. 1:18-19)*

✶ **1:18**
- ■ God's fierce wrath is revealed against all ungodliness (sins against his person) and unrighteousness (sins against his will). The first category is vertical while the second is horizontal in nature.

LESSON 21: THE BOOK OF ROMANS—PART 1

- This wrath is manifested in a three-fold way:
  - In the biblical account itself (John 3:36)
  - In the cross of Calvary (Matt. 27:46;1 Pet. 3:18)
  - In the natural world (through tornadoes, earthquakes, famines, etc.)

> B. The defendants:
> 1. A heathen—The pagan (Rom. 1:18-32)
> 2. A hypocrite—The moral person (Rom. 2:1-16)
> 3. A Hebrew—The religious person (Rom. 2:17-3:8)
> C. The detailed indictment
> 1. First indictment—Ingratitude *(Read Rom. 1:21)*

✷ **1:21** The fall of both Lucifer and Adam through pride and self-will was doubtless prompted by their thankless hearts. Thus, the real antidote or cure for pride in the life of the believer is not humility, but thanksgiving. A thankful person is automatically a humble person. (See 1 Thess. 5:18; Phil. 4:6.)

> 2. Second indictment—Insolence *(Read Rom. 1:22)*

✷ **1:22** They thought themselves to be wise. The Greek word for "became fools" here is *moraino*, a verb form of *moros*, from which we get our word "moron." This was the beginning of human philosophy, a term ill-named, for it means "a lover of wisdom." (See Acts 17:18-21; 1 Cor. 1:18-21; 1 Tim. 6:3-5, 20; 2 Tim. 3:7; 4:4.)

> 3. Third indictment—Idolatry *(Read Rom. 1:23)*

✷ **1:23**
- They preferred idols to the living God and *exchanged* (not changed, for no man, angel, or demon can do this) his glory for that of:
  - Humans—The Greeks worshiped the human body, as does Hollywood today.
  - Birds—The Assyrians bowed down to birds.
  - Beasts—The Egyptians looked to cows and crocodiles.
  - Creeping things—The pagans worshiped snakes.
- We note the vivid downward trend of humanity described here in 1:23. The Bible teaches devolution, not evolution.

> 4. Fourth Indictment—Immorality *(Read Rom. 1:24-27)*
> a. Lesbianism *(Read Rom. 1:26)*
> b. Homosexuality *(Read Rom. 1:27)*

✷ **1:27** They gave their bodies over to sexual perversions (1:26-27). The sin of homosexuality is usually the final stage in those civilizations that turn from God. It was for this crime that God burned Sodom off the map of the Middle East (Gen. 19) and later ordered the destruction of Jericho, along with other Old Testament cities (1 Kings 14:24). In recent years the number of homosexuals in Western civilization has increased drastically. The so-called Gay Liberation movement is neither gay nor liberating.

> 5. Fifth indictment—Incorrigibility *(Read Rom. 1:28-32)*
> a. They enjoyed their wicked deeds *(Read Rom 1:29-31)*

★ **1:31** Note the nature of these wicked deeds, some 22 in number:
- Fornication—Sexual sins in general
- Wickedness—This word, first found in Genesis 6:5 is mentioned over 360 times in the Bible.
- Covetousness—The final of the Ten Commandments warns against this sin (Exod. 20:17). It was the specific sin that caused Paul to comprehend his fallen nature and need for redemption (Rom. 7:7).
- Maliciousness—Unusual cruelty
- Envy—Unlawfully desiring something belonging to another
- Murder—This is the only sin which cannot be forgiven by its victim.
- Debate—Contention and strife
- Deceit—The placing of a bait or snare
- Malignity—Malice—holding or harboring hatred
- Whisperers—Secret slanderings
- Backbiters—Open slanderings. The name "Satan" literally means, "the one who slanders."
- God-haters—This person begins by despising the authority of the Bible and winds up by hating its Author.
- Despiteful—Insolent and insulting
- Proud—Having to do with one's features
- Boasters—Having to do with one's words
- Inventors of evil
- Disobedient to parents—This is the beginning of lawlessness and anarchy.
- Without understanding—See Ephesians 4:18-19
- Covenant breakers
- Without natural affection
- Implacable—Unable to be satisfied
- Unmerciful

> b. They endorsed their wicked deeds *(Read Rom. 1:32)*

★ **1:32** They knew the seriousness of their crimes, but still continued and even encouraged others to join them (Mark 14:10-11; Rev. 11:10). For these crimes, God gave them over to a reprobate mind (a mind incapable of rational judgment) (Prov. 1:24-31; Rom. 1:24, 26, 28).

> D. The jury
>   1. The conscience of a person *(Read Rom. 1:19)*

★ **1:19** Conscience may be thought of as one of four main characteristics which make up the human soul. These are:
- Intellect—That aspect of the soul which tells me whether a given issue is right or wrong.
- Sensibility—That aspect which tells me what I would like to do about the issue.
- Conscience—That aspect which tells me what I should do.
- Will—That aspect which determines what I shall do.

> 2. The deeds of a person *(Read Rom. 2:6)*
> 3. The works of God *(Read Rom. 1:20)*

★ **1:20** All people have both the witness of conscience (1:19) and that of nature (1:20). (See Isa. 40:26; Psa. 8:3; 19:1-3; Acts 14:17; 17:29.) In other words, God does not reap wrath where he has not sown knowledge. These twin witnesses are thus unmistakable and universal. As a result, all people are exposed both to them and by them.

LESSON 21: THE BOOK OF ROMANS—PART 1

> 4. The Law of God *(Read Rom. 2:12)*
> E. The defense
>   1. The pagan's defense
>   a. His plea rendered—"I should be acquitted on the ground of ignorance."
>   b. His plea refuted—"You have the witness of conscience" (Rom. 1:19). "You have the witness of nature" (Rom. 1:20).
>   2. The moral person's defense
>   a. His plea rendered—"I should be acquitted on the ground of comparison; that is, that I'm not as bad as the pagan."
>   b. His plea refuted—"You do the same basic things, but in a more refined way." *"Therefore thou art inexcusable, O man, whosoever thou art that judgest: for wherein thou judgest another, thou condemnest thyself; for thou that judgest doest the same things" (Rom. 2:1).*

★ 2:1

- The plea refuted—"You do the same basic things, but in a more refined way." A classic example of one person judging another for the very thing he himself had committed was when David condemned a rich farmer who stole from a poor one (2 Sam. 11-12).
- The self-righteous moral person, like the unrighteous pagan, will be judged by the twin witnesses of nature and conscience (Rom. 1:19-20; 2:12-15). The Bible lists various kinds of conscience.
    - A good conscience (1 Tim. 1:5, 19)
    - A weak conscience (1 Cor. 8:12)
    - A convicting conscience (John 8:9)
    - A defiled conscience (Titus 1:15)
    - A seared conscience (1 Tim. 4:2)
- It should be noted that a person's conscience does not function legislatively, but only judicially. It is like an umpire that calls the strikes, but does not make the rules. Conscience, then, is a goad, but not a guide. Paul summarizes this section by saying: *"For as many as have sinned without law shall also perish without law; and as many as have sinned in the law shall be judged by the law" (Rom. 2:12;* see also Luke 12:47-48).

> c. His plea reviewed
>   (1) He was indifferent (Rom. 2:4-5).
>   (a) Concerning God's forbearance (God's act of holding back his wrath)
>   (b) Concerning God's goodness (God's act of holding forth his grace)
>   (2) He was ignorant.
>   (a) He knew nothing concerning *who* God would judge *(Read Rom. 2:6, 11)*
>   (b) He knew nothing concerning *how* God would judge *(Read Rom. 2:7-8, 12, 14)*
>   (c) He knew nothing concerning *when* God would judge *(Read Rom. 2:16)*

★ 2:16 An overview summary of the moral person's problems is as follows:
- Self-righteous people make one of two capital mistakes:
    - They misunderstand the height of God's Law.
    - They underestimate the depth of their own moral conduct.
- They desire the fruit of Christianity without the root.
- They underestimate the awesome knowledge of God (2:1). But God knows all the facts.
    - God knows the number of the stars (Psa. 147:4).
    - God knows our thoughts and words (Psa. 139:1-2, 4, 23-24).
    - God knows the number of hairs on one's head (Matt. 10:30).

- God knows the past, present, and future (Acts 15:18).
- God even knows what might have been (Matt. 11:23).
■ They despise his goodness and forbearance (2:4). To despise is to belittle, or to look down upon (Gen. 25:34; Heb. 12:2, 5). Thus, the moral person was despising:
  - God's forbearance; that is, his act of holding back his wrath.
  - God's goodness; that is, his act of holding forth his grace.
■ The moral person takes lightly both God's extended hand and his clenched fist.
■ They assume their morality will excuse them from his judgment (2:3). It has been suggested that there are four possible ways one might escape human punishment:
  - He might commit an undetected crime or remain an undetected criminal.
  - He might escape beyond the jurisdiction of the Law.
  - He might hire a smart lawyer and "beat the rap."
  - He might escape, after being put in prison.
■ But with God there is no escape (Heb. 2:3). Our only hope is to settle out of court. Without this settlement, all people will be judged concerning their *thoughts* (Rom. 2:16), *words* (Matt. 12:36), and *deeds* (Rev. 20:12). This will happen *"for there is no respect of persons with God" (2:11)*. (See also Deut.10:17; Acts 10:34; James 2:1, 9; Eph. 6:9; Col. 3:25.)

> 3. The religious person's defense (Rom. 2:17-3:8)
>   a. His plea rendered *(Read Rom. 2:17,19)*
>   b. His plea refuted—You simply do not practice what you preach *(Read Rom. 2:21-29)*
>   c. His plea reviewed
>   (1) Fact # 1: The Jew had a national advantage, but no spiritual advantage (Rom. 3:1-2)
>   (2) Fact # 2: Even though Israel had rejected Christ, God's promises would not fail (Rom. 3:3-4)
>   (3) Fact # 3: Israel's unrighteousness had simply demonstrated God's righteousness (Rom. 3:5)
>   (4) Fact # 4: Israel would be punished for its unrighteousness (Rom. 3:6-8)

★ **3:8** An overview summary of the religious person's problems is as follows:
  ■ His law could not save him (2:17-24). The Jew had defiled this law and his knowledge of God and had become a horrible testimony to the Gentiles (2:24; also Gen. 34:30; Ezek. 36:17, 20). It was performance of God's will, and not the possession of his Law which averted judgment. Israel had simply not kept the Law (Matt. 21:13; 23:4-36; Acts 15:10).
  ■ His circumcision could not save him (2:25-27). The Jews believed Abraham (the first to be circumcised—see Gen. 17:11) stood at the gate of hell to assure that no circumcised Jew would ever enter there. While circumcision was indeed the seal of God's promise, inward faith alone was the source. (See Deut. 10:12, 16; 30:6.) The rite of circumcision had already been set aside in Acts 15. His birth could not save him (2:28-29). Salvation comes not through place, face, or race, but by grace. (See John 8:39, 44.)
  ■ Paul then quickly summarizes the case against Israel (3:1-8)—Even though the Jews had a national advantage over the Gentiles *"because that unto them were committed the oracles of God" (Rom. 3:2)*, they had no spiritual advantage whatsoever. Even though Israel's unrighteousness had simply "commended the righteousness of God" (that is, showed it in a clearer light), God would still judge them along with the uncircumcised Gentiles. The end *never* justifies the means.

> F. The verdict (Rom. 3:9-23) *(Read Rom. 3:9, 10-11, 19)*
>   1. Man's character is depraved *(Read Rom. 3:12)*

★ **3:12** All had become unprofitable. This is a reference to something originally good which goes bad, like sour milk, rotten meat, or moldy bread (Isa. 1:6). Thus, people are unrighteous, unreasonable, unresponsive, and unrepentant.

LESSON 21: THE BOOK OF ROMANS—PART 1

2. People's conversation is depraved *(Read Rom. 3:13-14)*
3. People's conduct is depraved (Rom. 3:15-18).
    a. They murder their brothers *(Read Rom. 3:15-17)*
    b. They mock their God *(Read Rom. 3:18)*
G. The sentence *(Read Rom. 6:23)*

★ 6:23 The sentence: Spiritual death, to be forever separated from God to suffer throughout all eternity in the lake of fire (Rom. 6:23; Rev. 20:11-15). The greatest crime of all can only be punished by the greatest penalty of all, if justice is to prevail.

H. The miracle *(Read Rom. 3:21-31; 6:23)*
    1. The nature of this miracle (Rom. 3:24)

★ 3:24 Up to this point the case of God against the accused has pretty well followed the format of earthly jurisprudence. But suddenly something totally different and unexpected takes place that would surely cause every earthly court reporter to gasp in utter amazement. After the Judge has carefully heard all the evidence and patiently listened to all the pleas, he finds no other choice but to invoke the supreme penalty, lest true justice be denied. But before the terrible sentence can be carried out, this same Judge quietly closes the case book, lays down the heavenly gavel, rises to his feet, takes off his judicial robes, and goes out to die for these three convicted defendants. This and this alone is justification. The corrupt, doomed, and naked sinner may now be cleansed, delivered, and clothed in the very righteousness of Christ himself.

2. The persons in this miracle—The Father and Son *(Read Rom. 3:25)*
3. The source of this miracle (Rom. 3:24, 28)
    a. *"Freely by his grace"* (Rom. 3:24)
    b. *"By faith"* (Rom. 3:28)
    c. *"Without the deeds of the law"* (Rom. 3:28)
4. The scope of this miracle—unlimited in scope (Rom. 3:22, 29)
    a. *"Unto all ... for there is no difference"* (Rom. 3:22)
    b. *"The God of the Jews ... of the Gentiles also"* (Rom. 3:29)
5. The bestowal of this miracle—limited in bestowal (Rom. 3:22, 26)
    a. *"Upon them that believe"* (Rom. 3:22)
    b. *"Him which believeth in Jesus"* (Rom. 3:26)
6. The witnesses of this miracle *(Read Rom. 3:21)*

★ 3:21 "The law and the prophets"—The Mosaic Law required two witnesses to attest to any fact (Deut. 19:15). This righteousness was often foreshadowed by the Law through the temple priesthood and offerings. This righteousness was often foretold by the prophets through their writings (Isa. 53; Luke 24:25-27; John 5:46; 1 Pet. 1:10-11).

7. The legal accomplishments of this miracle—*Question:* How to reconcile God's justice and his mercy. Note the two problem words in *Romans 3:25:* "Whom God hath set forth to be a propitiation through faith in his blood, to declare his righteousness for the remission of sins that are past, through the forbearance of God."

★ 3:25 The word *propitiation* means "satisfaction" and is a reference to the Old Testament temple mercy seat. It was upon this golden seat that the priest sprinkled the blood of a lamb to separate God's wrath from man's sin. (See 1 John 2:2; 4:10; Heb. 10:11-12.) Why did Christ die? Among other reasons, to preserve and vindicate the justice of God.

a. Remission: To let something pass by (that is, the sins of the Old Testament saints)
b. Forbearance: To hold something back (that is, God's wrath upon those sins).
8. Answer: *"Christ Jesus ... whom God hath set forth to be a propitiation"* (Rom. 3:24-25). *"That he might be just, and the justifier of him which believeth in Jesus"* (Rom. 3:26).
9. The harmony seen in this miracle *(Read Rom. 3:31)*
I. The two spokesmen for the court—The Judge introduces two well-known faith experts who swear to the fact that they both anticipated and experienced the miracle of justification centuries ago (Rom. 4:1-25).
1. Abraham, Israel's racial father (Rom. 4:1-5, 9-25)
a. Abraham and his salvation
(1) The method of his salvation *(Read Rom. 4:3 and Rom. 4:16a)*

✶ **4:3** The Old Testament Scripture quoted here is Genesis 15:6. This word *counted* could also be translated "imputed." To impute is to add something to someone's account. There are three major imputations in the Bible.
- First, the imputation of Adam's sin to the human race (Rom. 3:23; 5:12; 1 Cor. 15:22)
- Second, the imputation of the race's sin upon Christ (Isa. 53:5; Heb. 2:9; 2 Pet. 2:24; 2 Cor. 5:14)
- Third, the imputation of God's righteousness to all believers (Phil. 3:9) *"Through the righteousness of faith"* (Rom. 4:13b). *"Therefore it is of faith, that it might be by grace"* (Rom. 4:16a).

(2) The time of his salvation *(Read Rom. 4:10)*

✶ **4:10** When was Abraham saved? Was he saved before or after circumcision? In Genesis 15:6, Abraham is said to have been justified. At this time he was 85 years old (Gen. 16:16). In Genesis 17:24 we are told of his circumcision, at the age of 99. Thus, he was justified by faith and a child of God nearly 14 years before he was circumcised.

(3) The seal of his salvation *(Read Rom. 4:11)*

✶ **4:11** Why was Abraham saved? *"That he might be the father of all them that believe"* (4:11). This includes both the uncircumcised (believing Gentiles) and the circumcision (believing Jews). Paul here once again points out that circumcision was merely the *seal* of Abraham's faith, while justification was the *source*.

Dr. Allen Johnson writes: "A good illustration of this is the old twenty-dollar gold piece. The seal of the United States was imprinted on the coin as a sign that it was U.S. currency, but the value of the coin remained the same even if it was melted down and the seal obliterated. Now the same seal can be impressed on an iron slug, but the presence of the sign doesn't alter the intrinsic worthlessness of the slug" (*The Freedom Letter*, p. 76).

b. Abraham and his seed
(1) His earthly seed *(Read Rom. 4:17-22)*—Isaac was his earthly seed.
(2) His spiritual seed *(Read Rom. 4:11-12, 16, 23-25)*—Believers are his spiritual seed.
2. David, Israel's royal father *(Read Rom. 4:6-8)*
a. The felonies of David—He was guilty of adultery and murder (see 2 Sam. 11-12).
b. The forgiveness of David—He was forgiven by faith in God's grace. See Psalms 51 and 52.

LESSON 22

> **III. The Court Review (Rom. 5:1-21)**
>   A. A summary of justification (Rom. 5:1-11)
>   1. The believer has peace with God *(Read Rom. 5:1)*
>   2. The believer has access to God *(Read Rom. 5:2)*

✷ 5:2
- Access to God (5:2)—The believer can now approach God because of his new standing. In the Bible there is a distinction between our standing and our state.
  - Our *standing* refers to our position in heaven and never changes (1 Cor. 15:1; 2 Cor. 5:17).
  - Our *state* refers to our condition on earth and may change (for better or worse) daily (Phil. 2:19; Col. 4:7).
- Our new standing now gives us that blessed privilege not experienced by either Jew or Gentile in the Old Testament. We now have access to God's throne itself. In the Old Testament there was very little of this. Consider:
  - A Gentile was barred at the gates of the temple.
  - A Jewish woman was stopped at the woman's court.
  - A non-Levite Hebrew could not enter the inner court.
  - The high priest himself could only enter into the holy of holies once a year. But on Calvary this veil separating us from God's glory was rent in two by Christ. (See Matt. 27:51; Heb. 10:19.)

>   3. The believer receives assurance from God *(Read Rom. 5:3-4)*

✷ 5:4
- Patience (see Heb. 10:36; James 1:3)—This leads to:
- Experience (see Psa. 94:12; 2 Cor. 1:3-5; Gal. 4:19; Eph. 4:14-15)—This leads to:
- Hope—There are three requirements of an earthly hope:
  - It must concern the future.
  - It must concern something good in the future.
  - It must concern something possible in the future.
- This hope fulfills all three requirements (Eph. 1:17-22; 1 Pet. 1:3-4; Titus 2:11). There are two kinds of hope, a verb and a noun.
  - The verb "hope" says, "I hope to have" (earthly hope).
  - The noun "hope" says, "I have a hope" (heavenly hope).
- This assurance from God once prompted Andrew Murray to write: "First, He brought me here, it is by His will I am in this strait place; in that fact I will rejoice. Next, He will keep me here in His love, and give me grace as His child. Then, He will make the trial a blessing, teaching me the lessons He intends for me to learn, and working in me the grace He meant to bestow. Last, in His good time He can bring me out again-how and when He knows. Thus: I am (1) here by God's appointment, (2) in His keeping, (3) under His training, and (4) for His time."

>   4. The believer is indwelled by God *(Read Rom. 5:5)*

✷ 5:5
- There are three separate and distinct words for love in the Greek New Testament. In Romans Paul uses all three.
  - Storgos—A natural, gravitational love; an instinctive concern for one's offspring, found in both animals and humans. Only the negative form, astorgos, is used in Scripture (Rom. 1:31).

- Philos—A beautiful and friendly love. Paul describes this love in Romans 12:10.
- Agapao—A divine love, found only in God. This love is not dependent upon the beauty of the object being loved. It is found 320 times in the Greek New Testament, but rarely in classical writings. (Homer used it ten times and Euripedes three times.)

    This love is never found in the heart of any man prior to the ascension of Christ. In fact, Jesus asks Peter on three occasions (John 21:15-19) if he really loves him. The first two times Jesus uses the third kind of love and asks the following question; "Peter, do you *agapao* me?" On both occasions Peter answers by choosing the second word. He says, "Lord, you know I *phileo* you."

    Finally, our Lord uses the second word also. The reason for all this (as Peter would later find out) is explained in Romans 5:5 by Paul: "The love (*agapao*) of God is shed abroad in our hearts by the Holy Ghost which is given unto us." Thus, the reason why Peter answered the way he did was because the Holy Spirit had not yet come at Pentecost and it was therefore impossible for him to love Christ with this divine *agapao* love. In John 11 we have a similar case in which we are told that Lazarus loved Jesus with a *phileo* love, but that Jesus loved Lazarus with an *agapao* love (11:3, 5).
- There are two beloved New Testament passages in which this *agapeo* love is in view. (See John 3:16; Eph. 5:25.)

> 5. The believer is preserved in God (Rom. 5:6-11).
>   a. Through Christ's past work on Calvary's cross *(Read Rom. 5:6-8)*
>   b. Through Christ's present work at God's right hand *(Read Rom. 5:9-10)*

✱ 5:10

- The Bible records many clear statements about Christ's blood.
    - It was innocent blood (Matt. 27:4, 19, 24)—This was the testimony of Judas, Pilate's wife, and Pilate.
    - It was shed blood (Matt. 26:28).
    - It was precious blood (1 Pet. 1:18-19).
    - It was cleansing blood (1 John 1:9).
    - It was condemning blood (Matt. 27:25).
- Why did Christ shed his precious blood?
    - To show forth God's love
    - To save us from God's wrath
        - This includes present-day wrath (John 3:36; Rom. 1:18).
        - This includes tribulational wrath (1 Thess. 1:10; 5:9).
        - This includes eternal wrath (Rev. 20:15).
- This has been called the chapter of the "much mores." (See 5:9-10, 15, 17, 20.) My salvation was purchased by his bleeding and is preserved through his interceding (see Heb.1:3; 6:18-20; 7:25; 9:24).

> B. A summary of condemnation (Rom. 5:12-21)—In these verses Paul contrasts the work of Adam (the father of all) with the work of Christ (the Savior of all).
>   1. The work of Adam
>   a. The reality of his act *(Read Rom. 5:12)*

✱ 5:12 Adam brought sin into the world. At this point it may prove helpful to review both the origin and meaning of sin.

- The origin of sin: In the universe, it was introduced by Satan. (See Ezek. 28:11-19; Isa. 14:12-15; Luke 10:18; 1 John 3:8; Rev. 12:3-4.) In the world, it was introduced by Adam. (See Gen. 2:16-17; Rom. 5:12; 1 Cor. 15:22; 1 Tim. 2:14.)
- The meaning of sin
    - First meaning—"To miss the mark" (Greek is *hamartia*). Here sin may be pictured as any attitude or act of a person which does not hit the bull's-eye of God's glory target (Rom. 3:23). The secular use of its verbal form is illustrated in Judges 20:16.

- Second meaning—"To overstep the forbidden line" (Greek is *parabasis*. See 1 John 3:4; Acts 1:25; James 2:11.) Sin thus covers both our inability to do right and our inclination to do wrong.

> b. The scope of his act *(Read Rom. 5:12b)*
> c. The nature of his act *(Read Rom. 5:19)*
> d. The results of his act
>   (1) Immediate judgment upon himself
>   (2) Imputed judgment upon his posterity *(Read Rom. 5:14)*

✶ **5:14** He brought death into the world.
- This includes physical death (Gen. 3:19; 5:5; Psa. 90:10).
- This includes spiritual death (Matt. 7:23; 25:41; Rev. 2:11; 20:6, 14; 21:8).

> 3) Eternal judgment upon all unsaved *(Read Rom. 5:18)*

✶ **5:18**
- There are several theories about Adam's sin and its relationship to me.
  - The Pelagian view—This says that Adam's sin affected only himself, and merely resulted in a bad moral example.
  - Semi-Pelagian view—That Adam's sin merely weakened the will not to sin.
  - Federal (or Augustinian) view—That because of the unity of the human race, Adam's sin was imputed to posterity; corrupt nature begets corrupt nature. This position is taken by Paul, both here in Romans 5 and in 3:23: *"For all have sinned* |aorist tense, a once-for-all act in history| *and come short* |imperfect tense, repeatedly coming short| *of the glory of God."*
- The Bible thus distinguishes between sin (the *root* of my problem, caused by Adam) and sins (the *fruit* of my problem, caused by myself). I am therefore not a sinner because I sin, but I sin because I am a sinner.

> e. The relationship of the Law to his act *(Read Rom. 5:20)*
> 2. The work of Christ
>   a. The reality of his act—He introduced grace and righteousness into the world.
>   (1) These blessings were free (Rom. 5:16).
>   (2) These blessings were abundant (Rom. 5:17).
>   b. The scope of his act *(Read Rom. 5:15b; Rom. 5:18)*
>   c. The nature of his act *(Read Rom. 5:19b)*
>   d. The results of his act
>   (1) Justification—*"The free gift ... unto justification"* (Rom. 5:16b).
>   (2) Sanctification—*"They which receive ... grace and ... righteousness shall reign in life"* (Rom. 5:17b).
>   (3) Glorification—*"Even so might grace reign ... unto eternal life by Christ Jesus our Lord"* (Rom. 5:21b).
>   e. The relationship of sin to his act—*"But where sin abounded, grace did much more abound"* (Rom. 5:20b).

The Power Plant of Grace: God's Way (Sanctification and Preservation)—Romans 6-8

Paul does discuss the sanctification of a saint. But from this point on, he does not discuss the justification of a sinner. It will prove helpful here to contrast these two words:
1. *Justification* is an act, while *sanctification* (which simply means "to set apart") is a work.
2. Justification is the means, while sanctification is the end.
3. The first removes the guilt and penalty of sin, while the second removes the growth and power of sin.

4. The former works for us, while the latter works in us.
5. The one declares us righteous, while the other makes us righteous.
6. Justification furnishes the track which leads to heaven, while sanctification furnishes the train.

We have already noted that sanctification simply means "to set apart." Thus, in the Bible:
1. Physical objects were said to be sanctified (Exod. 40: 10-11; 19:23).
2. People could sanctify themselves (Exod. 19:22).
3. One person could sanctify another (Exod. 13:2).
4. Evildoers could sanctify themselves to do iniquity (Isa. 66:17).
5. God sanctified Christ (John 10:36).
6. Christ sanctified himself (John 17:19).
7. A believer could sanctify an unbeliever (1 Cor. 7:14).
8. Carnal Christians are said to be sanctified (1 Cor. 1:2; 3:1-2).
9. Believers are commanded to sanctify God (1 Pet. 3:15). Chapters 6-8 go to make up the second "building" in the book of Romans. There are three "floors" to this power plant of grace.

I. The Plan—First Floor of Sanctification (Rom. 6:1-23)
In this chapter Paul lists God's three-fold method leading to sanctification.
A. Know ye (Rom. 6:1-10)— *"Know ye not" (Rom. 6:3).* Paul wants us to know three things.
   1. That we have been baptized with Christ into his death (Rom. 6:3)

★ **6:3** Here Paul states not only that Christ died *for* me, but *as* me. The word "baptism" simply means "identification." This identification with Christ on Calvary is one of many "dry baptisms" in the Bible. Others would include:
- The baptism of sin and suffering upon Christ (Matt. 20:22)
- The baptism of the Holy Spirit upon believers at Pentecost (Acts 1:5)
- The baptism of believers into the body of Christ (1 Cor. 12:13)
- The baptism "for the dead" (1 Cor.15:29). Note: This is thought to refer to that act of living believers identifying themselves with martyred believers by picking up their fallen banners.
- The baptism "unto Moses" (1 Cor. 10:2)
- The baptism of judgment during the tribulation (Matt. 3:11-12)

   2. That we have been planted together in the likeness of his resurrection *(Read Rom. 6:5)*

★ **6:5** The believer has now been "transplanted" three times:
- To the Garden of Eden where he sinned with Adam
- To the cross, where he died with Christ
- To the tomb, where he arose with Christ

   3. That because of these two facts, the believer is:
      a. Delivered from his sin *(Read Rom. 6:2, 6-7)*

★ **6:7** Death cancels all obligations. Sin here is personified as a cruel tyrant who taxes his subjects beyond all endurance. The only way to pay is to die. This, then, renders inactive (but does not remove) the body of sin and makes it powerless (see also Eph. 4:22-24; Col. 3:9-10).

      b. Delivered to his Savior *(Read Rom. 6:8-10)*
B. Reckon ye *(Read Rom. 6:11-12)*

✱ **6:11** This simply means that by *faith* we are to act upon these facts regardless of any personal *feelings*.

> C. Yield ye (Rom. 6:13-15)
>   1. The rationale for this yielding
>   a. The *who* of the matter—a *"Yield yourselves unto God as those that are alive from the dead"* (Rom. 6:13).

✱ **6:13**
- We are to stop yielding (present tense) our body members as instruments of unrighteousness.
- We are to once for all (aorist tense) yield our body members as instruments of righteousness.

> b. The *what* of the matter *(Read Rom. 6:13,19)*
> c. The *why* of the matter *(Read Rom. 6:14-16)*
>   2. The rewards of this yielding *(Read Rom. 6:22-23)*

✱ **6:23** *"Being made free from sin"* (6:22). This marks the sixth time Paul has stated this fact. (See 6:2, 6-7,14,18). There are three Latin theological terms which may help clarify this precious doctrine. These are:
- Non posse non pecare—Not able not to sin. This refers to believers before their salvation.
- Posse non pecare—Able not to sin. This describes them after their salvation. They now have the power to live victorious lives.
- Non posse pecare—Not able to sin. This describes existence after the Rapture.

> **II. The Pain—The Second Floor of Frustration (Rom. 7:1-25)**
> *Paul now discusses what part the Law plays in God's plan of sanctification.*
>   A. The spiritual man and the Law (Rom. 7:1-6)
>   1. His relationship to the Law
>   a. He is as a widow, being freed from her husband (Rom. 7:1-3).
>   b. He is as a dead man, being freed from his lust (Rom. 7:5).

✱ **7:5** The Greek speaks of a violent death here: that of Calvary. In a sense it may be said it was necessary for both Christ and the believer to die in order to get together. Ponder the following:
- In the Old Testament, Christ was married to unfaithful Israel. (See the book of Hosea.)
- In the New Testament, sinners are bound by the power of sin and the chains of the Law.
- Then, Christ died, freeing him of his Old Testament relationship with sinful Israel (during this dispensation of the church). At the same time the believer died, freeing him from the Law and sin.
- This blessed relationship will be fully consummated at the marriage of the Lamb. (See Rev. 19:7-8.)

>   2. His relationship to the Savior
>   a. He has been raised by Christ (Rom. 7:4).
>   b. He will be married to Christ (Rom. 7:4).
>   c. He is now able to produce fruit through Christ (Rom. 7:4). Thus, the spiritual person is delivered from the Law.
>   B. The natural person and the Law (Rom. 7:7-13)—Here the Law is used in a twofold manner.
>   1. The condemnation usage—Sin uses the Law to rekindle the sinfulness of the flesh *(Read Rom. 7:7-11)*

✱ **7:11**
- The Law was used by sin to slay Paul (7:9-11). This may have been a reference to his bar mitzvah (a religious ceremony observed by all 13-year-old Jewish boys) at which time he formally took upon him the solemn responsibilities of the Law. His carefree days of childhood were then over. He was accountable to God for his actions.

- The Law was used by sin to work in him "all manner of concupiscence [forbidden and evil desires]" (7:8). In other words, the Law both *revealed* and, as used by sin, *revived* Paul's sin nature. Sin thus used the Law as its basis of operation in its war against Paul.

> 2. The illustration usage—God uses the Law to reveal the sinfulness of the flesh *(Read Rom. 7:12-13)*

✶ 7:13
- The Law in itself is *not* evil, but rather is *"holy, and just, and good" (7:12)*.
  - It is holy because it came from God (7:14).
  - It is just because it rightfully condemns the sinner.
  - It is good because it prepared the sinner for Christ (Gal. 3:24).
- The Law was ineffective only because of the weakness of the flesh (7:18). Herein is the real problem. The finest and most experienced football coach in America would lose every single game if he had a team composed of crippled and blind players. Thus, the natural person is doomed by the Law.

> C. The carnal person and the Law (Rom. 7:14-25)
> 1. Any attempt to keep the Law will lead to carnality *(Read Rom. 7:14,18-19)*
> 2. No attempt to keep the Law can lead to spirituality.
>   a. The agony of Paul's problem *(Read Rom. 7:22-24)*

✶ 7:24
- This may have been a spiritual comparison to the Roman act of punishing a murderer binding to him the corpse of his victim, thus using its very rot and stench to execute the killer.
- Paul thus realizes that the believer cannot control, change, cleanse, conquer, command, correct, or crucify the flesh.

> b. The answer to Paul's problem *(Read Rom. 7:25)*

- Thus, the carnal person is defeated by the Law. Paul ends chapter 6 with the statement that eternal life comes only through Jesus Christ (6:23). He ends chapter 7 by concluding that the victorious life can come only through Jesus Christ.
- Note: Before leaving chapter 7 it may prove helpful to briefly summarize the purpose and ministry of the Old Testament Law. The Law consisted of three sections:
  - The Ten Commandments (Exod. 20:3-17; Deut. 5:7-21)
  - The social regulations concerning the people (Exod. 21-23)
  - The religious ordinances concerning the tabernacle (Exod. 24-40).
- The Law followed the Abrahamic covenant by some five centuries, and therefore did not in any way abrogate God's previous promises (Gen. 12:1-3; Gal. 3:17-18). It was a way *of* life, but not a way *to* life (see Gal. 2:15-16; 3:21; 2 Cor. 3:7,9). Why did not Christ come during Abraham's time? Faith was then present (see Gen. 15; Rom. 4). The answer is that the chief meaning of the Law lies in the developing of an expectation of the Redeemer by revealing human sinfulness. It was therefore an addition, because the covenant with Abraham lacked a sufficient emphasis on sin. God used the ministry of two men to fully develop the meaning of faith repentance which leads to salvation. Note these two men:
  - Moses introduced the curse (Gal. 3:13).
  - Abraham introduced the blessing (Gal. 3:9, 14).
  - Moses pointed to the system of death (2 Cor. 3:6; Rom. 7: 9-10).
  - Abraham pointed to the system of life (Rom. 4:17-25; Heb. 11:19).
  - Moses led to the crucifixion (Gal. 2:19-20; 3:13).

- Abraham led to the resurrection (Heb. 11:19; Rom. 4:17, 19, 23-25). "But they both belong together, for the sinner is to be redeemed, and to this end renewal and new birth are needful. But the new birth has man's conversion as a presupposition, and conversion is two-fold: a turning from and a turning to, a *NO* to oneself and a *YES* to God, or, as the New Testament puts it, *repentance* and *faith!* Only here is revealed to us the true meaning of the Old Testament histories.
- Throughout centuries God spoke the word 'faith' into the history of salvation—this is the meaning of the Covenant with Abraham. Throughout 2,000 years it was an education in faith. Throughout centuries God spoke the word 'repent' into the history of salvation—this is the meaning of the law of Moses. For some 1,500 years it was an education in repentance" (Erich Sauer, *Dawn of World Redemption*, pp. 122-123). Then came Jesus "into Galilee, preaching the gospel of the kingdom of God, and saying, The time is fulfilled, and the kingdom of God is at hand: repent ye, and believe the gospel" (Mark 1:14-15). Thus, in one statement, Jesus joins perfectly both the message of Moses and that of Abraham (see also Acts 20:21.) We may therefore conclude that the Law functioned as:

    1. A *bridle*, whereby God could control Israel from above.
    2. A *hedge*, which separated Israel from the nations of the world.
    3. A *mirror*, revealing the true condition of human beings.
    4. A *stimulant*, bringing to surface the hidden sin of human beings.
    5. A *schoolteacher*, preparing us for, and delivering us to, Christ (Gal. 3:19, 24; Rom. 3:20; 7:7).

III. The Prize—Third Floor of Preservation (Rom. 8:1-39).

- Paul has thus far discussed the following: *One:* Why does the sinner need to be saved? Answer: Condemnation. *Two:* How is the sinner saved? Answer: Justification. *Three:* What is to happen after the sinner gets saved? Answer: Sanctification. *Four:* Will the sinner remain saved? This is the question answered in Romans 8, and the answer is yes, he or she will, indeed, because of preservation.

It has been observed that if the Bible were likened to a beautiful ring set with jewels, the book of Romans would be the most beautiful jewel in the ring, and the eighth chapter the most beautiful facet in the jewel. Romans 8 is in essence an amplification of John 5:24 and Revelation 21:5. *(Read John 5:24 and Rev. 21:5).* Will the believing sinner remain saved? He will, because of seven new things:

A. The believer has a new position (Rom 8:1-8).
    1. His position in regard to the Son of God: He is now in Christ *(Read Rom. 8:1).*

★ **8:1** Note: We observe that Paul does not say there is no fault, or sin, or imperfection, but no condemnation. We also observe the time element—it is now no condemnation.

    2. His position in regard to the law of God—He now fulfills its demands through Christ.
        a. The failure involved *(Read Rom. 8:7-8)*
        b. The facts involved *(Read Rom. 8:2-3)*
        c. The fruit involved *(Read Rom. 8:4-6)*
B. The believer has a new guest *(Read Rom. 8:9-13)*
C. The believer has a new adoption (Rom. 8:14-17)—"*Ye have received the Spirit of adoption*" (Rom. 8:15).

★ **8:15**
- This verse contains the first of but five references to the word adoption in the Bible. All five come from the pen of Paul. These are: Romans 8:15, 23; 9:4; Galatians 4:5; Ephesians 1:5.

- Here is an overview of biblical adoption:
  - The theology of adoption: Defined, the word literally means "the placing of a son." Adoption logically follows regeneration. Regeneration gives one his nature as a child of God, whereas adoption gives him his position as a son of God (Rom. 8:15-23; Gal. 4:4-6; Eph. 1:5; 2 Cor. 6:18).
  - Contrasted—How spiritual adoption differs from civil adoption:
    - We never adopt our own children, but God never adopts any other than his own.
    - Civil adoption provides comfort for the childless, but God had a beloved Son (Matt. 3:17; 17:5) prior to adopting us.
    - There are usually many pleasing characteristics in a civil-adopted child, but not in God's children prior to their adoption (Rom. 3:10-18).
    - Civil adoption could never give a child the same nature of the Father, but God's adopted are given the very mind of Christ (1 Cor. 2:16).
    - In some cases, civil adoption could be declared null and void, but God's adopted are absolutely secure.
  - Compared—How spiritual adoption compares with civil adoption:
    - The Father must begin the action leading to adoption (Isa. 1:18; John 3:16).
    - Both adoptions give an inheritance to one who previously had none (Rom. 8:17; 1 Pet. 1:1-9).
    - Both adoptions provide a new name (Rev. 2:17; John 1:42).

> 1. We have an intimacy with the Father *(Read Rom. 8:15)*
> 2. We have an inheritance with the Son *(Read Rom. 8:17)*
> 3. We have an illumination by the Spirit (Rom. 8:14,16)
>   a. He walks with us *(Read Rom. 8:14)*
>   b. He witnesses to us *(Read Rom. 8:16)*
> D. The believer has a new hope (Rom. 8:18-25)—The nature of this hope is the full and final redemption of all things. This includes:
>   1. The Christian himself *(Read Rom. 8:18, 23)*
>   *"We ourselves, having the first fruits of the Spirit ... groan within ourselves, waiting eagerly for our adoption as sons, the redemption of our body" (Rom. 8:23, NASB).*

✶ **8:23**
- It will be a body like Christ's body (1 John 3:2).
- It will be a body of flesh and bone (Luke 24:39). Our Lord both spoke (John 20:17) and ate and drank (Luke 24:30, 41-43; John 21:13) in his resurrected body.
- It will be a recognizable body (1 Cor. 13:12). Jesus was recognized by all believers after his resurrection.
- It will be a body in which the Spirit predominates (1 Cor. 15:44, 49).
- It will be a body unlimited by time and space (John 20:19).

> 2. The creation itself (Rom. 8:19-22)—*"For the anxious longing of the creation waits eagerly for the revealing of the sons of God. For the creation was subjected to futility, not of its own will, but because of him who subjected it, in hope that the creation itself also will be set free from its slavery to corruption into the freedom of the glory of the children of God. For we know that the whole creation groans and suffers the pains of childbirth together until now" (Rom. 8:19-22, NASB).*
> E. The believer has a new prayer helper (Rom. 8:26-27)
>   1. The identity of this helper—The Holy Spirit himself
>   2. The necessity for this helper *(Read Rom. 8:26a)*

✶ 8:26a
- In the Greek, the word infirmities is in the singular. Paul had but a single infirmity in mind here: our ignorance and inability in prayer. *"For we know not what we should pray for as we ought"* (8:26).
- The word helpeth should not be overlooked at this point. It means "to aid in the completion of a task." The same word is used in Luke 10:40. All this simply means the Holy Spirit expects the believer to do his share of praying also.

> 3. The intensity of this helper *(Read Rom. 8:26)*

✶ 8:26b This is the third "groan" mentioned in chapter 8.
- The groan of nature (8:22)
- The groan of the believer (8:23)
- The groan of the Holy Spirit (8:26)

> 4. The infallibility of this helper—He cooperates with Christ *(Read Rom. 8:27)*
> F. The believer has a new confidence *(Read Rom. 8:28)*

✶ 8:28 Here we should note two things this verse does not say:
- It does not say all things in and by themselves are good, but rather that they work together for good. A classic Old Testament example of this is Joseph's testimony to his brothers. (See Gen. 45:5-8; 50:20. See also Psa. 76:10.) Jacob (Joseph's father) did not always understand this principle; thus his troubled conclusion in Genesis 42:36.
- It does not say that this is true for all people, but only for God-lovers. But for these, it is an all-inclusive statement. It covers the good and the bad, the bright and the dark, the sweet and the bitter, the easy and the hard, the happy and the sad. It may be depended upon in prosperity and poverty, in health and sickness, in the calm and in the storm, in life and in death.

> G. The believer has a new destiny (Rom. 8:29-39).
> 1. The nature of this goal *(Read Rom. 8:29)*

✶ 8:29 God has one supreme purpose on this earth today, and that is to conform the largest number of people in the least amount of time into the image of his dear Son.

> 2. The steps involved in this goal—We have been foreknown, predestinated, called, justified, and glorified already in the mind of God. These five words form a golden chain of God's grace and glory, linking up from eternity past to eternity future.
> 3. The guarantee of this goal
>   a. Question: *"Who shall separate us from the love of Christ?"* (Rom. 8:35a).
>   b. Answer: No one. This is true in the face of tribulation, distress, persecution, famine, nakedness, peril, sword, death, life, and includes angels, principalities, powers, things present, things to come, height, depth, or any other creature (see Rom. 8:35, 38-39). *"What shall we then say to these things? If God be for us, who can be against us? Who shall lay any thing to the charge of God's elect? It is God that justifieth. Nay, in all these things we are more than conquerors through him that loved us"* (Rom. 8:31, 33, 37).

✶ 8:37 When the staunch believer John Chrysostom was brought before the Roman Emperor in the fifth century and threatened with banishment for his faith, he replied, "Thou canst not banish me, for this world is my Father's house." "But I will slay thee," said the Emperor. "Nay, thou canst not," said the noble champion of the faith, "for my life is hid with Christ in God." "I will drive thee away from man and thou shalt have no friend left." "Nay, thou canst not, for I have a friend in heaven from whom thou canst not separate me! I defy thee, for there is nothing that thou canst do to hurt me!"

LESSON 22: THE BOOK OF ROMANS—PART 2

c. Reason: Because of the three-fold work of Christ
   (1) His death guarantees it *(Read Rom. 8:32)*
   (2) His resurrection guarantees it *(Read Rom. 8:34a)*
   (3) His intercession guarantees it *(Read Rom. 8:34b)*

LESSON 23

The Synagogue of Israel—God's Wisdom (Explanation & Vindication) Romans 9-11

Paul writes these chapters to answer two questions. First, how does God look upon Israel's rejection of their Messiah? Second, how does Israel fit into God's plan for the church?

> **I. The Sovereignty of God and Israel's Selection in the Past (Rom. 9)** *(Read Rom. 9:1-3)*

✶ 9:3 Paul shared the compassion of both Moses (Exod. 32:31-32) and Christ (Matt. 23:37) over Israel's sinful condition. (See also Gal. 1:84)

> A. The nine spiritual advantages of this sovereign selection (Rom. 9:4-5)
> 1. They were Israelites (a special nation).
> 2. They had been adopted by God.
> 3. They had the glory cloud—This is a reference to the shekinah cloud, that visible luminous appearance of God's presence.
>   a. It led them across the wilderness (Exod. 13:21-22; Num. 9:17-22).
>   b. It protected them at the Red Sea (Exod. 14:19-20, 24).
>   c. It filled the tabernacle during Moses' dedication (Exod. 40:34-38).
>   d. It filled the temple during Solomon's dedication (1 Kings 8:10-11; 2 Chron. 5:13-14).
>   e. It was removed during Ezekiel's time (Ezek. 10).
> 4. They had the covenants.
>   a. The Abrahamic covenant—Promising a mighty nation (Gen. 12:2-3, 7; 13:14-17; 15:5, 18; 17:8).
>   b. The Palestinian covenant—Promising a land (Deut. 30:3).
>   c. The Davidic covenant—Promising an eternal kingdom (2 Sam. 7:12-16; 23:5; 2 Chron. 13:5).
>   d. The New Covenant—Promising new hearts (Jer. 31:31-34).
> 5. They had the Law.
> 6. They performed services for God (ministering in both tabernacle and temple).
> 7. They had the messianic promise.
> 8. They had a regenerate ancestry (Abraham, Moses, David, etc.).
> 9. They were the people from which Christ came.
> B. The historical example of this sovereign selection (Rom. 9:6-29)
> 1. The example of Ishmael and Isaac *(Read Rom. 9:6-9)*—God chose Isaac (Abraham's son through Sarah) over Ishmael (his son through Hagar).
> 2. The example of Esau and Jacob *(Read Rom. 9:10-13)*

✶ God chose Jacob (second-born twin of Isaac) over Esau (firstborn twin). Some have been troubled over Paul's statement here in verse 13: *"As it is written, Jacob have I loved, but Esau have I hated."* It should be noted that the statement obviously does not refer to the two boys, but to the nations they founded, namely, Israel and Edom. This Old Testament prophet Obadiah clearly tells us why God hated Edom. In each case here (9:6-13), God rejected men who had been firstborn into patriarchal families. In each case the parent wished to see the rejected one inherit the problem. Abraham pleaded for Ishmael (Gen. 17:18) and Isaac attempted to pass the blessing on to Esau (Gen 27:1, 4, 30, 33).

> 3. The example of Pharaoh (Rom. 9:14-24)
>   a. The facts
>   (1) God determined to pardon sinful Israel with undeserved grace *(Read Rom. 9:15-16)*.
>   (2) God determined to punish sinful Pharaoh with deserved judgment *(Read Rom. 9:17)*.

✶ **9:17**
- Some would claim that he was unfair in hardening Pharaoh's heart. It should be noted that on at least seven occasions in the book of Exodus we are told that God hardened the heart of Pharaoh (4:21; 7:3; 9:12; 10:1, 20, 27; 11:10). How are we to understand this? A partial (and only partial) answer may be found in the following observation: The manner in which a given object will react when confronted by an outside influence is wholly dependent upon the nature of that object. For example, imagine a winter scene and a frozen river. On either side is a bank of yellow clay. Suddenly the sun comes from behind the clouds and shines brightly down upon the river and the banks. What happens next? The reaction is this: The ice will melt but the clay will harden. Thus we see in nature the same outside, heavenly influence softening one object but hardening the other.
- Furthermore, it should be pointed out that on four occasions we are informed that Pharaoh hardened his own heart (Exod. 7:22; 8:15, 19; 9:35). The word "hardeneth" in 9:18 (*kabed*) is translated "heavy" in Exodus 17:12; 18:18; Psalm 38:4; and Isaiah 1:4. Thus, God left his heart heavy with iniquities.

>   b. The fairness—Paul answers two questions here.
>   (1) Is God righteous? Yes *(Read Rom. 9:14, 21-24)*

✶ **9:21** Paul spends little time on this objection, simply pointing out that the potter has power over the clay he works with in choosing the kind of vessel he makes. It should be noted here (9:21) that Paul does not say God made the clay as it was, but that he worked with it. (See Jer. 18:1-6; Isa. 45:9; 64:6-8.) Two kinds of vessels are described here: "The vessels of wrath fitted to destruction" (9:22). This is in the middle voice, meaning "to fit oneself." *"The vessels of mercy, which he had afore prepared unto glory" (9:23)*. The conclusion of the matter is that hell (destruction) is the deserved destination of the sinful person, while heaven (glory) is the undeserved destination of the saved person.

>   (2) Are we responsible? Yes *(Read Rom. 9:19-20)*
>   4. The example from Hosea *(Read Rom. 9:25-26)*
>   5. The example from Isaiah *(Read Rom. 9:27-29)*

✶ **9:29**
- In Hosea's example, God's sovereignty is seen in reference to the saved Gentiles (1 Pet. 2:9-10).
- In Isaiah's example, God's sovereignty is seen in reference to the saved Israelite remnant.

> C. The two conclusions concerning this sovereign selection (Rom. 9:30-33)
>   1. Through faith the Gentiles had attained righteousness without even seeking it (Rom. 9:30).
>   2. Through the Law Israel had not attained righteousness even after seeking it (Rom. 9:31-33).

✶ **9:33** They looked for a bold lion; but God sent them a bleeding lamb. They wanted a throne; they were offered a cross.

> **II. The Righteousness of God and Israel's Rejection at the Present (Romans 10)**
> *Introduction: Romans 9 and 10 should always be read together. Chapter 9 shows why some Jews are saved; and chapter 10 explains why most are lost.*
>   A. The prayer for God's righteousness (Rom. 9:1-3; 10:1-2)—At the beginning of chapters 9 and 10 Paul reveals his great soul agony over Israel's lost condition *(Read Rom. 10:1-2)*.

> B. The source of God's righteousness *(Read Rom. 10:4-5)*

★ **10:4** We might reword this verse to say that Christ is the end of the Old Testament Law to the believer after the Cross, as George Washington was the end of the British law to the American after the Revolutionary War. (See 2 Cor. 3:6-11; Heb. 7:11-19; Gal. 3:24; Eph. 2:15; Col. 2:14.)

> C. The availability of God's righteousness *(Read Rom. 10:6-8)*—This is true because of two historical facts.
>   1. The incarnation of Christ *(Read Rom. 10:6)*
>   2. The resurrection of Christ *(Read Rom. 10:7)*
> D. The method of God's righteousness *(Read Rom. 10:9-10)*

★ **10:9-10** Some have made oral confession a condition of salvation on the basis of *10:10*: "For with the heart man believeth unto righteousness; and with the mouth confession is made unto salvation." The Bible, of course, does not impose this limitation. Paul evidently was stressing the same truth found in James 2:20; that is, a genuine possession of Christ in one's heart will surely lead to a confession of Christ with one's mouth. The fruit will prove the root. (See Matt. 10:32; Luke 12:8; John 12:42-43; Matt. 12:34.) The method, then, of righteousness, is faith in Christ.

> E. The scope of God's righteousness *(Read Rom. 10:11-13)*

★ **10:13** Paul had earlier shown that all were lost. He now says that all can be saved. Compare the "whosoever" mentioned here with that in Revelation 20:15.

> F. The presentation of God's righteousness *(Read Rom. 10:14-15)*. There are three reasons why God sends preachers.
>   1. A sinner must call upon the Lord to be saved.
>   2. He must believe in order to call.
>   3. He must hear in order to believe.
> G. The rejection of God's righteousness (Rom. 10:16-21)
>   1. Isaiah had prophesied this rejection *(Read Rom. 10:16, 20-21)*
>   2. Moses had prophesied this rejection *(Read Rom. 10:19)*

III. The Wisdom of God and Israel's Restoration in the Future (Rom. 11)
> *Paul here just discussed the rejection of Israel in chapter 10. He will now show that this rejection was neither total nor final (vv 26-36).*
>   A. This restoration is assured because Israel's rejection was not total (Rom. 11:1-25).
>   1. The factions of Israel (Rom. 11:1-10)
>   a. The minority group *(Read Rom. 11:1-5)*. This group is represented by Paul (Rom. 11:1) and Elijah (Rom. 11:2-4).

★ **11:4** Elijah felt he was the only believer during his day, and he actually made "intercession to God against Israel" (11:2). But God (who will never answer this kind of prayer, regardless of who prays it) quickly informed him that: "I have reserved to myself seven thousand men, who have not bowed the knee to the image of Baal" (Rom. 11:4; see also 1 Kings 19:10, 14, 18).

>   b. The majority group *(Read Rom. 11:6-10)*

★ **11:7** Both Isaiah and David predicted this. Present-day Israel is thus plagued with a three-fold blindness:
- The blindness caused by the fall of Adam (Eph. 4:18)
- The blindness caused by Satan (2 Cor. 4:4)
- The blindness caused by God (Rom. 11:8)

(1) Isaiah: *Compare Romans 11:8 with Isaiah 29:10*
(2) David: *Compare Romans 11:9-10 with Psalm 69:22-23*
2. The fullness of the Gentiles (Rom. 11:11-25)
   a. The definition of this period (as contrasted to the times of the Gentiles) *(Read Luke 21:24)*
      (1) The *fullness* refers to that time span involved in the completing of the body of Christ consisting of both saved Jews and Gentiles from Pentecost to the Rapture (see Acts 15:14; 1 Cor. 12:12-13; Eph. 4:11, 13).
      (2) The *times* refers to that time span from the Babylonian Captivity until the end of the tribulation. (See Deut. 28:28-68; 2 Chron. 36:21; Dan. 9:24-27.)
   b. The details of this period
      (1) The *facts*—Paul offers a parable from nature
         (a) An olive tree—Symbolizing the faith of Abraham *(Read Rom. 11:16,18)*
         (b) Some natural branches broken off—Symbolizing unbelieving Israel (Rom. 11:17), a past event
         (c) Some wild branches grafted on—Symbolizing believing Gentiles (Rom. 11:17, 19), a present event
         (d) Some natural branches grafted back on—Symbolizing believing Israel (Rom. 11:23-24), a future event
      (2) The *fiction*—This parable does not teach that the church has replaced Israel. This parable does not teach that a believer can lose his salvation. He is simply saying that since God did not spare the nation Israel when they were apostate, he will likewise not spare an apostate church. Christendom is going in the same direction today as Israel once did, and God will reject and judge them for it. (See 1 Tim. 4:1-3; 2 Pet. 2:1-22; Rev. 3:14-22; 17:3-18.)
      (3) The *future*
         (a) Israel's unbelief once led to the riches of the Gentiles (Rom. 11:12).
         (b) Israel's belief will lead to the redemption of the globe *(Read Rom. 11:15)*
B. This restoration is assured because Israel's rejection was not permanent (Rom. 11:26-36).
  1. The Israel of God (Rom. 11:26-32)
     a. To be restored through their promised Christ *(Read Rom. 11:26)*

★ **11:26** Note: In the previous verse (11:25), Paul describes this future restoration as a mystery.
- A mystery in the Bible is a previously hidden truth, not revealed in the Old Testament, but declared and, at times, explained in the New Testament.
- There are 12 such mysteries. Without amplification, these are:
  - The mystery of the kingdom of heaven (Matt. 13:3-50; Mark 4:1-25; Luke 8:4-15)
  - The mystery of the Rapture (1 Cor. 15:51-52; 1 Thess. 4:16)
  - The mystery of the church as the body of Christ (Eph. 3: 1-11; 6:19; Col. 4:3; Rom. 16:25)
  - The mystery of the church as the bride of Christ (Eph. 5: 28-32)
  - The mystery of the indwelling Christ (Gal. 2:20; Col. 1:26-27)
  - The mystery of the incarnate Christ (Col. 2:2, 9; 1 Cor. 2:7)
  - The mystery of godliness (1 Tim. 3:16)
  - The mystery of iniquity (2 Thess. 2:3-12; Matt. 13:33)
  - The mystery of Israel's present blindness (Rom. 11:25)
  - The mystery of the seven stars (Rev. 1:20)
  - The mystery of Babylon the harlot (Rev. 17:5, 7)
  - The mystery of God (Rev. 10:7; 11:15-19)
- In Romans 11:25 the mystery is that *"blindness in part is happened to Israel until the fullness of the Gentiles be come in."*

     b. To be restored through their promised covenant *(Read Rom. 11:27, 29)*
  2. The God of Israel *(Read Rom. 11:33-36)*

The Temple of God: God's Will (Transformation and Exhortation)—Romans 12-16

> I. **Personal Responsibilities for All the Redeemed (Rom. 12:1-15:13)**
>   A. The believer and self (Rom. 12:1-2)
>   1. What he is to offer: Body dedication *(Read Rom. 12:1)*

✷ **12:1**
- Note: Paul does not issue a curt command, but rather a pleading request. Loving service simply cannot be commanded. This is the language of grace and the method of the apostle. (See also 1 Cor. 4:16; Eph. 4:1; 1 Tim. 2:1; contrast this with Luke 12:20.)
- What is the believer invited to do? He is to present his body *"a living sacrifice, holy, acceptable unto God."* Note:
  - It is to be his body. God is not primarily interested in our time, talents, or treasury. The only gift which satisfies the Redeemer Creator is the body of his redeemed creature. (See 1 Cor. 3:16; 6:19-20; 2 Cor. 8:5.)
  - It is to be his living body. Sometimes it is easier to die for the Lord than it is to live for him.
  - It is to be a separated (holy) living body.
- Why is the believer invited to do this?
  - Because he has already experienced God's mercy. All other faiths make sacrifice the root of mercy, but Christianity makes it the flower. (Contrast this with 1 Kings 18:26-29; 2 Kings 3:26-27.)
  - Because it is not only the proper and requested course of action, but also the practical and reasonable route.
    - ✦ To the sinner, God says, *"Come now, and let us reason together, saith the Lord: Though your sins be as scarlet, they shall be as white as snow; though they be red like crimson, they shall be as wool"* (Isa. 1:18). The proper and practical thing for the sinner to do is to give God his heart.
    - ✦ To the saint, God says, *"Present your bodies ... unto God, which is your reasonable service."* The proper and practical thing for the saint to do is give God his body.

>   2. What he is to avoid: Worldly conformation *(Read Rom. 12:2a)*
>   3. What he is to achieve: Godly transformation *(Read Rom. 12:2b)*

✷ **12:2** The word "transformed" is *metamorpheo* in the Greek, from whence we get our word *metamorphosis*, that biological change whereby a caterpillar becomes a butterfly. The same word is used in the transfiguration of Jesus in Matthew 17:2. (See also 2 Cor. 3:18.) This transformation refers to that act of a believer arranging his outward position so that it agrees with his inward condition. (See 1 Pet. 1:14; 1 John 2:15.) The renewing of the mind here in 12:2 is probably a reference to constant Bible study and prayer (Eph. 4:23; Col. 3:10). This daily renewing is the only safeguard against failure (1 Cor. 9:24-27).

>   B. The believer and service (Rom. 12:3-21)
>   1. The tools for Christian service—Seven gifts of the spirit *(Read Rom. 12:4-8)*
>   a. Foretelling and forthtelling (Rom. 12:6)
>   b. Serving (Rom. 12:7a)
>   c. Teaching (Rom. 12:8b)
>   d. Exhorting (Rom. 12:8)
>   e. Giving (Rom. 12:8)
>   f. Ruling (Rom. 12:8b)
>   g. Mercy showing (Rom. 12:8c)
>   2. The techniques of service—A list of 24 commands from the Spirit *(Read Rom. 12:9-21)*

✷ **12:9** "To dwell above, with saints in love, that will indeed be glory; to dwell below with saints we know, well, that's a different story!"

> a. How to deal with one's friends *(Rom. 12:10, 13-15)*

✱ **12:15** We are to *"rejoice with them that do rejoice, and weep with them that weep."* Jesus did this (John 2; 11). (The theological reason for this is discussed in 1 Cor. 12:26.)

> b. How to deal with one's foes *(Read Rom. 12:17-21)*

✱ **12:20** We are to "destroy" our enemies. The way we are to do this is to make them our friends (12:18-21). Two classic Old Testament examples of this are found in David's treatment of King Saul (1 Sam. 24, 26) and Joseph's attitude toward his brothers (Gen. 45).

> C. The believer and society (Rom. 13:1-14)
>   1. The *what* of the matter
>   a. His duties toward the rulers of the state *(Read Rom. 13:1-7)*

✱ **13:1-7**
- He is to be in subjection to the higher powers, for *"the powers that be are ordained of God" (13:1)*. The Bible teaches that a child of God is not to love the systems of this world, or be conformed to its patterns, but nevertheless is to obey its laws. The Scriptures present both a separation from and a submission to the state on the part of the Christian (Titus 3:1; 1 Pet. 2:13). The Jews of the Roman Empire were notoriously bad citizens. They refused to obey and used Deuteronomy 17:14-15 as their proof text. However, Paul taught subjection to the state in spite of the shameful and shabby treatment he had often received at its hands (Acts 16:22-24, 37-38; see Prov. 8:15-16; Dan. 2:21; 4:17; John 19:10-11). Thus, human government is a divine institution given by God after the flood (Gen. 9) to assure order and prevent anarchy (see Judg. 17:6).
- He is to know that *"whosoever therefore resisteth the power, resisteth the ordinance of God" (13:2)*. It should be noted that Paul is here establishing general principles to guide the Christian living in a society governed by laws. He does not deal with what action the believer is to take when these laws are immoral or unscriptural. This question is answered in another passage (Acts 5:29).
- He is to render tribute (federal and local taxes), and custom (sales taxes to the coffers of the state), and fear and honor to the keepers of that state (13:7). A man once stopped D. L. Moody in Chicago and asked him where he was going. The great evangelist replied, "To cast my vote in the forthcoming elections." Somewhat shocked, the man admonished him, "But, brother Moody, don't you realize you are a citizen of heaven and that this world is not your final home?" Moody smiled and said, "That's true, but in the meanwhile I pay my taxes in Cook County!"

>   b. His duties toward the rest of the state *(Read Rom. 13:8-10)*

✱ **13:8-10** This passage does not prohibit a Christian from buying a home or car on the installment plan. Taken in context, it simply says we are to pay our debts to society. Paul has already said, however, that all believers owe the Gospel to the unsaved with whom they come into contact (Rom. 1:14).

>   2. The *why* of the matter *(Read Rom. 13:11-12)*

✱ **13:12** Paul speaks of the night as almost over, while Jesus says it is yet to come (John 9:4). Both are right. To the saint, the day breaks; but to the sinner, the night comes. This present world is the only hell the Christian will ever know, and it is the only heaven the unsaved will experience. This long night of sin has extended for thousands of years, beginning with Adam's rebellion. But the Morning Star has already appeared (Luke 2). Soon the Sun of Righteousness will arise with healing in his wings. Every single New Testament epistle writer believed this. (See 1 Cor. 15:51; 1 Thess. 4:16; James 5:8; 1 Pet. 4:7; 1 John 2:18, 28; Jude 18.) Especially to be noted is Paul's phrase, *"the day is at hand"* in verse 12. This is the first of at least ten important "days" in the Bible, all future. These are:

- The day of the Rapture (Rom. 13:12; Eph. 4:30; Phil. 1:6, 10; 2:16; Heb. 10:37; 2 Pet. 1:19)—This may be regarded as a literal 24-hour day.
- The judgment seat of Christ day (1 Cor. 3:13; 5:5; 2 Tim. 1:18; 4:8; 1 John 4:17)—This may be regarded as a literal 24-hour day and will include only Christians.
- The Day of the Lord (Joel 1:15; 2:1-2, 11, 31; Acts 2:20; 2 Thess. 2:3; Rev. 6:17)—This "day" covers the entire tribulation, a period of seven years.
- The day of Christ's second coming (Matt. 24:36; 26:29; 1 Thess. 5:2-4; 2 Thess. 1:10)—This may be regarded as a literal 24-hour day.
- The day of Armageddon (Rev. 16:14)—This may be regarded as a literal 24-hour day.
- The "resurrection of the just" day (John 6:39-40, 44, 54; 11:24)—This may be regarded as a literal 24-hour day and includes all Old Testament saints and tribulational believers.
- The "fallen angel" judgment day (Jude 6)—This may be regarded as a literal 24-hour day.
- The day of Christ (1 Cor. 1:8; 2 Cor. 1:14; 2 Tim. 1:12)-This "day" covers the entire millennium, a period of 1,000 years.
- The great white throne judgment day (Matt. 7:22; 11:22; John 12:48; Acts 17:31; Rom. 2:5, 16; 2 Pet. 2:9)—This may be regarded as a literal 24-hour day.
- The "new creation" day (2 Pet. 3:7-13)—This may be regarded as a literal 24-hour day. Paul then exhorts the believer to "put on the armor of light" (13:12; see Eph. 6:10-17 for the specific pieces of this armor).

> 3. The *who* of the matter *(Read Rom. 13:14)*
> D. The believer and weaker saints (Rom. 14:1-23)
>   1. No believer is to be judged by another down here.
>   a. We are not to criticize his legalism *(Read Rom. 14:1-9)*
>   (1) Don't judge in matters of diet (Rom. 14:2-3)
>   (2) Don't judge in matters of days (Rom. 14:5-6)
>   b. We are not to corrupt our liberty *(Read Rom. 14:13-23)*
>   2. All believers will be judged up there *(Read Rom. 14:10-12)*

★ **14:12** There are some 14 special categories of judgment in the Bible. In the book of Romans Paul refers to at least four of these.
- The Garden of Eden judgment of Adam (Rom. 5:12)
- The Calvary judgment of Christ (Rom. 4:25)
- The judgment seat of Christ (Rom. 14:10)
- The tribulational judgment of Satan (Rom. 16:20)

> E. The believer and the Savior (Rom. 15:1-13)—The earthly ministry of Christ is presented here as a pattern for Christians. (See also 1 Pet. 2:21-25.)
>   1. It was a sacrificial ministry *(Read Rom. 15:1-3a)*
>   2. It was a suffering ministry *(Read Rom. 15:3b)*
>   3. It was a sharing ministry *(Read Rom. 15:1, 7)*
>   4. It was a settling ministry *(Read Rom. 15:4, 13)*
>   5. It was a sure ministry (Rom. 15:8-12).
>   a. To the Jews *(Read Rom. 15:8)*
>   b. To the Gentiles *(Read Rom. 15:8-12)*

> **II. Personal Remarks to the Roman Redeemed (Rom. 15:14-16:27)**
>   A. Paul reviews his past (Rom. 15:14-21).
>   1. He mentions his specialized ministry *(Read Rom. 15:16)*
>   2. He mentions his miracles *(Read Rom. 15:19a)*

✷ **15:19a** The book of Acts records many of Paul's miracles:
- Striking a sorcerer with blindness in Paphos of Cyprus (13:11-12)
- Various miracles in Iconium (14:3-4)
- Healing a cripple in Lystra (14:8-18)
- Curing a demoniac girl in Philippi (16:16-18)
- Healing many of diseases and demons at Ephesus (19:11-12)
- Raising Eutychus at Troas (20:9-10)
- Restoring Publius's father of a fever and healing others on the Isle of Melita (28:8-9)

>   3. He mentions his mission field *(Read Rom. 15:19b)*
>   4. He mentions his *modus operandi* *(Read Rom. 15:20)*
>   B. Paul previews his future.
>   1. He determines to visit them at a later time, as he goes to Spain (Rom 15:22-24, 28-29).

✷ **15:29** The Pillars of Hercules, the westernmost reaches of mainland Europe, and the civilized world in his day, beckoned to Paul. Did he later get to Spain? Just before his death he would write, *"I have finished my course" (2 Tim. 4:7)*. Since Spain was on his itinerary we assume he did indeed get there.

>   2. He desires their prayers at the present time, as he goes to Jerusalem (Rom. 15:25-27, 30-32).
>   a. The request for their prayers *(Read Rom. 15:30)*
>   b. The reason for their prayers *(Read Rom. 15:31)*
>   3. He delivers greetings to his many Roman friends.
>   a. Special greetings to three *(Read Rom. 16:1-3)*
>   b. General greetings to 25 *(Read Rom. 16:4-16)*

✷ **16:3** Paul briefly leaves the mountain peaks of doctrine to come down to the pavements of Rome. He began his epistle by saying that *"without ceasing I make mention of you always in my prayers"* (1:9). At the end of his letter he mentions no less than 28 of them by name.

>   4. He denounces troublemakers *(Read Rom. 16:17-18)*.

✷ **16:17**
- The New Testament gives three reasons for dismissing a member from the fellowship of a local church.
  - For troublemaking (Rom. 16:17; 2 Thess. 3:6; Prov. 6:19). Note: When Paul finally reached Rome, he found those troublemakers hard at work. (See Phil. 1:14-18; 3:18.)
  - For immorality (1 Cor. 5)
  - For heresy (Titus 3:10)
- The procedure for dismissing such a person is described in 1 Corinthians 5:4 and Matthew 18:15-17. (See also 2 Thess. 3:14-15.)

>   5. He declares the doom of Satan *(Read Rom. 16:20)*.

✷ **16:20** This prophecy of the bruising of Satan will be fulfilled in a two-fold manner:
  - When he is cast into the bottomless pit for a thousand years during the millennium (Rev. 20:1-3)
  - When he is cast into the lake of fire forever after the millennium (Rev. 20:10)

> 6. He delivers his final benediction *(Read Rom. 16:24-27).*

✷ **16:24** Paul both begins and concludes this as he does with all others by commending his readers to the grace of God. Note:
  - The introduction to his epistles:
    - *Romans 1:7b* – "Grace to you and peace from God our Father, and the Lord Jesus Christ."
    - *1 Corinthians 1:3* – "Grace be unto you, and peace, from God our Father, and from the Lord Jesus Christ."
    - *2 Corinthians 1:2* – "Grace be to you, and peace from God our Father, and from the Lord Jesus Christ."
    - *Galatians 1:3* – "Grace be to you and peace from God the Father, and from our Lord Jesus Christ."
    - *Ephesians 1:2* – "Grace be to you, and peace, from God our Father, and from the Lord Jesus Christ."
    - *Philippians 1:2* – "Grace be unto you, and peace, from God our Father, and from the Lord Jesus Christ."
    - *Colossians 1:2b* – "Grace be unto you, and peace, from God our Father, and the Lord Jesus Christ."
    - *1 Thessalonians 1:1b* – "Grace be unto you, and peace from God our Father, and the Lord Jesus Christ."
    - *2 Thessalonians 1:2* – "Grace unto you, and peace, from God our Father and the Lord Jesus Christ."
    - *1 Timothy 1:2b* – "Grace, mercy, and peace, from God our Father and Jesus Christ our Lord."
    - *2 Timothy 1:2b* – "Grace, mercy, and peace, from God the Father and Christ Jesus our Lord."
    - *Titus 1:4b* – "Grace, mercy, and peace, from God the Father and the Lord Jesus Christ our Saviour."
    - *Philemon 3* – "Grace to you, and peace, from God our Father and the Lord Jesus Christ."
  - The conclusion to his epistles:
    - *Romans 16:24* – "The grace of our Lord Jesus Christ be with you all."
    - *1 Corinthians 16:23* – "The grace of our Lord Jesus Christ be with you."
    - *2 Corinthians 13:14* – "The grace of the Lord Jesus Christ, and the love of God, and the communion of the Holy Ghost be with you all."
    - *Galatians 6:18* – "Brethren, the grace of our Lord Jesus Christ be with your spirit. Amen."
    - *Ephesians 6:24 (NIV)* – "Grace to all who love our Lord Jesus Christ with an undying love."
    - *Philippians 4:23 (NIV)* – "The grace of the Lord Jesus Christ be with your spirit."
    - *Colossians 4:18* – "Grace be with you."
    - *1 Thessalonians 5:28* – "The grace of our Lord Jesus Christ be with you."
    - *2 Thessalonians 3:18* – "The grace of our Lord Jesus Christ be with you all."
    - *1 Timothy 6:21b* – "Grace be with thee."
    - *2 Timothy 4:22* – "The Lord Jesus Christ be with thy spirit. Grace be with you."
    - *Titus 3:15b* – "Grace be with you all."
    - *Philemon 25* – "The grace of our Lord Jesus Christ be with your spirit."

LESSON 24
INTRODUCTION TO FIRST CORINTHIANS

GOD'S MEDICAL JOURNAL—
A DESCRIPTION OF AND PRESCRIPTION FOR VARIOUS LOCAL CHURCH DISEASES

    A. This is what 1 Corinthians is all about: The church at Corinth had been infected by a number of both satanic and fleshly viruses.
    B. There is almost no modern-day church problem that is not covered in 1 Corinthians. The church was filled with theological and personal problems.
        1. They had perverted the doctrine of baptism (chapter 1).
        2. They were bragging about what little human wisdom they had (chapter 1).
        3. They were carnal to the core (3:1).
        4. They had deceived themselves (3:18).
        5. They had defiled their bodies (3:17).
        6. They were puffed up (4:18).
        7. They were tolerating horrible immorality (5:1).
        8. They were suing each other in heathen courts (6:1).
        9. They were confused about marriage (7:1).
        10. They had abused the doctrine of Christian liberty (8:9).
        11. They were not dressing properly in the house of God (11:6).
        12. They had made a mockery of the Lord's Supper (11:30).
        13. They had corrupted the gifts of the Spirit, especially tongues (chapter 14).
        14. They were confused on the subject of the resurrection (chapter 15).
        15. They had let down on their offerings.
    It has been said that if sins were horses, this church could have filled many stables.
    C. The greatest human missionary of all times was the Apostle Paul. This ex-Pharisee, who had once hated and hounded Christians, made three great missionary trips, during which he established dozens of local New Testament churches. Thus the former vicious "wolf of the flock" became one of God's finest "sheepdogs."
    D. The fact is that the New Testament is made up basically of some letters Paul wrote to some of these churches he started, and to their pastors. This list would contain:
        1. The epistle to Rome (Romans)
        2. The epistle to Ephesus (Ephesians)
        3. The epistle to Colosse (Colossians)
        4. The epistle to Philippi (Philippians)
        5. The Epistle to Galatia (Galatians)
        6. The two epistles to Thessalonica (1 and 2 Thessalonians)
        7. The two epistles to a pastor named Timothy (1 and 2 Timothy)
        8. The epistle to a pastor named Titus (Titus)

9. The two epistles to Corinth (1 and 2 Corinthians)
E. Here, then, we have an amazing fact: Out of the 27 New Testament books, no less than 12 were written by Paul to his beloved mission churches.
F. Paul would have had little time, it would seem, for those modern "Christian movements" that bypass, downplay, and outright ignore the ministry and importance of local churches.
G. Of all his church letters, Romans is no doubt the most important, but 1 Corinthians is probably second in importance. This is so because of its great section on the resurrection of Christ and the believer (1 Cor. 15), and, if for no other reason, because of its sheer bulk, for 1 Corinthians is by far the longest epistle written by Paul.
H. In a nutshell, through Paul's efforts, the church was now in Corinth, but somehow Corinth had gotten into the church. This is probably the second most carnal New Testament church. The church at Laodicea was undoubtedly the worst. (See Rev. 3:14-22.)
I. This then is Paul's description of their problem. He therefore offers the proper prescription for their problems.
   1. The reminder *(Read 6:19)*
   2. The solution *(Read 1:10; 10:31; 15:58)*
J. Background to the founding of the church at Corinth
   1. It was founded by Paul during his second missionary journey.
   2. Acts 18 relates the "ground breaking" ceremonies.
      a. He leaves on his second trip with Silas (Acts 15:40).
      b. At Lystra they pick up Timothy (Acts 16:1).
      c. At Troas Paul receives his Macedonian vision (Acts 16:9).
      d. At Philippi a woman named Lydia, a demon-possessed girl, and a Roman jailer are all three saved (Acts 16:14-34).
      e. From Philippi Paul moves to Thessalonica (Acts 17:1).
      f. From there to Berea (Acts 17:10).
      g. From Berea to Athens (Acts 17:15).
      h. From Athens, finally to Corinth (Acts 18:1).
   3. In Corinth Paul soon meets Aquila and Priscilla. Crispus, the chief ruler of the synagogue, is saved (Acts 18:8).
   4. God comforts Paul in a vision (Acts 18:9-10).
   5. Paul stays at least 18 months in Corinth before departing (Acts 18:11).
   6. The Corinthian church was then pastored by a man called Apollos.
K. Background of Paul's first letter to the church at Corinth
   1. During the summer of A.D. 53, Paul starts on his third missionary journey, apparently alone (Acts 18:23).
   2. He arrives at Ephesus and spends three years there (Acts 20:31).
   3. While at Ephesus he is visited by a delegation from Corinth with news concerning the tragic situation in their local church.
   4. With a heavy heart, Paul sits down and writes 1 Corinthians.
L. The most exciting single word in the Bible is found here in 1 Corinthians: MARANATHA! (16:22).
M. The book also includes perhaps the greatest verse on temptation in an apostolic church (10:13).
N. In essence, 1 Corinthians provides the most amount of information on the following subjects.
   1. Characteristics of the natural, carnal, and spiritual person (2:14-3:4)
   2. The judgment seat of Christ (3:9-15)
   3. Rules concerning the married and single life (7)
   4. Christian liberty (8-10)

5. Communion (11:17-34)
   6. Rules for personal conduct in God's house (11:1-6)
   7. Spiritual gifts in general (12)
   8. The gift of tongues in particular (14)
   9. The importance of love (13)
   10. The doctrine of the resurrection (15)
O. There are quotations or allusions in 1 Corinthians from 18 Old Testament books; 1 Corinthians is the seventh longest New Testament book, and 28th longest biblical book, with 16 chapters, 437 verses, and 9,489 words.
P. Great passages would include:
   1. 1:18-31
   2. 6:19-20
   3. 9:24-27
   4. 10:13
   5. 12:12-26
   6. 13:1-13
   7. 15:21-28
   8. 15:51-58

Overview of the Book of First Corinthians

Part One: The eight corruptions committed by the Corinthian church

I. First Corruption — They were following human leaders
  A. The leaders involved
  B. The lunacy involved

II. Second Corruption — They were favoring earthly wisdom
  A. The reaction to God's wisdom
  1. "It is the program of a fool!" (the conclusion of the unsaved)
  2. "It is the power of God!" (the conclusion of the saved)
  B. The revelation concerning God's wisdom
  C. The results of God's wisdom
  1. To the Jews, who demanded signs, it was a stumbling block
  2. To the Greeks, who demanded earthly wisdom, it was senseless
  3. To all believers, who demanded nothing, it is salvation
  D. The reasons for God's wisdom
  E. The review of God's wisdom
  1. That the message of the cross is not of this world
  2. That the message of the cross had been ordained before the world
  3. That the message of the cross is reserved for the heirs of this world

III. Third Corruption — They were floundering in the flesh
  A. The corpse (the natural person)
  B. The crybaby (the carnal person)
  C. The conqueror (the spiritual person)

IV. Fourth Corruption — They were forgetting future judgment
  A. The meaning of this judgment
  B. The individuals in this judgment
  C. The purpose of this judgment
  D. The materials to be tested in this judgment
  E. The method of testing at this judgment
  F. The results of this judgment
  G. The admonition in light of this judgment

V. Fifth Corruption — They were flattering themselves
  A. Their two-fold problem
  1. They were overestimating their own abilities
  2. They were underestimating the abilities of others

VI. Sixth Corruption — They were failing to discipline
  A. The need for discipline

    B. The breakdown in discipline
    C. The authority to discipline
    D. The seriousness of discipline
    E. The reason for discipline
    F. The extent of discipline
    G. The procedure in discipline
    H. The results of discipline

VII. Seventh Corruption — They were fragmenting the body of Christ
    A. This action was improper
        1. Because of whom they were judging
        2. Because of whom they someday would judge
    B. This action was illegal
    C. This action was inconsistent

VIII. Eighth Corruption — They were falling into sexual immorality
Paul condemns this terrible sin, pointing out:
    A. That our bodies are members of the Savior
    B. That our bodies are temples of the Spirit

Part Two: The six questions submitted by the Corinthian Church

I. Question Number One: What about marriage?
    A. The two problems connected with this chapter
        1. Did Paul consider marriage to be unproductive?
        2. Did Paul consider his writings to be uninspired?
    B. The five persons considered in this chapter
        1. Singles
        2. Christian couples
        3. Unmarried, widowers, and widows
        4. Mixed couples
        5. The father (or guardian) of a young virgin

II. Question Number Two: What about Christian liberty?
    A. A current example — The Corinthian believers
        1. The confusion
        2. The clarification
        3. The conclusion
        4. The challenge
    B. A personal example — The Apostle Paul
        1. The basis of his rights
        2. The extent of his rights
        3. The employment of his rights
    C. An Old Testament example — The nation Israel
        1. The narration
        2. The application
        3. The summation

III. Question Number Three: What about church conduct?
    A. Rules concerning clothing
        1. The man's appearance
        2. The woman's appearance
    B. Rules concerning communion
        1. The person of communion
        2. The perversion of communion
        3. The purposes of communion
        4. The partakers of communion
        5. The penalty of communion

IV. Question Number Four: What about spiritual gifts?
    A. Definition of a spiritual gift
    B. Number of spiritual gifts
        1. Gift of wisdom
        2. Gift of knowledge
        3. The gift of faith
        4. The gift of healing
        5. The gift of miracles
        6. The gift of prophecy
        7. The gift of discernment
        8. The gift of tongues
        9. The gift of interpretation of tongues
        10. The gift of apostleship
        11. The gift of teaching
        12. The gift of helps
        13. The gift of administration
    C. Extent of the spiritual gifts
        1. Each believer possesses at least one spiritual gift
        2. No believer possesses all the spiritual gifts
    D. Abuse of the spiritual gifts
        1. Action abuses
        2. Attitude abuses
    E. Purpose of spiritual gifts
    F. Analogy of the spiritual gifts
        1. Each member in both bodies performs a vital task, appointed by God himself
        2. No member is to be independent of the other members
        3. Every member is to rejoice and suffer with the other members
    G. Indispensable ingredient in the spiritual gifts — This element is love
        1. The importance of love
        2. The impeccability of love
        3. The indestructibility of love
    H. Comparison of the spiritual gifts
        1. The gift of prophecy
        2. The gift of tongues

V. Question Number Five: What about the resurrection?
    A. The prominence of the resurrection

  1. It is the focal point in reference to salvation
  2. It is the focal point in reference to the scriptures
 B. The proof of the resurrection
  1. First proof — The manifestations of Christ
  2. Second proof — The salvation of Paul
 C. The priority of the resurrection
  1. Concerning Christ
  2. Concerning the gospel preachers
  3. Concerning believers
 D. The program of the resurrection
  1. The villain
  2. The victors
  3. The victory
  4. The vindication
 E. The prompting of the resurrection
  1. The resurrection factor should motivate me to pick up the fallen banner of departed believers
  2. The resurrection factor should motivate me to serve as a martyr if God's will so directs
  3. The resurrection factor should motivate me toward holy living
 F. The pattern of the resurrection
  1. To be resurrected the grain is planted in the ground
  2. At the resurrection of the new stalk retains the likeness of the grains
 G. The perfection of the resurrection
  1. Paul contrasts the new body to the old body
  2. Paul contrasts the new body with brute bodies
  3. Paul contrasts the new body with heavenly bodies
 H. The promise of the resurrection
  1. Concerning the bodies belonging to living believers
  2. Concerning the bodies belonging to departed believers
 I. The purpose of the resurrection
 J. The practical value of the resurrection

VI. Question Number Six: What about the collection?
 A. The offering taken
  1. The source of the offering
  2. The time of the offering
  3. The amount of the offering
  4. The purpose of the offering
  5. The custodian of the offering
 B. The offering taker
  1. His circumstances
  2. His commitment
  3. His coworkers
  4. His challenge
  5. His closing words

The Book of First Corinthians

PART ONE: The eight corruptions committed by the Corinthian church (1 Cor. 1-6)

Introduction:
"*Paul, called to be an apostle of Jesus Christ through the will of God, and Sosthenes our brother, unto the church of God which is at Corinth, to them that are sanctified in Christ Jesus, called to be saints, with all that in every place call upon the name of Jesus Christ our Lord, both theirs and ours: Grace be unto you, and peace, from God our Father, and from the Lord Jesus Christ. I thank my God always on your behalf, for the grace of God which is given you by Jesus Christ; that in every thing ye are enriched by him, in all utterance, and in all knowledge; even as the testimony of Christ was confirmed in you: so that ye come behind in no gift; waiting for the coming of our Lord Jesus Christ: who shall also confirm you unto the end, that ye may be blameless in the day of our Lord Jesus Christ. God is faithful, by whom ye were called unto the fellowship of his Son Jesus Christ our Lord*" (1 Cor. 1:1-9).

✶ **1:9** The following is an overview of these first 9 verses:
- Paul and Sosthenes send their regards. This Sosthenes may have been the same one referred to in Acts 18:17. He was the chief ruler of the synagogue in Ephesus who instigated a riot against Paul. It backfired, however, and he himself was beaten by some angry Greeks. This apparently led to his salvation.
- Paul says (1:2): "*With all that in every place call upon the name of Jesus.*" Thus, this epistle was written for all believers, as were his others (see 1 Thess. 5:27; Col. 4:16).
- "*The Lord Jesus Christ*" (1:3)—This great name is mentioned six times in the first ten verses of the epistle, doubtless because the church had not honored this grand title. Here is the reason why any local church has difficulties.
- "*Ye are enriched ... in all utterance and. .. knowledge*" (1:5). The Corinthian believers knew the truth and could speak the truth. They simply were not practicing the truth.
- "*Ye come behind in no gift*" (1:7)—The Bible lists some 18 gifts. The church at Corinth apparently had all of them.
- Verse 8 is one of the greatest "security of the believer" statements in the entire Bible. Note the wording:
  - Confirm—This means to establish and make absolutely secure. The same verb is used in Romans 15:8, where Paul states that God confirmed in Christ the promises made in the Old Testament.
  - Blameless—A legal term meaning "not called into court, uncharged, unaccused." It does not mean sinless, but chargeless. (See also Col. 1:22, 1 Tim. 3:10.)
  - To the end ... in the day—A reference to the Rapture. Conclusion: Paul is writing to one of the most backslidden, carnal, confused, and selfish churches on record. He thus could only predict their eventual salvation because of God's eternal security, in spite of their pitiful condition.
- "*God is faithful*" (1:9)—A brief summary of his faithfulness would include:
  - He is faithful in defending his people *(Read Psa. 89:20, 24, 22)*.
  - He is faithful in times of temptation *(Read 1 Cor. 10:13)*.
  - He is faithful in keeping the Christian saved *(Read 2 Thess. 3:3; 1 Thess. 5:23-24)*.
  - He is faithful in chastening his children *(Read Psa. 119:75; Heb. 12: 6)*.
  - He is faithful in forgiving confessed sin *(Read 1 John 1:9)*.
  - He is faithful in hearing our prayers *(Read Psa. 143:1)*. Thus, their calling was through God, and since he is faithful, their salvation was sure. We note with sadness that Paul says nothing about their present condition (as in letters to other churches), but only mentions their past and future.

- *"The fellowship of his Son Jesus Christ" (1:9)*—Christians the world over love to talk and write and sing about this fellowship, and well they should; but it should be kept in mind that sometimes this fellowship involves suffering also. As Paul writes: *"That I may know him, and the power of his resurrection, and the fellowship of his sufferings, being made conformable unto his death" (Phil. 3:10).*

  Too often it would seem we want the first without the second. But there can be no power of the resurrection without the fellowship of his sufferings.

> **I. First Corruption—They were following human leaders (1 Cor. 1:10-17)**—*"Now I beseech you, brethren, by the name of our Lord Jesus Christ, that ye all speak the same thing, and that there be no divisions among you; but that ye be perfectly joined together in the same mind and in the same judgment. For it hath been declared unto me of you, my brethren, by them which are of the house of Chloe, that there are contentions among you" (1 Cor. 1:10-11).*

✶ **1:11**
- *"No divisions among you" (1:10).* Greek scholar W. E. Vine lists four distinct steps which may lead downward from harmony to a tragic breakup of Christian unity. These are:
  - Stasis—A strong disagreement, a dissension. (See Acts 15:2; 23:7, 10.)
  - Dichostasia—A standing apart. (See Gal. 5:20; Rom. 16:17.)
  - Schisma—A severe rent, a tear. (See 1 Cor. 11:18; John 7:43; 9:16; 10:19.)
  - Hairesis—A mature and established separation. (See Acts 5:17; 24:5, 14; 26:5; 2 Pet. 2:1; Titus 3:10.) Here the third word is used by Paul, *schisma*, thus suggesting the Corinthian church was in danger of complete breakup.
- *"But that ye be perfectly joined together" (1:10).* The phrase *"perfectly joined together"* in this verse comes from one Greek word. That word is *katartizo*. This word is used in three other important New Testament passages:
  - *"Through faith we understand that the worlds were framed by the Word of God" (Heb. 11:3).* Here the word *katartizo* is translated "framed."
  - *"Wherefore when he cometh into the world he saith, sacrifice and offering thou wouldst not, but a body hast thou prepared me" (Heb. 10:5).* Here the word is translated "prepared."
  - *"And going on from thence, he saw ... James ... and John his brother in a ship with Zebedee their father, mending their nets (Matt. 4:21).* In this final passage the word is translated "mending." The point of all the above is simply this: God is desirous that church believers be joined together: As perfectly as the sun, moon, and stars fit together (Heb. 11:3). As perfectly as God formed the body for Jesus to use (Heb. 10:5). As perfectly as a mended net is. Souls are not saved in a church plagued with problems, simply because the net is broken and they get away.
- Paul begins by naming his source of information—*"For it hath been declared unto me ... of Chloe." (See 1:11.)* All too often unsigned critical letters are received by Christian leaders, finding fault with either the pastor or some other member in the church. How many times has vicious gossip from the mouths of nameless (and spineless) church members led to the destruction of their own church!

> A. The leaders involved *(Read 1 Cor. 1:12)*
> B. The lunacy involved *(Read 1 Cor. 1:13-15, 17)*

✶ **1:17**
- In verses 12 through 17 Paul writes to straighten out their first basic problem, that of baptism. How many churches have, since that time, been split right down the middle over the subject of baptism. Here the argument, however, was not over the mode or even the purpose, but concerning the different men who had baptized some of these Corinthian believers.
  - Paul had baptized some of them, of course (but very few in reality), when he established the church.
  - Apollos later pastored the church and also baptized some.
  - Peter (Cephas) had apparently baptized a few, although we know nothing as to when or where this might have taken place. Some believe it could have happened at Pentecost.

- Christ is also mentioned in this list. As with Peter, we have no knowledge whatsoever as to where, when, and indeed *if* he ever did this.
■ At any rate, here is a local New Testament church hopelessly divided into four groups, with each group claiming superiority over the other three because of the man who had baptized them.
  - The Paulite group—The "claim to fame" of the first group was this: "We are of Paul and therefore better than you. Anyone knows Paul is a great doctrinal preacher, and that's the only kind to have."
  - The Apollosite group—The second group would probably retort, "We are of Apollos, and anyone with any sense at all will agree that Apollos is an eloquent preacher and can preach circles around Paul any day."
  - The Cephasite group—The third group might then answer, "We are of Cephas, and you can brag about doctrine and eloquence all you want to, but there's just nobody as down-to-earth and practical as Peter."
  - The Christite group—The fourth group could thereupon be pictured as looking down at the other three and piously saying, "We are of Christ, and therefore look to no human preacher to lead us and feed us."
■ *"Was Paul crucified for you?" (1:13)*. We note Paul hits his own fan club first. It is easy to rebuke a group if they are wrong, especially if that group is against you anyway, but it is another thing to criticize sharply those who sing your praises the loudest. Paul was truly "sold out" for Jesus.
■ *"For Christ sent me not to baptize, but to preach the gospel" (1:17)*. This is probably the strongest verse in the Bible refuting the doctrine of baptismal regeneration (the unscriptural teaching which says one must be baptized to be saved). We would note here that Paul did not say that Christ had forbidden him to baptize, for the apostle often did baptize his converts (see Acts 16:15, 33; 18:8; 19:5). What he is saying here is simply this: Water baptism is not a part of the gospel of Christ. Later in this same epistle, Paul defines the gospel: *"Moreover, brethren, I declare unto you the gospel ... how that Christ died for our sins according to the scriptures; and that he was buried, and that he rose again the third day according to the scriptures" (1 Cor. 15:1, 3-4)*. This, then, by itself, is the gospel.

II. Second Corruption—They were favoring earthly wisdom (1 Cor. 1:18-2:13). In verses 1:18-31 Paul contrasts false worldly wisdom (which the Corinthians so highly prized but did not themselves have—see 1:26) with true godly wisdom which centers in the cross of Christ.
  A. The reaction to God's wisdom
    1. "It is the program of a fool!" (the conclusion of the unsaved) *(Read 1 Cor. 1:18a)*
    2. "It is the power of God!" (the conclusion of the saved) *(Read 1 Cor. 1:18b)*

✱ **1:18b**
  ■ Note: In the original it states that the unbelievers are perishing and the believers are being saved. Both salvation and damnation are put in the present tense. (See John 3:18, 26 in regard to the unsaved.) Concerning the saved, the New Testament describes their salvation in three tenses:
    - Past tense—Romans 8:24 (justification)
    - Present tense—1 Corinthians 1:18 (sanctification)
    - Future tense—Romans 5:9 (glorification)
  ■ Dr. Harry Ironside was once asked by a stranger if he was saved. The famous pastor replied, "Yes, I have been, I am being, and I shall be!"

  B. The revelation concerning God's wisdom *(Read 1 Cor. 1:19-21, 25-26)*

✱ **1:26**
  ■ Concerning 1:19 — In both 1:19 and 3:19 Paul quotes from two Old Testament passages comparing God's wisdom with human wisdom:
    - *"For it is written, I will destroy the wisdom of the wise" (1:19)*. (See Isa. 29:14.)

- *"For it is written, He taketh the wise in their own craftiness" (3:19).* (See job 5:13.) For three classic New Testament examples of just this very thing, see Matthew 21:23-27 (concerning the baptism of John); Matthew 22:15-22 (concerning the tribute to Caesar); and John 8:1-11 (concerning an adulterous woman). In his eternal wisdom, God chose instead the method of the cross to save people.

■ Concerning 1:26—Paul tactfully reminds the church that it was a good thing God did not choose the intellect and prestige of the world. *"For ye see your calling, brethren, how that not many wise men after the flesh, not many mighty, not many noble, are called" (1:26).* The great John Wesley was often helped during his ministry by a noble lady of high English society named Lady Huntington. This gracious woman who gave so much of her time, talent, and treasure to Christ would often testify as follows: "I am only going to heaven through the letter M. How thankful I am that Paul did not say that not any noble are called, but rather not many noble are called. Therefore, I am only going to heaven through the letter M!"

> C. The results of God's wisdom
> 1. To the Jews, who demanded signs, it was a stumbling block (1 Cor. 1:22-23).
> 2. To the Greeks, who demanded earthly wisdom, it was senseless (1 Cor. 1:22-23).

✶ **1:23** Note: Israel had rejected God's plan in spite of the fact that he had provided them with certain signs. (See John 3:2; 20:30; Acts 2:19, 43; 5:12.)

> 3. To all believers, who demanded nothing, it is salvation *(Read 1 Cor. 1:24, 30)*
> D. The reasons for God's wisdom *(Read 1 Cor. 1:27-29)*

✶ **1:29** Thus, in manifesting his own glory, God delighted in choosing:
- ■ The foolish things of this world
  - A bleeding lamb in Exodus 12
  - A smitten rock in Exodus 17
  - A brass snake in Numbers 21
- ■ The weak things of this world
  - A rod to defeat the Egyptians in Exodus 4
  - A sling to defeat a mighty giant in 1 Samuel 17
  - A bone to defeat the Philistines in Judges 15
- ■ The base things of this world
  - A harlot's son who became a mighty judge in Judges 11
  - A heathen girl who became David's great-grandmother in Ruth 4
  - An immoral woman who became a great soul winner in John 4

> E. The review of God's wisdom (1 Cor. 2:1-13)—In these verses Paul reviews his past visit to their city during which time he established the churches at Corinth. He reminds them:
> 1. That the message of the cross is not of this world *(Read 1 Cor. 2:1-6)*

✶ **2:4** Prior to his visit in Corinth, Paul had spoken to the Greek philosophers on Mars Hill in Athens (Acts 17:16-34). Here he delivered a powerful and eloquent message, using philosophy, poetry, and history along with great scriptural truths. The sermon, however, produced little fruit. Some (but not all) have therefore concluded that the apostle here in 1 Corinthians 2:1-4 is recording his determination to depend henceforth only and always upon the Holy Spirit and not to rely at all upon eloquence, philosophy, etc. Others have felt that his condition as described in 2:3 was purely physical, perhaps due to nervous exhaustion. (See also 2 Cor. 7:5.)

2. That the message of the cross had been ordained before the world *(Read 1 Cor. 2:7-8)*
  3. That the message of the cross is reserved for the heirs of this world (1 Cor. 2:9-13)
     a. This inheritance is concealed to unbelievers *(Read 1 Cor. 2:9)*
     b. This inheritance is revealed to believers *(Read 1 Cor. 2:10)*
III. **Third Corruption—They were floundering in the flesh (1 Cor. 2:14-3:7)**. In these remarkable verses Paul divides all people into three spiritual categories. These are:
  A. The corpse (the natural person) *(Read 1 Cor. 2:14)*—Controlled by Satan

★ **2:14** Characteristics of the natural person:
  - He may not be totally depraved (as evil as he could possibly be), but he is totally helpless to comprehend God's Word (see Acts 8:31).
  - He thus concludes that the Scriptures are senseless (see Acts 17:18, 32; 26:24).
  - He is dead and must be resurrected, for he cannot be revived (see Rom. 5:12; Eph. 2:1).

  B. The crybaby (the carnal person) *(Read 1 Cor. 3:1-6)*—Controlled by the flesh

★ **3:6** Characteristics of the carnal person:
  - He is helpless, as a newborn infant. The word "babes" used here is *nepios* in the original, and carries with it weakness without power of speech, immaturity and inexperience. This condition is also pictured in *Ephesians 4:14*. *"That we henceforth be no more children, tossed to and fro, and carried about with every wind of doctrine"* (see also Gal. 4:3; 2 Pet. 1:9).
  - He is unable to receive anything but milk (3:2). This condition always suggests either infancy or infirmity. Milk is proper for awhile (1 Pet. 2:2), but *"strong meat belongeth to them that are of full age, even those who by reason of use have their senses exercised to discern both good and evil"* (Heb. 5:14; see also Heb. 5:11-13).
  - He walks and talks like an unsaved person. *"Are ye not carnal and walk as men?" (3:3b)*. All believers should consider this pointed question: "If you were arrested and charged with being a 'Christian,' would there be enough evidence to convict you?" It would seem the Corinthians, to a large extent, would get off scot-free.
  - He compares spiritual leaders instead of spiritual truths. (See 2:13 as opposed to 3:4.) Paul answers this by saying: *"I have planted, Apollos watered; but God gave the increase" (3:6)*. Only God can do this (see also 1 Kings 18:30-38).

  C. The conqueror (the spiritual person) *(Read 1 Cor. 2:15)*—Controlled by the Spirit

★ **2:15** Characteristics of the spiritual person:
  - He (or she) is not sanctimonious.
  - This person is not superior (in matters of brains, strength, background, money, etc.).
  - She is **not** sensational.
  - He is **not** sugary sweet.
  - This person is **not** straightlaced.
  - He is **not** segregated from society.
  - She is **not** superficial.
  - He is **not** spineless.
  - He or she **is** spiritual. To be spiritual is to be in harmony with God, as are his laws (Rom. 7:14). Thus, a spiritual person is simply one controlled and motivated by the Holy Spirit. (See 1 Cor. 15:46; Gal. 5:16, 25.) Because of this, he or she can correctly judge *"all things" (2:15)*. (See also 2 Tim. 2:15 as opposed to 2 Pet. 3:14-17.) Paul states that *"we have the mind of Christ" (2:16)*. All believers enjoy this positionally (2 Cor. 5:17), but the spiritual person has it experientially (Phil. 2:5).

IV. Fourth Corruption—They were forgetting future judgment (1 Cor. 3:8-23). *"Every man's work shall be made manifest: for the day shall declare it" (1 Cor. 3:13a).*
  A. The meaning of this judgment—This is the same judgment mentioned by Paul in two other passages *(Read Rom. 14:10b and 2 Cor. 5:10a).*

✱ **2 Corinthians 5:10a** The Greek word *bema* (translated "judgment seat" in the King James Version) was a familiar term to the people of Paul's day. Dr. Lehman Strauss writes: "In the large Olympic arenas, there was an elevated seat on which the judge of the contest sat. After the contests were over, the successful competitors would assemble before the *bema* to receive their rewards or crowns. The *bema* was not a judicial bench where someone was condemned; it was a reward seat. Likewise, the Judgment Seat of Christ is not a judicial bench ... the Christian life is a race, and the divine umpire is watching every contestant. After the church has run her course, he will gather every member before the *bema* for the purpose of examining each one and giving the proper reward to each" (*God's Plan for the Future*, p.111).

  B. The individuals in this judgment—Only believers will be included *(Read 1 Cor. 3:9)*
  C. The purpose of this judgment—It is to determine the quality of my service for Christ from the moment of my salvation until my death or Rapture.

✱ ■ Negative considerations
  ● The purpose of the *bema* judgment is not to determine whether a particular individual enters heaven or not, for every person's eternal destiny is already determined before he leaves this life.
  ● The purpose of the *bema* judgment is not to punish believers for sins committed either before or after their salvation. The Scriptures are very clear that no child of God will have to answer for his sins after this life. *"He hath not dealt with us after our sins, nor rewarded us according to our iniquities. For as the heaven is high above the earth, so great is his mercy toward them that fear him. As far as the east is from the west, so far hath he removed our transgressions from us" (Psa. 103:10-12). "But thou hast in love to my soul delivered it from the pit of corruption: for thou hast cast all my sins behind thy back" (Isa. 38:17b). "I have blotted out ... thy transgressions and ... thy sins" (Isa. 44:22a). "Thou wilt cast all their sins into the depths of the sea" (Micah 7:19b). "For I will be merciful ... and their sins and their iniquities will I remember no more" (Heb. 8:12). "The blood of Jesus Christ his Son cleanseth us from all sin" (1 John 1:7b).*
■ Positive considerations—What, then, is the purpose of the *bema* judgment? In 1 Corinthians 4:2, Paul says that all Christians should conduct themselves as faithful stewards of God: *"Moreover it is required in stewards, that a man be found faithful."* The Apostle Peter later writes in a similar way: *"Minister ... as good stewards of the manifold grace of God" (1 Pet. 4:10).* In the New Testament world, a steward was the manager of a large household or estate. He was appointed by the owner and was entrusted to keep the estate running smoothly. He had the power to hire and fire and to spend and save, being answerable to the owner alone. His only concern was that periodic meeting with his master, at which time he was required to account for the condition of the estate up to that point. With this background in mind, it may be said that someday at the *bema* judgment all stewards will stand before their Lord and Master and be required to give an account of the way they have used their privileges and responsibilities from the moment of their conversion. In conclusion, it can be seen that:
  ● In the past, God dealt with us as sinners (Eph. 2:1-3; 1 Cor. 6:9-11; Rom. 5:6-8).
  ● In the present, God deals with us as sons (Rom. 8:14; Heb.12:5-11; 1 John 3:1-2).
  ● In the future, God will deal with us (at the *bema*) as stewards.

  D. The materials to be tested in this judgment *(Read 1 Cor. 3:10-12)*
  E. The method of testing at this judgment *(Read 1 Cor. 3:13)*
  F. The results of this judgment *(Read 1 Cor. 3:14-15)*

★ **3:15**
- A two-fold consideration concerning the *bema* judgment:
  - Negative considerations—It should be noted immediately that this passage does not teach the false doctrine known as purgatory, for it is the believer's works and not the believer himself that will be subjected to the fires.
  - Positive considerations—From these verses it is apparent that God classifies the works of believers into one of the following six areas: gold, silver, precious stones, wood, hay, stubble. There has been much speculation about the kinds of work down here that will constitute gold or silver up there. But it seems more appropriate to note that the six objects can be readily placed into two categories:
    - Those indestructible and worthy objects which will survive and thrive in the fires. These are gold, silver, and precious stones.
    - Those destructible and worthless objects which will be totally consumed in the fires. These are the wood, hay, and stubble.
- A two-fold conclusion concerning the *bema* judgment:
  - Those who receive rewards
    - The basis for these rewards—Though it is difficult to know just what goes to make up a "golden work" or a "stubble work," we are nevertheless informed of certain general areas in which God is particularly interested.
      - How we treat other believers (Heb. 6:10; Matt. 10:41-42)
      - How we exercise our authority over others (Heb. 13:17; James 3:1)
      - How we employ our God-given abilities (2 Tim. 1:6; 1 Cor. 12:4, 11; 1 Pet. 4:10). To these verses can be added the overall teaching of Jesus' parables of the ten pounds (Luke 19:11-26) and the eight talents (Matt. 25:14-29).
      - How we use our money (1 Tim. 6:17-19; 2 Cor. 9:6-7; 1 Cor. 16:2)
      - How we spend our time (Eph. 5:16; Col. 4:5; 1 Pet. 1:17)
      - How much we suffer for Jesus (Matt. 5:11-12; Mark 10:29-30; Rom. 8:18; 2 Cor. 4:17; 1 Pet. 4:12-13)
      - How we run that particular race which God has chosen for us (1 Cor. 9:24; Phil. 3:13-14; Heb. 12:1; Phil. 2:16)
      - How effectively we control the old nature (1 Cor. 9:25-27)
      - How many souls we witness to and win for Christ (Prov. 11:30; 1 Thess. 2:19-20; Dan. 12:3)
      - How we react to temptation (James 1:2-3; Rev. 2:10)
      - How much Christ's second coming means to us (2 Tim. 4:8)
      - How faithful we are to the Word of God and the God of the Word (1 Pet. 5:2-4; 2 Tim. 4:1-2; Acts 20:26-28)
    - The nature of these rewards
      - The incorruptible crown—Given to those who master the old nature (1 Cor. 9:25-27)
      - The crown of rejoicing—Given to soul winners (Prov. 11:30; 1 Thess. 2:19-20; Dan. 12:3)
      - The crown of life—Given to those who successfully endure temptation (James 1:2-3; Rev. 2:10)
      - The crown of righteousness—Given to those who especially love the doctrine of the Rapture (2 Tim. 4:8)
      - The crown of glory—Given to faithful preachers and teachers (1 Pet. 5:2-4; 2 Tim. 4:1-2; Acts 20:26-28). It has been suggested that these "crowns" will actually be talents and abilities with which to glorify Christ. Thus, the greater the reward, the greater the ability.
  - Those who suffer loss
    - *"If any man's work shall be burned, he shall suffer loss" (1 Cor. 3:15)*. This word for "suffer" is *zemioo* in the Greek New Testament, and is used again by Paul in Philippians chapter 3, where he describes those things which were the greatest source of pride to him prior to salvation. He tells us, *"For I went through the Jewish initiation ceremony when I was eight days old, having been born into a pure-blooded Jewish home that was a branch of the old original Benjamin family. So I was a real Jew if there ever was one! What's more, I was a member of the Pharisees who demand the strictest obedience to every Jewish law and custom. And sincere?*

Yes, so much so that I greatly persecuted the church; and I tried to obey every Jewish rule and regulation right down to the very last point" (Phil. 3:5-6, TLB).

✦ But after his conversion, Paul writes, *"For whom I have suffered the loss of all things ... that I may win Christ"* (Phil. 3:8). The point of all these teachings is simply this: at the *bema* judgment the carnal Christian will suffer the loss of many past achievements, even as Paul did, but with one important exception: Paul was richly compensated, since he suffered his loss to win Christ, while the carnal believer will receive nothing to replace his burned-up wood, hay, and stubble. Before leaving this section, the question may be asked, "Is it possible for someone who has earned certain rewards down here to lose them somehow through carnality?" Some believe this to be tragically possible on the basis of the following verses: *"Look to yourselves, that we lose not those things which we have wrought, but that we receive a full reward"* (2 John 8). *"Behold, I come quickly; hold that fast which thou hast, that no man take thy crown"* (Rev. 3:11). *"Let no man beguile you of your reward"* (Col. 2:18).

✦ The passage in 3:14-17 actually lists three kinds of builders:
  ◆ The wise builder (3:14)
  ◆ The worldly builder (3:15)
  ◆ The wicked builder (3:17)—The wicked builder, of course, will not stand before the *bema*, but will be at the great white judgment throne (Rev. 20:11-15). The word "destroy" in 3:17 is *phtheiro* in the original and is often associated in the Greek New Testament with false doctrine and corrupt teachers. (See 1 Cor. 15:33; Eph. 4:22; 2 Pet. 2:12; Jude 10; Rev. 19:2.)

✦ It should also be observed that we shall account for not only what we did but what we could have done if we would have (Rev. 3:1-3; Luke 12:48; 1 Cor. 4:1), and what we would have done if we could have (Matt. 26:41; 1 Kings 8:18).

G. The admonition in light of this judgment— *"Know ye not that ye are the temple of God, and that the Spirit of God dwelleth in you? If any man defile the temple of God, him shall God destroy; for the temple of God is holy, which temple ye are.... Therefore let no man glory in men. For all things are yours.... And ye are Christ's; and Christ is God's"* (1 Cor. 3:16-17, 21, 23).

LESSON 25

> **V. Fifth Corruption — They were flattering themselves.**
>   A. Their two-fold problem
>   1. They were overestimating their own abilities *(Read 1 Cor. 4:7-8)*

✶ **4:8** David Lowery writes: "The posture of humility should be taken by all Christians. Paul set forth the pattern of Christ's life to the Philippians (Phil. 2:5-11). It was marked first by humiliation and then crowned by exaltation. The Corinthians had apparently dispensed with the first half. They wanted their exaltation immediately—no more sickness, no more suffering, no more pain. This is no more possible today than it was when Paul wrote to these self-deluded Corinthians, but nonetheless, many follow in their train. The Corinthians thought they had all they wanted (1 Cor. 4:8a), but they should have been hungering and thirsting for the practical righteousness they so desperately needed (Matt. 5:6). They thought of themselves as kings in need of nothing, when in fact, they were as needy as the foolish king in the children's tale of the emperor's new clothes, who blithely paraded nakedly before his subjects (cf. Rev. 3:17-18)" (*Bible Knowledge Commentary*, p. 513).

>   2. They were underestimating the abilities of others *(Read 1 Cor. 4:6)*
>   B. Paul's three-fold solution
>   1. He offers a prophetical reminder—The judgment seat of Christ, at which time the Lord would deal with them *(Read 1 Cor. 4:1-6)*
>   2. He announces a planned visit—At which time he would deal with them *(Read 1 Cor. 4:18-21)*
>   3. He points to a personal example—his own sufferings for Christ (1 Cor. 4:8-17).
>   a. The facts of his sufferings *(Read 1 Cor. 4:9,11-13)*

✶ **4:13** It has been observed that the trouble with Christians in our country today is that no one is trying to kill them.

>   b. The (hoped for) fruits from his sufferings *(Read 1 Cor. 4:14-17)*

✶ **4:17** We note Paul admonishes them to *"be ye followers of me."* He repeats this request on at least three other occasions (see 1 Cor. 11:1; 2 Thess. 3:9; Phil. 3:17). In light of this it is unscriptural for a pastor or Christian leader (however sincere) to admonish his people, saying: "Don't look at my life, don't do as I do or say. Don't even look at men as your examples, look only to Christ!" See the words of Jesus on this in Matthew 5:13-16. Also to be noted are Paul's words, *"I have begotten you" (4:15)*, which may be compared with those found in Galatians 4:19 and 1 Thessalonians 2:11.

> **VI. Sixth Corruption—They were failing to discipline (1 Cor. 5:1-13).**
>   A. The need for discipline *(Read 1 Cor. 5:1)*

✶ **5:1** The Greek word for fornication is *porneia* (root word of English pornography). Paul uses this word 17 times in all his writings. Eleven of these are found in 1 Corinthians. Here the sin involved a man living with his stepmother in a sexual way. We note:
  ■ He was a church member. This is implied:
    ● Because his sinning partner is not rebuked Paul is here only concerned with that sin committed by a member. The woman was apparently not a member.
    ● Because Paul orders him to be dismissed from the fellowship of the church
  ■ He was guilty as charged—*"It is reported commonly"* (5:1).
  ■ He was unrepentant.

> B. The breakdown in discipline *(Read 1 Cor. 5:2)*

★ **5:2**
- They were puffed up, not because of the sin itself, but because of their tolerance and pride. At times tolerance can be downright treason.
- Paul rebukes them for not mourning over this tragedy. How much better had the vain Corinthians heeded the advice of the following verses: *"Be afflicted and mourn and weep: let your laughter be turned to mourning and your joy to heaviness" (James 4:9). "The sacrifices of God are a broken spirit: a broken and a contrite heart, O God, thou wilt not despise" (Psa. 51:17).*
- But regardless of their brazen attitude, this church corruption had broken the tender heart of Paul, who would later write: *"For out of much affliction and anguish of heart I wrote unto you with many tears" (2 Cor. 2:4).*

> C. The authority to discipline *(Read 1 Cor. 5:4)*

★ **5:4** Although the individual Christian is warned not to sit in judgment upon another Christian (1 Cor. 4:5), the assembled church does indeed have this right and responsibility. (See also Matt. 18.20.)

> D. The seriousness of discipline *(Read 1 Cor. 5:5)*

★ **5:5**
- What does it mean to do this? The Greek word for *destruction* here is *olethros*, a reference to the act of spoiling or marring something. Apparently Paul was saying this: "If this fellow is having so much fun in his sin, then remove him entirely from your fellowship and let Satan kick him around a little. Let him taste what it's like to face a hostile world without the prayers and ministry of a local church!"
- Thus, when a local Bible-believing church removes a person like this, it literally fulfills the divine command of *Job 2:6*: *"The Lord said unto Satan, Behold, he is in thine hand; but save his life."*
- Paul was forced to take this drastic action against two other individuals at a later date *(Read 1 Tim. 1:19-20)*.

> E. The reason for discipline *(Read 1 Cor. 5:6-7)*

★ **5:7** At least three reasons can be listed for this church discipline:
- To help the man find his way back to God. It worked, too, for the fellow did indeed repent (see 2 Cor. 2:6-8).
- To keep the sin from spreading throughout the church— *"Know ye not that a little leaven leaveneth the whole lump?" (5:6b).* Leaven is a type of evil in the Bible (see Matt. 166; Gal. 5:9).
- To maintain the standards of Christ to a watching world. (See Acts 5:1-13.) One reason why the church has so little influence in the world today is because the world has so much influence in the church.

> F. The extent of discipline *(Read 1 Cor. 5:9-13)*—Here Paul says church discipline is to be limited to church members.

★ **5:13**
- Negative—The church is not to judge the outside world; that is, to nag and rebuke unbelievers for their smoking, card playing, etc., but rather to lead them to Christ.
- Positive—The New Testament lists at least three types of individuals to be dismissed from the fellowship of a local church.
  - A constant troublemaker (Prov. 6:19; 2 Thess. 3:6, 11, 14)
  - An immoral person (as seen here in 1 Cor. 5)
  - A heretic (one who denies the virgin birth, etc.; Titus 3:10; Rom. 16:17-18)

G. The procedure in discipline. (See Matt. 18:15-20.)

✱ ■ First step: *"Go and tell him his fault between thee and him alone"* (Matt. 18:15a). At this initial stage the spirit of Galatians 6:1 should prevail: *"Brethren, if a man be overtaken in a fault, ye which are spiritual, restore such a one in the spirit of meekness; considering thyself, lest thou also be tempted"* (Gal. 6:1).
  ■ Second step: *"If he will not hear thee, then take with thee one or two more, that in the mouth of two or three witnesses every word may be established"* (Matt. 18:16).
  ■ Third step: *"If he shall neglect [literally, disregard] to hear them, tell it unto the church"* (18:17a).
  ■ Fourth step: *"If he neglect to hear the church, let him be unto thee as an heathen man and a publican"* (Matt. 18:17). *"Yet count him not as an enemy, but admonish him as a brother"* (2 Thess. 3:15).

H. The results of discipline—In this case, it worked. (See 2 Cor. 2:6-8.)
VII. **Seventh Corruption—They were fragmenting the body of Christ (1 Cor. 6:1-11)**. The Corinthians had been unjustly taking fellow believers to court in legal matters.
   A. This action was improper (1 Cor. 6:1-7).
      1. Because of whom they were judging—Namely, fellow believers *(Read 1 Cor. 6:1)*

✱ **6:1** Paul is not condemning the court system here as an institution, for he himself had used it (see Acts 25:10-11). What he is saying is that feuding believers should use every means at their disposal to settle their legal difficulties and not drag each other before pagan courts.

      2. Because of whom they someday would judge—Namely, this world, and fallen angels *(Read 1 Cor. 6:2-3)*

✱ **6:3** See Daniel 7:18, 22; Matthew 19:28; 2 Peter 2:4; Revelation 20:4.

   B. This action was illegal *(Read 1 Cor. 6:8)*

✱ **6:8** In other words, they not only refused to settle their petty problems out of court, but now planned to cheat one another in court.

   C. This action was inconsistent *(Read 1 Cor. 6:9-11)*—They had apparently conveniently forgotten their own terrible past prior to their salvation.
VIII. **Eighth Corruption—They were falling into sexual immorality (1 Cor. 6:12-20)**. Paul condemns this terrible sin, pointing out:
   A. That our bodies are members of the Savior *(Read 1 Cor. 6:15-16)*

✱ **6:16** The believer is thus forbidden to unscripturally involve himself in the systems of this present evil world. The child of God is to flee from unlawful involvements in sex (1 Cor. 6:18; 2 Tim. 2:22), silver (1 Tim. 6:10-11), and society (idolatry; see 1 Cor. 10:14).

   B. That our bodies are temples of the Spirit *(Read 1 Cor. 6:18-20)*

PART TWO: The six questions submitted by the Corinthian Church (1 Cor. 7-16):

I. **Question Number One: What about marriage? (1 Cor. 7)**
   A. The two problems connected with this chapter

1. Did Paul consider marriage to be unproductive?
   a. The fiction—Paul thought lightly of marriage, as indicated by the following verses: *"But I would have you without carefulness. He that is unmarried careth for the things that belong to the Lord, how he may please the Lord: But he that is married careth for the things that are of the world, how he may please his wife" (1 Cor. 7:32-33).*
   b. The facts—This error Paul himself amply refutes.
      (1) Refuted by his other writings. (See Eph. 5:22-33; 1 Tim. 3:2; 4:1-5; 5:14; Titus 1:6; 2:4-5; Heb, 13:4.)
      (2) Refuted by his comments in this same chapter *(Read 1 Cor. 7:17, 24, 26)*. The "present distress" phrase in verse 26 is thought to be a reference to a particular kind of persecution the Corinthian believers were suffering at that time in history.
2. Did Paul consider his writings to be uninspired?
   a. The fiction—Paul admitted his thoughts on marriage to be uninspired, as indicated by the following verses: *"But I speak this by permission, and not of commandment.... But to the rest speak I, not the Lord: If any brother hath a wife that believeth not, and she be pleased to dwell with him, let him not put her away.... Now concerning virgins I have no commandment of the Lord: yet I give my judgment, as one that hath obtained mercy of the Lord to be faithful.... But she is happier if she so abide, after my judgment: and I think also that I have the Spirit of God" (1 Cor. 7:6, 12, 25, 40).*
   b. The facts
      (1) The word *permission* is literally "a joint opinion" and may refer to the inspired considered opinion of both Paul and Sosthenes. At any rate, Paul was simply saying that this opinion was not a command but rather a divine suggestion. (For a comparable passage, see Rom. 12:1.)
      (2) Verse 12 can be explained by comparing it with verse 10. In verse 10, Paul quotes a command uttered by the Lord Jesus himself while he was upon the earth (see Matt. 19:6). But here is a group situation (one partner saved, one unsaved) to whom Jesus issued no command while on earth, but now does so in heaven through Paul's inspired pen.
      (3) The same answer given for verse 12 also applies here in verse 25.
      (4) The word *think* here could be translated "persuaded" (1 Cor. 7:40). (See Matt. 22:42; 1 Cor. 8:2 where the same Greek word is used. See also Paul's statements in 1 Tim. 3:16; 1 Cor. 2:4.)
B. The five persons considered in this chapter
   1. Singles *(Read 1 Cor. 7:1)*
   2. Christian couples (1 Cor. 7:2-7, 10-11)

★ **7:5** Both partners are to render "due benevolence" to each other (7:3). This phrase is translated "good will" in Ephesians 6:7. Neither partner is to "defraud" the other (7:5). The context shows this to be in regard to sexual rights. Paul reminds both that neither has "power" over his own body. This is to say that separate ownership of oneself does not exist in the marriage state. No partner may rightfully quote the words of Matthew 20:15 to the other partner: *"Is it not lawful for me to do what I will with mine own?"* Thus, to defraud (deny) sexual rights one to the other is to invite being tempted by Satan. (See also 2 Cor. 2:11; 1 Pet. 5:8.)

   a. Rules for the husband
      (1) He is to render his duty to his wife (1 Cor. 7:3).
      (2) He is to render his body to his wife (1 Cor. 7:4).
      (3) He must not divorce her (1 Cor. 7:11).
   b. Rules for the wife
      (1) She is to remain with her husband if at all possible (1 Cor. 7:10).
      (2) She is to remain his wife even if separation becomes necessary (1 Cor. 7:11).

(3) She is to attempt reconciliation after the separation (1 Cor. 7:11).
(4) She is to render her duty to her husband (1 Cor. 7:3).
(5) She is to render her body to her husband (1 Cor. 7:4).
　　c. Rules for both *(Read 1 Cor. 7:5)*
3. Unmarried, widowers, and widows
　　a. The unmarried
　　　　(1) If possible, feel free to remain unmarried *(Read 1 Cor. 7:7-8)*
　　　　(2) If impossible, feel free to become married *(Read 1 Cor. 7:9, 28)*.
　　b. The widowers and widows *(Read 1 Cor. 7:27-28, 39)*.
4. Mixed couples *(Read 1 Cor. 7:12-16)*. The saved partner is to remain with the unsaved spouse if at all possible. Two reasons are given for this.
　　a. Because of the sanctity of marriage itself (1 Cor. 7:14)
　　b. Because of the sanctification of the lost partner (1 Cor. 7:14)—The Holy Spirit can more easily work in the heart of an unsaved spouse if the other partner is a believer.
5. The father (or guardian) of a young virgin (1 Cor. 7:36-38)
　　a. He may feel it best for her marriage to be performed.
　　b. He may feel it best for her marriage to be prevented or postponed.

II. Question Number Two: What about Christian liberty? (1 Cor. 8-10). Can a Christian do any lawful thing he or she desires to do? Paul answers this in these chapters by employing three examples:
　A. A current example—The Corinthian believers (1 Cor. 8)
　　1. The confusion—Should a Christian eat meat that had previously been sacrificed to pagan idols?

✱ There were many pagan temples at Corinth upon which tons of animal meat was sacrificed daily. Some of this meat was consumed by the priests while the remainder was placed on sale in the various city meat markets. It probably sold cheaper, due to its previous usage. Some believers, spotting a bargain, were apparently buying this meat for their table. Other Christians were shocked at this. Here, then, was the question: Should saved people eat meat which had previously been sacrificed to idols?

　　2. The clarification *(Read 1 Cor. 8:8)*
　　3. The conclusion *(Read 1 Cor. 8:7, 13)*
　　4. The challenge
　　　　a. Avoid becoming a stumbling stone *(1 Cor. 8:9, 11-12)*

✱ **8:12**
■ The Scriptures declare that a Christian is responsible to at least five classes of people.
　● The world in general (Matt. 5:16; 1 Tim. 3:7)
　● His or her immediate family (Eph. 5-6)
　● All believers in general (Eph. 4:32)
　● Weaker believers in particular (Rom. 14:1; 15:1) He is thus to be careful:
　　✦ Lest he cause a weaker brother to defile his conscience (1 Cor. 8:7, 10)
　　✦ Lest he cause a weaker brother to sin against Christ (8:12)
　● The local church (1 Tim. 3:10; 1 Cor. 10:32)
■ How, though, can one decide upon that which is right or wrong? The Bible declares an action may be wrong on two counts.
　● Because of an inherent sin factor. There are certain things that are always wrong because they go against the very grain of God's holiness. Such things would be murder, lying, adultery, stealing, idolatry, etc.

- Because of an acquired sin factor. There are certain things that, in and by themselves, are harmless, but through time and custom have acquired the taint of being evil. An example of this would be the wearing of cosmetics, which was once considered sinful, but now (if modestly applied) is generally accepted among Christian women.

The first factor is character sin, and the second can be referred to as reputation sin. The child of God is to avoid both.

> b. Attempt becoming a stepping stone *(Read 1 Cor. 8:1)*

✸ 8:1

- The Greek word for "edifieth" is *oikodomeo* and speaks of that action which builds a house (see John 2:20; Matt. 7:24). The New Testament teaches that:
    - The believer is to build himself up (see Jude 20).
    - He is to build up other Christians (see 1 Thess. 5:11; Rom. 14:19).
    - He is to help build up the entire church (see 1 Cor. 14:12).
- The word "puffeth up" is found but seven times in the Greek New Testament, six of which are used here in 1 Corinthians. (See 4:6, 18-19; 5:2; 8:1; 13:4.) In every case it is associated with worldly knowledge. Note the following three quotes: *"And if any man think that he knoweth anything, he knoweth nothing yet as he ought to know" (1 Cor. 8:2).* "Knowledge is that act of passing from a state of unconscious ignorance to a state of conscious ignorance" (L. S. Chafer). "I do not know what I may appear to the world; but to myself I seem to have been like a boy playing on the seashore and diverting myself, now and then finding a smoother pebble or a prettier shell than ordinary, while the great ocean of truth lay all undiscovered before me" (Sir Isaac Newton).

> B. A personal example—The Apostle Paul (1 Cor. 9)—Here Paul points out that no one had more right to exercise Christian liberty than he did.
>   1. The basis of his rights *(Read 1 Cor. 9:1)*
>   2. The extent of his rights
>   a. To enjoy food *(Read 1 Cor. 9:4)*
>   b. To enjoy family life *(Read 1 Cor. 9:5)*
>   c. To enjoy financial support *(Read 1 Cor. 9:9, 14)*
>   (1) A soldier is paid, and he was Christ's warrior—*"Who goeth a warfare any time at his own charges?" (1 Cor. 9:7).*
>   (2) A husbandman enjoys the fruit from his field, and he had planted many vineyards—*"Who planteth a vineyard, and eateth not of the fruit thereof?" (1 Cor. 9:7).*
>   (3) A shepherd drinks of the milk of his flock and he had nurtured many lambs—*"Or who feedeth a flock, and eateth not of the milk of the flock?" (1 Cor. 9:7).*
>   (4) A priest lives off the temple gifts, as did God's minister to the Gentiles—*"Do ye not know that they which minister about holy things live of the things of the temple? and they which wait at the altar are partakers with the altar?" (1 Cor. 9:13).*
>   3. The employment of his rights
>   a. The *what* of the matter—*"Nevertheless we have not used this power; but suffer all things" (1 Cor. 9:12b).* *"I preach the gospel ... of Christ without charge" (1 Cor. 9:18).*
>   b. The *who* of the matter
>   (1) Concerning the Jew—*"And unto the Jews I become as a Jew" (1 Cor. 9:20a).* This he did, however, without being *legalistic*.
>   (2) Concerning the Gentiles—*"To them that are without law, as without law" (1 Cor. 9:21).* This he did, however, without being *lawless*.

> (3) Concerning the weak—*"To the weak became I as weak" (1 Cor. 9:22).*
> This he did, however, without being *limp*.
>
> c. The *why* of the matter—Paul explains the reasons for using his Christian rights sparingly. *"We ... suffer all things, lest we should hinder the gospel of Christ" (1 Cor. 9:12b). "For though I be free from all men, yet have I made myself servant unto all, that I might gain the more" (1 Cor. 9:19). "I am made all things to all men, that I might by all means save some" (1 Cor. 9:22b).*

★ **9:22b** His life was a living testimony of these statements. Thus:
- In ministering to the Jews (9:20)—He circumcised Timothy in Lystra because the Jews in that area knew the young man's father was a Greek. He later preached in Hebrew before a mob of Jews in Jerusalem (see Acts 16 and 22).
- In ministering to the Gentiles (9:21)—He stood to preach, a practice of the Gentiles, while delivering a message in Antioch. He quoted from Greek literature when addressing some Greeks on Mars Hill (see Acts 13 and 17).
- In ministering to the weak believers (9:22)—He refrained from eating meat, and commanded that weak Christians everywhere be received into full fellowship (see 1 Cor. 8:13; Rom. 14:1; 15:1).

> d. The *how* of the matter *(Read 1 Cor. 9:26-27)*

★ **9:27** Here the word "castaway" is *adokimos* in the Greek, meaning "disapproved." The same word is found in 2 Timothy 2:15.

> e. The *when* of the matter—Here Paul refers to the judgment seat of Christ *(1 Cor. 9:24-25)*
> C. An Old Testament example—The nation Israel (1 Cor. 10). Paul here records what happened to Old Testament Israel when that nation abused its liberty and blessings from God.
> 1. The narration (10:1-10).
>   a. The review of this freedom *(Read 1 Cor. 10:1-4)*
>   b. The rebellion against this freedom (1 Cor. 10:5-10)
>   (1) They were guilty of idolatry *(Read 1 Cor. 10:7)*
>   (2) They were guilty of immorality *(Read 1 Cor. 10:8)*
>   (3) They were guilty of insubordination *(Read 1 Cor. 10:9-10)*
>   c. The removal of this freedom *(Read 1 Cor. 10:5)*
>   (1) Their idolatry was punished by the sword *(Read Exod. 32:26-28)*
>   (2) Their immorality was punished by a scourge *(Read Num. 25:9)*

★ **Numbers 25:9** Note: A contradiction has been imagined here, for Moses tells us 24,000 were killed in this plague (Num. 25:9), while Paul says 23,000 died (1 Cor. 10:8). However, the apostle limits his number to those who "fell in one day," while Moses gives the total death figure for the entire period.

>   (3) Their insubordination was punished by serpents *(Read Num. 21:5-6)*
> 2. The application (1 Cor. 10:11-13)
>   a. This was recorded to remind us concerning our fallibility *(Read 1 Cor. 10:12)*

★ **10:12** Especially important here are Paul's two words, "Take heed." In the Bible God commands us to take heed concerning:
- Our speech (Psa. 39:1)
- Overconfidence (1 Cor. 10:12)
- Being deceived by others (Matt. 24:4)
- Our ministry to others (Acts 20:28; 1 Tim. 4:16; Col. 4:17)

LESSON 25: THE BOOK OF FIRST CORINTHIANS—PART 2

> b. This was recorded to reassure us concerning God's dependability *(Read 1 Cor. 10:13)*

★ **10:13** It will prove helpful at this point to review the biblical doctrine of temptation.
  ■ The definition of temptation
   ● To entice to do evil—Satan tempted Christ and tempts Christians this way. (See Matt. 4:1; Heb. 2:18; 4:15; James 1:13.)
   ● To test or prove with the intent of making one stronger—God "tempts" his children this way. (See Gen. 22:1.)
   ● To presume upon the goodness of God Israel tempted God in this manner, as believers can today. (See Psa. 78:18; Acts 5:9; Matt. 4:7.)
  ■ The source of temptation
   ● The world (see Matt. 13:22; John 16:33; Titus 2:12; 2 Pet. 1:4; Gal. 1:4; 2 Tim. 4:10; 1 John 2:15).
   ● The flesh (see Matt. 26:41; Rom. 7:18; Gal. 5:19-21).
   ● The devil (see 1 Chron. 21:1; Eph. 4:27; 6:11; 1 Tim. 3:6-7; James 4:7.)
  ■ The purpose of temptation—As we have already seen, God allows temptation to strengthen his children. It is therefore not a sin to be tempted. (See James 1:2, 12; 1 Pet. 1:6-7.)
  ■ The victory over temptation. (See 1 Pet. 4:19; 2 Pet. 2:9.)

> 3. The summation (1 Cor. 10:14-33)—Paul summarizes this entire section on Christian liberty by the following statements.
>   a. What our actions should be *(Read 1 Cor. 10:14-22; 25-29)*
>   (1) Beware, lest our conduct among unbelievers be compromised (1 Cor. 10:14-22)
>   (2) Beware, lest our conscience among believers be compromised (1 Cor. 10:25-29)
>   b. What our attitude should be *(Read 1 Cor. 10:23-24, 31-32)*

LESSON 26

III. Question Number Three: What about church conduct (1 Cor. 11)? *"Be ye followers of me, even as I also am of Christ. Now I praise you, brethren, that ye remember me in all things, and keep the ordinances, as I delivered them to you" (1 Cor. 11:1-2).*
  A. Rules concerning clothing (1 Cor. 11:1-16)
    1. The man's appearance
      a. His head was to be uncovered *(Read 1 Cor. 11:4)*
        (1) Demonstrating his relationship to his Savior *(Read 1 Cor. 11:7)*

★ **11:7** Thus, no male in a Christian service should wear a hat, as did the Roman priests and Jewish Rabbis, who wore a head covering called a tallis. The custom began due to a misinterpretation of Moses and his veil. (Compare Exod. 34:33 with 2 Cor. 3:13.)

        (2) Demonstrating his relationship to his wife— *"And the head of the woman is the man" (1 Cor. 11:3b). "But the woman is the glory of the man" (1 Cor. 11:7b). "For the man is not of the woman; but the woman of the man. Neither was the man created for the woman; but the woman for the man" (1 Cor. 11:8-9).*
      b. His hair was to be cut— *"Doth not even nature itself teach you, that, if a man have long hair, it is a shame unto him?" (1 Cor. 11:14).* This demonstrated his relationship to society. Back then one of the marks of a homosexual was his long hair.
    2. The woman's appearance
      a. Her head was to be covered (1 Cor. 11:5, 10).
        (1) Demonstrating her submission to her husband (1 Cor. 11:5)
        (2) Demonstrating her spirituality to the angels *(Read 1 Cor. 11:10)*

★ **11:10** Some believe this passage suggests church members may share their pews with angels. (See Psa. 138:1; Eph. 3:10; 1 Tim. 5:21; Heb. 1:14; 1 Pet. 1:10, 12.)

      b. Her hair was not to be cut— *"For if the woman be not covered, let her also be shorn: but if it be a shame for a woman to be shorn or shaven, let her be covered. But if a woman have long hair, it is a glory to her: for her hair is given her for a covering" (1 Cor. 11:6, 15).* This demonstrated her standards to the world. In those days only female slaves and harlots wore short hair.
  B. Rules concerning communion (1 Cor. 11:17-34)
    1. The person of communion—The Lord Jesus Christ. The table of the Lord is to magnify the Lord of the table *(Read 1 Cor. 11:23, 25a).*

★ **11:25** Paul did not receive his information concerning the historical details of the Last Supper from any of the apostles who attended, but from Christ himself. This was also true concerning the details surrounding the preaching, death, and resurrection of the Savior. (See 1 Cor. 15:3; Acts 20:35; Gal. 1:11, 22.)

    2. The perversion of communion
      a. The Corinthian error *(Read 1 Cor. 11:18, 20-21)*

✶ **11:21** At their communion service the fickle and self-centered Corinthians had so involved themselves in the supper that they had totally ignored both other saints and the Savior. As a result some (the well-to-do) would stuff themselves with food and drink while others (the poor) would go away hungry. Many things happened on that momentous night in the Upper Room, but here in 11:23, Paul singles out Jesus' betrayal by Judas, which may have been a hint describing what the Corinthians were actually doing also. It should be noted that Paul does not teach here (11:22) against having fellowship banquets in a church basement.

b. The current errors

(1) That the bread and cup are sacraments—This is refuted by *1 Corinthians 11:24. "This do in remembrance of me."*

(2) That the bread and cup are changed to flesh and blood—This is refuted by 1 Corinthians 11:28 where they remain the same.

3. The purposes of communion

a. It serves as a backward look to the **Cross** *(Read 1 Cor. 11:26)*

b. It serves as an inward look to the **conscience** *(Read 1 Cor. 11:28)*

c. It serves as a forward look to the **crown** *(Read 1 Cor. 11:26)*

4. The partakers of communion

a. Generally speaking—All believers, but only believers

b. Specifically speaking—Two groups are forbidden to partake.

(1) The unsaved sinner—He may qualify by obeying John 3:16.

(2) The unclean saint—He may qualify by obeying 1 John 1:9.

5. The penalty of communion *(Read 1 Cor. 11:29-30)*

✶ **11:30** Here several words deserve our consideration.

■ Unworthily—The word here is an adverb and not an adjective. Paul does not say, "If anyone who is not worthy partakes," but rather, "If anyone partakes in an unworthy manner."

■ Damnation—In the Greek this is the word *krima*, and should here be translated "judgment." (See Rom. 11:33; 1 Pet. 4:17; and Rev. 20:4, where the same word appears.) This judgment may be manifested in a two-fold manner:

- Through physical sickness (11:30)
- Through physical death— *"And many sleep" (11:30)*. The Greek word for sleep here is *koimao* and refers to physical death. (See John 11:11-12; Acts 7:60; 1 Cor. 15:6, 18, 20, 51.)

6. The profit of communion

a. It can be used for the judging of ourselves *(Read 1 Cor. 11:31-32)*

b. It can be used for the giving of ourselves *(Read 1 Cor. 11:33)*

IV. Question Number Four: What about spiritual gifts (1 Cor. 12-14)? *"Now concerning spiritual gifts, brethren, I would not have you ignorant" (1 Cor. 12:1).*

A. Definition of a spiritual gift—It is a supernatural ability given by Christ through the Holy Spirit to the believer at salvation. (See 1 Cor. 12:7; Eph. 4:7-13.)

✶ Dr. Charles Ryrie has written the following: "Many think of a spiritual gift as an office in the church which only a privileged few can ever occupy. Or else they consider gifts so out of reach of the ordinary believer that the best he can hope for is that someday he might happen to discover some little gift and be allowed to exercise it in some small way. Both of these conceptions are wrong. A spiritual gift is primarily an ability given to the individual. This means that the gift is not a place of service, for the gift is the ability, not where that ability is exercised. The gift of pastor, for instance, is usually associated with the office or position a person may occupy in the pastorate. But the gift is the ability to give shepherdlike care to people, regardless of where this is done. Of course, the man who occupies the office of a pastor should have and exercise the gift of pastor, but so should a dean of men in a Christian school. Indeed (though this may seem shocking at first), why shouldn't a Christian woman be given the gift of pastor to use among the children in her neighborhood or in her Sunday school class or as dean of women? Now I did not say that women should become pastors of churches to do the preaching and take the leadership of the people. I think that the office or position of the pastorate is reserved for men only; but this does not mean that the gift or the ability cannot be given to women" (*Balancing the Christian Life*, pp. 95-96).

> B. Number of spiritual gifts—In this chapter Paul lists 13 of these gifts. They are:
> 1. Gift of wisdom (1 Cor. 12:8)

★ There are four kinds of wisdom mentioned in the Bible:
- Natural wisdom (Acts 5:38)
- Worldly wisdom (1 Cor. 1:14-31)
- Sanctifying wisdom (James 1:5)
- Stewardship wisdom—This is the wisdom Paul speaks of here in 1 Corinthians 12:8. It can be defined as the ability to apply spiritual principles to contemporary problems.

> 2. Gift of knowledge (1 Cor. 12:8)

★ There are (at least) three theories concerning this gift:
- The supernatural ability to systematically organize the great theological truths in the Word of God for purposes of study, teaching, and preaching.
- The supernatural ability to receive a divine revelation of truth.
- The supernatural ability to function as one of the eight authors of the New Testament.

> 3. The gift of faith (1 Cor. 12:9)

★ The Bible describes three kinds of basic faith:
- Saving faith—Given to all repenting sinners (Acts 16:31; Rom. 4:5; 5:1; 10:17)
- Sanctifying faith—Available to all believers (Gal. 2:20; 3:11; 5:22; Eph. 6:16; Rom. 1:17; Heb. 10:38)
- Stewardship faith—Given to some believers (Rom.12:3; 1 Cor. 12:9). This is the gift kind of faith and is a supernatural ability to believe and expect great things from God.

> 4. The gift of healing (1 Cor. 12:9, 28)

★ A supernatural ability to cure human ills, whether of physical, mental, or demonic origin—There is evidence that the sign gifts were phased out during the latter part of the first century at the completion of the scriptural canon. Paul decidedly possessed the gift of healing (Acts 14:10; 16:18; 19:12; 20:10; 28:8-9), but for some reason did not employ it during the final months of his ministry. (See Phil. 2:26-27; 1 Tim. 5:23; 2 Tim. 4:20.)

Here it should be emphasized that the removal of the sign gifts does not mean God cannot and will not supernaturally heal a believer today. It does mean, however, that the gift of healing through an individual has ceased. God's present-day plan for healing is found in James 5:14-16.

> 5. The gift of miracles (1 Cor. 12:10, 28)

✱ A supernatural ability to perform those events outside and beyond the realm of nature; the ability to set aside for a time the regular laws of nature—In the Bible there are five periods which witnessed a great outpouring of miracles.
  - During the time of Moses and Joshua
  - During the time of Elijah and Elisha
  - During the time of Daniel
  - During the time of Christ
  - During the time of Peter and Paul

> 6. The gift of prophecy (1 Cor. 12:10, 28)

✱ There were two aspects to this gift.
  - To foretell the future—The supernatural ability to receive and transmit a revelation from God, especially that which concerns itself with future events. (See Matt. 13:14; 2 Pet. 1:20-21; Rev. 1:3; Acts 11:27-28; 21:10-11.)
  - To forthtell the present.

> 7. The gift of discernment (1 Cor. 12:10)

✱ The supernatural ability to distinguish between demonic, human, and divine works. (See 1 John 4:1.) Both Peter (Acts 8:23) and Paul (Acts 13:10; 16:16-18) possessed this gift.

> 8. The gift of tongues (1 Cor. 12:10, 28)

✱ See notes under H.2. on 1 Corinthians 14.

> 9. The gift of interpretation of tongues (1 Cor. 12:10)

✱ The supernatural ability to clarify and interpret those messages spoken in tongues

> 10. The gift of apostleship (1 Cor. 12:28)

✱ A reference to certain men called by Christ himself (John 15:16) and endowed with special authority to function as the official "charter members" of the early church.
  - The requirements—According to both Peter (Acts 1:22) and Paul (1 Cor. 9:1) one must have seen the resurrected Christ to qualify.
  - The number:
    - The original Twelve (Luke 6:13)
    - Matthias (Acts 1:26)
    - Paul (Rom. 1:1)
    - Barnabas (Acts 14:14; Gal. 2:9)
    - James (1 Cor. 15:7; Gal. 1:19)

> 11. The gift of teaching (1 Cor. 12:28)

✱ The supernatural ability to inform, interpret, and inspire concerning the details of the Word of God.
  - Apollos had this gift (Acts 18:24-25).
  - Aquila and Priscilla possessed it (Acts 18:26)

> 12. The gift of helps (1 Cor. 12:28)

★ The supernatural ability to render practical help in both physical and spiritual matters.
- Dorcas had this gift (Acts 9:36-39).
- Phebe had this gift (Rom. 16:1-2).

> 13. The gift of administration (1 Cor. 12:28)
> 14. In other passages Paul adds at least five more gifts to the list given here. (See Rom. 12:6-8; Eph. 4:7-8.)

★ The supernatural ability to organize, administer, and promote either people or projects. (See Titus 1:4-5; see also the book of Nehemiah.)

> C. Extent of the spiritual gifts
> 1. Each believer possesses at least one spiritual gift *(Read 1 Cor. 12:7, 11)*.
> 2. No believer possesses all the spiritual gifts *(Read 1 Cor. 12:29-30)*
> D. Abuse of the spiritual gifts
> 1. Action abuses
> a. Attempting to employ that gift not given to us *(Read 1 Cor. 14:34)*
> b. Refusing to employ that gift given to us (1 Cor. 14:1, 12, 23)
> c. Not employing our gift in love *(Read 1 Cor. 13:1)*
> 2. Attitude abuses
> a. The sin of envy *(Read 1 Cor. 12:15-16)*
> b. The sin of pride *(Read 1 Cor. 12:21)*
> E. Purpose of spiritual gifts
> 1. To edify the saints *(Read 1 Cor. 14:4)*
> 2. To glorify the Savior *(Read 1 Cor 14:2)*
> F. Analogy of the spiritual gifts—In 12:12-27, Paul links the body of Christ and its many spiritually gifted members to that of the human body with its many physical members *(Read 1 Cor. 12:15-16)*.
> 1. Each member in both bodies performs a vital task, appointed by God himself *(Read 1 Cor. 12:18, 25)*.
> 2. No member is to be independent of the other members.
> a. The foot and the ear are not to show envy toward the hand and the eye (1 Cor. 12:15-17).
> b. The eye and the head are not to show pride toward the hand and the feet (1 Cor. 12:21).
> 3. Every member is to rejoice and suffer with the other members *(Read 1 Cor. 12:26)*.
> G. Indispensable ingredient in the spiritual gifts—This element is love (1 Cor. 13).

★
- The spiritual gifts may be thought of as God's divine bricks to be used in the construction of his holy and earthly temple. In the analogy, charity (love) serves as the "celestial cement" which holds the bricks together. Paul ends the previous chapter with the words: *"But covet earnestly the best gifts: and yet show I unto you a more excellent way" (12:31)*. Thus, chapter 13 is this more excellent way.
- It should furthermore be noted that God used Paul, the mighty theologian, to write the greatest poem on love in the history of the world. Each Christmas season the National Safety Council issues the following admonition: "If you drink, don't drive, and if you drive, don't drink, because alcohol and gasoline don't mix." Some have erroneously concluded the same about theology and love. But God has commanded that they are not to be separated (see Rev. 2:1-4). Theology without love leads to dead orthodoxy. Love without theology leads to outright heresy.

LESSON 26: THE BOOK OF FIRST CORINTHIANS—PART 3

> 1. The importance of love *(1 Cor. 13:1-3)*
>   a. The gift of tongues is useless without it (1 Cor. 13:1).
>   b. The gift of prophecy is useless without it (1 Cor. 13:2).
>   c. The gift of knowledge is useless without it (1 Cor. 13:2).
>   d. The gift of faith is useless without it (1 Cor. 13:2).
>   e. The gift of giving is useless without it (1 Cor. 13:3).
> 2. The impeccability of love *(Read 1 Cor. 13:4-7)*
>   a. In relationship to saints (1 Cor. 13:4a)—It is patient, kind, and not jealous.
>   b. In relationship to self (1 Cor. 13:4b-5a)—It does not brag, is not arrogant, never acts unbecomingly, nor seeks its own.
>   c. In relationship to sin (1 Cor. 13:5b-6)—It is not provoked, nor does it hold grudges. It refuses to rejoice in unrighteousness, but finds its joy in truth.
>   d. In relationship to circumstances (1 Cor. 13:7)
> 3. The indestructibility of love *(Read 1 Cor. 13:8-13)*

★ **13:13** Note: Paul does not say here that love is more durable than faith and hope, but simply is greater. In some divine manner we will continue using these three virtues even in heaven. Love is greater because:
- It is the root of faith and hope.
- It is for others, while faith and hope are largely personal.
- It is the very essence of God himself.

>   a. Unlike the other gifts, love is permanent (1 Cor. 13:8)
>   b. Unlike the other gifts, love is complete (1 Cor. 13:9-12)
>   H. Comparison of the spiritual gifts (1 Cor. 14)—In this chapter Paul contrasts and compares two particular gifts, that of tongues, and the gift of prophecy.
>   1. The gift of prophecy
>   a. Meaning of the gift—This gift was two-fold:
>   (1) Forthtelling or proclaiming
>   (2) Foretelling or predicting *(Read 1 Cor. 14:29-30)*
>   b. Importance of the gift—It is more important than the gift of tongues *(Read 1 Cor. 14:4-6, 19, 39)*
>   c. Purpose of the gift (1 Cor. 14:3-4, 19, 22)
>   (1) Foretelling aspect—To reveal new divine truths
>   (2) Forthtelling aspect—To build up, to stir up, and to cheer up *(Read 1 Cor. 14:3)*
>   d. Regulations of the gift
>   (1) Only three prophets allowed for each service (1 Cor. 14:29)
>   (2) Only one of them to speak at any given time (1 Cor. 14:4)
>   (3) Forthtelling was to take a back seat to foretelling (1 Cor. 14:30).
>   2. The gift of tongues
>   a. Meaning of the gift—Three explanations have been given:
>   (1) The supernatural ability to speak previously unlearned human languages

★ This view says that all accounts of New Testament tongue-speaking refer to the same event, that is, the supernatural ability to suddenly speak in previously unlearned human languages. The following are arguments for this view.
- Because of the usage of the same vocabulary—Dr. John Walvoord writes: "The use of identical terms in reference to speaking with tongues in Acts and First Corinthians leaves no foundation for distinction. In all passages, the same

vocabulary is used: *laleo* and *glossa*, in various grammatical constructions. On the basis of the Greek and the statement of the text, no distinction is found" (*The Holy Spirit*, p. 183). It is also pointed out that the word *glossa* is found 50 times in the Greek New Testament. Of these, 16 times it refers to the physical organ (see James 3:5); once it refers to flames of fires (Acts 2:3); 33 times it refers to human language.

- Because the word rendered "interpret" in 1 Corinthians 14:13 is *diermeneuo*, and literally means "to translate." Out of the 21 occasions where this word is found in the New Testament, 18 definitely refer to translation. (See Acts 9:36.)
- Because of the description of the events at Pentecost (Acts 2:6-11). Also, Peter says (Acts 11:15) that the tongue-speaking he witnessed at Caesarea was identical to that at Pentecost.
- Because ecstatic gibberish could not be a sign to unbelievers (1 Cor. 14:22)
- Because Jesus warned against tongue-babbling—The Greek words *batta* and *logeo* in Matthew 6:7 refer to the act of babbling, or speaking without thinking
- Because Paul offers no redefinition or clarification of Acts 2 when he writes 1 Corinthians 14
- Because Paul quotes Isaiah 28:11-12 in 1 Corinthians 14:21, which reference is definitely connected to human language. A brief background of Isaiah 28 is needed here. In 721 B.C. the northern kingdom was destroyed. Isaiah warns the southern kingdom (Judah) that the same thing will happen to them unless they repent. He is ridiculed by a group of drunken priests and prophets who disbelieve the warning. Isaiah responds by saying that since they would not listen when God spoke to them in Hebrew, they would when he spoke to them (through enemy soldiers) in the Assyrian language. (See also Moses' words in Deut. 28:15-68, especially v. 49.) (Concerning Titus' invasion in A.D. 70, see Jeremiah 5:15.) Thus, to be addressed in other tongues was a symbol of judgment to the Hebrew mind.
- Because of the advent of higher criticism in the eighteenth and nineteenth centuries In other words, the critics of the Bible rejected the miracle of speaking unlearned human languages and advocated the ecstatic utterance view, thus identifying biblical tongues with other ancient mystery religions.

> (2) The supernatural ability to speak in a heavenly nonhuman language

★ This position holds that the language spoken is decidedly nonearthly; rather, it is heavenly in its structure. Arguments supporting this view are:
- The tongue-speaking disciples at Pentecost are accused of drunkenness (Acts 2:13), a charge which would not be made if the language was of an earthly nature.
- Paul says tongues would cease (1 Cor. 13:8), a ridiculous statement if the gift is simply speaking unlearned human language.
- Because of Paul's words in 1 Corinthians 14:2, *"For he that speaketh in an unknown tongue speaketh not unto men, but unto God: for no man understandeth him."*
- Paul had the gift of tongues (1 Cor. 14:18), yet he could not understand the human speech of Lycaonia in Acts 14:11.
- Because of the distinction made between mind and spirit in 1 Corinthians 14:14-15. Here it is claimed (by some) that God uses the mind to reveal certain revelation in human language and employs the human spirit to reveal other information in nonhuman language.
- Because of the phrase "other tongues" in Acts 2:4. This is a translation of the Greek word *heteros*, which means, "another of a different kind." (See also Gal. 1:6-7).
- Because of the suggestion in 1 Corinthians 13:1: "Though I speak with the tongues of men and of angels." Note: Here it may be asked what kind of language angels speak. While talking to people on earth they have been known to speak both Hebrew (Gen. 19) and Greek (Luke 1). Even during their heavenly ministry they spoke languages which were understandable. (See Isa. 6; Rev. 4-5.)

> (3) A combination of the first two—Purpose of the gift

★ ■ Negative
- It was not for church edification (1 Cor.14:4,19).
- It was not for personal edification. Here an objection may be raised, for does not Paul say, *"He that speaketh in an unknown tongue edifieth himself"*? He does indeed (1 Cor. 14:4). However, a problem is seen here. If tongues are for personal edification, and if the church house was filled with tongue-speaking (as the context definitely indicates-14:23), then how do we explain that, apart from the church at Laodicea (Rev. 3:14-18), this group at Corinth was the most carnal and confused church in the entire Bible? No gift was to be used for personal edification in a selfish way. Here Paul may actually be rebuking them for their unscriptural use of this gift.
- It was not to demonstrate Spirit baptism. (This erroneous concept is totally refuted in 1 Cor. 12:13; Rom. 6:3-4; Col. 2:9-12; Eph. 4:5; Gal. 3:27-28.)

■ Positive
- To validate the authority of the apostles and early Christians
- To demonstrate God's judgment upon unbelieving Israel
- To serve as a sign to seeking (but lost) individual Jews *(Read 1 Cor. 14:20-22)*
  - ✦ Here Paul quotes from Isaiah 28:11-12. In that chapter, Isaiah warned sinful Israel as follows:
    - ◆ God could not get their attention when he spoke to them in Hebrew.
    - ◆ God would get their attention when he spoke to them in a foreign tongue.
  - ✦ By this Isaiah referred to the language used by the Babylonian soldiers in their impending invasion and destruction of the city of Jerusalem.
  - ✦ Thus, for Israel to be addressed by God in a foreign (non-Hebrew) language was in essence to be judged by God. Both Moses (Deut. 28:49) and Jeremiah (Jer. 5:15) had also warned of this.
- To impart new truths prior to the completion of the canon. When Paul wrote 1 Corinthians there were but four New Testament books in existence (James, 1 and 2 Thessalonians and Galatians). There was no written record available concerning such important issues as:
  - ✦ The doctrine of the church (later discussed in Ephesians and Colossians)
  - ✦ The doctrine of justification, sanctification, and glorification (later written about in Romans)
  - ✦ The doctrine of apostasy (Jude)
  - ✦ Christian forgiveness (Philemon)
  - ✦ The priesthood of Christ (Hebrews)
  - ✦ The life of Christ (the four Gospels)
  - ✦ Practical Christian service (1 and 2 Peter)
  - ✦ Christian love (as found in 1, 2, and 3 John)
  - ✦ Advice to pastors and deacons (as discussed in 1 and 2 Timothy and Titus) — In view of all this, no believer could quote or claim the blessed truth in 2 Timothy 3:16-17, simply because it had not yet been written.

b. Regulations of the gift
   (1) No more than three tongue speakers are to speak in any given service (1 Cor. 14:27).
   (2) No more than one may speak at the same time (1 Cor. 14:27).
   (3) An interpreter must translate for all utterances (1 Cor. 14:28) — Paul now lists three analogies to demonstrate the absolute importance of the tongues translator.
       (a) First analogy: From the world of music (1 Cor. 14:7) — *"Yet even lifeless things, either flute or harp, in producing a sound, if they do not produce a distinction in the tones, how will it be known what is played on the flute or on the harp?" (1 Cor. 14:7, NASB)*
       (b) Second analogy: From military warfare *(Read 1 Cor. 14:8)*
       (c) Third analogy: From daily conversation *(Read 1 Cor. 14:9-11)*

(4) All tongue speaking must be done in an orderly manner *(Read 1 Cor. 14:33, 40)*

(5) No woman is permitted to speak in tongues *(Read 1 Cor. 14:34)*

★ **14:34** In 1 Corinthians 11:3-10 Paul allowed a woman to speak in her natural and native tongue; but here he forbids her to use foreign tongues.

V. Question Number Five: What about the resurrection (1 Cor. 15)?

★ Without doubt this chapter (along with Rom. 8) simply must be considered as one of the two greatest in the entire Word of God. Here we have the oldest written account of Christ's resurrection.

A. The prominence of the resurrection (1 Cor. 15:1-4)
  1. It is the focal point in reference to salvation *(Read 1 Cor. 15:1-2)*
  2. It is the focal point in reference to the scriptures *(Read 1 Cor. 15:3-4)*

★ **15:4**
- The time element in Christ's resurrection— *"The third day" (15:4)*. There are two main theories concerning this phrase.
  - He was crucified on Friday. The well-known custom of the Jews was to count a part of a day as a whole day. Thus, he would be in the tomb a portion of Friday (from 3:00 P.M. to 6:00 P.M.), all day Saturday, and a part of Sunday.
  - He was crucified on Wednesday. If Matthew 12:40 is to be taken at face value, then Wednesday is the only day which would allow the necessary three full days and nights.
- The reason for the resurrection of Christ: *"For our sins" (15:3)*. Christ was not a martyr dying for his faith, but a Savior dying for our sins. He did not say, "I am finished," but, *"It is finished."* All three persons in the Trinity were involved in his death and resurrection.
  - The Father (John 3:16; Acts 2:24)
  - The Son (John 10:11, 18).
  - The Holy Spirit (Heb. 9:14; Rom. 1:4)
- The results of the resurrection of Christ— *"By which also ye are saved"* (15:2).

B. The proof of the resurrection (1 Cor. 15:5-22)
  1. First proof—The manifestations of Christ (1 Cor. 15:5-8). There were actually 10 postresurrection appearances of Christ. Paul lists but six (counting himself) in this passage.
     a. To Peter (1 Cor. 15:5)
     b. To the apostles, with Thomas being absent (1 Cor. 15:5)
     c. To 500 disciples (1 Cor. 15:6)
     d. To James, the half-brother of Christ (1 Cor. 15:7)
     e. To the apostles, with Thomas being present (1 Cor. 15:7)
     f. To Paul (1 Cor. 15:8)
  2. Second proof—The salvation of Paul *(Read 1 Cor. 15:9-11)*
C. The priority of the resurrection (1 Cor. 15:12-19)— *"Now if Christ be preached that he rose from the dead, how say some among you that there is no resurrection of the dead?" (1 Cor. 15:12)*. Obviously some were saying this very thing. Paul then lists many horrible conclusions one must be forced to hold **if** this statement were true.
  1. Concerning Christ—The Easter story is a lie. *"But if there be no resurrection of the dead, then is Christ not risen" (1 Cor. 15:13)*.
  2. Concerning the gospel preachers—They continue to lie. *"Yea, and we are found false witnesses of God; because we have testified of God that he raised up Christ: whom he raised not up, if so be that the dead rise not" (1 Cor. 15:15)*.

LESSON 26: THE BOOK OF FIRST CORINTHIANS—PART 3

3. Concerning believers—They swallow the lie.
   a. We are still in our sins—*"And if Christ be not raised, your faith is vain; ye are yet in your sins" (1 Cor. 15:17)*.
   b. Our departed loved ones will never be raised—*"Then they also which are fallen asleep in Christ are perished" (1 Cor. 15:18)*.
   c. We will never be raised (1 Cor. 15:13, 15).
   d. We have no hope in this life—*"If in this life only we have hope in Christ, we are of all men most miserable" (1 Cor. 15:19)*.
   e. The sensual way is the only way (1 Cor. 15:32)—*"If the dead rise not ... let us eat and drink; for tomorrow we die" (1 Cor. 15:32)*.
D. The program of the resurrection (1 Cor. 15:20-28)—*"But now is Christ risen from the dead, and become the firstfruits of them that slept. For since by man came death, by man came also the resurrection of the dead. For as in Adam all die, even so in Christ shall all be made alive" (1 Cor. 15:20-22)*.

★ **15:20-22** In these verses Paul refers to the third of seven Jewish feasts mentioned in Leviticus 23. It was called the Feast of the First Fruits. Note:
- On the first day, selected delegates marked out the spot in the grain field from which the sheaf would be cut.
- On the second day the sheaf was cut and brought into the temple.
- On the third day it was presented to the Lord as a pledge sample.

1. The villain—*"The last enemy that shall be destroyed is death" (1 Cor. 15:26)*.
2. The victors—*"But every man in his own order: Christ the firstfruits; afterward they that are Christ's at his coming" (1 Cor. 15:23)*.

★ **15:23** The Greek word for "order" here is *tagma*, a military term referring to troops in order of rank, as in a parade. Thus we see:
- The resurrection of Christ (Mark 16:2-8; Matt. 28:5-8; Luke 24:1-8)—His resurrection leads the parade, for it was the very first of its kind. The miracle Christ performed upon Lazarus (John 11), or example, was not true resurrection, but simply the restoration of a dead mortal body to that of a living mortal body. Lazarus died again at a later date. But ultimate resurrection carries with it immortality.
- The Rapture resurrection—*"Afterward they that are Christ's at his coming" (15:23b)*. These "troops" follow behind the head of the parade. (See 1 Cor. 15:53; 1 Thess. 4:16.)
- The premillennial resurrection of Old Testament and tribulation saints—*"Then cometh the end" (15:24a;* see John 5:24; Dan. 12.2; Rev. 20:5-6).

a. *"Christ the first fruits"*—His own resurrection (1 Cor. 15:23)
b. *"Afterward they that are Christ's at his coming"*—The Rapture resurrection (1 Cor. 15:23b)
c. *"Then cometh the end"*—Premillennial resurrection of Old Testament and tribulational saints (1 Cor. 15:24b)
3. The victory *(Read 1 Cor. 15:24-25)*
4. The vindication *(Read 1 Cor. 15:28)*
E. The prompting of the resurrection (1 Cor. 15:29-34)
   1. The resurrection factor should motivate me to pick up the fallen banner of departed believers *(Read 1 Cor. 15:29)*.

★ **15:29** This verse has been somewhat of a problem.
- Negative: Whatever its meaning, it does not support the totally unscriptural practice of the Mormon church of living people being baptized by proxy for dead people. To die lost is to forever remain lost. (See Luke 16:19-31; Heb. 2:3; Rev. 22:11.)

- Positive: Inasmuch as baptism refers to identification, Paul may be saying here that, if there is no resurrection of the dead, then what is the purpose of living believers picking up the standard left by departed believers?

>   2. The resurrection factor should motivate me to serve as a martyr if God's will so directs (1 Cor. 15:30-32)
>   3. The resurrection factor should motivate me toward holy living *(Read 1 Cor. 15:33-34)*
>   F. The pattern of the resurrection *(Read 1 Cor. 15:35-38)*—Paul illustrates the resurrection by a grain of wheat.
>   1. To be resurrected the grain is planted in the ground.
>   2. At the resurrection the new stalk retains the likeness of the grains.

* ■ Paul doesn't describe the method God used in raising the dead, but instead gives a glorious example, a grain of wheat (15:37).
  ■ Several thrilling conclusions can be drawn from this illustration.
    ● The old body, like a grain of wheat, has no power to change itself. Only God can grow wheat and raise the dead.
    ● The old body, like a grain of wheat, must die to be changed *(Read John 12:24)*. Thus death does not suppress the grain, but simply releases it.
    ● The new body, like a grain of wheat, does not lose its identity. Both still retain a certain likeness of the former state (1 Cor. 13:12).

>   G. The perfection of the resurrection *(Read 1 Cor. 15:39-50)*
>   1. Paul contrasts the new body to the old body.
>   a. The old body—It is sown a perishable body, sinful by nature, dominated by the flesh, and bounded by time and gravity. It is likened to the sinful body of the first Adam.
>   b. The new body—It is raised an imperishable body, sinless by nature, dominated by the spirit, and unbounded by time and gravity. It is likened to the sinless body of the last Adam.

* ■ In verse 44 Paul writes, *"There is a natural body and there is a spiritual body."* What is the difference? Consider a book with a sheet of plain white paper stuck inside it. In this illustration the book is human body and the paper sheet is the spirit. Down here the book "bosses" the spirit. It has the final say. This is the natural body, governed by the physical laws of gravity and time.
  ■ But now take the white sheet out of the book and wrap it around the book like a cover. Now the sheet (spirit) is on top. It has the final say. This is the spiritual body, which is unaffected by the physical laws of gravity or time, but enjoys the blessings of eternity.

>   2. Paul contrasts the new body with brute bodies (1 Cor. 15:39)—It is as different as human flesh is from animal flesh.
>   3. Paul contrasts the new body with heavenly bodies (1 Cor. 15:40-41)—It is as different as the sun is from the moon.
>   H. The promise of the resurrection (1 Cor. 15:51-54)
>   1. Concerning the bodies belonging to living believers—They will be changed without dying *(Read 1 Cor. 15:51-53)*.

* **15:53b**
  ■ *"I shew you a mystery."* What mystery? Let us suppose you began reading the Bible in Genesis chapter 1, and read through 1 Corinthians chapter 14. If you stopped your reading here, you would already have learned about many important facts, such as creation, sin, the flood, Bethlehem, Calvary, the resurrection, and the existence of heaven and hell. But you would be forced to conclude that a Christian could go to heaven only after physically dying. You would, of course, note the two exceptions of Enoch (Gen. 5:24) and Elijah (2 Kings 2:11); but apart from these it would be clear that believers have to travel the path of the grave to reach the goal of glory. But now the secret is out, and here it is: Millions of Christians will someday reach heaven without dying. *"Behold I shew you a mystery; we shall not all sleep, but we shall all be changed"* (1 Cor. 15:51). This, then, is the mystery of the Rapture.

- *"We shall all be changed."* Observe the word all. The Bible does not support a partial Rapture theory.
- *"In the twinkling of an eye."* This occurs as quickly as a gleam of light shines in the eye, about one fifth of a second.

> 2. Concerning the bodies belonging to departed believers—They'll be raised without corruption *(Read 1 Cor. 15:52-53)*.
> I. The purpose of the resurrection *(Read 1 Cor. 15:54-57)*

★ 15:57

- The purpose of the resurrection should be clearly understood by Christians. It is a tragic fact that our world is indeed a materialistic one. Materialism has been defined as the art of knowing the price of everything, but the value of nothing. On occasion, however, in an attempt to avoid this philosophy, believers go to the other extreme and conclude that God is interested only in nonphysical matters. This sad error is sometimes seen in our churches in the separate deacon and trustee boards. Often this attitude imposes a higher moral standard upon deacons than on trustees, for, after all, aren't the "spiritual" matters more important than the "physical" areas? The truth of the matter is that God is very much interested in physical things, especially in the bodies of Christians. (See 1 Cor. 6:19-20; 2 Cor. 6:16; Eph. 5:28-29; Rom. 12:1-2.)
- What, then, is the purpose of the resurrection? Among other things, it is to destroy man's final enemy. Paul has already written: "The last enemy that shall be destroyed is death" (15:26). Mankind has five natural enemies:
  - The world (Gal. 1:4; 1 John 2:15; James 4:4).
  - The flesh (Rom. 7:18; 8:8; Gal. 5:17; 1 John 2:16).
  - The devil (Matt. 13:39; Eph. 6:11).
  - Spiritual death (John 5:24; 8:51; Rev. 2:11).
  - Physical death (Psa. 55:4; Heb. 2:15).
- Here death is pictured as a venomous serpent and its poisonous fang is sin. But someday God will destroy both the rattler and its fang. Note also the twin phrases:
  - "O death, where is thy sting?" This may refer to living believers who will escape physical death at Christ's coming.
  - "O grave, where is thy victory?" This may refer to departed believers, whose bodies the graves will be forced to give up.

> J. The practical value of the resurrection *(Read 1 Cor. 15:58)*

VI. Question Number Six: What about the collection (1 Cor. 16)?

★ **16:1** The location of the offering: the churches of Galatia. The mention of "the churches of Galatia" is to be noted. The New Testament never speaks of the church in or of a country or province. The official "state church" institution in various countries today is totally foreign to the Bible.

> A. The offering taken *(Read 1 Cor. 16:1-4)*
> 1. The source of the offering—*"Let every one of you"* (1 Cor. 16:2)

★ **16:2b** The local church is to be supported by its members. We note also that it was to be done by everyone.

> 2. The time of the offering—*"Upon the first day of the week"* (1 Cor. 16:2a)

★ **16:2a** This, of course, means on Sunday. (See Mark 16:2, 9; Luke 24:1; John 20:1,19; Acts 20:7.)

> 3. The amount of the offering—*"As God hath prospered him"* (1 Cor. 16:2c)

✷ **16:2c** Although no actual proportion is laid down, it is unthinkable that a believer would give less to God than that amount he tips a waitress in a restaurant.

> 4. The purpose of the offering—*"For the saints" (1 Cor. 16:1)*
> 5. The custodian of the offering—*"Whomsoever ye shall approve" (1 Cor. 16:3)*

✷ **16:3** In all financial affairs of an assembly, the responsibility should be in the hand of more than one brother, to avoid the slightest suspicion of improper handling.

> B. The offering taker (1 Cor. 16:5-24)
>   1. His circumstances
>   a. To visit Corinth later (1 Cor. 16: 5-7)
>   b. To stay at Ephesus until June (1 Cor. 16:8)
>   2. His commitment—*"For a great door and effectual is opened unto me, and there are many adversaries" (1 Cor. 16:9).*
>   3. His coworkers—Paul sends greetings from and expresses his appreciation for the following individuals.
>   a. Timothy (1 Cor. 16:10-11)
>   b. Apollos (1 Cor. 16:12)
>   c. Stephanas, Fortunatus, and Achaicus (1 Cor. 16:15-18)
>   d. Aquila and Priscilla (1 Cor. 16:19)
>   4. His challenge—*"Watch ye, stand fast in the faith, quit you like men, be strong. Let all your things be done with charity" (1 Cor. 16:13-14)*.
>   5. His closing words (1 Cor. 16:21-24)—*"If any man love not the Lord Jesus Christ, let him be Anathema Maranatha" (1 Cor. 16:22).*

✷ **16:22**
- The word *anathema* means "fitted for destruction." (See Rom. 9:3; Gal. 1:8-9.)
- The word *maranatha* means "the Lord comes." (See Phil. 4:5; James 5:7-8; Rev. 1:7; 3:11.)

LESSON 27

INTRODUCTION TO SECOND CORINTHIANS

A MUST READING FOR THE MINISTRY: THE MOST INTIMATE ACCOUNT EVER WRITTEN OF THE DUTIES AND DEMANDS, JOYS AND SORROWS, TRIALS AND TRIUMPHS, PAIN AND PRIVILEGES INVOLVED IN THE WORK OF GOD.

A. This book, 2 Corinthians, may be compared with 1 Corinthians. In 1 Corinthians we see the congregation in the pews; but here in 2 Corinthians can be viewed the preacher in his pulpit.

B. Paul had organized the Corinthian church during his second missionary trip (Acts 18:1-18).

C. During his third missionary trip he visits the church (2 Cor. 12:14; 13:1).

D. He sends Titus to Corinth to organize a special love offering for the poverty-stricken saints in Jerusalem (1 Cor. 16:1; 2 Cor. 8:6, 10). Titus does this and returns to Paul.

E. He writes a letter (now lost) to the Corinthian church (1 Cor. 5:9). We must keep in mind that God did not choose to inspire all of the many letters written by Paul and early church leaders, but only those which are found in the New Testament.

F. After a while, Paul writes another letter. This letter is the 1 Corinthians of the New Testament. There were two basic reasons why he wrote this epistle.

   1. To rebuke the church—Paul had heard about some tragic church factions from the household of Chloe, living there in Corinth (1 Cor. 1:11).
   2. To instruct the church—Paul was visited while in Ephesus by a three-man delegation from Corinth, who handed him a list of questions the church had for him (1 Cor. 7:1; 8:1; 12:1; 16:17).

G. He then sends Timothy to Corinth with this New Testament epistle (1 Cor. 4:17; 16:10-11).

H. Timothy returns to Paul in Ephesus—This young preacher was apparently unable to straighten things out in Corinth (2 Cor. 1:1).

I. Paul desires to visit the church himself at this time, but is unable to (2 Cor. 1:15-17).

J. He soon hears that his work there is being undermined by some legalistic Judaizers who had just arrived from Jerusalem (2 Cor. 3:1;10:12-18;11:22-23).

K. He now sends Titus back to Corinth with orders to straighten things out and meet him in Troas (2 Cor. 2:12-13; 7:6-7).

L. Paul comes to Troas, but does not find Titus. After a restless period, he departs to Macedonia (2 Cor. 2:12-13).

M. Here he meets Titus, who gives him a favorable report concerning the work at Corinth.

N. With great relief, Paul writes 2 Corinthians (2 Cor. 7:5-15).

O. Paul is finally able to visit Corinth at a later date for a period of three months. Here he writes the epistle of Romans (Acts 20:3; Rom. 15:22-29; Rom. 16:1, 23).

P. One of the reasons Paul had written 1 Corinthians was to instruct the church to remove an unrepentant member (1 Cor. 5:1-8).

Q. He then wrote 2 Corinthians, instructing the church to receive back that one who had since become repentant (2 Cor. 2:6-11).
R. Paul lists no less than 15 characteristics of the gospel ministry. One of the most important reasons why God allows a Christian to suffer is explained in this book (1:1-6). In no other epistle does Paul refer to his own sufferings as in this letter (4:8-10; 6:4-10;11:24-33).
S. He also provides the most concise reason why God uses us to do his work (4:7).
T. The most extended discussion of the grace of giving is found in 2 Corinthians (see 8-9).
U. Paul was the first of two human beings allowed to visit paradise and return again. John the apostle was the other. In fact the phrase, "the third heaven," is found but once in the Bible (2 Cor. 12:2).
V. The book of 2 Corinthians also serves as an expose on the person and work of Satan. (See 2:10-11; 4:4; 11:3,13-15; 12:7.
W. At least four names for Christians are given in this book which are not found anywhere else in the Bible. These are:
  1. Living epistles (3:2-3)
  2. A sweet savor of Christ (2:15)
  3. Treasure-carrying earthen vessels (4:7)
  4. Ambassadors for Christ (5:20)
X. The book of 2 Corinthians is the only epistle in which Paul takes the time to defend his apostleship against the lies of his enemies. (See 10-11.)
Y. There are quotations or allusions in 2 Corinthians from 14 Old Testament books. The book of 2 Corinthians is the tenth longest New Testament book, and 33rd longest biblical book, with 13 chapters, 257 verses, and 6,092 words.
Z. Great passages would include:
  1. 1:2-5
  2. 4:1-18
  3. 5:1-10
  4. 5:17-21
  5. 6:14-18
  6. 7:10
  7. 8:9
  8. 9:6
  9. 9:15
  10. 12:9-10

Overview of the Book of Second Corinthians

I. Consolation
 A. The person of consolation and comfort
 B. The purpose of consolation and comfort
 C. The pattern of consolation and comfort

II. Explanation
 A. Concerning Paul's travel to Asia
  1. His trials
  2. His testimony
 B. Concerning Paul's trip to Macedonia
  1. His anticipated trip
  2. His abandoned trip
  3. His actual trip
 C. Concerning Paul's tears in Ephesus
  1. In the past, the Corinthian church had refused to rebuke an unrepentant believer
  2. At the present, the Corinthian church had refused to restore the repentant believer

III. Characterization
 A. It is a triumphal one
 B. It is a sincere one
 C. It is a divinely approved one
  1. His authority came from the saints
  2. His authority came from the Spirit
 D. It is a dependent one
 E. It is a superior one
  1. Its priests are superior
  2. Its program is superior
  3. Its person is superior
  4. Its purpose is superior
 F. It is an open one
 G. It is a satanically opposed one
 H. It is a Christ-honoring one
  1. It stresses who Christ is
  2. It stresses what Christ has done
  3. It stresses why Christ uses us
 I. It is a suffering one
  1. The nature of this suffering
  2. The victory through this suffering
  3. The results from this suffering

J. It is a confident one
   1. The basis of our confidence
   2. The vehicle of our confidence
   3. The goal of our confidence
K. It is a compelling one
   1. The judgment of saints
   2. The need of sinners
   3. The terror of the Lord
   4. The love of Christ
   5. The power of the gospel
L. It is a representative one
   1. Paul speaks of Christ's work (His atonement)
   2. Paul speaks of Christ's workers (His ambassadors)
M. It is (to be) a blameless one
   1. Being offensive in nothing
   2. Being approved in all things
N. It is a paradoxical one
   1. "As deceivers, and yet true"
   2. "As unknown, and yet well known"
   3. "As dying, and behold, we live"
   4. "As chastened, and not killed"
   5. "As sorrowful, yet always rejoicing"
   6. "As poor, yet making many rich"
   7. "As having nothing, and yet possessing all things"
O. It is to be a separated one
   1. The nature of this separation
   2. The logic of this separation
   3. The reason for this separation
   4. The blessings of this separation

IV. Gratification
A. Upon seeing Titus
B. Upon hearing Titus
   1. The church had favorably received Paul's message
   2. The church had favorably received Paul's messenger

V. Solicitation
A. The examples of giving
   1. The Macedonians
   2. The Savior
   3. The Father
B. The characteristics of giving
   1. It is initiated by God himself
   2. It is to be done purposefully
   3. It is to be voluntary

4. It is to be liberal
   5. It is to be preceded by a giving of self to the Lord
   6. It is to come from our joy in Christ
   7. It is to be based on what we have
   8. It is related to one of the spiritual gifts
   9. It is therefore to be regarded as a ministry
  C. The results of giving
   1. It serves as an example for others
   2. It shows our love for God
   3. It guarantees our own spiritual growth
   4. It assures us our own need will be provided for
   5. It results in God giving us more that we might in turn give back more
   6. It provides for the needs of deserving saints
   7. It results in God receiving glory from those needy saints who have been ministered to
   8. It enriches the giver as he is prayed for by the saints he has helped

VI. Vindication
  A. His methods were superior
   1. He did not use a fleshly system
   2. He did not use a false standard
  B. His mission field was superior
  C. His motives were superior
   1. His jealousy over the church
   2. His fear for the church
   3. His unselfish service to the church
   4. His warning to the church
   5. His sufferings for the church
  D. His miracles were superior
   1. Paul's supernatural sight
   2. Paul's supernatural strength
   3. Paul's supernatural signs
  E. His future meeting would be superior
   1. The spirit he would bring with him when he came
   2. The spirit he would expect from them when he came

THE BOOK OF SECOND CORINTHIANS

"Paul, an apostle of Jesus Christ by the will of God, and Timothy our brother, unto the church of God which is at Corinth, with all the saints which are in all Achaia: Grace be to you and peace from God our Father, and from the Lord Jesus Christ" (2 Cor. 1:1-2).

> **I. Consolation (2 Cor. 1:3-7)**
>   A. The person of consolation and comfort *(Read 2 Cor. 1:3)*

✶ **1:3**
- These two words, "comfort" and "consolation" (both from the same Greek word), are found ten times in the first seven verses. Paul begins this epistle (1:3) and ends it (13:11) with the word comfort. Each member of the blessed Trinity is a Comforter.
    - The Father (2 Cor. 1:3; Isa. 49:13)
    - The Son (John 14:1; Isa. 61:2; 2 Thess. 2:16)
    - The Holy Spirit (John 14:16, 26; 15:26; 16:7)
- The word for "comfort" comes from two Greek words, *para* (alongside) and *kaleo* (to call). Thus, to comfort a person is to answer his call and walk alongside him to cheer him, guide him, and, on occasion, to defend him. The Greek word was often used in a court of justice to denote a legal counsel for the defense, one who would plead another's cause. (See 1 John 2:1.) Furthermore, it may be stated that God is the only source of real comfort. The prophetical prayer of Jesus on the cross as given in the Psalms (69:20) perfectly describes all human beings: *"Reproach hath broken my heart; and I am full of heaviness: and I looked for some to take pity, but there was none; and for comforters, but I found none."*
- There are two types of people which need no comfort: the unborn and the dead (see Isa. 40:1-2). C. H. Spurgeon said that the preacher who prepared his sermons for heartbroken people would never lack for an audience.

> B. The purpose of consolation and comfort *(Read 2 Cor. 1:4-5)*

✶ **1:5** There is a vast difference between sympathy and empathy. The first can only say, "I'm sorry for what you're going through"; but the second may state, "I know exactly what you're going through." Thus, because our Lord Jesus suffered all things, he is able to offer all comfort. (See Heb. 2:14-18; 4:14-16.) The Savior not only comforts us, but suffers with us (Acts 9:4). The spiritual rule therefore is this: The more one suffers for Christ, the more comfort he receives from Christ, and the more ability he has to comfort other suffering people. Thus, he who has suffered much speaks many languages.

> C. The pattern of consolation and comfort *(Read 2 Cor. 1:6)*
> **II. Explanation (2 Cor. 1:8-2:13)**
>   A. Concerning Paul's travel to Asia (2 Cor. 1:8-14)
>   1. His trials *(Read 2 Cor 1:8)*
>   2. His testimony *(Read 2 Cor. 1:9-10)*

✶ **1:10** Paul's faith here was like that of Isaac and Abraham in the Old Testament. (See Gen. 22:1-18; Heb. 11:17-19.) Note his testimony concerning God's threefold deliverance.
- "Who delivered us." This speaks of justification.
- "Who doth deliver." This speaks of sanctification.
- "Who will yet deliver." This speaks of glorification.

> B. Concerning Paul's trip to Macedonia (2 Cor. 1:8-24; 2:1, 12-13)
>   1. His anticipated trip (2 Cor. 1:15-16)—He intended to visit the Corinthian church on the way back to Judea.
>   2. His abandoned trip (2 Cor. 1:23, 2:1)—He realized the carnal church would not be receptive to his ministry at that time.
>   3. His actual trip (2 Cor. 2:12-13)
> C. Concerning Paul's tears in Ephesus (2 Cor. 2:2-11)—*"For out of much affliction and anguish of heart I wrote unto you with many tears; not that ye should be grieved, but that ye might know the love which I have more abundantly unto you"* (2 Cor. 2:4).
>   1. In the past, the Corinthian church had refused to rebuke an unrepentant believer (see 1 Cor. 5).
>   2. At the present, the Corinthian church had refused to restore the repentant believer.
>   a. Paul tells the church what they were to do *(Read 2 Cor. 2:6-8)*
>   b. Paul tells the church why they were to do it *(Read 2 Cor. 2:11)*

✴ **2:11** There were at least five things that Paul did not want his readers to be ignorant concerning:
- The fact of Israel's past rejection (1 Cor. 10:1)
- The fact of Israel's future restoration (Rom. 11:25)
- The fact and nature of spiritual gifts (1 Cor. 12:1)
- The fact and nature of the Rapture (1 Thess. 4:13)
- The fact and nature of Satan's deception (2 Cor. 2:11)

> **III. Characterization (2 Cor. 2:14-6:18)**—Paul here lists 15 desired characteristics of the gospel ministry.
>   A. It is a triumphal one *(Read 2 Cor. 2:14-16)*

✴ **2:14** God has thus assured us of victory—total victory:
- Regardless of when the problems arise (always)
- Regardless of where the problems arise (every place). To illustrate this promise, Paul likens the ministry to a victorious Roman parade during which the successful general (in this case, Jesus) would lead both conquerors (the saved) and captives (the unsaved) to their respective destinies. From the marching parade there would ascend a sweet fragrance, caused by the burning of incense. Thus: *"To the one [captives] we are the savour of death unto death; and to the other [conquerors] the savour of life unto life"* (2:16). In the Old Testament, Joseph's presence was death for the baker (Gen. 40:16-19, 22), but life for the butler (Gen. 40:9, 13, 21). Likewise, in the New Testament, Jesus' presence meant death for the unrepentant thief (Luke 23:39), but life for the repentant thief (Luke 23:40-43).

> B. It is a sincere one *(Read 2 Cor. 2:17)*

✴ **2:17** The word "corrupt" means to peddle, or to huckster the Word of God. All false prophets are guilty of this horrible sin. (See Acts 8:18-23; 2 Pet. 3:14-16.)

> C. It is a divinely approved one (2 Cor. 3:1-3)—*"Do we begin again to commend ourselves? or need we, as some others, epistles of commendation to you, or letters of commendation from you?"* (2 Cor. 3:1). Unlike his enemies the Judaizers, Paul needed no letters of recommendation from finite and carnal people.
>   1. His authority came from the saints *(Read 2 Cor. 3:2)*
>   2. His authority came from the Spirit *(Read 2 Cor. 3:3)*

✴ **3:3** The legalistic Judaizing teachers who plagued Paul's work carried formal and impressive letters of introduction from Jerusalem. Prior to his conversion, the apostle had done this also (Acts 9:2). But now all that had changed. Paul's letters were:
- Personal—*"Ye are our epistle."*

- Permanent—*"Written in our hearts"*
- Public—*"Known and read of all men."*

> D. It is a dependent one *(Read 2 Cor. 3:4-5)*
> E. It is a superior one (2 Cor. 3:6-18)—The apostle now contrasts the gospel of grace with the Law of Moses.
>   1. Its priests are superior *(Read 2 Cor. 3:6)*
>   2. Its program is superior (2 Cor. 3:7-13)—The glory of grace will never fade away, as did the glory of the Law. (See Exod. 34:29-35) *(Read 2 Cor. 3:13)*

✶ **3:13** Here Paul refers back to Exodus 34:29-35, when Moses came down from Mount Sinai after receiving the Ten Commandments. On that occasion his face had so radiated God's glory that he wore a veil, so he wouldn't frighten the waiting Israelites below. But in 2 Corinthians 3:13 Paul explains that the real reason for the veil was to prevent Israel from viewing the glory which soon faded away. But God's new program is superior to that of Moses, for its glory, as given by Christ, will never fade away. (See also Matt. 26:28; Heb. 8:8, 13.)

> 3. Its person is superior *(Read 2 Cor. 3:17)*
> 4. Its purpose is superior (2 Cor. 3:14-18)
>   a. Concerning the Israel of God—To remove the veil, that is, to take away the unbelief from their hearts *(Read 2 Cor. 3:15-16)*
>   b. Concerning the child of God—To renew the vision; that is, to transform believers into the image of Christ *(Read 2 Cor. 3:18)*

✶ **3:18** Thus, the supreme goal of the believer on this earth is to become as much like Jesus as possible. This, of course, is God's ultimate goal throughout all eternity, but he wants to start this process now.

Dr. H. A. Ironside writes in his book on 2 Corinthians: "You remember Hawthorne's story of 'The Great Stone Face.' He tells of a lad who lived in the village below the mountain, and there upon the mountain was that image of the great stone face, looking down so solemnly, so seriously, upon the people. There was a legend that some day someone was coming to that village who would look just like the great stone face, and he would do some wonderful things for the village and would be the means of great blessing. The story gripped this lad, and he used to slip away and hour after hour would stand looking at that great stone face and thinking of the story about the one that was coming. Years passed, and that one did not come, and still the young man did what the boy had done, and went to sit and contemplate the majesty, the beauty of that great stone face. By and by youth passed away and middle age came on, and still he could not get rid of that legend; and then old age came, and one day as he walked through the village someone looked at him and exclaimed, 'He has come, the one who is like the great stone face!' He became like that which he contemplated. If you want to be Christlike, look at Jesus. If you want to grow in grace, contemplate Jesus. You find Him revealed in the Word, so read your Bible and meditate upon it."

> F. It is an open one *(Read 2 Cor. 4:1-4)*

✶ **4:2** This openness is vital, for sinners are already blinded by Satan and should not suffer additional harm by the lives of deceitful Christians. The strongest argument against the Bible is the life of a carnal Christian, while the strongest argument for the Bible is the life of a godly Christian.

> G. It is a satanically opposed one (2 Cor. 4:3-4)
> H. It is a Christ-honoring one (2 Cor. 4:5-7)
>   1. It stresses who Christ is *(Read 2 Cor. 4:5)*
>   2. It stresses what Christ has done *(Read 2 Cor. 4:6)*
>   3. It stresses why Christ uses us *(Read 2 Cor. 4:7)*

LESSON 27: THE BOOK OF SECOND CORINTHIANS

★ **4:7** One of the world's largest and most famous diamonds (108.3 carats), presented to Queen Victoria in 1850 [which can be viewed inside a thick bullet-proof glass case in the Tower of London], rests upon a simple and inexpensive black cloth. This background thus serves by way of contrast to bring out to the fullest all the dazzling glory of that magnificent national treasure. In similar fashion God has entrusted in earthen vessels (bodies of believers) heaven's most prized treasure, the Lord Jesus Christ, "that the excellency of the power may be of God."

> I. It is a suffering one (2 Cor. 4:8-18).
>   1. The nature of this suffering (2 Cor. 4:8-16)
>   a. Troubled on every side (2 Cor. 4:8)
>   b. Perplexed (2 Cor. 4:8)
>   c. Persecuted (2 Cor. 4:9)
>   d. Cast down (2 Cor. 4:9)
>   e. Perishing outer man (2 Cor. 4:16)
>   2. The victory through this suffering
>   a. Troubled, yet not crushed
>   b. Perplexed, but not in despair
>   c. Persecuted, but not forsaken
>   d. Struck down, but not destroyed
>   e. Perishing outer person, but renewed inner person
>   3. The results from this suffering
>   a. Immediate blessings
>   (1) We experience the power of God *(Read 2 Cor. 4:10)*
>   (2) We exhibit the glory of God *(Read 2 Cor. 4:15)*
>   b. Future blessings
>   (1) The assurance of our bodily resurrection *(Read 2 Cor. 4:14)*
>   (2) The assurance of our bountiful reward *(Read 2 Cor. 4:17-18)*
> J. It is a confident one (2 Cor. 5:1-9)—*"Therefore we are always confident"* (2 Cor. 5:6). *"We are confident, I say"* (2 Cor. 5:8).
>   1. The basis of our confidence—*"Now he that hath wrought us for the selfsame thing is God, who also hath given unto us the earnest of the Spirit"* (2 Cor. 5:5)
>   2. The vehicle of our confidence—*"For we walk by faith, not by sight"* (2 Cor. 5:7)
>   3. The goal of our confidence
>   a. To please our heavenly Father down here *(Read 2 Cor. 5:8-9)*
>   b. To receive our heavenly frame up there *(Read 2 Cor. 5:1)*
> K. It is a compelling one (2 Cor. 5:10-17)—There were five factors which caused Paul to work night and day in the gospel ministry.
>   1. The judgment of saints *(Read 2 Cor. 5:10)*
>   2. The need of sinners *(Read 2 Cor. 5:14)*
>   3. The terror of the Lord *(Read 2 Cor. 5:11a)*

★ **5:11** Here Paul refers to that reverential fear and respect which should characterize every believer. Paul's fear was that he might displease his glorious Master.

> 4. The love of Christ *(2 Cor. 5:14-15)*

★ **5:15** This glorious gospel therefore assures us that:
■ We might live through Christ (1 John 4:9).

- We might live with Christ (1 Thess. 5:10).
- We might live for Christ (2 Cor. 5:15).

> 5. The power of the gospel *(Read 2 Cor. 5:17, 21)*
> L. It is a representative one (2 Cor. 5:18-20).
>   1. Paul speaks of Christ's work (his atonement) *(Read 2 Cor. 5:18-19)*
>   2. Paul speaks of Christ's workers (his ambassadors) *(Read 2 Cor. 5:20)*

★ **5:20** There are three facts concerning an ambassador:
- An ambassador must be a citizen of the state he represents (Phil. 3:20; Col. 3:1-2).
- He is chosen (John 15:16).
- He is called home before war is declared (1 Thess. 1:10; 5:1-10).

> M. It is (to be) a blameless one (2 Cor. 6:1-7).
>   1. Being offensive in nothing—*"Giving no offence in any thing, that the ministry be not blamed"* (2 Cor. 6:3).
>   2. Being approved in all things—*"But in all things approving ourselves as the ministers of God, in much patience"* (2 Cor. 6:4a).
>   a. During the hardships imposed by circumstances—*"In afflictions, in necessities, in distresses"* (2 Cor. 6:4b).
>   b. During the hardships imposed by sinners—*"In stripes, in imprisonments, in tumults"* (2 Cor. 6:5a).
>   c. During the hardships imposed by self-discipline—*"In labors, in watchings, in fastings"* (2 Cor. 6:5b).
> N. It is a paradoxical one (2 Cor. 6:8-10).

★ A paradox is an apparent (but not real) contradiction. There are a number of paradoxes in the Bible concerning both the saint and the Savior.
- Concerning the saint
  - Of finding one's life, yet eventually losing it (John 12:25)
  - Of losing one's life, yet eventually finding it (Matt. 10:39)
  - Of being unknown, yet being well known (2 Cor. 6:9a)
  - Of dying, yet possessing life (2 Cor. 6:9b)
  - Of being sorrowful, yet always rejoicing (2 Cor. 6:10)
  - Of dying, yet able to give life (John 12:24)
  - Of being poor, yet making many rich (2 Cor. 6:10)
  - Of having nothing, yet possessing all things (2 Cor. 6:10)
  - Of hearing words that cannot be expressed (2 Cor. 12:4)
  - Of being strong when one is weak (2 Cor. 12:10)
  - Of knowing the love of Christ which surpasses knowledge (Eph. 3:19)
  - Of seeing the unseen (2 Cor. 4:18)
- Concerning the Savior—It may be concluded that the very life and ministry of our blessed Savior was itself a divine paradox.
  - He hungered, yet fed multitudes (Matt. 4:2; John 6).
  - He thirsted, yet is the water of life (John 19:28; 4:14).
  - He wearied, yet is our rest (John 4:6; Matt. 11:29-30).
  - He paid tribute, yet is the King of kings (Matt. 17:27; Rev. 19:16).
  - He prayed, yet hears our prayers (Mark 14:32, 35, 39; John 14:12, 14).
  - He wept, yet dries our tears (John 11:35; Rev. 21:4).
  - He was sold for 30 pieces of silver, yet redeems the world (Matt. 26:15; 1 Pet. 1:18-19).
  - He was led as a sheep to the slaughter, and yet is the Good Shepherd (Isa. 53:7; John 10:11).
  - He was put to death, yet raises the dead (John 19:30).

1. *"As deceivers, and yet true"* (2 Cor. 6:8)
2. *"As unknown, and yet well known"* (2 Cor. 6:9)
3. *"As dying, and, behold, we live"* (2 Cor. 6:9).
4. *"As chastened, and not killed"* (2 Cor. 6:9)
5. *"As sorrowful, yet always rejoicing"* (2 Cor. 6:10)
6. *"As poor, yet making many rich"* (2 Cor. 6:10)
7. *"As having nothing, and yet possessing all things"* (2 Cor. 6:10)
O. It is to be a separated one (2 Cor. 6:11-18).
   1. The nature of this separation— *"Be ye not unequally yoked together with unbelievers"* (2 Cor. 6:14a).

★ **6:14a** This separation would no doubt cover such human ties as:
- Marriage
- Certain business partnerships
- Unsound ecclesiastical organizations

   2. The logic of this separation
      a. What partnership has righteousness with lawlessness (2 Cor. 6:14)?
      b. What fellowship has light with darkness (2 Cor. 6:14)?
      c. What harmony has Christ with Belial (2 Cor. 6:15)?
      d. What has a believer in common with an unbeliever (2 Cor. 6:15)?
      e. What agreement has the temple of God with idols (2 Cor. 6:16)?
   3. The reason for this separation— *"For ye are the temple of the living God"* (2 Cor. 6:16b).
   4. The blessings of this separation (2 Cor. 6:16-18)— *"As God hath said, I will dwell in them, and walk in them: and I will be their God, and they shall be my people"* (2 Cor. 6:16c).
IV. **Gratification (2 Cor. 7:1-16)**—Paul is profoundly thankful to God for two things:
   A. Upon seeing Titus—He was practically beside himself when Titus did not appear either in Troas or Macedonia as originally planned (See 2 Cor. 2:12-13) *(Read 2 Cor. 7:5-6)*.
   B. Upon hearing Titus (2 Cor. 7:7-16)—Titus, who had been sent by Paul to Corinth, now brings back a twof-old report.
      1. The church had favorably received Paul's message—He had previously sent them a letter (probably 1 Corinthians) of rebuke, attempting to straighten out the mess in their congregation. It had worked, according to Titus, and led to their repentance *(Read 2 Cor. 7:10)*.
      2. The church had favorably received Paul's messenger *(Read 2 Cor. 7:13, 15)*
V. **Solicitation (2 Cor. 8:1-9:15)**— *"I have shewed you all things, how that so labouring ye ought to support the weak, and to remember the words of the Lord Jesus, how he said, It is more blessed to give than to receive"* (Acts 20:35).
   A. The examples of giving
      1. The Macedonians (2 Cor. 8:1-5)
         a. They surrendered their bodies to the Lord— *"But first gave their own selves to the Lord"* (2 Cor. 8:5).
         b. They submitted their wills to the apostle— *"And unto us by the will of God"* (2 Cor. 8:5).
         c. They sacrificially shared their wealth with the saints— *"How that in a great trial of affliction the abundance of their joy and their deep poverty abounded unto the riches of their liberality"* (2 Cor. 8:2).
      2. The Savior— *"For ye know the grace of our Lord Jesus Christ, that, though he was rich, yet for your sakes he became poor, that ye through his poverty might be rich"* (2 Cor. 8:9).

★ **8:9** Thus, our Lord became what he was not (poor), that we might become what we were not (rich). The sinless Son of God became the Son of man that sinful sons of men might become the sons of God.

3. The Father— *"Thanks be unto God for his unspeakable gift"* (2 Cor. 9:15).
   B. The characteristics of giving
   1. It is initiated by God himself *(Read 2 Cor. 8:1; 9:8)*.
   2. It is to be done purposefully *(Read 2 Cor. 9:7)*
   3. It is to be voluntary (2 Cor. 8:3-4, 8, 12; 9:7)—*"They [the Macedonians] were willing"* (2 Cor. 8:3). *"For if there be first a willing mind, it is accepted"* (2 Cor. 8:12). *"Not grudgingly, or of necessity"* (2 Cor. 9:7).
   4. It is to be liberal *(Read 2 Cor. 8:2; 9:6)*
   5. It is to be preceded by a giving of self to the Lord (2 Cor. 8:5).
   6. It is to come from our joy in Christ (2 Cor. 8:2; 9:7).
   7. It is to be based on what we have *(Read 2 Cor. 8:12)*
   8. It is related to one of the spiritual gifts *(Read 2 Cor. 8:7)*
   9. It is therefore to be regarded as a ministry *(Read 2 Cor. 9:1)*
   C. The results of giving
   1. It serves as an example for others *(Read 2 Cor. 9:2)*
   2. It shows our love for God *(Read 2 Cor. 8:8, 24)*
   3. It guarantees our own spiritual growth *(Read 2 Cor. 9:9-10)*
   4. It assures us our own need will be provided for *(Read 2 Cor. 9:11)*
   5. It results in God giving us more that we might in turn give back more *(Read 2 Cor. 9:8)*
   6. It provides for the needs of deserving saints *(Read 2 Cor. 9:12)*
   7. It results in God receiving glory from those needy saints who have been ministered to *(Read 2 Cor. 9:12-13)*
   8. It enriches the giver as he is prayed for by the saints he has helped *(Read 2 Cor. 9:14)*
VI. Vindication (2 Cor. 10-13)—Paul writes these chapters to defend his name and ministry. Both were being undermined by some envious Judaizers who had probably come to Corinth from Jerusalem to stir up trouble. In his defense he lists a fivefold superiority of his divinely given ministry as contrasted to the false Judaizers.
   A. His methods were superior.
   1. He did not use a fleshly system *(Read 2 Cor. 10:3-5)*

✱ **10:4** In defeating Satan one cannot fight fire with fire. He must use blood (see Rev. 12:11).

   2. He did not use a false standard *(Read 2 Cor. 10:12, 17-18)*

✱ **10:18**
- All too often both saved and unsaved people are guilty of this false measurement system.
  - The unsaved person can usually find some poor miserable wretch who is worse than he is, thus relieving his own uneasy conscience and causing him to conclude that his "superior morality" is sufficient, apart from Christ's righteousness.
  - Sometimes Christian leaders fall victim to this snare also by comparing their own ministry to that of another believer's work. This can lead to envy (if his work is bigger than mine) or pride (if the opposite is true).
- But Paul carefully avoided this trap. Note his words: *"But he that glorieth, let him glory in the Lord. For not he that commendeth himself is approved, but whom the Lord commendeth"* (10:17-18).
- In this Paul was supported by both Old and New Testament teachings.
  - *1 Samuel 16:6-7*—*"And it came to pass, when they were come, that he looked on Eliab, and said, Surely the LORD'S anointed is before him. But the Lord said unto Samuel, Look not on his countenance, or on the height of his stature; because I have refused him: for the Lord seeth not as man seeth; for man looketh on the outward appearance, but the LORD looketh on the heart."*
  - *John 7:24*—*"Judge not according to the appearance, but judge righteous judgment."*

  B. His mission field was superior *(Read 2 Cor. 10:16)*
  C. His motives were superior—Especially was this true concerning the church. Paul was the concerned shepherd, while his enemies were cruel hirelings.
    1. His jealousy over the church *(Read 2 Cor. 11:2)*

★ 11:2 At this point let us distinguish between jealousy and envy.
- Jealousy: "The desire to possess one's own things." Contrary to popular opinion, this is a good and natural trait, if kept in proper bounds.
- Envy: "The desire to possess the things of another." This is always wrong.

    2. His fear for the church *(Read 2 Cor. 11:3)*
    3. His unselfish service to the church—Even though he was an apostle, Paul functioned as a servant among them *(Read 2 Cor. 11:5)*
     a. He gave much to them *(Read 2 Cor. 11:8)*
     b. He took nothing from them *(Read 2 Cor. 11:9)*
    4. His warning to the church—He warns the church about their enemies.
     a. Who they were *(Read 2 Cor. 11:13)*
     b. Where they came from *(Read 2 Cor. 11:14-15)*
     c. What they did—"For you bear with anyone if he enslaves you, if he devours you, if he takes advantage of you, if he exalts himself, if he hits you in the face" (2 Cor. 11:20, NASB).
    5. His sufferings for the church (2 Cor. 11:23-33)
     a. Backbreaking labor (2 Cor. 11:23, 27)
     b. Beatings
      (1) Beaten with 39 lashes on five occasions (2 Cor. 11:24)
      (2) Beaten with rods on three occasions (2 Cor. 11:25)
     c. Stonings (2 Cor. 11:25)
     d. Three shipwrecks (2 Cor. 11:25)—During one of these he was afloat on the sea.
     e. Wearisome travels (2 Cor. 11:26)
     f. Constant dangers (2 Cor. 11:26)
      (1) From swollen rivers
      (2) From robbers
      (3) From his own countrymen
      (4) From Gentiles
      (5) From false brethren
     g. Narrow escapes *(Read 2 Cor. 11:32-33)*
     h. Physical deprivations
      (1) Lack of food and water (2 Cor. 11:27)
      (2) Lack of warm clothing (2 Cor. 11:27)
      (3) Lack of proper rest (2 Cor. 11:27)
     i. The daily pressure of caring for his local churches (2 Cor. 11:28)
  D. His miracles were superior.
    1. Paul's supernatural sight *(Read 2 Cor. 12:1-4)*

★ 12:4 Note: We cannot even speculate upon what Paul actually witnessed on this occasion. At a later date John the apostle apparently viewed a similar sight. (See Rev. 10:4.) Some believe Paul actually died during his stoning at Lystra (Acts 14:19) and that during this time he experienced the vision here in 2 Corinthians 12, prior to being raised again from the dead by God.

> 2. Paul's supernatural strength *(Read 2 Cor. 12:7-10)*

★ **12:10**
- Note: This passage marks the fifth reference to Satan by Paul in 2 Corinthians. From these verses we learn:
  - His title: The god of this world (4:4)
  - His tactics:
    - To take advantage of believers (2:11)
    - To inflict suffering upon believers (12:7) — See especially Job 1-2.
    - To blind unbelievers (4:4)
  - His treachery-Disguising himself as an angel of light (11:14)
  - His trustees — False ministers (11:15)
- What was the nature of this thorn in the flesh? There are various views. The main theory is that he suffered from chronic ophthalmia, a disease of the eyes — not extremely painful, but at times repulsive. It came upon Paul 14 years prior to his writing this epistle, which was about the time of his entrance into Galatia. This was occasioned by some sort of physical infirmity. (See also Gal. 4:13-15; 6:11.)
- It should also be remembered that he was blinded for a while at his conversion (Acts 9:9). Satan thus may have exploited a natural infirmity.

> 3. Paul's supernatural signs *(Read 2 Cor. 12:12)*
> E. His future meeting would be superior—His enemies had met with the Corinthians, but only to confuse and corrupt. His planned meeting would be different.
>   1. The spirit he would bring with him when he came *(Read 2 Cor. 12:14)*
>   2. The spirit he would expect from them when he came *(Read 2 Cor. 12:20; 13:5, 11-14)*

LESSON 28

INTRODUCTION TO GALATIANS

THE IMPERATIVE—
WARNING: DO NOT MIX THE INGREDIENTS UNDER ANY CIRCUMSTANCES
THE LAW OF GOD AND THE GRACE OF GOD

A. The book of Galatians is the Magna Charta of the early church. It is Scripture's strongest declaration and defense of the doctrine of justification by faith.
B. One of the problems in dating the book concerns its destination. Was the letter written to the churches in northern Galatia (where Paul visited during his second and third missionary trips) or to the churches in southern Galatia (where he preached during his first trip)?
C. The Galatians themselves were an emotional and intense Celtic people. Caesar said: "They are fickle in their resolves, fond of change, and not to be trusted." This is demonstrated during Paul's first visit to them. In the morning they attempted to worship him, and in the afternoon to murder him (Acts 14). They were a branch of Gauls, originally from north of the Baltic Sea, who had split off from a main migration westward to France and had settled in Asia Minor during the third century B.C.
D. This is probably Paul's first epistle. The book of 2 Timothy would be his last. Paul's work in Galatia had been highly successful. Great multitudes of people, mostly Gentiles, had accepted Christ. But after he left, the Judaizers from Jerusalem (a group of legalistic gospel-perverting Jews) had come to Galatia, teaching that Gentiles must put themselves back under the bondage of the law to be saved. The Galatians had thus received their message with the same zeal that they had accepted Paul's. There was then a general epidemic of circumcision among them.
E. The Judaizers had not only attacked the message of Paul, but also his apostleship.
F. Galatians may have been the only book written personally by the apostle without the aid of a stenographer (see 6:11).
G. It is, next to 2 Corinthians, the most autobiographical of Paul's letters and the only epistle by Paul addressed to a group of local churches.
H. The key word is *liberty*, used 11 times in the letter. This is more than all his other epistles combined.
I. It has been said that Judaism was the cradle of Christianity and very nearly its grave. But God raised up Paul as the Moses of the Christian church to deliver believers from bondage. Galatians finishes what Paul will begin in 2 Corinthians (concerning his apostleship), and begins what Paul will finish in Romans (concerning justification by faith).
J. There is a striking parallel between Galatians and Romans. At least 19 passages may be favorably compared. Galatians is a rough sketch of which Romans is the finished picture.
K. J. Vernon McGee aptly summarizes Galatians: "It is a stern, severe and solemn message (Gal. 1:6-9; 3:1-5). It does not correct conduct, as the Corinthian letters do, but it is corrective—the Galatian believers were in grave peril. Because the foundations were being attacked, everything was threatened."
"It is the strongest declaration and defense of the doctrine of justification by faith in or out of the

scripture. It is God's polemic on behalf of the most vital truth of the Christian faith against any attack. Not only is a sinner saved by grace through faith, but the saved sinner lives by grace. Grace is a way to life and a way of life" *(Through the Bible*, p. 108).

L. Paul reveals more about his early Christian life activities in this book than in any other of his writings (1:13-2:14). Among these events is the account when he confronted Peter concerning Simon's sinful legalism.

M. Galatians is the first chronological New Testament book to quote Habakkuk 2:4: *"The just shall live by faith" (Gal. 3:11)*. The other two instances are Romans 1:17 and Hebrews 10:38. Chapters 3 and 4 provide the most extensive explanation on the function of the Law of God in all Scripture. The book also contains the greatest contrast between the fruit of the flesh and that of the spirit in the Bible. (See 5:19-23.)

N. There are quotations and allusions in Galatians from ten Old Testament books. Galatians is the 11th longest New Testament book, and 40th longest biblical book, with six chapters, 149 verses, and 3,098 words.

O. Great passages would include:
1. 2:20
2. 3:26-29
3. 4:4-5
4. 5:22-26
5. 6:14

Overview of the Book of Galatians

I. **Justification by Faith: The Foundation**
    A. The source of our justification
    B. The sacrifice for our justification

II. **Justification by Faith: The Aberration**
    A. The concern of Paul
    B. The curse from Paul

III. **Justification by Faith: The Revelation**
    A. The uniqueness of this revelation
        1. It was not of man, that is, human flesh did not compile it for Paul
        2. It was not from man, that is, human flesh did not communicate it to Paul
    B. The need for this revelation
    C. The trips following this revelation
        1. Traveling to Arabia and Damascus
        2. Traveling to Jerusalem
    D. The purpose of this revelation
    E. The recognition of this revelation
        1. The when of the matter
        2. The what of the matter
    F. The enemies of this revelation

IV. **Justification by Faith: The Confrontation**
    A. The rebuke involved
    B. The reason involved
    C. The rationale involved

V. **Justification by Faith: The Clarification**

VI. **Justification by Faith: The Transformation**

VII. **Justification by Faith: The Argumentation**
    A. The argument from their own experience
        1. He reminds them how they first received the message of justification
        2. He reminds them how they first received the messenger of justification
    B. The argument from the life of Abraham
    C. The argument from the Law
        1. The Law and sinners
        2. The Law and the promise
        3. The Law and Israel

       4. The Law and Christ
       5. The Law and believers
       6. The Law and the Galatians

VIII. Justification by Faith: The Allegorization
    A. Hagar (an allegory of the Law)
    B. Sarah (an allegory of grace)

IX. Justification by Faith: The Application
    A. Assuring us of the freedom of the Son
       1. Keeping us from the legalism of the Jews
       2. Keeping us from the license of the Libertines
       3. Keeping us in the love of the Lord
    B. Assuring us the fruit of the Spirit
       1. As demonstrated by our fruitbearing
       2. As demonstrated by our burden-bearing
       3. As demonstrated by our seed-bearing
       4. As demonstrated by our brand-bearing

THE BOOK OF GALATIANS

"Paul, an apostle, (not of men, neither by man, but by Jesus Christ, and God the Father, who raised him from the dead;) and all the brethren which are with me, unto the churches of Galatia" (Gal. 1:1-2).

> **I. Justification by Faith—The Foundation (Gal. 1:3-5)**
>   A. The source of our justification *(Read Gal. 1:3)*
>   B. The sacrifice for our justification *(Read Gal. 1:4-5)*
> **II. Justification by Faith—The Aberration (Gal. 1:6-9)**
>   A. The concern of Paul *(Read Gal. 1:6-7)*
>   B. The curse from Paul *(Read Gal. 1:8)*

✶ **1:8**
- This "gospel" was really not an *allos* (Greek word meaning "another of the same kind"), but a *heteros* (Greek word meaning "another of a different kind").
- This "gospel" was not to be received, even though it came from an angel or from Paul himself.
- This "gospel," if received and believed, would result in divine judgment and damnation upon its recipients. The word "accurse" here is *anathema* in the Greek. (See also Acts 23:14; 1 Cor. 12:3; Rom. 9:3; 2 Thess. 1:9.)

> **III. Justification by Faith—The Revelation (Gal. 1:10-2:10)**
>   A. The uniqueness of this revelation (Gal. 1:11-12, 17-19)
>   1. It was not of man, that is, human flesh did not compile it for Paul *(Read Gal. 1:11)*
>   2. It was not from man, that is, human flesh did not communicate it to Paul *(Read Gal. 1:12)*

✶ **1:12** The Savior also revealed to Paul those facts concerning:
- The Last Supper (1 Cor. 11:23)
- The death and resurrection of Christ (1 Cor. 15:3-4)

>   B. The need for this revelation *(Read Gal. 1:13-14)*

✶ **1:14** Here Paul gives his testimony and tells of the horrible life he lived prior to his conversion. The apostle loved to relate this testimony. (See Acts 22:1-16; 26:1-20; 1 Tim. 1:12-16.)

>   C. The trips following this revelation
>   1. Traveling to Arabia and Damascus (Gal. 1:17)
>   2. Traveling to Jerusalem
>   a. The *when* of the matter— "... after three years I went up to Jerusalem ... and abode ... fifteen days" (Gal. 1:18).
>   b. The *who* of the matter— "To see Peter" (Gal. 1:18). "... saw I none, save James the Lord's brother" (Gal. 1:19).
>   D. The purpose of this revelation (Gal. 2:1-2, 9) *(Read Gal. 1:15-16)*

✶ **1:16** Two other unborn babies also experienced this early call.
- Jeremiah the prophet (Jer. 1:4-10)
- John the Baptist (Luke 1:15-17)

> E. The recognition of this revelation (Gal. 2:1-2, 9)
>   1. The *when* of the matter *(Read Gal. 2:1)*

✲ 2:1 He visits Jerusalem again along with Barnabas and Titus (Gal. 2:1-10; Acts 11:29-30). It has now been 14 years since his conversion. At this point in the record the Judaizers begin putting pressure upon Paul to mix their devilish legalism with God's pure grace, but they would run into a brick wall in this. James, Peter, and John encourage Paul to keep preaching God's grace to the Gentiles.

>   2. The *what* of the matter *(Read Gal. 2:2, 7, 9)*
> F. The enemies of this revelation *(Read Gal. 2:3-5)*
> **IV. Justification by Faith: The Confrontation (Gal. 2:11-14)**
>   A. The rebuke involved *(Read Gal. 2:11)*

✲ 2:14
- It is difficult to know just when this confrontation took place. Some would feel it happened at a later date, following the Jerusalem Council. At any rate, Peter had allowed the ever-present Judaizers to pressure him into withdrawing from all Gentile believers upon the arrival of some influential Jews from Jerusalem. Paul soundly rebukes Peter for this. By doing what he did, Peter was denying five major doctrines.
  - The unity of the church (2:14)
  - Justification by faith alone (2:15-16)
  - Freedom from the Law (2:17-18)
  - The all-sufficiency of the indwelling Christ (2:19-20)
  - The grace of God (2:21)
- Peter's immediate reaction to this rebuke is not recorded. He very obviously did repent and bore Paul no ill will for it (see 2 Pet. 3:15).

>   B. The reason involved *(Read Gal. 2:12-13)*
>   C. The rationale involved *(Read Gal. 2:14)*
> **V. Justification by Faith: The Clarification (Gal. 2:15-19)**
> **VI. Justification by Faith: The Transformation (Gal. 2:20-21)**
> **VII. Justification by Faith: The Argumentation (Gal. 3:1-4:20)** — In chapters 3 and 4 Paul offers a series of arguments that prove the sufficiency of justification by faith alone.
>   A. The argument from their own experience (Gal. 3:1-2; 4:12-20).
>   1. He reminds them how they first received the message of justification (Gal. 3:1-5) — *"You foolish Galatians, who has bewitched you, before whose eyes Jesus Christ was publicly portrayed as crucified? This is the only thing I want to find out from you: Did you receive the Spirit by the works of the Law, or by hearing with faith? Are you so foolish? Having begun by the Spirit, are you now being perfected by the flesh? Did you suffer so many things in vain—if indeed it was in vain? Does He then who provides you with the Spirit and works miracles among you, do it by the works of the Law, or by the hearing with faith?"* (Gal. 3:1-5, NASB).

✲ 3:5 Warren Wiersbe writes: "The illustration of human birth is appropriate here. Two human parents are required for a child to be conceived and born, and two spiritual parents are required for a child to be born into God's family: the Spirit of God and the Word of God (James 3:1-8; 1 Pet. 1:22-25). When a normal child is born, he has all that he needs for life; nothing need be added. When the child of God is born into God's family, he has all that he needs spiritually; nothing need be added! All that is necessary is that the child have food, exercise, and cleansing that he might grow into maturity. It would be strange if the parents had to take the child to the doctor at one month to receive ears, at two months to receive toes, and so on" (*Be Free*, p. 57).

> 2. He reminds them how they first received the messenger of justification (Gal. 4:12-20)—"*But you know that it was because of a bodily illness that I preached the gospel to you the first time; and that which was a trial to you in my bodily condition you did not despise or loathe, but you received me as an angel of God as Christ Jesus Himself. Where then is that sense of blessing you had? For I bear you witness, that if possible, you would have plucked out your eyes and given them to me. Have I therefore become your enemy by telling you the truth?*" (Gal. 4:13-16, NASB).
> B. The argument from the life of Abraham (Gal. 3:6-9)
> C. The argument from the Law (Gal. 3:10-4:11)
>   1. The Law and sinners (Gal. 3:10-12)

★ **3:11**
- God not only pardons sinners by faith, but then preserves them by faith: "*The just shall live by faith*" (3:11). This all-important statement is taken from the Old Testament book of Habakkuk (2:4) and is used three times in the New Testament. (See Rom. 1:17 and Heb. 10:38.)
- The New Testament author of the book of James had already written: "*For whosoever shall keep the whole law, and yet offend in one point, he is guilty of all*" (James 2:10). Thus the Old Testament Law may be likened to a long chain. To break this chain, a person need only snap a single link, and the entire chain is broken.

>   2. The Law and the promise (Gal. 3:15-26)
>   a. The law cannot change the promise (Gal. 3:15-18)
>   b. The Law is inferior to the promise (Gal. 3:19-20)—His argument here is that God used a mediator (angels) in giving the law, but gave the promise of faith personally to Abraham.
>   c. The Law is not contrary to the promise (Gal. 3:21-26)
>   3. The Law and Israel
>   a. It was given to Israel 430 years after the promise (Gal. 3:17).

★ **3:17** Warren Wiersbe writes: "The 430 years of verse 16 has puzzled Bible students for many years. From Abraham's call (Gen. 12) to Jacob's arrival in Egypt (Gen. 46) is 215 years. This may be computed as follows:
- Abraham was 75 years old when God called him and 100 years when Isaac was born (Gen. 12:4; 21:5). This gives us 25 years.
- Isaac was 60 when Jacob was born (Gen. 25:26).
- Jacob was 130 years old when he arrived in Egypt (Gen. 47:9). Thus, 25 + 60 + 130 = 215 years.
- But Moses tells us that Israel sojourned in Egypt 430 years (Exod. 12:40); so the total number of the law is 645 years, not 430.
- The length of stay in Egypt is recorded also in Genesis 15:13 and Acts 7:6, where the round number of 400 years is used. Several solutions have been offered to this puzzle, but perhaps the most satisfying is this: Paul is counting from the time Jacob went into Egypt, when God appeared to him and reaffirmed the Covenant (Gen. 46:1-4). The 430 years is the time from God's confirmation of His promise to Jacob until the giving of the law at Sinai" (*Be Free*, pp. 77-78.)

>   b. It was an insertion, given because of sin (Gal. 3:19).
>   c. It was ordained by angels (Gal. 3:19).

★ **3:19** Note the following verses which attest to this fact of angelic activity on Mount Sinai at the giving of the Law. "*The Lord came from Sinai ... and he came with ten thousands of saints. From his right hand went a fiery law for them*" (Deut. 33:2). "*The chariots of God are twenty thousand, even thousands of angels; the Lord is among them, as in Sinai, in the holy place*" (Psa. 68:17). "*Who [sinful Israel] have received the law by the disposition of angels, and have not kept it?*" (Acts 7:53). "*For the word spoken by angels [the law] was stedfast*" (Heb. 2:2).

> d. It thus acted as a divine custodian *(Read Gal. 3:23-24)*

★ **3:24** It thus acted as Israel's "schoolmaster" (child-discipliner, from the Greek word *paidagogos*). *"Wherefore the law was our schoolmaster to bring us unto Christ"* (3:24). J. Vernon McGee writes: "The key word here is schoolmaster and has nothing to do with a school teacher in a present-day context. The term designated a slave or servant in a Roman home who had charge of any child born in the home. He fed, dressed, bathed, blew the nose of and paddled, the son born in the home. When the little fellow reached school age, he took him by the hand and led him to school. This is where he got the name of *paidagogos* (child leader). The law took mankind by the hand, led him to the cross of Christ and said, 'Little man, you need a Saviour.' The law turns us over to Christ. We are under Christ now and not under the law" (*Through the Bible*, p. 110).

> 4. The Law and Christ
> a. He has redeemed us from its curse *(Read Gal. 3:13)*

★ **3:13** McGee observes: "This was a very strange law since the method of capital punishment under the law was by stoning. But if the crime was aggravated and atrocious, the body of the criminal was taken after death and hung up to display the seriousness of the crime" (*Through the Bible*, p. 110).

> b. He did this at God's appointed time through a human body *(Read Gal. 4:4-5)*

★ **4:5** Paul here, of course, does not mean that the Law makes us children of God, while Christ makes us sons of God. But he does contrast the differences between a child and a son under the Roman legal system of the day.
- Childhood refers to my condition in God's family, while adoption speaks of my position.
- Through regeneration one enters into the family; but by adoption he enjoys the family.
- The circumstances leading to childhood are private, while those dealing with adoption are public.
- A child is under guardians, while an adopted adult has full liberty.

> c. He thus guaranteed our full adoption as sons of God (Gal. 4:1-7)—*"And because ye are sons, God hath sent forth the Spirit of his Son into your hearts, crying, Abba, Father. Wherefore thou art no more a servant, but a son; and if a son, then an heir of God through Christ"* (Gal. 4:6-7).

★ **4:7** Paul contrasts the differences between a son and a servant (4:7).
- A servant retains his old nature, while a son enjoys that of his father.
- A servant has a master, while a son has a father.
- A servant obeys out of law and fear, but a son out of liberty and love.
- A servant is promised no inheritance, while a son can legally expect to inherit all things.

> 5. The Law and believers *(Read Gal. 3:25-29)*

★ **3:29** There were three great divisions in the Roman world:
- Racial and religious—Jew and Greek
- Social and class—bond and free
- Man's world and woman's world—But in Christ there is no spiritual distinction whatsoever.

> 6. The Law and the Galatians (Gal. 4:8-20)
> a. Paul rebukes them for their faithlessness *(Read Gal. 4:8-10)*

★ **4:10** After being released from spiritual slavery, why did they now desire to put back on their chains of bondage again (4:9-10)? They were doing exactly this by observing days (Jewish holy days such as weekly sabbaths and special feast days), months (celebrations of new moons which began each month of the Jewish lunar calendar), times (seasons of week-long festivals such as the feast of tabernacles, unleavened bread, etc.), and years (Sabbatical and Jubilee years).

> b. Paul reminds them of his faithfulness *(Read Gal. 4:11-16, 19)*

★ **4:19**
- Where was that happy spirit once enjoyed between the apostle and the Galatians (4:11-15)? He reminds them of their past affection for him, which had made them willing (if it were possible) to pluck out their eyes for him. Some connect this statement in 4:15 with that in 2 Corinthians 12:7 concerning Paul's thorn in the flesh.
- Why had they thus turned from him, viewing him, their real spiritual mother, as their enemy, and attached themselves to false legalizing teachers (4:16-20)? In perhaps no other single verse does the apostle display more of his agony and aspiration for all his converts than he does here in *4:19: "My little children, of whom I travail in birth again until Christ be formed in you."*

VIII. Justification by Faith: The Allegorization (Gal. 4:21-31)—In these verses Paul uses Hagar and Sarah, two Old Testament women, to allegorize the Law of Moses and the grace of God.
  A. Hagar (an allegory of the Law)
   1. She was a bondwoman.
   2. Her marriage to Abraham was fleshly directed.
   3. Her son, Ishmael, was naturally born.
   4. This son persecuted Abraham's second son, Isaac.
   5. Her child was not considered as Abraham's rightful heir.
   6. Hagar represented the Mount Sinai Covenant as she bore a slave child (Israel would also be slaves for awhile).
   7. She corresponded to earthly Jerusalem (in Paul's day) due to her slavery (Jerusalem was occupied by the Romans at that time).
  B. Sarah (an allegory of grace)
   1. She was a freewoman.
   2. Her marriage to Abraham was spirit-directed.
   3. Her son Isaac was supernaturally born.
   4. This son was persecuted by Ishmael.
   5. Her child was considered as Abraham's rightful heir.
   6. Sarah represented the New Covenant, as she bore a free son.
   7. She corresponded to heavenly Jerusalem.

IX. Justification by Faith: The Application (Gal. 5:1-15)
  A. Assuring us of the freedom of the Son (Gal. 5:1-15)
   1. Keeping us from the legalism of the Jews (Gal. 5:1-12)—*"Stand fast therefore in the liberty wherewith Christ hath made us free, and be not entangled again with the yoke of bondage. Behold, I Paul say unto you, that if ye be circumcised, Christ shall profit you nothing. For I testify again to every man that is circumcised, that he is a debtor to do the whole law. Christ is become of no effect unto you, whosoever of you are justified by the law; ye are fallen from grace"* (Gal. 5:1-4).

★ **5:4** What does it mean to refuse this glorious liberty in Christ?
- It means to trade the blessed yoke of Christ for the burdensome yoke of the Law (5:1). Note the contrast between these two yokes.

LESSON 28: THE BOOK OF GALATIANS

- The yoke of Christ— *"Come unto me, all ye that labour and are heavy laden, and I will give you rest. Take my yoke upon you, and learn of me; for I am meek and lowly in heart: and ye shall find rest unto your souls. For my yoke is easy, and my burden is light" (Matt. 11:28-30).*
- The yoke of the Law— *"Now therefore why tempt ye God, to put a yoke upon the neck of the disciples, which neither our fathers nor we were able to bear?" (Acts 15:10).*

■ It means to become debtor to the entire Mosaic Law (3:3; see also Deut. 27:26). Warren Wiersbe writes: "Imagine a motorist driving down a city street and either deliberately or unconsciously driving through a red light. He is pulled over by a policeman who asks to see his driver's license. Immediately the driver begins to defend himself. 'Officer, I know I ran that red light—but I have never robbed anybody. I've never committed adultery. I've never cheated on my income tax!' The policeman smiles as he writes out the ticket, because he knows that no amount of obedience can make up for one act of disobedience. It is one law, the same law that protects the obedient man and punishes the offender. To boast about keeping part of the law while at the same time breaking another part is to confess that I am worthy of punishment" (*Be Free*, pp. 118-119).

■ It means to fall from grace (5:4). This, of course, does not mean they had lost their salvation, for in the book of Galatians Paul refers to his readers as:
- Brethren (nine times; see 1:2, 11; 3:15; 4:12, 31; 5:11, 13; 6:1, 18)
- Children of God (3:26)
- Sons of God (4:6)
- Heirs of the promise (3:29)—The Greek word here translated "fallen" is *ekpipto*, and is found in Acts 27:17,26, 29, 32, where it refers to a ship not under control. This is the meaning here in Galatians. To put oneself back under the Law means to deny the sweet and sure control of God's grace. Paul has already stated that it is tragically possible to frustrate (literally, to nullify, to make of none effect) the grace of God. (See Gal. 2:21.)

2. Keeping us from the license of the Libertines (Gal. 5:13)

★ **5:13** Paul now warns against the opposite of legalism, which is lawlessness.
■ In Romans 7 (as here in Gal. 5) Paul connects the commandments of God with the corruption of the flesh. This he does by pointing out the following: The law in itself is good (Rom. 7:7). The trouble came when sin used the Law to make him feel guilty by arousing all kinds of evil and forbidden desires within him (7:8). He concludes by saying: *"For I was alive without the law once: but when the commandment came, sin revived, and I died. And the commandment, which was ordained to life, I found to be unto death" (Rom. 7:9-10).*
■ Here now in Galatians 5 he lists some 17 works of the flesh, resulting from an illegal use of the Law. These are:
- Adultery (sexual sins between married people)
- Fornication (sexual sins between unmarried people)
- Uncleanness (impurity)
- Lasciviousness (sensuality)
- Idolatry (worship of idols)
- Witchcraft (Greek is *pharmakeia*, which can refer to sorcery and/or drugs)
- Hatred (enmity)
- Variances (Greek is *eris*, referring to the god of strife)
- Emulations (rivalry, jealousy)
- Wrath (temper, outburst of anger)
- Strife (factions, cliques)
- Seditions (divisions, dissensions)
- Heresies (sects)
- Envyings (coveting)
- Murders (unlawful killing)

- Drunkenness (rendered helpless by strong drink)
- Revelings (carousings, orgies)

> 3. Keeping us in the love of the Lord *(Read Gal. 5:14)*
> B. Assuring us the fruit of the Spirit (Gal. 5:15-23)
>   1. As demonstrated by our fruitbearing (Gal. 5:16-26)
>   a. Negative: The fruit of the flesh *(Read Gal. 4:19-21)*
>   b. Positive: The fruit of the Spirit *(Read Gal. 5:22-23)*

✴ 5:23
- Warren Wiersbe writes: "The contrast between works and fruit is important. A machine in a factory works, and turns out a product, but it could never manufacture fruit. Fruit must grow out of life, and in the case of the believer, it is the life of the Spirit. When you think of 'works' you think of effort, labor, strain, and toil; when you think of 'fruit' you think of beauty, quietness, the unfolding of life. The flesh produces 'dead works' (Heb. 9:14), but the Spirit produces living fruit. ... the New Testament speaks of several kinds of fruit: people won to Christ (Rom. 1:13), holy living (Rom. 6:22), gifts brought to God (Rom. 15:16-18), good works (Col. 1:10), and praise (Heb. 13:15). The fruit of the Spirit listed in our passage has to do with character" (*Be Free*, pp. 133-134).
- Note now the various aspects of this Spirit-produced fruit.
  - Love (divine concern for others)
  - Joy (inward peace and sufficiency)
  - Peace (a confidence and quietness of the soul)
  - Longsuffering (patience, endurance without quitting)
  - Gentleness (kindness)
  - Goodness (love in action)
  - Faith (dependability)
  - Meekness (subdued strength)
  - Temperance (self-control)

> 2. As demonstrated by our burden-bearing *(Read Gal. 6:1-6)*
> 3. As demonstrated by our seed-bearing *(Read Gal. 6:7-10)*
> 4. As demonstrated by our brand-bearing *(Gal. 6:14-17)*

✴ 6:17 J. Sidlow Baxter writes: "This Galatian epistle was written to groups of believers scattered through a rural area, in which most of the people were agricultural workers of one sort or another. In keeping with the mentality and circumstances of the Galatians, Paul uses language and metaphors which are specially appropriate to them. There were four kinds of 'bearing' with which the Galatians were familiar above all else. These were: fruit-bearing, burden-bearing, seed-bearing, and brand-bearing (for as many of the agricultural labourers were slaves, they were branded to indicate whose property they were). See now how Paul makes use of these things in expounding the true liberty of the Spirit:
- Fruit-bearing: *'The fruit of the Spirit is love, joy, peace, longsuffering,'* etc. (5:22-23).
- Burden-bearing: *'Bear ye one another's burdens and so fulfill the law of Christ'* (6:2).
- Seed-bearing: *'Whatsoever a man soweth,'* etc. (6:7). 'Let us not be weary in well doing, for ... we shall reap' (6:9).
- Brand-bearing: *'I bear in my body the marks* [or brands] *of the Lord Jesus'* (6:17). There were five classes of person who were branded, i.e, slaves (as a mark of ownership), soldiers (as a mark of allegiance), devotees (as a mark of consecration), criminals (as a mark of exposure), and the abhorred (as a mark of reproach). The marks of the Lord Jesus in the body of Paul were all these five in one!" (*Explore the Book*, Vol. 6, pp. 153-154, 158).

(See 2 Cor. 11:23-28 for a history of some of these marks.)

LESSON 29

INTRODUCTION TO EPHESIANS

SIX STRIKING SYMBOLS OF THE CHRISTIAN CHURCH

- A. The church is likened to:
  1. A body (Eph. 1)
  2. A temple (Eph. 2)
  3. A mystery (Eph. 3)
  4. A new man (Eph. 4)
  5. A bride (Eph. 5)
  6. A soldier (Eph. 6)
- B. This is what Ephesians is all about. Ephesians and Colossians have some similarities.
  1. Both were written by the same author—Paul.
  2. Both were written during the same period of time.
  3. Both are prison epistles.
  4. Ephesians emphasizes the body of Christ, which is the church.
  5. Colossians emphasizes the head of that body, which is Christ himself.
- C. Note J. Vernon McGee's introduction to this book of Ephesians: "A quartet of men left Rome in the year A.D. 62, bound for the province of Asia, which was located in what is currently designated as Asia Minor."
  This quartet of men and their respective places of abode can be identified as:
  1. Epaphroditus from Philippi (Phil. 4:18) had the epistle to the Philippians.
  2. Tychicus from Ephesus (Eph. 6:21) had the epistle to the Ephesians.
  3. Epaphras from Colosse (Col. 4:12) had the epistle to the Colossians.
  4. Onesimus, a slave from Colosse (Philem. 10) had the epistle to Philemon (who was his master).
- D. Ephesus is the only New Testament church to receive a letter from more than one Bible writer. John the apostle also had a message for them (Rev. 2:1-7).
- E. This church had more famous preachers than did any other church. This would include men such as Paul, Apollos, John, and Timothy.
- F. Ephesians is the Joshua book of the New Testament.
- G. It has been called "Paul's third heaven epistle." It has been referred to as the Alps of the New Testament, the Mount Whitney of the High Sierras of all Scripture.
- H. In no other epistle is our preconversion position in the world and postconversion in Christ so vividly described as in this book.
  1. Our preconversion position (2:1-3, 11-13)
  2. Our postconversion position (1:3-14; 2:4-10,14-22)
- I. Ephesians provides the most beautiful New Testament passages describing Christ's relationship to and love for his church. (See 5:22-33.)
- J. The Ephesian church was founded by Paul during his second missionary trip.
- K. After spending 18 months in Corinth (Acts 18:11), he visited Ephesus with Aquila and Priscilla (Acts 18:18).

L. Paul stayed there for only a short time, but promised to return (Acts 18:19-21).
M. Aquila and Priscilla remained in Ephesus where God led them to instruct a powerful Bible preacher named Apollos in the details of the Word of God (Acts 18:24-26).
N. Paul returned during his third missionary trip and stayed three years (Acts 19:8-10; 20:31).
O. He is later visited by the Ephesian elders during a layover at Miletus, en route to Jerusalem (Acts 20:16-38).
P. It is thought that this epistle may be the one referred to by Paul in Colossians 4:16.
Q. It gives the most detailed description and presentation of the believer as a soldier of Jesus (6:11-17).
R. Two of Paul's greatest prayers for the church are found in this book (1:15-18; 3:14-21).
S. It includes the last of three New Testament passages speaking of spiritual gifts (4:11). Compare with Romans 12:3-8; 1 Corinthians 12:1-31.
T. According to John's letter (Rev. 2:1-7), this church:
   1. Worked hard and possessed patience
   2. Had high church standards
   3. Hated the deeds of the licentious Nicolaitanes
   4. Had left their first love
   5. Needed to repent and return to Christ
U. Ephesians is the 12th longest New Testament book, and 41st longest biblical book, with six chapters, 155 verses, and 3,039 words. There are quotations or allusions from 13 Old Testament books in Ephesians.
V. Great passages would include:
   1. 1:17-23
   2. 2:1-10
   3. 2:19-22
   4. 3:17-21
   5. 4:1-6
   6. 5:16-33
   7. 6:10-17

OVERVIEW OF THE BOOK OF EPHESIANS

I. **The Church is likened to a Body**
   A. The creation of this body
      1. It was wrought and planned by the Father
      2. It was bought and purchased by the Son
      3. It was taught and preserved by the Spirit
   B. The consecration of this body
      1. Paul prays that the church may know the God of glory
      2. Paul prays that the church may know the glory of God
         a. As it is seen in his saints
         b. As it is seen in his Son
         c. As it is seen in his church

II. **The Church is likened to a Temple**
   A. What we once were
      1. Dead in sin
      2. Influenced by Satan
      3. Controlled by lust
      4. Separated from Christ
      5. Excluded from the promises
      6. Hopeless in the world
   B. What God did
      1. He loved us
      2. He liberated us
   C. Why God did it
   D. How God did it
      1. By the grace of God
      2. By the blood of Christ
   E. What we now are
      1. We are products of God's workmanship
      2. We are partners with Israel in God's Son
      3. We are parts of God's temple

III. **The Church is likened to a Mystery**
   A. The time element of his mystery
      1. Not known in the Old Testament
      2. Make known in the New Testament
   B. The nature of this mystery
   C. The recipient of this mystery
      1. Paul, the man
      2. Paul, the meek

        3. Paul, the messenger
    D. The basis of this mystery
    E. The reasons for this mystery
        1. That God's wisdom might be experienced by the church
        2. That God's wisdom might be illustrated to the angels
    F. The results of this mystery
        1. Believers have access to the throne of God
        2. Believers are strengthened by the Spirit of God
        3. Believers can know the love of God
        4. Believers can request the power of God
        5. Believers can display the glory of God

IV. The Church is likened to a New Man
    A. The position of the new man
        1. The unity of his new position—Seven great stabilizers
        2. The unifier of his new position—One great Savior
    B. The disposition of the new man
        1. His walk
        2. His words
        3. His works

V. The Church is likened to a Bride
    A. The bride: Her duties as the church
        1. To be separated
        2. To be circumspect
        3. To be Spirit-filled
        4. To be single minded
        5. To be submissive
    B. The bridegroom: His devotion to the church
        1. This devotion, as illustrated by marriage
        2. This devotion, as demonstrated on the cross
        3. This devotion, as consummated by the Rapture

VI. The Church is likened to a Soldier
    A. Boot camp training
        1. Example of children and parents
        2. Example of servants and master
    B. Front line fighting
        1. Our enemy—The devil
        2. Our endeavors—The game plan
        3. Our equipment—The armor of God
        4. Our examples—Paul and Tychius

THE BOOK OF EPHESIANS

I. The Church Is Likened to a Body (Eph. 1) — *"Which is his body, the fulness of him that filleth all in all" (Eph. 1:23).*
  A. The creation of this body (Eph. 1:1-14)
    1. It was wrought and planned by the Father *(Read Eph. 1:1-6)*

✻ 1:3
- Paul writes to those "at Ephesus, and to the faithful in Christ Jesus." Dr. J. Vernon McGee has written: "The little preposition in (en), when it precedes Christ, is the most important word of this epistle. Theologians have amassed an array of imposing theological words to define our salvation—such as redemption, atonement, justification, reconciliation, propitiation, and the vicarious substitutionary sacrifice of Christ. All of these are fine, and each presents one aspect of the many facets of our salvation. None, however, seems entirely adequate. What does it mean to be saved? This is a question which is answered in utmost simplicity by the Bible term, 'in Christ.' To be saved means to be in Christ. A sinner who has trusted Christ for his salvation has as much right in heaven as has Christ—or he has no right there at all, for he is in Christ!" (*Exploring Through Ephesians*, p.11).
- Paul writes: *"Blessed be the God and Father of our Lord Jesus Christ" (see v. 3).* The word "blessed" is *eulogetos*, and means "to speak well of, to praise, to celebrate." This adjective is used only of God. (See Mark 14:61; Luke 1:68; Rom.1:25; 9:5; 2 Cor.1:3;11:31; Eph. 1:3; 1 Pet. 1:3.) When the word "blessed" is used of a person, the Greek term is *makarios*, and means "to pronounce happy." (See Matt. 5:3-11.) Thus, God desires for his children to bless him by saying nice things about him. Furthermore, God hears and records these things in his book of remembrance. (See Mal. 3:16.) We note also that Paul carefully distinguishes the difference between Christ's relationship to the Father and our relationship to the Father. See also John 20:17 where Jesus does the same thing. (See also John 1:14, 18; 3:16, 18; 1 John 4:9; Rev. 1:5.)

>   a. He elected us.
>   (1) The time involved— *"Before the foundation of the world" (Eph. 1:4).*
>   (2) The purpose involved— *"That we should be holy and without blame before him" (Eph. 1:4).*
>   b. He predestinated us.
>   (1) The method—Through Jesus Christ
>   (2) The basis— *"According to the good pleasure of his will" (Eph. 1:5).*
>   (3) The reason— *"To the praise of the glory of his grace" (Eph. 1:6).*
>   2. It was bought and purchased by the Son (Eph. 1:7-12).
>   a. Redeemed by his blood— *"In whom we have redemption through his blood, the forgiveness of sins, according to the riches of his grace" (Eph. 1:7).*
>   b. Gathered in his name— *"That in the dispensation of the fulness of times he might gather together in one all things in Christ, both which are in heaven, and which are on earth; even in him" (Eph. 1:10).*

✻ 1:10
- Special note: The word translated *dispensation* here, *oikonomia*, is employed three times by the Greek text of Ephesians. The apostle writes concerning:
  - The dispensation of the fullness of time (1:10)
  - The dispensation of the grace of God (3:2)

LESSON 29: THE BOOK OF EPHESIANS

- The dispensation (translated by the word "fellowship" in the King James Version) of the mystery (3:9)
■ It may prove helpful at this point to briefly define the concept of dispensationalism as developed by Paul.
■ The Greek word *oikonomia* is found some 19 times in the New Testament. It is translated by the following English words:
  - Steward (Luke 12:42;16:11;1 Cor. 4:1-2; Titus 1:7; 1 Pet. 4:10)
  - Stewardship (Luke 16:2-4)
  - Dispensation (1 Cor. 9:17; Eph. 1:10; 3:2; Col. 1.25)
  - Fellowship (Eph. 3:9)
  - Edifying (1 Tim. 1:4)
■ Note the following definitions of a dispensation: "It is a period of time during which man is tested in respect of obedience to some specific revelation of the will of God" (from the *Scofield Bible*). Thus the central idea in the word dispensation is that of managing or administering the affairs of a household. "As far as the use of the word in Scripture is concerned, a dispensation may be defined as a stewardship, administration, oversight or management of others' property. As we have seen, this involves responsibility, accountability, and faithfulness on the part of the steward ... A dispensation is primarily a stewardship arrangement and not a period of time (though obviously the arrangement will exist during a period of time. .. a dispensation is basically the arrangement involved, not the time involved; and a proper definition will take this into account). A concise definition of a dispensation is this: 'A dispensation is a distinguishable economy in the outworking of God's purpose'" (*Dispensationalism Today*, pp. 25, 29, 31.)
■ To summarize: Dispensationalism views the world as a household run by God. In this household world, God is dispensing or administering its affairs according to his own will and in various stages of revelation in the process of time. These various stages mark off the distinguishably different economies in the outworking of his total purpose, and these economies are the dispensations.

> c. Predestinated for his glory— "*In whom also we have obtained an inheritance, being predestinated according to the purpose of him who worketh all things after the counsel of his own will: That we should be to the praise of his glory, who first trusted in Christ*" (Eph. 1:11-12).
> 3. It was taught and preserved by the Spirit (Eph. 1:13-14).
>   a. The *what* of the matter— "*In whom ye also trusted, after that ye heard the word of truth, the gospel of your salvation: in whom also after that ye believed, ye were sealed with that holy Spirit of promise*" (Eph. 1:13).

★ **1:13** He seals us. This indicates the following:
■ Ownership (1 Cor. 6:19-20; 2 Tim. 2:19)
■ Security (Eph. 4:30)
■ Completed transaction (Jer. 32:9-10; John 17:4; 19:30)

> b. The *why* of the matter— "*Which is the earnest of our inheritance until the redemption of the purchased possession, unto the praise of his glory*" (Eph. 1:14).

★ **1:14** He becomes our earnest. An earnest is something of value (like money) given as a down payment for a purchased possession. This all happens at the time of salvation. Note: He is called "that holy Spirit of promise" (1:13) because Jesus himself has promised he would come. (See John 14:16-17;16:7,13; Acts 1:4-5.) Verse 14 is the third and final doxology in these first few verses. (See verses 6,12,14.)

> B. The consecration of this body (Eph. 1:15-23)
>   1. Paul prays that the church may know the God of glory— "*That the God of our Lord Jesus Christ, the Father of glory, may give unto you the spirit of wisdom and revelation in the knowledge of him*" (Eph. 1:17).
>   2. Paul prays that the church may know the glory of God.

> a. As it is seen in his saints *(Read Eph. 1:18-19)*
> b. As it is seen in his Son *(Read Eph. 1:20-21)*
> c. As it is seen in his church *(Read Eph. 1:22-23)*

✷ **1:23** Thus, the believer is fighting from a victory and not for a victory. The divine "cards" have already been stacked; we have already won. (See also Matt. 28:18; Psa. 8:6; 110:1; 1 Cor. 15:25-26.)

> **II. The Church Is Likened to a Temple**—"*In whom all the building fitly framed together groweth unto an holy temple in the Lord*" (Eph. 2:21).
>   A. What we once were (Eph. 2:1-3, 11-12)
>   1. Dead in sin (Eph. 2:1)
>   2. Influenced by Satan *(Read Eph. 2:2)*
>   3. Controlled by lust (Eph. 2:3)
>   4. Separated from Christ (Eph. 2:12)
>   5. Excluded from the promises (Eph. 2:12)
>   6. Hopeless in the world (Eph. 2:12)
>   B. What God did (Eph. 2:4-6, 18)
>   1. He loved us *(Read Eph. 2:4)*
>   2. He liberated us *(Read Eph. 2:5-6)*
>   C. Why God did it *(Read Eph. 2:7)*
>   D. How God did it (Eph. 2:8-9, 13)
>   1. By the grace of God *(Read Eph. 2:8-9)*
>   2. By the blood of Christ *(Read Eph. 2:13)*
>   E. What we now are (Eph. 2:10, 14-22)
>   1. We are products of God's workmanship *(Read Eph. 2:10)*

✷ **2:10** We are the workmanship of God. The Greek word for workmanship (2:10) is *poema*, from whence our English word "poem" comes. God has two treasured poems in this universe:
- The poem of creation (see Rom. 1:20; Rev. 4:11)
- The poem of salvation (see Eph. 2:10; Rev. 5:9) Thus, we are saved to be sure. This salvation is apart from works (2:8-9) but unto works (2:10).

>   2. We are partners with Israel in God's Son (Eph. 2:14-18)—"*For He Himself is our peace, who made both groups into one, and broke down the barrier of the dividing wall, by abolishing in His flesh the enmity, which is the Law of Commandments contained in ordinances, that in Himself He might make the two into one new man, thus establishing peace*" (Eph. 2:14-15, NASB).

✷ **2:16** We are (as Gentiles) united with Israel in Christ, that he might reconcile both unto God in one body (2:16). Chrysostom once wrote: "He does not mean that He has elevated us to that high dignity of theirs, but He has raised both of us and them to one still higher. I will give you an illustration. Let us imagine that there are two statues, one of silver and other of lead, and then that both shall be melted down, and the two shall come out gold. So thus He has made the two one."

>   3. We are parts of God's temple *(Read Eph. 2:19-22)*
> **III. The Church Is Likened to a Mystery (Eph. 3)**—"*For this cause I Paul, the prisoner of Jesus Christ for you Gentiles, If ye have heard of the dispensation of the grace of God which is given me to you-ward: how that by revelation he made known unto me the mystery; (as I wrote afore in few words, whereby, when ye read, ye may understand my knowledge in the mystery of Christ)*" (Eph. 3:1-4).

LESSON 29: THE BOOK OF EPHESIANS

    A. The time element of this mystery
        1. Not known in the Old Testament *(Read Eph. 3:5)*
        2. Made known in the New Testament *(Read Eph. 3:5b)*
    B. The nature of this mystery *(Read Eph. 3:6)*

★ **3:6** In the Old Testament, Gentile salvation was known, but not without becoming Jews by proselytization (see Isa. 11:10; 42:6; 60:3; Zech. 2:11; Mal. 1:11). (Compare these Old Testament verses with Eph. 3:5-6; Rom. 16:25; Col. 1:26.)

    C. The recipient of this mystery (Eph. 3:1-4, 7-9)
        1. Paul, the man *(Read Eph. 3:3)*
        2. Paul, the meek *(Read Eph. 3:8)*
        3. Paul, the messenger *(Read Eph. 3:9)*
    D. The basis of this mystery *(Read Eph. 3:11)*
    E. The reasons for this mystery (Eph. 3:10)
        1. That God's wisdom might be experienced by the church—*"In order that the manifold wisdom of God might now be made known through the church"* (Eph. 3:10, NASB).
        2. That God's wisdom might be illustrated to the angels—*"To the rulers and authorities in the heavenly places"* (Eph. 3:10, NASB).

★ **3:10** Thus this world becomes a university wherein both demons and angels might study the grace of God. (See also Eph. 1:21; 6:12; Col. 1:16; 2:15; 1 Pet. 1:12.)

    F. The results of this mystery
        1. Believers have access to the throne of God *(Read Eph. 3:12)*
        2. Believers are strengthened by the Spirit of God *(Read Eph. 3:14, 16)*
        3. Believers can know the love of God *(Read Eph. 3:17-19)*

★ **3:19** There are two great prayers in this epistle.
- In 1:15-23, Paul prays for the eyes of the believers: *"That ... the eyes of your understanding being enlightened"* (1:18). Here he wanted them to know the tremendous power of God.
- In 3:14-21, Paul prays for the hearts of the believers: *"That Christ may dwell in your hearts"* (3:17). Here he wanted them to know the tender love of Christ.

        4. Believers can request the power of God *(Read Eph. 3:20)*
        5. Believers can display the glory of God *(Read Eph. 3:21)*
IV. The Church Is Likened to a New Man (Eph. 4:13-24)— *"Till we all come in the unity of the faith, and of the knowledge of the Son of God, unto a perfect man, unto the measure of the stature of the fulness of Christ: and that ye put on the new man, which after God is created in righteousness and true holiness"* (Eph. 4:13, 24).
    A. The position of the new man
        1. The unity of his new position-Seven great stabilizers (Eph. 4:4-6)
            a. One body

★ One body (Christ's body—the church). (See I Cor. 12:12, 27; Eph. 5:30.)

            b. One spirit

★ One Spirit (the Holy Spirit). (See I Cor. 12:4.)

> c. One hope

★ One hope—The Scriptures declare this hope to be:
- Good (2 Thess. 2:16)
- Better (Heb. 7:19)
- Blessed (Titus 2:13)
- Glorious (Col. 1:27)
- Lively (1 Pet. 13)
- Firm (Heb. 3:6; 6:11)
- Eternal (Titus 3:7)

> d. One Lord

★ One Lord (the Savior) (1 Cor. 12:5)

> e. One faith

★ One faith (Jude 3; 2 Cor. 13:5; 1 Cor. 16:13; Gal. 1:23; Phil. 1:27; 1 Tim. 1:2; 4:1; 5:8; 2 Tim. 4:7: Titus 1:4)

> f. One baptism

★ One baptism (into Christ's body) (Rom. 6:3-4; 1 Cor. 12:13; Col. 2:9-12; Gal. 3:27-28; 1 Pet. 3:21)

> g. One God and Father
> 2. The unifier of his new position—One great Savior (Eph. 4:7-16)
>   a. His gifts to believers— *"But to each one of us grace has been given as Christ apportioned it. This is why it says: 'When he ascended on high, he led captives in his train and gave gifts to men.' (What does 'he ascended' mean except that he also descended to the lower, earthly regions? He who descended is the very one who ascended higher than all the heavens, in order to fill the whole universe.) It was he who gave some to be apostles, some to be prophets, some to be evangelists, and some to be pastors and teachers"* (Eph. 4:7-11, NIV).

★ **4:11** Dr. Homer Kent writes the following concerning these verses: "Paul first issues a statement that God has bestowed gifts to believers to enable them to accomplish the goal of walking in unity (4:7). The previous paragraph has emphasized the fact of unity by pointing to the oneness of believers in various respects. Now Paul shows that each believer is an individual participant and recipient of the divine graces which he needs. Each person's grace is in proportion to what Christ in His sovereign wisdom has freely given. Not all receive the same gifts, or the same number of gifts, or the same amount of any one gift. Christ dispenses as He deems best. The scriptural proof (4:8-10) cited for the above assertion is drawn from Psalm 68:18. 'When he ascended up on high, he led captivity captive, and gave gifts unto men.' The historical circumstances of the psalm are uncertain. It depicts a victorious and triumphant return, probably of David to Mount Zion. If the psalm was intended to be Messianic (as this usage in Ephesians certainly suggests), then David is regarded as typical of his greater Son whose passion victory was followed by the ascension. The chief points in the quotation which were significant to the author were the victorious ascent and the dispensing of gifts to men. Certain other features, however, are also of special interest. 'He led captivity captive' is translated 'he captured prisoners' (*Jerusalem Bible*), 'he took many captives with him' (*TEV*), and 'he led a host of captives' (*RSV*). Messianically interpreted, this usually referred to Christ's conquering of His enemies: Satan, sin, death, the curse. Others (a minority, but including many of the ancient Fathers) explain these 'captives' as friends, either the redeemed on earth, or Old Testament saints in hades (Heb., sheol). In support of this last interpretation, arguments such as the following are given:

- That which is led captive is taken to heaven. This is not true of Satan, sin, death, or the curse.
- The past tense (aorist) 'led captive' does not fit the regeneration of subsequent believers as well as some prior action.
- The interpretation that this refers to the descent of Christ to the realm of the dead at His death accords well with 1 Peter 3:19-20.
- It fits Matthew 27:50-53, where the visible release of some Old Testament saints from hades may imply the spiritual release of all such.
- This harmonizes with the apparent change in location of paradise, which in the New Testament era is stated as being above, and equated with heaven (2 Cor.12:2-4)" (*Ephesians, the Glory of the Church*, pp. 68-69).

> b. His goal for believers (Eph. 4:12-16)
>   (1) That we be equipped *(Read Eph. 4:12)*
>   (2) That we be unified *(Read Eph. 4:13,16)*
>   (3) That we be settled *(Read Eph. 4:14)*
> B. The disposition of the new man
>   1. His walk
>   a. Adopt the spiritual walk *(Read Eph. 4:1-3)*

★ **4:3**
- In lowliness (Phil 2:3; Matt. 11:29)
- In meekness (2 Cor. 10:1)
- In longsuffering (Gal. 5:22)
- In forebearing (Col. 3:13)
- In unity (John 17:21; 1 Cor. 12:13)

>   b. Avoid the sensual walk *(Read Eph. 4:17-19)*
>   2. His words *(Read Eph. 4:15, 25, 29, 31)*

★ Chrysostom wrote the following concerning 4:25: *"Let not the eye lie to the foot, nor the foot to the eye. If there be a deep pit and its mouth covered with reeds shall present to the eye the appearance of solid ground, will not the eye use the foot to ascertain whether it is hollow underneath, or whether it is firm and resists? Will the foot tell a lie and not the truth as it is? And what, again, if the eye were to spy a serpent or a wild beast, will it lie to the foot?"*

>   3. His works
>   a. Put off the old man *(Read Eph. 4:22)*
>   (1) Don't lose your temper *(Read Eph. 4:26)*

★ **4:26** D. L. Moody once remarked that he wouldn't give a dime for a Christian without a temper, but he also wouldn't give a nickel for a believer who couldn't control that temper. There is, of course, righteous anger (see Mark 3:5). However, Satan loves to use uncontrolled anger.

>   (2) Don't give place to the devil *(Read Eph. 4:27)*
>   (3) Don't steal *(Read Eph. 4:28)*

★ **4:28** Dr. Homer Kent observes: "Paul's actual expression is 'the one stealing.' It is a present participle and can hardly be relegated to the one who 'stole' before he was converted. Rather, it seems to depict the continuing practice of pilfering that still characterized some of these Christians. We must recognize that many of the early Christians came from the ranks of slaves, where pilfering was a way of life. Conversion does not remove all such habits instantaneously, especially in matters where no great conscience has developed.

"Furthermore, let us recognize that stealing in the broad sense is not unknown among present day Christians. Deans of students in any Christian school can elaborate on this problem at some length. Income tax returns, insurance claims, and examinations in school are only a few examples of situations where Christians are many times less than honest. The scriptural injunction is not merely that stealing cease, nor even that restitution be made. The Christian principle is laid down that each man should toil honestly at that which is good, not merely to meet his own needs and thus avoid temptation to thievery, but to be able to amass a surplus to help others in need. This is in stark contrast to the prevalent attitude which assumes that one is entitled to the supply of needs, whether or not he wishes to work. By working diligently, the individual removes some of the temptation to steal, and by assisting others in need, he helps remove the temptation from them also" (*Ephesians, the Glory of the Church*, p. 83).

> (4) Don't grieve the Holy Spirit *(Read Eph. 4:30)*
>   b. Put on the new man *(Read Eph. 4:23-25, 29, 31-32)*
> **V. The Church Is Likened to a Bride (Eph. 5)** — *"For the husband is the head of the wife, even as Christ is the head of the church: and he is the saviour of the body" (Eph. 5:23).*
>   A. The bride: Her duties as the church (Eph. 5:1-23)
>   1. To be separated *(Eph. 5:1-13)*
>   a. To the Lord *(Read Eph. 5:1-2, 8-10)*
>   b. From the world *(Read Eph. 5:3-7, 11-13)*
>   2. To be circumspect *(Read Eph. 5:14-16)*
>   3. To be Spirit-filled *(Read Eph. 5:17-18)*

★ **5:18** Note: This verse does not encourage "moderate drinking," as some have supposed. The word translated "excess" is *asotia* in the Greek and refers to a riotous and unruly way of life.

>   4. To be singing *(Read Eph. 5:19)*
>   5. To be singleminded *(Read Eph. 5:20)*
>   6. To be submissive *(Read Eph. 5:21-22)*
>   B. The bridegroom: His devotion to the church (Eph. 5:23-33)
>   1. This devotion, as illustrated by marriage *(Read Eph. 5:23-24, 28-33)*
>   2. This devotion as demonstrated on the cross *(Read Eph. 5:25)*
>   3. This devotion, as consummated by the Rapture *(Read Eph. 5:26-27)*
>   a. A bride without spot—No worldly imperfections
>   b. A bride without blemish—No fleshly imperfections
> **VI. The Church Is Likened to a Soldier (Eph. 6)** — *"Put on the whole armour of God, that ye may be able to stand against the wiles of the devil" (Eph. 6:11).*
>   A. Boot camp training (Eph. 6:1-9)
>   1. Example of children and parents *(Read Eph. 6:1-4)*
>   a. As a soldier, the child is to honor and obey his parents.

★ Both Samson and Absalom are sad warnings to those who would disobey this command. (See Judg. 14:1-3; 2 Sam. 15:1-12; 18:15.)

>   b. As a commander, the parent is to discipline and instruct his or her children.

★ The parent is to instruct and admonish children in the Lord. (See Prov. 13:24; 19:18; 22:15; 23:13-14; 29:15,17; Deut. 6:6-7.)

> 2. Example of servants and master *(Read Eph. 6:5-9)*
>   a. The servant is to serve his master as he would serve Christ.
>   b. The master is to treat his servant as he would treat Christ.
> B. Front line fighting (Eph. 6:10-24)
>   1. Our enemy—The devil
>   a. His cohorts *(Read Eph. 6:12)*

✷ 6:12
- Principalities—A possible reference to Satan's "generals" who have the oversight of entire nations (see Dan. 10).
- Powers—May refer to his "troops" who possess human beings (see Mark 5; Matt. 17).
- World rulers—Those demons in charge of Satan's worldly business.
- Spiritual wickedness—Those demons in charge of worldly religion.

> b. His cunning (Eph. 6:11)— *"The wiles [schemes] of the devil."*

✷ 6:11 Greek scholar Kenneth Wuest writes: "Wiles is methodeia in the Greek, referring to 'cunning arts, deceit, craft, trickery.' It means to follow up, or investigate by method and settled plan, to follow craftily, frame devices, deceive" (*Ephesians and Colossians*, p. 141). (See also 1 Tim. 3:7; 2 Cor. 2:11.)

> c. His cruel tactics (Eph. 6:16)— *"The fiery darts [flaming missiles] of the wicked."*

✷ 6:16 This is a reference to arrows tipped with tow, pitch, or such material, then set on fire before they are discharged. (See also 1 Pet. 1:7; 4:12.)

> 2. Our endeavors—The game plan
>   a. We are to obey (Eph. 6:10)— *"Finally, my brethren, be strong in the Lord, and in the power of his might."*
>   b. We are to stand (Eph. 6:11, 14).

✷ 6:14 We are to stand. No less than four times does Paul exhort us to do this (vv. 11, 13-14). The believer is never told to attack the devil, but to withstand and resist him. (See 1 Pet. 5:8-9.) Thus, when tempted to do wrong, we should flee as did Joseph (Gen. 39:12); but when attacked by Satan for doing right, we should stand firm as did Daniel's three friends (Dan. 3). It has been observed that as pilgrims we walk, as witnesses we talk, as contenders we run, but as fighters we stand.

> c. We are to pray (Eph. 6:18)— *"Praying always with all prayer and supplication in the Spirit."*

✷ 6:18 We are to pray. (See Matt. 17:21; Jude 20; 1 Tim. 2:8; 1 Thess. 5:17.)

> d. We are to watch (Eph. 6:18).

✷ We are to watch. (See 1 Cor. 16:13; 2 Cor. 6:5; 11:27; Matt. 24:43; Luke 12:37-40; Acts 20:31; 1 Thess. 5:6; 1 Pet. 4:7; 2 Tim. 4:5; Rev. 3:2; 16:15.) We may thus conclude that both watching and praying are the divine twin secrets for overcoming:
- The world (see Mark 13:33)
- The flesh (see Mark 14:38)
- The devil (see Eph. 6:18)

   e. We are to persevere (Eph. 6:18).
  3. Our equipment—The armor of God *(Read Eph. 6:11)*
   a. The girdle of truth (Eph. 6:14)
   b. The breastplate of righteousness (Eph. 6:14)
   c. The sandals of the gospel (Eph. 6:15)
   d. The shield of faith (Eph. 6:16)
   e. The helmet of salvation (Eph. 6:17)
   f. The sword of the Spirit (Eph. 6:17)

★ Let us carefully note each piece of armor mentioned here. Paul very obviously takes those pieces of armor worn by the Roman soldier and makes spiritual application to each one.

- The girdle of truth—*Expositors' Commentary* says: "First in the list of these articles of equipment mentioned is the girdle. Appropriately so; for the soldier might be furnished with every other part of his equipment, and yet, wanting his girdle, would be neither fully clothed nor securely armed. His belt was no mere adornment of the soldier, but an essential part of his equipment. Passing round the loins and by the end of the breastplate (in later times supporting the sword), it was of special use in keeping other parts in place, and in securing the proper soldierly attitude and freedom of movement." Truth, as mentioned here, probably refers to truthfulness as found in a Christian. Thus a believer whose life is tainted with deceit and falsehood forfeits the very thing which holds other pieces of his armor together.
- The breastplate of righteousness—This speaks of right acts as practiced by the believer. The breastplate was to protect the heart of the soldier. Thus, unrighteous acts committed by a Christian rob him of this vital protection and expose his spiritual heart to Satan. (See Heb. 10:22; 13:9; James 1:26; 4:8; 1 John 3:19-22.)
- The sandals of the gospel—The Roman soldier wore sandals which were bound by thongs over the instep and around the ankle, and the soles were thickly studded with nails. This gave him a firm footing in time of attack. This may refer to the assurance and confidence which comes from knowing the great doctrinal truths associated with the gospel. (See 1 Pet. 3:15; Eph. 4:14.)
- The shield of faith—K. Wuest writes: "The word shield used here designated the shield of the heavy infantry, a large, oblong one, four by two and one-half feet, sometimes curved on the inner side." Hebrews 11 is a commentary on this piece of armor.
- The helmet of salvation—The helmet, of course, protected the head and brain. This piece (like the sandals) may refer to the intake of Bible doctrine, lest one's eyes be blinded, his ears deafened, and his mind confused with the attacks from the world, the flesh, and the devil.
- The sword of the Spirit—Here is the only offensive weapon listed among the various pieces of armor. The rest are defensive in nature. The sword of the Spirit is identified as the Word of God. (See Heb. 4:12.) This, then, is the armor the Christian is commanded to wear. Kenneth Wuest writes concerning the command in 6:13, "Wherefore take unto you the whole armour of God": " 'Take unto you' is *analambano*, meaning, 'to take up in order to use.' The verb is aorist imperative, which construction issues a command given with military snap and curtness, a command to be obeyed at once and once for all. Thus, the Christian is to take up and put on all the armor of God as a once-for-all act and keep that armor on during the entire course of his life, not relaxing the discipline necessary for the constant use of such protection. The historian Gibbon relates how the relaxation of discipline and disuse of exercise rendered soldiers less willing and less able to support the fatigue of service. They complained of the weight of armor, and obtained permission to lay aside much of it" (*Ephesians and Colossians*, p. 142).

  4. Our examples—Paul and Tychicus (Eph. 6:19-24)
   a. Paul, the chained ambassador *(Read Eph. 6:19-20)*
   b. Tychicus, the coming ambassador *(Read Eph. 6:21-22)*

★ **6:22** Dr. Homer Kent writes: "In closing this letter, Paul explains that he will be sending it by his messenger Tychicus, who was also the bearer of the epistles to Philemon and to the Colossians (Col. 4:7). It is most probable that all three letters were carried on the same trip. Tychicus was one of Paul's most trusted colleagues. He was from the province of Asia (Acts 20:4), and could have been from Ephesus, the capital. He had traveled with Paul on the third missionary journey and presumably accompanied him to Jerusalem with the collection. Now he was at Rome with the apostle, and would have the responsible task of delivering these important letters to their destinations, as well as conducting the runaway slave Onesimus safely to his master in Colosse. Years later he would be sent by Paul to Ephesus once again (2 Tim. 4:12). To call him a 'beloved brother' was to emphasize Paul's personal attachment to him. To describe him as a 'faithful minister' points to his trustworthy performance of spiritual responsibilities. 'In the Lord' belongs to both expressions and denotes the spiritual realm in which Paul and Tychicus find the basis for their association" (*Ephesians, the Glory of the Church*, p.125).

LESSON 30

INTRODUCTION TO PHILIPPIANS

CAN IT BE? IS IT POSSIBLE TO OFFER UP PRAISE IN A PRISON
AND TO WRITE OF JOY FROM A JAILHOUSE?

- A. It is indeed, as demonstrated by the wonderful book of Philippians. The words of joy and rejoicing are found no less than 18 times in Philippians, more than any other biblical book for its size. The secret and source of this joy is Christ, which name in various forms appears some 70 times in this epistle.
- B. The church at Philippi was founded as a result of a supernatural vision experienced by Paul while at Troas during his second missionary trip (see Acts 16:8-10).
- C. It was apparently Paul's favorite church. During his brief stay there he and Silas saw God work marvelously in the lives of at least three individuals.
    1. An Asian businesswoman named Lydia whom God saved from Judaism (Acts 16:13-15)
    2. A Greek soothsayer whom God saved from demonism (Acts 16:16-18)
    3. A Roman jailer whom God saved from emperorism (the worship of Caesar, Acts 16:27-32)
- D. Thus this church, conceived in a vision, would reach its apex in a prison. Strange and wonderful indeed are the ways of God.
- E. For its size, Philippians speaks more about Christian unity than any other biblical book. (See 2:1-4; 3:15-17; 4:1-3.)
- F. It also describes the second (of two) kinds of peace in the Bible.
    1. The peace *with* God, experienced by all believers (Rom. 5:1)
    2. The peace *of* God, experienced by Spirit-filled believers (Phil. 4:7)
- G. This book contains the greatest passage on the humility and exaltation of Christ in the entire Word of God (see 2:5-11).
- H. The city of Philippi was founded by Philip of Macedon (father of Alexander the Great) in 357 B.C., and named after him. It was some 700 miles from Rome and enjoyed full Roman citizenship privileges.
- I. In A.D. 57, at the end of his third missionary trip (some five years after his first visit), Paul seems to have paid two brief visits to Philippi (see 2 Cor. 1:16; Acts 19:21; 20:1-3).
- J. The year A.D. 62 finds the apostle a prisoner in Rome. Acts 28:30-31 indicates that he was confined to his own hired house, being chained to various Roman soldiers every six hours. Although he could not preach in public, he was allowed to write (Eph. 6:20; Phil. 1:7, 14, 16; Col. 4:18; Philem. 1, 10, 13).
- K. It was therefore at this time, some ten years after his original visit to Philippi, that Paul wrote the epistle of Philippians to his favorite church.
- L. This church, upon learning of his imprisonment in Rome, had sent a love offering by way of Epaphroditus. They had already sent him two other love gifts years back for his missionary endeavors in Thessalonica (Phil. 4:15-16).
- M. While in Rome, Epaphroditus had become very ill and nearly died. But God spared his life. Paul thus writes Philippians both to thank them for their gift and also to report the good news of Epaphroditus's recovery.

N. Philippians is the 17th longest New Testament book, and 49th longest biblical book, with four chapters, 104 verses, and 2,002 words. There are quotations or allusions from nine Old Testament books in Philippians.
O. Great passages would include:
    1. 1:21-22
    2. 2:1-11
    3. 3:7-14
    4. 3:20-21
    5. 4:4-8
    6. 4:11-13

Overview of the Book of Philippians

I. Christ is Life's Purpose
   A. He could rest in God's security
      1. Paul's greetings to the saints
      2. Paul's thanksgiving for the saints
      3. Paul's prayer concerning the saints
      4. Paul's explanation to the saints
   B. He could rejoice in great suffering
      1. The cause of his fetters
      2. The circumference of his faith
      3. The courage of his friends
      4. The carnality of his foes
      5. The confidence in his future
   C. He could remain in glad service
      1. God's will for the apostle
      2. God's will for the Philippians

II. Christ is Life's Pattern
   A. The exhortation to these virtues
      1. They are available
      2. They are attainable
   B. The examples of these virtues
      1. The example of Christ
      2. The example of the Father
      3. The example of Paul
      4. The example of Timothy

III. Christ is Life's Prize
   A. The corrupters of this prize
      1. Who they were
      2. What they were
      3. Where they were headed
   B. The cost of this prize
   C. The crown of this prize
      1. He gained a new knowledge
      2. He gained a new righteousness
      3. He gained a new power
      4. He gained a new goal
      5. He gained a new role
      6. He gained a new hope

IV. Christ is Life's Power
   A. This power can unify
   B. This power can fortify
   C. This power can purify
   D. This power can exemplify
   E. This power can satisfy
   F. This power can ratify
   G. This power can sanctify
   H. This power can multiply
   I. This power can glorify

THE BOOK OF PHILIPPIANS

I. Christ Is Life's Purpose (Phil. 1)— *"For to me to live is Christ, and to die is gain" (Phil. 1:21).* The knowledge of this wonderful truth allowed Paul to accomplish three things.
  A. He could rest in God's security *(Read Phil. 1:6)*
    1. Paul's greetings to the saints *(Read Phil. 1:1-2)*

✶ 1:2 Dr. John Walvoord writes: "The mention of bishops and deacons indicates the advanced state of organization of the Church at Philippi now composed of mature and gifted believers from whom recognized leaders had come. As A. R. Fausset notes, 'This is the earliest epistle where bishops and deacons are mentioned, and the only one where they are separately addressed.' Of course, as early as Acts 6, men were appointed in the church to serve in a way similar to deacons. Although not called deacons, the prominence of this appointment of men to special service in Acts seems to recognize its significance. Elders were appointed in every church as early as Acts 14:23, and are mentioned in Acts 11:30; 20:27-28; 1 Thess. 5:12-13)" (*Philippians, Triumph in Christ*, p. 24).

Greek scholar Kenneth Wuest writes in a similar manner: "The word *bishop* is the translation of a Greek word used in secular pursuits of an overseer in any capacity, for instance, the official in charge of the repairing of a temple or an officer in an army. The word itself means 'to look upon.' Paul uses it as another name for an elder, the latter being the title of the office so far as statutes in the church are concerned, the former being the title that indicated the responsibility and activity of the office, that of overseeing the spiritual welfare of the local church. He brings the two names together as designating one individual in Acts 20:17, 28. The word *deacon* is the English spelling of a Greek word that was used as a general term to designate a servant. It covered both slaves and hired servants. It represented a servant, not in his relation to his master, but in his activity. The same word is translated 'minister' in I Corinthians 3:5; 2 Corinthians 3:6; Ephesians 3:7. Here it refers to a distinct class of officers in the apostolic church. The origin of the office is given us in Acts 6" (*Word Studies in Philippians*, p. 28).

As a final note here, consider the comments of J. Dwight Pentecost: "The word 'deacon' comes from a compound Greek word that means 'to stir up the dust.' It presents the picture of one who is moving so rapidly through the dusty lanes of the villages of Palestine to discharge his duty that his feet kick up dust as he goes. There was so much for the deacons to do they could not loiter nor tarry. They went about their ministry with such diligence that they were stirring up the dust; thus those who were set apart to this ministry were called 'those who stir up the dust' or deacons" (*The Joy of Living*, p. 114).

    2. Paul's thanksgiving for the saints *(Read Phil. 1:3-8)*
    3. Paul's prayer concerning the saints *(Read Phil. 1:9-11)*

✶ 1:11
  ■ The word "approve" here means to place one's OK upon something after a period of testing. It was used by the Greeks to describe doctors who had passed their examinations. They were then certified physicians.
  ■ The "joy of Christ" phrase is no doubt a reference to the Rapture (1 Thess. 4:14-18; 1 Cor. 15:51-53; Heb. 9:24-28; Rev. 4:1).

    4. Paul's explanation to the saints *(Read Phil. 1:12)*
  B. He could rejoice in great suffering (Phil. 1:13-20).
    1. The cause of his fetters— *"So that my imprisonment in the cause of Christ" (Phil. 1:13).*
    2. The circumference of his faith— *"Has become well known throughout the whole praetorian guard and to everyone else" (Phil. 1:13, NASB).* "All the saints salute you, chiefly they that are of Caesar's household" (Phil. 4:22).

LESSON 30: THE BOOK OF PHILIPPIANS

✴ **4:22** John Walvoord writes: "Paul was guarded by imperial soldiers who were the cream of the Roman army, and the time of this writing was while he was in Rome, the center of the Roman government. Whether in Rome or elsewhere, however, according to the custom, the apostle was probably chained to a Roman soldier twenty-four hours a day, with a new guard every six hours. No doubt this was a most trying experience which subjected Paul to all the evil characteristics and whims of his guard even when he talked to his friends, when he prayed or when he attempted to write. Always there was this Roman guard. The circumstances, however, also afforded him the priceless opportunity of witness, and each guard heard Paul's story. The claims of the grace of God and the transformation it afforded in his life subjected him to the scrutiny of each guard to see whether his testimony was genuine. The slightest deviation, impatience, or irritation would disqualify his testimony to the guard, and any lack of consistency in life would soon be communicated to others. The apostle's sincerity and his glowing account of God's grace manifested to him apparently were effective as guard after guard came to know Jesus Christ in an effective way."

"Only God knows what went on in the rented room in which Paul was permitted to live. There the guards heard the conversation of Paul with his intimate friends and were able to ask questions about the strange words which they heard from their prisoner. In the lonely hours of the dark night, illuminated only by the moon, many a guard probably heard the testimony of Paul—his early career as a Pharisee, his antagonism and persecution of Christians, his remarkable conversion, and the causes of his imprisonment. No doubt all this was the subject of much conversation in the praetorian guard, and raised sympathy among the soldiers as they understood his unjust imprisonment. His chains had become an effective line of communication to the elite soldiers of the Roman Empire who, if converted, could carry the gospel to the ends of the earth as they were moved from place to place. It reminds us that every circumstance of life is a platform on which the transforming grace of God can be manifested in the life of the Lord's own" (*Philippians: Triumph in Christ*, pp. 37-38).

> 3. The courage of his friends *(Read Phil. 1:14)*

✴ **1:14** Paul's imprisonment had apparently jolted some of his timid believer friends into a bolder approach in presenting the gospel. One possibility for this may have been the conversion of several elite Roman soldiers. Thus their testimony would doubtless have given new courage to those regular church members in Rome.

> 4. The carnality of his foes
>   a. Their rebellion *(Read Phil. 1:15-17)*

✴ **1:17** The psalmist once wrote: *"Surely the wrath of man shall praise thee"* (Psa. 76:10). In other words, inspite of the impure and insincere motives of his enemies in proclaiming the gospel, Paul nevertheless rejoiced. The greatest problem of the world, then, as it is today, is not when the gospel is imperfectly preached, but when it is not preached at all.

> b. His reaction *(Read Phil. 1:18)*
> 5. The confidence in his future (Phil. 1:19) — *"For I know that this shall turn out for my deliverance through your prayers and the provision of the Spirit of Jesus Christ"* (Phil. 1:19, NASB).

✴ **1:19** The King James Version speaks of the "supply of the Spirit of Jesus Christ." Warren Wiersbe writes: "The word supply gives us our English word chorus. Whenever a Greek city was going to put on a special festival, someone had to pay for the singers and dancers. The donation called had to be a lavish one, and so this word came to mean 'to provide generously and lavishly.' Paul was not depending upon his own dwindling resources; he was depending on the generous resources of God, ministered by the Holy Spirit" (Be Joyful, p. 36).

> C. He could remain in glad service (Phil. 1:21-30) — *"For to me to live is Christ, and to die is gain"* (Phil. 1:21).
>   1. God's will for the apostle *(Read Phil. 1:20)*

★ **1:20** Through Paul's body the Savior would be magnified. How can this be done? It has been observed that through the telescope a distant object can be brought near, and through the microscope a small object can be made big. Thus, by rightly applying these instruments in a spiritual way, the believer can, through his body, cause Christ to become both big and near in the eyes of watching saints and sinners alike.

> a. His desire was to depart and be with the Savior *(Read Phil. 1:23)*

★ **1:23** Note: Paul speaks of death as a departure (see also 2 Tim. 4:6). This word depart was used by:
  - Soldiers, when they took down their tent and moved on.
  - Politicians, when they set a prisoner free.
  - Farmers, when they unyoked their oxen.

> b. His decision was to remain and minister to the saints *(Read Phil. 1:24)*
> 2. God's will for the Philippians *(Read Phil. 1:27-30)*
> **II. Christ Is Life's Pattern (Phil. 2)**— *"Let this mind be in you, which was also in Christ Jesus"* (Phil. 2:5). The pattern here to be copied by the saints incorporates the two beautiful Christian virtues of unity and humility.
>   A. The exhortation to these virtues (Phil. 2:1-4)
>   1. They are available (Phil. 2:1)—"Since therefore there is encouragement in Christ, since there is consolation of love, since there is fellowship of the Spirit [and] affection and compassion" *(my personal translation)*.
>   2. They are attainable *(Read Phil. 2:2-4)*

★ **2:4** Plato defined "lowliness" as follows: "That state of mind which submits to the divine order of the universe, and does not impiously exalt itself." The word is used in a secular document of the Nile River at its low stage. How many tragic church splits would be avoided if only this principle was observed.

> B. The examples of these virtues (Phil. 2:5-30)
>   1. The example of Christ *(Read Phil. 2:5-8)*

★ **2:8** Surely these verses rank among the greatest in all Scripture. What exactly did Christ do?
  - He left heaven's glory (John 17:5; 2 Cor. 8:9).
  - He made himself of no reputation. The Greek word here in 2:7 is *kenoo* and means "to empty." Just what did Christ empty himself of?
    - Negative—He did not lay aside in any sense of the word his deity. He was, is, and ever shall be the total Son of God. (See John 1:1; 17:5; 2 Cor. 4:4; Col. 1:15; 2:9; Heb. 1:3.)
    - Positive—He did, for awhile, hide his heavenly fame in an earthly frame. Even though he retained every single attribute of deity while on earth, He did, nevertheless, surrender to the Holy Spirit the independent exercise of those divine characteristics. (See Psa. 22:6; Isa. 53:3; Mark 9:12; Rom. 15:3.) Two phrases need to be examined at this point:
      - "The form of God"—This does not mean that Christ had a physical shape prior to the incarnation. It refers to that inner, essential, and abiding nature of a person or thing.
      - "Robbery to be equal with God"—That is, he did not hold or consider the outer manifestation of his deity in heaven as a treasure to be grasped and retained at all costs. Christ in his incarnation did not concern himself with retaining all this.
  - He was made in the likeness of human beings (John 1:14; Rom. 1:3; 8:3; Gal. 4:4; Heb. 2:14, 17). This simple but absolutely staggering fact cannot be even remotely grasped by human minds. The infinite holy Creator suddenly becomes in the likeness of his finite and sinful creatures (yet without sin). Who can comprehend such sacrifice? It is as if a mighty

and magnificent earthly king would determine to lay aside for awhile his fantastic storehouse of wealth and, leaving behind an adoring and amazed court, take upon himself the body of a lowly ant. "The Son of man" was, by the way, our Lord's favorite name for himself while on earth.

- He took upon himself the form of a servant. He did not come as a mighty human Caesar or some world-renowned human philosopher. Even this would have been a condescension of colossal proportions. He came, rather, as a lowly servant.
- He humbled himself. That is, he submitted to authority (see 1 Pet. 2:21-24). He agreed to talk our language, to wear our clothes, to eat our food, to breathe our air, and to endure our vile and vicious treatment. Contrast his statement in the Garden with that of Lucifer's statement (Matt. 26:39, 42; Isa. 14:13-14).
- He became obedient unto death (Matt. 26:39; John 10:18; Heb. 5:8;12:2).
- He died on a cursed cross. He did not just die, but suffered the worst kind of death both physically and judicially (Gal. 3:13; Isa. 53; Psa. 22).

> a. He gave up (for awhile) the glory of heaven.
> b. He emptied himself (he refused to use his divine attributes in an independent way).
> c. He was incarnated in the flesh.
> d. He took the form of a servant.
> e. He humbled himself.
> f. He became obedient unto death.
> g. He died on a cursed tree.
> 2. The example of the Father *(Read Phil. 2:9-11)*

✷ 2:11

- He has been highly exalted by the Father himself (Isa. 52:13; John 17:1; Acts 2:33; Heb. 2:9).
- He has been given a name (position and place of authority) above all other names (Eph.1:20; Heb.1:4).
- He will be universally acknowledged as Lord of all.
  - The methods of this acknowledgment—By the bowing of the knee and the confession of the tongue.
  - The creatures of this acknowledgment
    - "Those in heaven"—The world of angels
    - "Those on earth"—The world of saints and sinners
    - "Those under the earth"—The world of demons. (See Rev. 5:13; 7:9-12; 14:6-7; Isa. 45:23; Rom. 10:9-10.) Note: To confess him in this life as Lord means salvation, but to wait until the next life will result in damnation. Thus, the supreme question is not when a human being will do this, but rather where.

> 3. The example of Paul (Phil. 2:12-18)
> a. What the apostle had done— *"Holding fast the Word of life, so that in the day of Christ I may have cause to glory because I did not run in vain nor toil in vain. But even if I am being poured out as a drink offering upon the sacrifice and service of your faith, I rejoice and share my joy with you all"* (Phil. 2:16-17. NASB).
> b. What the Philippians were to do (Phil. 2:12-15,18)
> (1) They were to work out their salvation *(Read Phil. 2:12-14)*

✷ 2:14

- We note he did not say, "Work for your own salvation." The idea here is to complete something. The Greeks used this phrase in bringing a math problem to its logical conclusion and also to work a gold mine in a field.
- It is thus not by imitation, but by incarnation (Gal. 2:20). The Christian life is not to be a series of ups and downs, but rather of ins and outs. God works in; we are to work out.

> (2) They were to hold out their illumination *(Read Phil. 2:15)*

★ **2:16** Dr. J. Dwight Pentecost writes: "The apostle uses an interesting word when he says 'holding forth.' It has the idea of two travelers going through the night, one with a light and one without a light. The one extends his light on the other who is following, that light might fall on his footsteps ... God has set you as a light. The word Paul translates 'light' is the word for luminary. It is the word for a light giving heavenly body, a star if you please. This world is waiting for the sunrise of the Son of righteousness, but until he slips over the horizon to bring his light to this world again, there is a star to cast its light that men might not fall. You are a star to hold forth the word of life; therefore, do all things without murmuring and complaining" *(The Joy of Living*, pp. 101-102).

> 4. The example of Timothy (Phil. 2:19-24) — *"But I trust in the Lord Jesus to send Timotheus shortly unto you, that I also may be of good comfort, when I know your state" (Phil. 2:19).*
>   a. To the church he had served as a shepherd *(Read Phil. 2:20)*

★ **2:20** Timothy had a long and intimate contact with this church. (See Acts 16:3; 17:14-15; 19:22; 20:3-4; Phil. 2:19-23.)

> b. To the apostle, he had served as a son *(Read Phil. 2:22)*
> 5. The example of Epaphroditus (Phil. 2:25-30)
>   a. His service *(Read Phil. 2:25)*

★ **2:25**
- This man was a Gentile believer from Philippi. His name means "charming." He had been sent by the Philippian church to minister to Paul and bring him their offering.
- Note the three titles here:
  - "My brother" — Indicating they were bound by a common love
  - "My companion in labour" — Indicating they were bound by a common work
  - "My fellowsoldier" — Indicating they were bound by a common danger

> b. His sickness *(Read Phil. 2:27)*
> c. His sacrifice *(Read Phil. 2:30)*

★ **2:30** Warren Wiersbe aptly summarizes the life of this remarkable man. Wiersbe writes: "Epaphroditus was a balanced Christian! Balance is important in the Christian life. Some people emphasize 'fellowship' so much that they forget the furtherance of the Gospel. Others are so involved in 'defending the faith' of the Gospel that they neglect building fellowship with other believers. Epaphroditus did not fall into either of these traps. He was like Nehemiah, the man who rebuilt the walls of Jerusalem with his sword in one hand and his trowel in the other (Neh. 4:17). You cannot build with a sword nor battle with a trowel! It takes both to get the Lord's work accomplished. Dr. H. A. Ironside used to tell about a group of believers who thought only of 'fellowship.' They had little concern for reaching the lost or for defending the faith against its enemies. In front of their meeting place they hung a sign: 'JESUS ONLY.' But the wind blew away some of the letters, and the sign read 'US ONLY.' It was a perfect description of a group of people who were not balanced Christians" *(Be Joyful*, p. 76).

> **III. Christ Is Life's Prize (Phil. 3)** — *"Brethren, I count not myself to have apprehended: but this one thing I do, forgetting those things which are behind, and reaching forth unto those things which are before" (Phil. 3:13).*
>   A. The corrupters of this prize (Phil. 3:1-3, 18-19)
>   1. Who they were — The Judaizers. *"Beware of the dogs, beware of the evil workers, beware of the false circumcision" (Phil. 3:2, NASB).*

   2. What they were *(Read Phil. 3:18)*
   3. Where they were headed *(Read Phil. 3:19)*
 B. The cost of this prize—Becoming a Christian had cost Paul the many natural advantages of his background *(Read Phil. 3:4-6)*.

✶ 3:6 Robert Lightner writes: "Circumcision was named first probably because it was a big issue with the Judaizers. Paul's specific time, the eighth day, stressed that he was not a proselyte or an Ishmaelite but a pure-blooded Jew. Proselytes were circumcised later in life and Ishmaelites after age 13 (cf. Gen. 17:25-26). Paul was of the people of Israel, which describes his heritage. His parents were both true Jews, unlike some of the Judaizers. He could trace his family lineage all the way back to Abraham. He was a true member of the covenant people (cf. 2 Cor.11:22). He was also a Benjamite, from which tribe came Israel's first king.

✶ (1 Sam. 9:1-2). This tribe had a special place of honor and was viewed with great esteem. Even after the kingdom was disrupted the tribe of Benjamin remained loyal to the house of David. Hebrew was Paul's native tongue. Unlike some of the Israelites, he did not adopt Greek customs. He knew thoroughly both the language and customs of the people of God. He was a Hebrew son of Hebrew parents. In regard to the Law, Paul was a Pharisee, a member of the strictest sect among his people. In addition to the Law of Moses, the Pharisees added their own regulations which in time were interpreted as equal to the Law. What greater zeal for the Jewish religion could anyone boast of than that he persecuted the church? Paul did this relentlessly before his conversion to Christ (Acts 9:1-2). No Judaizer could match such zeal. "In 'legalistic righteousness' Paul also excelled. In fact in his own eyes he was faultless (amemptos; the same word is used in Phil. 2:15 where it is rendered 'blameless')" (*Bible Knowledge Commentary*, New Testament Volume, p. 660).

 C. The crown of this prize (Phil. 3:7-17, 20-21)
  1. He gained a new knowledge *(Read Phil. 3:7-8)*

✶ 3:8 Martyred missionary Jim Elliot once wrote: "He is no fool who gives up what he cannot keep to gain what he cannot lose" (See also Jer. 9:23; 1 Cor. 2:2.)

  2. He gained a new righteousness *(Read Phil. 3:9)*
  3. He gained a new power *(Read Phil. 3:10)*

✶ 3:10 Far too many Christians are excited about the implications of the first half of this famous verse but show little interest in the last part. But it must be kept in mind that there is no power of the resurrection without the fellowship of the suffering. These go hand-in-hand. To know Christ in this manner has been the goal of all godly believers throughout history. See the following testimonies:
- Moses—Exodus 33:13
- David—Psalm 42:1-2; 63:1-2
- Philip—John 1:45 (see also Rom. 6:3-5; 8:17)

  4. He gained a new goal *(Read Phil. 3:11-17)*

✶ 3:14
- John Walvoord writes: "He begins by saying, 'Not as though I had already attained, either were already perfect' (v. 12). The perfection he would have at the future resurrection was not yet attained, as he still had a sin nature, a sinful body, and was only too aware of the need for further spiritual progress. In stating that he was not already perfect, the apostle Paul used a Greek word, *teleioo*, meaning 'to reach a goal or fulfill a purpose.' The Greek word is the root of the English word *teleology* which refers to the design or purpose of the universe. The same word is found in Luke 13:32; John 17:23; 1 Corinthians 2:6; 2 Corinthians 12:9; Ephesians 4:12, and many other passages" (*Philippians, Triumph in Christ*, pp. 90-91).

- Note especially Paul's statement in 3:13: "This one thing I do." For other biblical examples, see:
  - Jesus and the rich young ruler (Mark 10:21)
  - Martha and Jesus (Luke 10:42)
  - An ex-blind man (John 9:25)
  - The psalmist (Psa. 27:4). (See also James 1:8.)
- Warren Wiersbe writes: "Consecration is the secret of power. If a river is allowed to overflow its banks, the area around it becomes a swamp. But if that river is dammed and controlled, it becomes a source of power" (*Be Joyful*, p. 97).
- Concerning Paul's phrase, "reaching forth unto those things which are before," see I Corinthians 9:24,26; 2 Timothy 4:7, 8; Hebrews 6:1; 12:1.

> 5. He gained a new role *(Read Phil. 3:17)*
> 6. He gained a new hope *(Read Phil. 3:20-21)*

★ **3:21** Paul was a citizen of Rome, but what he is saying here is "Our citizenship is in heaven." Or "We are a colony of heaven." What does that mean? It means that the believer, since he is a citizen of heaven, is to take his orders from up there. He is to obey the laws from heaven. Thus, just as Philippi was a colony of Rome on foreign soil, the church is a colony of heaven on earthly, foreign soil.

> **IV. Christ Is Life's Power (Phil. 4)** — *"I can do all things through Christ which strengtheneth me" (Phil. 4:13).*
> A. This power can unify *(Read Phil. 4:1-3)*
> B. The power can fortify *(Read Phil. 4:6-7)*

★ **4:7**
- Note the two golden rules concerning experiencing the peace of God here:
  - *"Be careful about nothing."* The word careful here means "to be pulled in different directions." Paul is not talking about concern here, but about panic. (See Psa. 55:22; 1 Pet. 5:7.)
  - Be prayerful about everything. Furthermore, our prayers should be both definite and devotional. It has been noted that there are but two areas over which the Christian is not to worry:
    - Those things which he himself can change. Here perspiration is the answer.
    - Those things which he himself cannot change. Here supplication is the answer.
- The word keep here was often used to describe someone or something which was carefully guarded by the elite Roman soldiers of Caesar's palace. All Christians enjoy the peace with God mentioned in Romans 5:1, but only those who have successfully substituted care for prayer can enjoy the peace of God which truly passes understanding. Thus we see that this peace guards:
  - Our hearts, protecting us from wrong feelings.
  - Our minds, protecting us from wrong thinking.
- We should observe here that the familiar sign "Prayer changes things" is not always true. But prayer does change us, by protecting against those matters which were driving us to despair. (See Isa. 26:3; Psa. 119:165; 2 Cor. 10:5.) This, then, is God's marvelous method for keeping peace.

> C. This power can purify *(Read Phil. 4:8)*
> D. This power can exemplify *(Read Phil. 4:9)*
> E. This power can satisfy *(Read Phil. 4:10-13)*

★ **4:12** Paul had learned in all of his circumstances "therewith to be content." It should be added, however, that contentment is not complacency; it is containment. The abiding Christ within Paul's body assured him of this satisfaction. Note the two kinds of Christians:

- The thermometer believer-His satisfaction is totally dependent upon outside circumstances. He simply registers the prevailing spiritual temperature.
- The thermostat believer. His satisfaction is totally independent of the outside circumstances. He is not only affected by it, but actually controls that area surrounding him.

> F. This power can ratify *(Read Phil. 4:15-16)*
> G. This power can sanctify *(Read Phil. 4:18)*
> H. This power can multiply *(Read Phil. 4:19)*
> I. This power can glorify *(Read Phil. 4:20)*

LESSON 31

INTRODUCTION TO COLOSSIANS

THE PREEMINENCE OF THE PREEMINENT ONE, THE GLORIES OF THE GLORIOUS ONE

    A. The book of Colossians is the most Christocentric book in the Bible. The greatest passage on the preexistent, omnipotent, exalted and eternal Son of God is found in Colossians. (See 1:15-19.)

    B. Colossians in a sense concludes that which Ephesians introduces. In Ephesians Paul dwells upon the body of the church, while in Colossians he writes of the head of that body. Because of this, both books are somewhat similar. For example, 78 out of the 95 verses in Colossians are nearly identical to those in Ephesians.

    C. It has been said that Colossians is to Ephesians what Galatians is to Romans.

    D. This book provides one of two New Testament commands for the church epistles to be exchanged and read before the various local assemblies (compare Col. 4:16 with 1 Thess. 5:27).

    E. Colossians is one of the epistles Paul wrote during his first Roman imprisonment. The others are Ephesians, Philippians, and Philemon.

    F. The church at Colosse was probably started during Paul's third missionary journey. Although he personally never visited the city (see Col. 2:1), he did spend two years teaching the Word of God in Ephesus at the house of Tyrannus (see Acts 19:9-10). Colosse was only 90 miles east of Ephesus. It is therefore suggested that one of his students during this time was a man from Colosse named Epaphras. After graduating from the two-year T.B.I. (Tyrannus Bible Institute), Epaphras may have gone back to evangelize the entire Lycus Valley. This valley, some ten miles long, contained three important cities: Laodicea, Hierapolis, and Colosse. Laodicea was only 12 miles from Colosse.

    G. It is therefore possible that Paul's zealous young student started both the church in Colosse and the one in Laodicea. (See also Col. 4:16 and Rev. 3:14-22.)

    H. The Colossian church was composed mainly of Gentile membership (see Col. 2:13).

    I. Paul intended to visit it upon his release from prison (Philem. 22).

    J. The church in Colosse may have met in the home of Philemon, for he lived at Colosse with one of his slaves, Onesimus (Col. 4:9 and the book of Philemon). Some time after its beginning, the church at Colosse was infected by a deadly virus known as Judaistic Gnosticism. This represented the worst of both the Jewish and Greek world of thought. The "J-G virus" consisted of the following:

        1. Salvation could be obtained only through knowledge. This meant only those with superior intellects could hope to achieve salvation. Faith (belief without materialistic proof) was silly and useless.

        2. Matter itself was evil. The J-G virus taught that the world was created by a series of angelic emanations. In other words, God (the original source) created an angel who in turn created another angel, who created yet a third, etc. Finally, the last of these angels created the world as we know it today.

        3. While this philosophy admitted to the *transcendence* of God (that he is above everything), it denied his *immanence* (that he is also in everything). This view immediately ruled out the incarnation of Christ, special divine creation, prayer, faith, miracles, the second coming, and the accuracy of the Bible.

4. The goal of human life was either morbid *asceticism* (avoiding all joys of life, and abusing the body for the spirit's sake) or that of unrestrained *licentiousness* (if it feels good, do it). The first was known as Stoicism, and the second view Epicureanism. Scofield once observed: "Pure Christianity lives between two dangers ever present: the danger that it will evaporate into a philosophy ... and the danger that it will freeze into a form."
5. In conclusion, it may be said that the J-G virus error included dietary and Sabbath observations, circumcision rites, worship of angels, and the practice of asceticism. (See Col. 2:11, 16; 2:18; 2:21-23.)

K. Epaphras was apparently unable to deal properly with this vicious strain and thus makes the dangerous and wearisome thousand-mile trip from Colosse to Rome to seek Paul's advice.

L. When he left Colosse, Archippus assumed the pastorate (Col. 4:17). Archippus may have been the son of Philemon (Philem. 2).

M. Upon reaching Rome and informing Paul, Epaphras was evidently also imprisoned (Philem. 23). This was doubtless because of bold preaching.

N. Paul writes the Colossian epistle to deal with the disease and sends it back by one of his trusted top lieutenants named Tychicus (Col. 4:7; cf. Acts 20:4; Eph. 6:21; 2 Tim. 4:12; Titus 3:12).

O. Colossians may be contrasted to other Pauline epistles. Thus:
1. In Romans we are *justified* in Christ.
2. In 1 Corinthians we are *enriched* in Christ.
3. In 2 Corinthians we are *comforted* in Christ.
4. In Galatians we are *free* in Christ.
5. In Ephesians we are *quickened* in Christ.
6. In Philippians we are *happy* in Christ.
7. In Colossians we are *complete* in Christ.

P. This book thus presents the glorious culmination of it all. We are complete in Christ. This completeness is fourfold:
1. Building *downward*—"Grounded and settled and ... not moved away from the hope of the gospel" *(1:23)*. This is the *deeper* life.
2. Building *upward*—"Built up in him, and stablished in the faith" *(2:7)*. This is the *higher* life.
3. Building *inward*—"For ye are dead, and your life is hid with Christ in God" *(3:3)*. This is the *inner* life.
4. Building *outward*—"Walk with wisdom toward them that are without, redeeming the time" *(4:5)*. This is the *outer* life.

Q. Colossians is the 18th longest New Testament book, and 50th longest biblical book, with four chapters, 95 verses, and 1,998 words. There are quotations or allusions from seven Old Testament books in Colossians.

R. Great passages would include:
1. 1:10-20
2. 2:14-15
3. 3:12-17
4. 3:18-23

Overview of the Book of Colossians

I. The Deity and Preeminence of the Savior
   A. The thanksgiving for this divine preeminence
      1. It was the source of Paul's praying
      2. It was the source of Paul's preaching
      3. It was the source of Paul's persecution
   B. The theology of this divine preeminence
      1. Christ's relationship to the Father
      2. Christ's relationship to the Church
      3. Christ's relationship to the universe

II. The Danger and Perversion of the Serpent
   A. The nature of these perversions
      1. Enticing words (persuasive argument)
      2. Philosophy
      3. Vain deceit (empty deception)
      4. Human tradition
      5. Worldly doctrines
      6. Legalism
      7. Self-abasement
      8. Worship of angels
      9. Receiving visions
     10. Self-made religion
   B. The answer to these perversions
      1. Know who Jesus is
      2. Know what he has done for you
      3. Know who you are
      4. Know what you are to do for him

III. The Duty and Performance of the Saints
   A. In relation to the Son of God
   B. In relation to the Word of God
   C. In relation to the work of God
      1. What to put off
      2. What to put on
   D. In relation to our talks with God
      1. Paul's command to pray
      2. Paul's request for prayer
   E. In relation to our testimony for God
      1. Before the unsaved

      2. In the home
      3. On the job
      4. In the church
  F. In relation to the ministers of God
      1. His greetings to the Colossians
      2. His request of the Colossians

THE BOOK OF COLOSSIANS

"Paul, an apostle of Jesus Christ by the will of God, and Timotheus our brother, to the saints and faithful brethren in Christ which are at Colosse: Grace be unto you, and peace, from God our Father and the Lord Jesus Christ" (Col. 1:1-2).

> **I. The Deity and Preeminence of the Savior (Col. 1)**
>   A. The thanksgiving for this divine preeminence
>   1. It was the source of Paul's praying (Col. 1:3-14)
>   a. He thanks the Father for the witness of the Colossians *(Read Col. 1:3-4, 12-14)*
>   b. He prays to the Father for the walk of the Colossians *(Read Col. 1:9-11)*
>   2. It was the source of Paul's preaching *(Read Col. 1:25-27)*

✶ 1:27 Paul speaks of "this mystery among the Gentiles." A biblical mystery is simply a sacred secret previously kept from people in the Old Testament. There are 11 such mysteries. Paul writes of eight of these; Matthew describes one; and John the apostle lists two. Out of the eight Pauline mysteries, no less than three are found here in Colossians. These are:
- The mystery that the body of Christ (the church) is to be composed of both saved Jews and Gentiles (Col. 4:3; see also Rom.16:25; Eph. 3:1-12; 6:19).
- The mystery of the indwelling Christ (Col. 1:27; see also Gal. 2:20).
- The mystery of the incarnation of Christ (Col. 2:2, 9; see also I Cor. 2:7).

> 3. It was the source of Paul's persecution—*"But part of my work is to suffer for you; and I am glad, for I am helping to finish up the remainder of Christ's sufferings for his body, the church" (Col. 1:24, TLB).*

✶ 1:24 Norman Geisler writes: "By this he did not mean that Christ's suffering on the cross was insufficient (cf. Rom. 3:21-26; Heb. 10:10-14). He was speaking not of salvation but of service. Christ's suffering alone procures salvation (1 Pet. 1:11; 5:1; Heb. 2:9). But it is a believer's privilege to suffer for Christ (2 Tim. 3:11; 1 Pet. 3:13-14; 5:9; Heb.10:32). The word 'affliction' (*thlipsis*)—never used in the New Testament of Christ's death—means 'distress,' 'pressure,' or 'trouble' (which Paul had plenty of; 2 Cor. 11:23-29). Ordinarily it refers to trials in life, not the pains of death. Christ does indeed continue to suffer when Christians suffer for Him. He asked Saul (later called Paul) on the Damascus Road, "Why do you persecute Me?" (Acts 9:4). Since the church is Christ's body, He is affected when it is affected. For the sake of Christ's body Paul willingly suffered (Phil. 1:29)." (*Bible Knowledge Commentary*, New Testament Volume, p. 675).

> B. The theology of this divine preeminence
>   1. Christ's relationship to the Father *(Read Col. 1:15, 19)*

✶ 1:19
- The word "image" here is used to express likeness, and refers to the visible manifestation of something invisible. Christ is not similar to God—he is God.
- The word "firstborn" is *prototokos*, a reference to the highest priority of position. It does not speak of time, but of title. Christ is thus ascribed as Lord of all creation. (See Psa. 89:27.) Norman Geisler observes: "First, Christ is the image of the invisible God. Besides the obvious meaning of likeness (cf. 2 Cor. 4:4), 'image' implies representation and manifestation. Like the head of a sovereign imprinted on a coin, so Christ is 'the exact representation of [the Father's] being' (Heb.

1:3). As Jesus said, 'Anyone who has seen Me has seen the Father' (John 14:9). Anyone who saw Christ, the visible manifestation of the invisible God, has thereby 'seen' God indirectly. For 'no one has ever seen God, but God the only Son ... has made Him known' (John 1:18). Paul wrote of the 'invisible' God (1 Tim. 1:17), but Christ is the perfect visible representation and manifestation of that God. Second, Christ's supremacy is shown in His relationship to Creation. He is the Firstborn over all Creation. Though it is grammatically possible to translate this as 'Firstborn in Creation,' the context makes this impossible for five reasons: (1) The whole point of the passage (and the book) is to show Christ's superiority over all things. (2) Other statements about Christ in this passage (such as Creator of all [1:16], upholder of Creation [v. 17], etc.) clearly indicate His priority and superiority over Creation. (3) The 'Firstborn' cannot be part of Creation if He created 'all things.' One cannot create himself. (Jehovah's Witnesses wrongly add the word 'other' six times in this passage in their New World Translation. Thus they suggest that Christ created all other things after He was created! But the word 'other' is not in the Greek). (4) The 'Firstborn' received worship of all the angels (Heb. 1:6), but creatures should not be worshiped (Exod. 20:4-5). (5) The Greek word for 'Firstborn' is *prototokos*. If Christ were the 'first-created,' the Greek word would have been *protoktisis*" (*Bible Knowledge Commentary*, New Testament Volume, 672-673).

   2. Christ's relationship to the Church *(Read Col. 1:18)*

★ **1:18**
- How can it be said that Christ was the firstborn from the dead when he himself had, before his own resurrection, brought back three individuals from the grave? These were:
  - The son of a widow at Nain (Luke 7:11-15)
  - Jairus's daughter (Luke 8:41-42, 49-56)
  - Lazarus (John 11:43)
- The answer is both simple and thrilling. Jesus is the firstborn from the dead because:
  - His resurrected body was a new body, not subjected to the laws of sin, time, or gravity.
  - His resurrected body was a permanent body, never to die again, as the three that were raised had to do.

   3. Christ's relationship to the universe
      a. He was its Creator *(Read Col. 1:16)*
      b. He is its Sustainer *(Read Col. 1:17)*
      c. He shall be its Reconciler *(Read Col. 1:20-22)*

★ **1:22** In relationship to the universe, Christ was its past Creator (1:16). He is its present Sustainer (1:17). He shall be its future Reconciler (1:20-22). Note:
- The nature of this reconciliation—Simply stated, it refers to the bringing about into a right relationship with the Father all those things within this sinful universe. This does not mean, of course, that all people (or any fallen angel) will be eventually saved. It does mean, however, that the glorious truth of Romans 8:28 will someday be totally realized.
- The time of this reconciliation—It began at the cross, but will be concluded with the sound of the seventh trumpet (see Rev. 11:15).

II. The Danger and Perversion of the Serpent (Col. 2)
   A. The nature of these perversions
      1. Enticing words (persuasive argument)—Verse 4

★ **2:4** This perversion would doubtless correspond favorably to the liberalism of the 20th century, which has promised so much but produced so little.

   2. Philosophy (Col. 2:8)

★ **2:8a** False philosophy is like a blind man looking in a dark room for a black cat that isn't there. It can also be described as that science of learning more and more about less and less until finally you know everything about nothing.

> 3. Vain deceit (empty deception)—(Col. 2:8)
> 4. Human tradition (Col. 2:8)

★ **2:8c** All traditions, of course, are not bad; but many are. Jesus soundly and severely denounced the wicked traditions of the godless Pharisees. (See Matt. 15:1-9.)

> 5. Worldly doctrines— *"Since you died with Christ to the basic principles of this world, why as though you still belonged to it, do you submit to its rules: Do not handle! Do not taste! Do not touch! These are all destined to perish with use, because they are based on human commands and teachings"* (Col. 2:20-22, NIV).
> 6. Legalism— *"Let no man therefore judge you in meat, or in drink, or in respect of an holy day, or of the new moon, or of the sabbath days"* (Col. 2:16). *"These are a shadow of the things that were to come; the reality, however, is found in Christ"* (Col. 2:17, NIV).

★ **2:17** A believer who puts himself back under legalism would be like a son admiring the photo of his father, but ignoring the father's actual presence.

> 7. Self-abasement (Col. 2:18, 23)
> 8. Worship of angels (Col. 2:18)
> 9. Receiving visions (Col. 2:18)
> 10. Self-made religion (Col. 2:23)
> B. The answer to these perversions
>   1. Know who Jesus is *(Read Col. 2:3, 9)*
>   2. Know what he has done for you *(Read Col. 2:1-2)*
>   a. The quickening *(Read Col. 2:13)*
>   b. The blotting *(Read Col. 2:14)*

★ **2:14**
- To expound upon the theological blessings of this verse, consider a statement found in Genesis 2:19: *"Adam called every living creature... the name thereof"* (Gen. 2:19b). Adam must have had a tremendous vocabulary. Ernest Mayr, America's leading taxonomist, lists the species existing today—3,500 mammals, 8,600 birds, and 5,500 reptiles and amphibians. In spite of all this, there were seven simple words unknown and unexperienced by Adam prior to his fall. These words were:
  - Death (Gen. 2:17)
  - Nakedness (3:7)
  - Cursed (3:14)
  - Sorrow (3:17)
  - Thorns (3:18)
  - Sweat (3:19)
  - Sword (3:24)
- After the fall, Adam soon added these bitter and bloody words to his vocabulary. The echo of these wicked words haunted Adam and mankind for over 40 centuries. Then came the second Adam (a name for Jesus).
- The New Testament tells us how he met and dealt with each word.
  - Death (John 11:25)

LESSON 31: THE BOOK OF COLOSSIANS

- Nakedness (John 19:23)
- Cursed (Gal. 3:13)
- Sorrow (John 12:27)
- Thorns (John 19:5)
- Sweat (Luke 22:44)
- Sword (John 19:34)

■ As a result of this, Paul literally shouts out the truth here in Colossians 2:14 that these terrible works of condemnation have forever been blotted out.

> c. The spoiling *(Read Col. 2:15)*
> d. The nourishing—*"The Head, from whom the entire body, being supplied and held together by the joints and ligaments, grows with a growth which is from God"* (Col. 2:19, NASB).
> 3. Know who you are *(Read Col. 2:10,12)*
> 4. Know what you are to do for him *(Read Col. 2:6-7)*
>
> **III. The Duty and Performance of the Saints (Col. 3-4)**
> A. In relation to the Son of God *(Read Col. 3:1-4)*

★ **3:4** Note two phrases in these verses:
- ■ *"Christ sitteth on the right hand of God"* (v.1b). This is but one of at least 13 references which speak of Christ being seated at God's right hand. The other instances are, as described by:
  - Jesus himself (Luke 22:69)
  - Peter (Acts 2:33; 5:31;1 Pet. 3:22)
  - Stephen (Acts 7:35)
  - Paul (Rom. 8:34; Eph.1:20)
  - Author of Hebrews (1:3, 13; 8:1; 10:12; 12:2)
- ■ *"Set your affection on things above, not on things on the earth"* (Col. 3:2).
  - Objection—"But isn't it possible for a Christian to be so heavenly minded that he is no earthly good?"
  - Observation—For every one believer so heavenly minded he's no earthly good there are doubtless ten believers so earthly minded that they are no heavenly good. A child of God functions both as a temporary pilgrim (down here) and a permanent citizen (up there). His pilgrimage thus should be governed by his citizenship.

> B. In relation to the Word of God *(Read Col. 3:16)*

★ **3:16** Colossians 3:16 is as vital to the sanctification of a saint as John 3:16 is to the justification of a sinner.

> C. In relation to the work of God *(Read Col. 3:17)*
> 1. What to put off *(Read Col. 3:5-9)*
> 2. What to put on *(Read Col. 3:10-12, 14)*
> D. In relation to our talks with God (Col. 4:2-4)
> 1. Paul's command to pray *(Read Col. 4:2)*
> 2. Paul's request for prayer *(Read Col. 4:3-4,18)*
> E. In relation to our testimony for God
> 1. Before the unsaved *(Read Col. 4:5-6)*
> 2. In the home (Col. 3:18-21)
>   a. Concerning wives *(Read Col. 3:18)*
>   b. Concerning husbands *(Read Col. 3:19)*

            c. Concerning children *(Read Col. 3:20)*
            d. Concerning fathers *(Read Col. 3:21)*
         3. On the job (Col. 3:22-25)
            a. Advice to servants *(Read Col. 3:22-24)*
            b. Advice to masters *(Read Col. 4:1)*
         4. In the church *(Read Col. 3:13)*
      F. In relation to the ministers of God (Col. 4:7-18)—Paul ends this epistle by sending greetings from eight men and by making a request.
         1. His greetings to the Colossians

- Tychicus—The carrier of the Colossian epistle
- Onesimus—The once runaway slave of Philemon
- Aristarchus— A fellow prisoner with Paul at this time
- John Mark—The author of Mark's Gospel
- Justus—Nothing known about him except that he was a coworker with Paul
- Epaphras—The imprisoned Colosse pastor
- Luke—Paul's beloved Greek physician and the author of Luke's Gospel and the book of Acts
- Demas—A coworker who would eventually forsake Paul (2 Tim. 4:10)
- Archippus—The Colossian believer who assumed Epaphras's place as pastor during Paul's imprisonment

         2. His request of the Colossians *(Read Col. 4:16)*

LESSON 32
INTRODUCTION TO FIRST THESSALONIANS

REPEATED RAPTURE REMINDERS

A. No other biblical book, regardless of its size, gives as much space to the Rapture as does 1 Thessalonians. This glorious event is referred to in each of its five chapters. (See 1:10; 2:19; 3:13; 4:13-18; 5:1-11, 23.) The passage in 4:13-18 is the most detailed single account of the Rapture in the Bible.

B. The church at Thessalonica was founded by Paul during his second missionary journey. (See Acts 17:1-10.) Of the many churches established by the apostle, only a few (six to be exact) would receive a New Testament epistle from Paul. Of the six, only the church at Corinth and the one in Thessalonica were blessed with two inspired letters.

C. Paul was hindered by Satan when he later attempted to visit this city (1 Thess. 2:18).

D. Paul spent at least three weeks in Thessalonica in the home of Jason (possibly a kinsman, see Rom. 16:21) organizing the church, working all the while as a tentmaker, that he might not be a burden to the believers. (See 1 Thess. 2:9; 2 Thess. 3:7-12.)

E. His visit there is short-lived, for the gospel is opposed by some unbelieving Jews. Thus, under cover of night, Paul, Timothy, and Silas leave for Berea.

F. He soon is driven from Berea by the same vicious Jews and heads for Athens. Timothy and Silas remain in Berea.

G. While in Athens he sends word to Timothy requesting that his young helper go back and strengthen the work at Thessalonica, which command Timothy obeys (1 Thess. 3:1-2).

H. From Athens, Paul goes to Corinth. Here at a later date both Silas and Timothy catch up with him. Timothy brings a good report concerning the work in Thessalonica. Paul is overjoyed and writes both 1 and 2 Thessalonians from Corinth at this time.

I. His first letter was written to encourage, establish, instruct, and inspire. The church was apparently composed of a great many Gentiles (Acts 17:4).

J. Henrietta Mears writes: "Paul's success in Thessalonica has not been the usual experience of missionaries among the heathen. Carey in India, Judson in Burma, Morrison in China, and Moffat in Africa waited each seven years for his first convert. But here, the Holy Spirit allowed Paul to reap a sudden harvest" *(What the Bible Is All About*, p. 532).

K. The church was noted for its soul winning zeal (1 Thess. 1:8).

L. The members were not, however, good Bible students (Acts 17:11).

M. There were difficulties in the congregation.
   1. Some were lazy (2 Thess. 3:10).
   2. Some were busybodies (2 Thess. 3:11).
   3. Some were disobedient (2 Thess. 3:14-15).

N. The book of 1 Thessalonians is the 19th longest New Testament book and 51st longest biblical book, with five chapters, 89 verses, and 1857 words. There are quotations or allusions from eight Old Testament books in 1 Thessalonians.

O. Great passages would include:
1. 3:12-13
2. 4:3-4
3. 4:13-18
4. 5:16-24

Overview of the Book of First Thessalonians

I. The Reputation of the Church
   A. It was an energetic church
   B. It was an elect church
   C. It was an exemplary church
      1. Paul's example to the church
      2. Their example to the world
   D. It was an evangelistic church
   E. It was an expectant church
      1. In the past — *"How ye turned to God from idols"*
      2. In the present — *"To serve the living and true God"*
      3. In the future — *"And to wait for his Son from heaven"*

II. The Review of the Church
   A. The activities of the shepherd in Thessalonica (what Paul says about himself)
      1. He was a suffering traveler
      2. He was a faithful steward
      3. He was a gentle mother
      4. He was a tireless laborer
      5. He was a consistent example
      6. He was a concerned father
      7. He was as a homesick brother
      8. He was an expectant soul winner
      9. He was as a missionary superintendent
     10. He was a prayer warrior
   B. The activities of the sheep in Thessalonica (what Paul says about his converts)
   C. The activities of the serpent in Thessalonica (what Paul says about his enemies)
      1. The Judaizers
      2. The devil

III. The Removal of the Church
   A. The challenges of this removal
      1. We are to know God's will (what he wants us to do)
      2. We are to know God's way (how he wants us to do it)
   B. The chronology of this removal
      1. A realization
      2. A repose
      3. A revelation
      4. A return
      5. A resurrection
      6. A Rapture

        7. A reunion
        8. A reassurance

IV. **The Responsibility of the Church**
    A. The God of purpose (what he wills for us to do)
        1. Be watchful
        2. Be helpful
        3. Be merciful
        4. Be respectful
        5. Be joyful
        6. Be prayerful
        7. Be thankful
        8. Be careful
    B. The God of peace (what he will do for us)

THE BOOK OF FIRST THESSALONIANS

"Paul, and Silvanus, and Timotheus, unto the church of the Thessalonians which is in God the Father and in the Lord Jesus Christ: Grace be unto you, and peace, from God our Father, and the Lord Jesus Christ. We give thanks to God always for you all, making mention of you in our prayers.... I charge you by the Lord that this epistle be read unto all the holy brethren" (1 Thess. 1:1-2; 5:27).

I. The Reputation of the Church (1 Thess. 1)
   A. It was an energetic church *(Read 1 Thess. 1:3)*

★ **1:3** The *New Scofield Bible* observes: "Even though Paul had ministered in Thessalonica for less than a month, many great doctrines of the Christian faith are alluded to in this Epistle: the Trinity (cf. 1:1 with 1:5-6); the Holy Spirit (1:5-6; 4:8; 5:19); Christ's second advent (1:10; 2:19; 3:13; 4:14-17; 5:23); the Day of the Lord (5:1-3); assurance (1:5); conversion (1:9); election (1:4); resurrection (4:14-18); sanctification (4:3; 5:23); and Christian behavior (2:12; 4:1)" (*New Scofield Reference Bible*, p. 1290).

   B. It was an elect church *(Read 1 Thess. 1:4)*

★ **1:4**
- Election is both individual and corporate. It covers both Christian and congregation. The latter is in view here. C. H. Spurgeon was once asked how he reconciled God's election with man's choice. He answered, "I never have to reconcile friends!"
- Both of these great theological truths are presented in the Bible. They are not contradictory, but complementary. The entire Trinity is directly involved in this election.
   - In regard to the Father: we were saved before the foundation of the world (Eph.1:4; 2 Tim. 1.9).
   - In regard to the Son: we were saved at the cross (Gal. 2:20).
   - In regard to the Holy Spirit: we were saved at the moment of our decision to accept Christ (1 Cor. 12:13; Titus 3:5).
- Thomas Constable writes: "That God has chosen to bless some individuals with eternal life is clearly taught in many places in both the Old and New Testaments (Deut. 4:37; 7:6-7; Isa. 44:1-2; Rom. 9; Eph.1:4-6, 11; Col. 3:12; 2 Thess. 2:13). Equally clear is the fact that God holds each individual personally responsible for his decision to trust or not to trust in Jesus Christ (cf. John 3; Rom. 5). The difficulty in putting divine election and human responsibility together is understanding how both can be true. That both are true is taught in the Bible. How both can be true is apparently incomprehensible to finite human minds; no one has ever been able to explain this antinomy satisfactorily. This task transcends human mental powers, much as seeing angels transcends human visual powers and hearing very high-pitched sounds transcends human auditory powers. The Thessalonians' response to the gospel message proved that God had chosen them for salvation" (*Bible Knowledge Commentary*, New Testament Volume, p. 691).

   C. It was an exemplary church (1 Thess. 1:5-7).
      1. Paul's example to the church *(Read 1 Thess. 1:5-6)*

★ **1:6** Paul speaks of preaching the gospel not only in word but in power also.
- God's Word is effective even though preached by a carnal believer (Isa. 55:11; Phil. 1:15-18). It is tragically possible for the divine message to be anointed while the human messenger is not.

■ God's will is that both his spokesmen and scriptures be in perfect harmony.

> 2. Their example to the world *(Read 1 Thess. 1:7)*
> D. It was an evangelistic church *(Read 1 Thess. 1:8)*

★ **1:8** Charles Ryrie comments: "The word translated 'sounded out' is very picturesque. The Greek letters, simply changed into English characters, spell our word echo. Thus the picture is of the message of the gospel so stirring the strings of the Thessalonians' hearts that it reverberated in strong and clear tones to all Greece and everywhere" (*First and Second Thessalonians*, p. 27). Thus, while waiting for the trumpet of Christ to sound, these Thessalonians were sounding out the trumpet for Christ (see I Thess. 4:16; see also Rom. 1:8).

> E. It was an expectant church (1 Thess. 1:9-10)—In these verses Paul summarizes the three spiritual stages of saved church members.
> 1. In the past—*"How ye turned to God from idols"* (1 Thess. 1:9).
> 2. In the present—*"To serve the living and true God"* (1 Thess. 1:9).
> 3. In the future—*"And to wait for his Son from heaven, whom he raised from the dead, even Jesus, which delivered us from the wrath to come"* (1 Thess. 1:10).

★ **1:10**
- ■ All this may be tied in beautifully with Paul's statement concerning them in 1:3 where he writes of their *"work of faith, and labour of love, and patience of hope."* Thus we see:
  - ● In the past—Turning, and looking to the Father. This was their work of faith (see John 6:28-29; Acts 20:21).
  - ● In the present—Serving, and looking on the fields. This was their labor of love (see John 4:35; 1 Cor. 15:58; Heb. 6:10).
  - ● In the future—Waiting, and looking for the Son. This was their patience of hope (see 2 Tim. 4:8).
- ■ Dr. John Walvoord writes: "Paul told how God had worked in the Thessalonians. It had resulted in their turning to God from idols to serve the living and true God. This is a very accurate expression and one we should understand. It does not say that they turned from idols to God. Rather, they turned to God from idols to serve the living and true God. It was not reformation first and faith in Christ second, but it was faith in Christ first with the result that idols were forsaken. The tense of the word turned, as it is found in the Greek New Testament, is in the aorist, which means that they turned once for all. It was a single, definite act" (*The Thessalonian Epistle*, p. 17).

> **II. The Review of the Church (1 Thess. 2-3)**—In these chapters the apostle reviews those circumstances involved in the founding of their church *(Read 1 Thess. 2:1)*.
> A. The activities of the shepherd in Thessalonica (what Paul says about himself)
> 1. He was a suffering traveler (1 Thess. 2:1-2)—*"But even after that we had suffered before, and were shamefully entreated, as ye know, at Philippi, we were bold in our God to speak unto you the gospel of God with much contention"* (1 Thess. 2:2). *"For verily, when we were with you, we told you before that we should suffer tribulation; even as it came to pass, and ye know"* (1 Thess. 3:4).

★ **2:2** The Greek word translated "contention" is *agonia*, from whence comes our English word agony.

> 2. He was a faithful steward *(Read 1 Thess. 2:2-6)*

★ **2:6** Here the apostle states that his message, motive, and method were all approved by God.

> 3. He was a gentle mother *(Read 1 Thess. 2:7-8)*

✱ **2:7** Dr. Charles Ryrie comments: "The word cherish means 'to warm' and is used of the way a mother bird covers her young (Deut. 22:6); its only other occurrence in the New Testament is our Lord's relationship to his church (Eph. 5:29)" (*First and Second Thessalonians*, p. 37). How a mother feeds her child is almost as important as what she feeds it. This is also brought out in Ephesians 4:15: "But speaking the truth [the what] in love [the how]."

> 4. He was a tireless laborer *(Read 1 Thess. 2:9)*

✱ **2:9** Richard Wolff writes: "Paul had learned to cut out and stitch the coarse goats' hair cloth used for making tents, shoes, and mats. It was customary for a Rabbi to learn a trade" (*General Epistles of First and Second Thessalonians*, p. 19).

> 5. He was a consistent example *(Read 1 Thess. 2:10)*

✱ **2:10** Note his three key words here:
- Holily—His testimony godward (spiritual)
- Justly—His testimony manward (social)
- Unblameably—His testimony selfward (personal). Thus, the upward, outward, and inward in Paul's life possessed that vital spiritual maturity a good leader simply must have.

> 6. He was a concerned father *(Read 1 Thess. 2:11-12)*

✱ **12:12** The apostle often pictures himself as a parent. (See 1 Cor. 4:14; 2 Cor. 6:13; Gal. 4:18-19; Phil. 1:10.)

> 7. He was as a homesick brother *(Read 1 Thess. 2:17)*
> 8. He was an expectant soul winner *(Read 1 Thess. 2:19-20)*

✱ **2:20**
- The Word of God mentions at least five possible rewards. These are:
  - The incorruptible crown—Given to those who master the old nature (1 Cor. 9:25-27).
  - The crown of life—Given to those who successfully endure temptation (James 1:2-3; Rev. 2:10).
  - The crown of righteousness—Given to those who especially love the doctrine of the Rapture (2 Tim. 4:8).
  - The crown of glory—Given to those faithful preachers and teachers (1 Pet. 5:2-4).
  - The crown of rejoicing—Given to soul winners (Prov.11:30;1 Thess. 2:19-20).
- Note Paul's statement in 2:19, "at his coming." The Greek word here is *parousia*, and is a technical term for the arrival or visit of a king. The word appears in many key New Testament prophecy passages. (See Matt. 24:3, 27, 37, 39; 2 Thess. 2:8; 1 Cor. 15:22-23; 1 Thess. 4:13-18; James 5:7-8; 1 John 2:28; 2 Pet. 1:16; 3:4.)

> 9. He was as a missionary superintendent *(Read 1 Thess. 3:1-5)*

✱ **3:2**
- Paul had previously been driven from Thessalonica and Berea by the unbelieving Jews. From Berea he went to Athens. While there he sent Timothy (who had remained in Berea) back to Thessalonica as a short-term missionary to strengthen the young church. In this passage he asks the Thessalonians not to pity him because of his manifold sufferings. The apostle declares that his trials had neither shaken nor surprised him, for, "we are appointed thereunto" (3:3; see also John 16:2; 1 Cor. 4:9; 2 Tim. 3:12; Acts 9:16).
- William MacDonald has written: "Paul reminds them that even when he was in Thessalonica, he used to tell them that Christians are appointed to afflictions. His predictions came true in their own lives; how well they knew it! Trials form a necessary discipline in our lives:

- They prove the reality of our faith, and weed out those who are mere professors (1 Pet. 1:7).
- They enable us to comfort and encourage others who are going through trials (2 Cor. 1:4).
- They develop certain graces, such as patience, in our character (Rom. 5:3).
- They make us more zealous in spreading the gospel (Acts 4:29; 5:27-29; 8:3-4).
- They help to remove the dross from our lives (Job 23:10)" (*Letters to the Thessalonians*, p. 44).

> 10. He was a prayer warrior (1 Thess. 2:13; 3:7-13).
>   a. The persistence of his prayers *(Read 1 Thess. 3:10)*
>   b. The purpose of his prayers *(Read 1 Thess. 3:10-13)*
> B. The activities of the sheep in Thessalonica (what Paul says about his converts) *(Read 1 Thess. 2:14; 3:6)*.
> C. The activities of the serpent in Thessalonica (what Paul says about his enemies)
>   1. The Judaizers *(Read 1 Thess. 2:15-16)*

✷ 2:16

■ Paul's worst enemies in Thessalonica (as in other places) had been the vicious Judaizers. How Satan had used them.
- They had already *"killed the Lord Jesus, and their own prophets"* (2:15). See also Acts 2:23; 3:15; 5:30; 7:52.
- They had *"persecuted us"* (2:15).
- They *"please not God, and are contrary to all men"* (2:15).
- They had forbidden Paul to *"speak to the Gentiles that they might be saved"* (2:16). See also Acts 13:50; 14:5, 19; 17:5; 18:12; 22:22.

■ Paul has been accused of being anti-Semitic, but this is totally unfounded. The apostle himself, of course, was an Israelite and proud of his background. (See Phil. 3:4-5.) Furthermore, his great heart practically bled for the conversion of his beloved nation. (See Rom. 9:1-3; 10:1.)

> 2. The devil *(Read 1 Thess. 2:18)*
> **III. The Removal of the Church (1 Thess. 4)**
>   A. The challenges of this removal
>   1. We are to know God's will (what he wants us to do) *(Read 1 Thess. 4:1, 3)*.

✷ 4:3 God has but one will for sinners, and that is that they become saved. (See I Tim. 2:4; 2 Pet. 3:9.) In like manner he has only one will for saints and that is that they be sanctified. Here Paul, of course, refers to a daily growing in grace and maturing in the faith. The first step in sanctification is consecration. (See Rom. 12:1-2.)

> 2. We are to know God's way (how he wants us to do it).
>   a. Concerning self—Purity *(Read 1 Thess. 4:3-5)*
>   b. Concerning saints—Charity (1 Thess. 4:6-10)
>   (1) The revelation of the matter *(Read 1 Thess. 4:6, 9)*
>   (2) The reasons for the matter *(Read 1 Thess. 4:7-8)*
>   c. Concerning sinners—Honesty (1 Thess. 4:11-12). "And to make it your ambition to lead a quiet life and attend to your own business and work with your hands just as we commanded you; so that you may behave properly toward outsiders and not be in any need" *(1 Thess. 4:11-12, NASB)*.
> B. The chronology of this removal (1 Thess. 4:13-18)

✷ In this great passage Paul answers a question that had bothered the Thessalonians. When he was among them (Acts 17) they had doubtless learned many precious truths about the glorious return of Christ to earth someday and the establishing of his kingdom. In fact, to some, this all seemed to be just around the corner. But since the apostle's departure, a number of believers had died. They obviously then would not be here on earth at the time of Christ's return. Did this mean they would miss everything? This then is the background and to the great Rapture passage before us here in chapter 4.

> 1. A realization *(Read 1 Thess. 4:13)*

✶ **4:13** This is but one of five key areas in which Paul would not have believers to be ignorant. The other four are:
- The events in the Old Testament (1 Cor. 10:1)
- The restoration of Israel (Rom. 11:25)
- The manifestation of spiritual gifts (1 Cor. 12:1)
- The devices of Satan (2 Cor. 2:11)

> 2. A repose *(Read 1 Thess. 4:14)*

✶ **4:14**
- The death of a believer is looked upon as a peaceful sleep. (See Matt. 27:52; John 11:11; Acts 7:60; 13:36; 1 Cor. 15:6,18,20,51; 2 Pet. 3:4.) However, it should be quickly stated that this verse in no way teaches soul sleep. That unscriptural doctrine is refuted by Matthew 17:3 and Revelation 6:9-11.
- The sleep here thus refers to the body of the believer, and not the believer himself. Paul makes this very clear in another passage: *"We are confident, I say, and willing rather to be absent from the body, and to be present with the Lord"* (2 Cor. 5:8).

> 3. A revelation *(Read 1 Thess. 4:15)*

✶ **4:15** Note Paul's use of the pronoun "we." The apostle apparently hoped to be there when Christ came. He would later know otherwise. (See 2 Tim. 4:6.)

> 4. A return *(Read 1 Thess. 4:16)*

✶ **4:16a**
- *"For the Lord himself"* — This glorious and personal return will be a fulfillment of the prophecy made at the time of Christ's ascension. *"And while they looked stedfastly toward heaven as he went up, behold, two men stood by them in white apparel; which also said, Ye men of Galilee, why stand ye gazing up into heaven? this same Jesus which is taken up from you into heaven, shall so come in like manner as ye have seen him go into heaven"* (Acts 1:10-11).
- *"The voice of the archangel"* — It is often supposed that Michael will be this archangel on the basis of Daniel 12:1-2. However, it is not unreasonable to suggest that Gabriel will be the angel involved at this time because of the vital part he played in those events surrounding the first coming of Christ. (See Luke 1:19, 26; Matt. 1:20; 2:13.)

> 5. A resurrection — *"And the dead in Christ shall rise first"* (1 Thess. 4:16b).

✶ **4:16b** This makes the second of three resurrections mentioned by Paul in 1 Corinthians 15:23-24:
- The resurrection of Christ (*"Christ the first fruits"*)
- The Rapture resurrection (*"they that are Christ's at his coming"*)
- The resurrection of Old Testament and tribulational saints (*"then cometh the end"*). See also Revelation 20:4, 6.

> 6. A Rapture — *"Then we which are alive and remain shall be caught up together."* (1 Thess. 4:17).
> 7. A reunion — *"With them in the clouds, to meet the Lord in the air: and so shall we ever be with the Lord"* (1 Thess. 4:17).
> 8. A reassurance — *"Wherefore comfort one another with these words"* (1 Thess. 4:18).

LESSON 32: THE BOOK OF FIRST THESSALONIANS

IV. The Responsibility of the Church (1 Thess. 5)
   A. The God of purpose (what he wills for us to do) (1 Thess. 5:1-22)
      1. Be watchful (1 Thess. 5:1-8)
         a. The action involved *(Read 1 Thess. 5:2)*

✸ **5:2**
- *"The day of the Lord"* — Here is the first reference in the New Testament to this period. It is found often in the Old Testament (e.g., Isa. 13:9-11; Joel 2:28-32; Zeph. 1:14-18; 3:14-15), or a title used to describe the coming great tribulation.
- *"As a thief in the night"* — Christ's second coming is often compared in this manner (Luke 12:39; 1 Thess. 5:4; 2 Pet. 3:10; Rev. 3:3; 16:15). These verses stress two great truths:
  - Regarding the suddenness of his return.
  - Regarding our watchfulness for his return.

         b. The reaction involved
            (1) The children of light *(Read 1 Thess. 5:4-6, 8)*

✸ **5:8** This is in contrast to the unsaved, who are described as the children of darkness. Someday the Sun of righteousness shall arise with healing in his wings (Mal. 4:2). It is therefore only logical that the children of light should await that glorious day.

            (2) The children of darkness *(Read 1 Thess. 5:3, 7)*
      2. Be helpful (1 Thess. 5:9-11, 14).
         a. The *why* of the matter *(Read 1 Thess. 5:9-10)*

✸ **5:10**
- Concerning verse 9: This is a reference to both external wrath (John 3:36; Col. 3:6) and tribulational wrath (Rev. 6:17; 15:1; 11:18). Paul begins and ends his epistle to the Thessalonian church with this precious promise. (Compare 1:9 with 5:9.)
- Concerning verse 10-William MacDonald writes: "This verse emphasizes the tremendous price our Lord paid to deliver us from wrath and insure our salvation. He died for us that whether awake or asleep we should live together with Him. There will be two classes of believers at His coming:
  - Those who have died.
  - Those who are living. The former are spoken of as being asleep, the latter as being awake. Whether we are among the living or the dead at the time of His return, we shall live with Him. Christians who die lose nothing. The Lord said the same thing, in effect, to Martha, 'I am the resurrection, and the life: he that believeth on me, though he die [i.e., a Christian who has died], yet shall he live [he will be raised at the Rapture]; and whosoever liveth and believeth on me [a believer alive at the time of the Rapture] shall never die (John 11:25-26)" (*Letter to the Thessalonians*, p. 68).

         b. The *who* of the matter *(Read 1 Thess. 5:11, 14)*

✸ **5:14**
- Warn the unruly. The Greek word here is *ataktos*, which referred to soldiers who deserted their ranks.
- Comfort the feebleminded. A better word here would be fainthearted.
- Support the weak, the immature. (See Rom. 14.)

      3. Be merciful *(Read 1 Thess. 5:15)*
      4. Be respectful *(Read 1 Thess. 5:12-13)*
      5. Be joyful *(Read 1 Thess. 5:16)*

✴ **5:16** This verse in the Greek is the shortest in the New Testament (and not John 11:35). It is often, however, one of the hardest to keep.

> 6. Be prayerful *(Read 1 Thess. 5:17)*

✴ **5:17** Charles Ryrie writes: "The Christian's joy puts him in the proper mood to pray without ceasing. Paul has already used the words without ceasing twice of his own remembrance of the Thessalonians (1:3; 2:13) and now he enjoins it on the believers. Outside the New Testament the word is used of a hacking cough and aptly illustrates what Paul has in mind here about prayer. Just as a person with a hacking cough is not always audibly coughing, though the tendency to cough is always there, so the Christian who prays without ceasing is not always praying audibly and yet prayer is always the attitude of his heart and life" (*First and Second Thessalonians*, p. 80).

> 7. Be thankful *(Read 1 Thess. 5:18)*

✴ **5:18** (See also Eph. 5:20; Col. 3:17.) The importance of this command cannot be overstated. The cure for pride in our lives is not to practice humility, lest we become proud of our piousness, but to be thankful. In Romans 1, Paul described the terrible final stages of Gentile world apostasy. The picture he paints is one of the most chilling in all the Bible. What horrible crime could possibly cause all this? Note his answer: *"Because, when they knew God, they glorified him not as God, neither were thankful"* (Rom. 1:21). Someone has offered the following little rule: Be careful for nothing, be prayerful in everything, and be thankful for anything.

> 8. Be careful (1 Thess. 5:19-22).
>   a. Concerning the Spirit of God— *"Quench not the Spirit"* (1 Thess. 5:19).

✴ **5:19** The Holy Spirit is like a fire. (See Matt. 3:11; Luke 3:16; Acts 2:3; Heb. 11:34.) To quench the Spirit is one of two sins a believer can commit against this blessed third person of the Trinity who lives in our hearts. The other is to grieve him. (See Eph. 4:30.) To quench him is not to do what he wants us to do, while to grieve him is to do what he does not want us to do.

>   b. Concerning the gifts of God— *"Despise not prophesyings"* (1 Thess. 5:20).
>   c. Concerning the Word of God— *"Prove all things; hold fast that which is good"* (1 Thess. 5:21).
>   d. Concerning my walk for God— *"Abstain from all appearance of evil"* (1 Thess. 5:22).
> B. The God of peace (what he will do for us) *(Read 1 Thess. 5:23-28)*

✴ **5:24**
- Verse 23 has been a main support for the doctrine of trichotomy, which teaches that we are a threefold being: spirit, soul, and body. Whatever else may be involved in this verse, Paul is praying that God would sanctify the total believer. God is not involved in "saving souls," but in sanctifying individuals. Jesus strongly brings this out. (See Matt. 22:36-40.)
- Note the final words in 5:23, *"...unto the coming of our Lord Jesus Christ."* Paul ends this chapter as he has done the previous four, with a reference to the second appearing of Christ. In the first chapter (1:10) he connects it with salvation; in the second (2:19-20), with service; in the third (3:13), with stability; in the fourth (4:18), with sorrow; and here with sanctification.
- This epistle, Paul commanded, was to *"be read unto all the holy brethren"* (5:27; see also Col. 4:16; 1 Tim. 4:13; Rev. 1:3).

LESSON 33
INTRODUCTION TO SECOND THESSALONIANS

THE SIN OF MAN AND THE MAN OF SIN

- A. In 2 Thessalonians Paul writes of both.
    1. General facts concerning the sin of man (1:8-9; 3:6-15)
    2. Specific facts concerning the man of sin (2:1-12)
- B. The New Testament's two most extended passages dealing with the coming Antichrist are 2 Thessalonians 2:1-12 and Revelation 13:1-8.
- C. This book is the shortest of Paul's epistles to local churches.
- D. The book of 1 Corinthians was his longest to a local assembly.
- E. Paul wrote 1 Thessalonians to tell his converts they had not missed the Rapture. He now writes this epistle assuring them they were not enduring the great tribulation.
- F. Merrill Tenney summarizes both 1 and 2 Thessalonians: "Practically every major doctrine in the catalogue of faith is represented in these two small epistles. Although they were not written as doctrinal treatises, nor primarily to present the author's general theological views, they contain a well-rounded body of theological teaching.
- G. The book of 2 Thessalonians is the 22nd longest New Testament book, and 60th longest biblical book, with three chapters, 47 verses, and 1,042 words. There are quotations or allusions from nine Old Testament books in this epistle.
- H. Great passages would include:
    1. 1:11-12
    2. 2:13-17
    3. 3:3-5

Overview of the Book of Second Thessalonians

I. Explanation — The Way of the Lord (A Pastoral Encouragement)
   A. God and the persecuted
      1. The saints and the benefits of persecution (we receive the good)
      2. The Savior and the benefits of persecution (he receives the glory)
   B. God and the persecutors
      1. The judge
      2. The judged
      3. The judgment

II. Tribulation — The Wrath of the Lord (A Prophetical Enlightenment)
   A. Facts concerning the day of the Lord
      1. The day of the Lord and the church
      2. The day of the Lord and the Antichrist
      3. The day of the Lord and the restrainer
      4. The day of the Lord and the unsaved
   B. Facts concerning the destined of the Lord
      1. The source and time of our salvation
      2. The method and means of our salvation
      3. The goal of our salvation
      4. The responsibilities of our salvation
      5. The reassurance of our salvation

III. Consecration — The Will of the Lord (A Practical Exhortation)
   A. Paul's request
   B. Paul's reassurance
   C. Paul's reprimand
      1. The recipients of this reprimand
      2. The recommendations in this reprimand

THE BOOK OF SECOND THESSALONIANS

"Paul, and Silvanus, and Timotheus, unto the church of the Thessalonians in God our Father and the Lord Jesus Christ: Grace unto you, and peace, from God our Father and the Lord Jesus Christ" (2 Thess. 1:1-2).

> I. Explanation—The Way of the Lord (A Pastoral Encouragement, 2 Thess. 1). In this chapter Paul explains (in part) just why God often allows believers to suffer persecution.
>   A. God and the persecuted
>   1. The saints and the benefits of persecution (we receive the good)
>   a. The benefit of sanctification
>   (1) Our faith in God is enlarged (2 Thess. 1:3).
>   (2) Our love for believers is enlarged (2 Thess. 1:3).

★ 1:3a Dr. Charles Ryrie states that this verb "groweth exceedingly" is a very strong compound one, found only here in the New Testament, and indicates organic growth, as a healthy plant.

> (3) Our example to all is enlarged (2 Thess. 1:4).
>   b. The benefit of preparation—*"All this is evidence that God's judgment is right, and as a result you will be counted worthy of the kingdom of God, for which you are suffering" (2 Thess. 1:5, NIV).*
>   2. The Savior and the benefits of persecution (he receives the glory) *(Read 2 Thess. 1:10, 12)*

★ 1:12 Dr. John Walvoord writes: "This is an expression often used but perhaps not always analyzed or understood as it should be. The Scriptures state: 'The heavens declare the glory of God; and the firmament sheweth his handiwork. Day unto day uttereth speech, and night unto night sheweth knowledge' (Psa. 19:1-2). What does it mean when it is said that the heavens declare the glory of God? The heavens declare that God is perfect. The heavens manifest his wisdom, his power, and his intelligent end. The heavens are manifesting the glory of God in the sense that they reveal what God is and what he can do. But the heavens are not designed to reveal the love of God, the grace of God, nor the righteousness of God. We are designed to show 'the exceeding riches of his grace in his kindness toward us through Christ' (Eph. 2:7)" (*The Thessalonian Epistles*, p. 112).

>   B. God and the persecutors (2 Thess. 1:7-9)
>   1. The judge *(Read 2 Thess. 1:7)*
>   2. The judged *(Read 2 Thess. 1:8)*

★ 1:8
- What a contrast is seen here in regard to angels concerning Christ's first coming and his second coming:
  - First coming—Angels are prohibited from delivering the Savior from the Calvary judgment (Matt. 26:52-53).
  - Second coming—Angels are permitted to deliver sinners to the final judgment.
- Note also the two categories of sinners here:
  - *"Them that know not God"*—These are probably those who may never have heard the spoken gospel, but did have both the witness of conscience and nature, and are therefore without excuse. (See especially Rom. 1:18-20; 2:12-16.)
  - *"Them ... that obey not the gospel of our Lord Jesus Christ."* Here is doubtless a reference to those who actually heard but then refused the gospel invitation.

> 3. The judgment *(Read 2 Thess. 1:9)*

✶ 1:9 William McDonald writes: "They shall suffer punishment. A god who doesn't punish sin is no god at all. The idea that a God of love must not punish sin overlooks the fact that God is also holy and must do what is morally right. The nature of the punishment is here defined as eternal destruction. The word translated eternal (*aionios*) is used 70 times in the New Testament. Three times it may mean ages of limited duration (Rom. 16:25; Titus 1:2). The other times it means eternal or endless. It is used in Romans 16:26 to describe the unending existence of God."

"Destruction never means annihilation. It means loss of well-being, or ruin as far as the purpose of existence is concerned. The wineskins which the Lord Jesus described in Luke 5:37 were destroyed (same word as used here). They did not cease to exist, but they were ruined as far as further usefulness was concerned."

"The punishment of the wicked also includes banishment from the presence of the Lord and from the glory of His might. To perish without Him is to be without Him forever" (*Letters to the Thessalonians*, pp. 87-88).

A final thought may prove helpful before leaving this chapter. In 1 Thessalonians Paul had dealt with the Rapture of Christ. (See 1 Thess. 4:13-18.) But here in the opening chapter of 2 Thessalonians, he describes the revelation of Christ. These two great events are not one and the same and should not be confused. William McDonald offers the following helpful distinction:

- **The Rapture**
  - Christ comes in the air (1 Thess. 4:17).
  - He comes for his saints (1 Thess. 4:16-17).
  - The Rapture is a mystery, i.e., a truth unknown in Old Testament times (1 Cor. 15:51).
  - Christ's coming for his saints is never said to be preceded by signs in the heavens.
  - The Rapture is identified with the day of Christ (1 Cor. 1:8; 2 Cor. 1:14; Phil. 1:6, 10).
  - The Rapture is presented as a time of blessing (1 Thess. 4:18).
  - The Rapture takes place in a moment, in the twinkling of an eye (1 Cor.15:52). This strongly implies that it will not be witnessed by the world.
  - The Rapture seems to involve the church primarily (John 14:1-4; 1 Cor. 15:51-58; 1 Thess. 4:13-18).
  - Christ comes as the bright and morning star (Rev. 22:16).
- **The Revelation**
  - He comes to the earth (Zech. 14:4).
  - He comes with his saints (1 Thess. 3:13; Jude 14).
  - The revelation is not a mystery; it is the subject of many Old Testament prophecies (Psa. 72; Isa. 11; Zech. 14).
  - Christ's coming with his saints will be heralded by celestial portents (Matt. 24:29-30).
  - The revelation is identified with the day of the Lord (2 Thess. 2:1-12, ASV).
  - The main emphasis of the revelation is on judgment (2 Thess. 2:8-12).
  - The revelation will be visible worldwide (Matt. 24:27; Rev. 1:7).
  - The revelation involves Israel primarily, then also the Gentile nations.
  - Christ comes as the sun of righteousness with healing in his wings (Mal. 4:2).

> **II. Tribulation—The Wrath of the Lord (A Prophetical Enlightenment—2 Thess. 2)**
> A. Facts concerning the day of the Lord (2 Thess. 2:1-12)—The day of the Lord as used here ("day of Christ" in the King James Version)

✶ We begin this section by noting that the expression "day of Christ" should be translated "day of the Lord." A vast difference separates these two biblical days. The day of the Lord refers to the coming seven-year tribulation. (See especially Joel 1:15; 2:1-2; Rev. 6:12-17.) The day of Christ points to the future millennium. (See 1 Cor. 1:8; 5:5; Phil. 1:6, 10; 2:16.) These believers had somehow been tricked by Satan into believing this dreadful day of the Lord had come.

1. The day of the Lord and the church (2 Thess. 2:1-3)
   a. The confusion— *"Now we request you, brethren, with regard to the coming of our Lord Jesus Christ, and our gathering together to Him, that you may not be quickly shaken from your composure or be disturbed either by a spirit or a message or a letter as if from us, to the effect that the day of the Lord has come"* (2 Thess. 2:1-2, NASB).

★ **2:2**
- *"Neither by spirit"* —That is, don't believe any false prophet who might receive this "through the spirit."
- *"Nor by word"* —That is, don't listen to any false teacher who might teach this.
- *"Nor by letter as from us"* —That is, don't accept any letter supposedly coming from me which would teach this, for such a letter is false.

   b. The clarification *(Read 2 Thess. 2:3)*

★ **2:3**
- Note the expression, "a falling away first." Some have translated this, "a catching away first," believing it to be a reference to the Rapture. This is a theological possibility, but the Greek word is *apostasia*, from whence our English word apostasy comes. It thus would seem more likely to mean the worldwide religious apostasy which Paul would later write (in past) about. (See 1 Tim. 4:1-3; 2 Tim. 3:1-5; 4:3-4.)
- Merrill F. Unger writes: "Before the day of the Lord bursts upon a Christ-rejecting world, there must first come the apostasy, or falling away. This is not simple departure from the faith often characterizing the church age (1 Tim. 4:1-5; 2 Tim. 3:1-8; Rev. 3:14-22), but the wholesale rebellion and thoroughgoing lapse into error and demonism of the period just preceding Christ's advent in glory (Luke 18:8; Rev. 9:20-21)" (*Unger's Bible Handbook*, p. 711).
- What then is the relationship between the church and the day of the Lord? It is simply this: the tribulation cannot begin until the church is removed from the earth.

2. The day of the Lord and the Antichrist (2 Thess. 2:3-5, 8-9)
   a. His titles
      (1) The man of sin (2 Thess. 2:3)
      (2) The son of perdition (2 Thess. 2:3)

★ **2:3** Some believe that Judas Iscariot will be the Antichrist, pointing out that the title, "son of perdition," is found but two times in the New Testament. Jesus himself had used it first in reference to Judas (see John 17:12), and now Paul calls the Antichrist by the same name. Such evidence is, of course, far from conclusive.

      (3) The mystery of iniquity (2 Thess. 2:7)

★ **2:7** The mystery of iniquity in one sense is the evil opposite of the mystery of godliness.
- The mystery of godliness refers to that historical event whereby all the fulness of God both indwelled and empowered Jesus Christ. (See 2 Cor. 5:19; Col. 2:9; 1 Tim. 3:16.)
- The mystery of iniquity refers to that prophetical event whereby all the fullness of Satan will both indwell and empower the Antichrist.

      (4) The wicked one (2 Thess. 2:8)
   b. His travesty *(Read 2 Thess. 2:4)*
   c. His trickery *(Read 2 Thess. 2:9)*

> d. His termination *(Read 2 Thess. 2:8)*
> 3. The day of the Lord and the restrainer (2 Thess. 2:6-7) — *"And you know what restrains him now, so that in his time he may be revealed. For the mystery of lawlessness is already at work; only he who now restrains will do so until he is taken out of the way" (2 Thess. 2:6-7,* NASB*).*

✷ **2:7** Who or what is this powerful restrainer? There are several theories:
- It is human government. However, this is unlikely, for Satan already exercises strong influence upon the kingdoms of mankind. (See Matt. 4:8.)
- It is angels. This too is remote. (See Jude 9.)
- It is the Holy Spirit. This is by far the most logical conclusion. Dr. Charles Ryrie writes: "The pretribulation argument is simply this. The restrainer is God, and the instrument of restraint is the God-indwelt church (cf. Eph. 4:6 for God indwelling; Gal. 2:20 for Christ indwelling; I Cor. 6:19 for the Spirit indwelling). It should be remembered that Christ said of the divinely indwelt and empowered church that 'the gates of hell shall not prevail against it' (Matt.16:18), so we can say that this indwelt, empowered church is an adequate restraining instrument against the forces of darkness. The church will not go through any of the tribulation because the restrainer will be removed before the Man of Sin is revealed, which revelation (with the signing of the covenant with the Jews, Dan. 9:27) begins the tribulation period. Since the restrainer is ultimately God, and since God indwells all Christians, either He must be withdrawn from the hearts of believers while they are left on earth to go through the tribulation, or else when He is withdrawn all believers are taken with Him. Since it is impossible for a believer to be 'disindwelt' the only alternative is that believers too will be taken out of the way before the appearance of the Man of Sin, which signals the start of the tribulation" *(First and Second Thessalonians*, p. 112).

> 4. The day of the Lord and the unsaved *(Read 2 Thess. 2:10-12)*

2:12 Note it is God who sends these strong delusions. God's divine sovereignty is seen even in the activities of unsaved people and apostate angels. (See Exod. 4:21; Gen. 50:20; Josh. 11:20; 1 Sam. 16:14; 1 Kings 22:19-23; Judg. 9:23.) Dr. John Walvoord writes: "Some understand from verse 11 that if a person in this present age of grace hears the gospel and does not receive Christ as Savior, then when Christ comes and takes His church home to glory these will find it impossible to be saved after the church is translated. It is unlikely that a person who rejects Christ in this day of grace will turn to Him in that awful period of tribulation. But the usual principle of Scripture is that while there is life there is hope. It is possible, though very improbable, that a person who has heard the gospel in this present age of grace will come to Christ after the Rapture. The Scriptures definitely teach that God will send strong delusion to those who do not believe after the church is gone. God will judge their hearts, and if they deliberately turn away from the truth He will permit them to believe a lie. They will honor the man of sin as their god and as their king, instead of acknowledging the Lord Jesus Christ. The result will be 'That they all might be damned who believed not the truth, but had pleasure in unrighteousness'" *(The Thessalonian Epistles*, p. 129).

> B. Facts concerning the destined of the Lord (2 Thess. 2:13-17) — After dealing with the eternal damnation of the lost, Paul now deals with the eternal salvation of the saved.
> 1. The source and time of our salvation *(2 Thess. 2:13)*
> 2. The method and means of our salvation — *"Through sanctification by the Spirit and faith in the truth" (2 Thess. 2:13,* NASB*).*

✷ **2:13b** It has been said that had it not been for the Father and Son, there would have been no salvation feast; and were it not for the Spirit, there would be no guests.

> 3. The goal of our salvation — *"And it was for this He called you through our gospel that you may gain the glory of our Lord Jesus Christ" (2 Thess. 2:14,* NASB*).*

★ **2:14** That is, that believers might one day share the splendor and honor that Jesus now enjoys, seated at the right hand of the Father. The intrinsic glory of Christ, however, will never be shared with any human being. (See Isa. 42:8; John 17:1, 5.)

> 4. The responsibilities of our salvation *(Read 2 Thess. 2:15)*

★ **2:15** Paul obviously felt this admonition was sorely needed, based upon the original evaluation of the church in Thessalonica, as given in Acts: *"And the brethren immediately sent away Paul and Silas by night unto Berea: who coming thither went into the synagogue of the Jews. These were more noble than those in Thessalonica, in that they received the word with all readiness of mind, and searched the scriptures daily, whether those things were so"* (Acts 17:10-11).

> 5. The reassurance of our salvation *(Read 2 Thess. 2:16-17)*
> **III. Consecration—The Will of the Lord (A Practical Exhortation, 2 Thess. 3)**
>   A. Paul's request *(Read 2 Thess. 3:1-2)*
>   B. Paul's reassurance *(Read 2 Thess. 3:3-5)*
>   C. Paul's reprimand *(2 Thess. 3:6-18)*
>   1. The recipients of this reprimand
>   a. The disorderly *(Read 2 Thess. 3:6,11)*
>   b. The busybodies *(2 Thess. 3:11)*
>   c. The loafers *(2 Thess. 3:7-10)*
>   (1) Paul's work record *(Read 2 Thess. 3:7-9)*
>   (2) Paul's work rule *(Read 2 Thess. 3:10)*
>   d. The disobedient *(Read 2 Thess. 3:14)*
>   2. The recommendations in this reprimand
>   a. First step—Identify them *(Read 2 Thess. 3:14)*
>   b. Second step—Admonish them *(Read 2 Thess. 3:12, 15)*
>   c. Third step—Excommunicate them *(Read 2 Thess. 3:6, 14b)*
>   d. Fourth step—Love them as a brother or sister through it all *(Read 2 Thess. 3:15)*

Three: LETTERS BY PAUL TO INDIVIDUALS

A study of the epistles of Paul, which he penned to different followers of God:

- ➤ I Timothy
- ➤ II Timothy
- ➤ Titus
- ➤ Philemon
- ➤ II Thessalonians

LESSON 34

INTRODUCTION TO FIRST TIMOTHY

FROM AN OLD MAN OF GOD TO A YOUNG MAN OF GOD

   A. The book of 1 Timothy is the first of three New Testament letters written especially to pastors. The other two are 2 Timothy and Titus. Paul probably wrote both this epistle and Titus between his first and second imprisonments.

   B. The New Testament has much to say concerning Timothy.

   C. His name appears some 24 times.

   D. He was from Lystra and probably was saved during Paul's first missionary trip (Acts 14:19-20; 16:1-2).

   E. His mother (Eunice) and grandmother (Lois) were godly Jewish women, but his father was a pagan Greek (Acts 16:1; 2 Tim. 1:5).

   F. He is invited by Paul to "join the team" during the apostle's second trip (Acts 16:3). This team would consist of Silas, Paul, and Luke.

   G. Timothy may have been chosen to take John Mark's place. (See Acts 13:5.)

   H. He is circumcised by Paul that he might have freedom to preach the gospel in the various Jewish synagogues (Acts 16:3; see also 1 Cor. 9:20).

   I. Timothy is formally ordained by Paul and the presbytery (1 Tim. 4:14; 2 Tim. 1:6).

   J. He also accompanies Paul during the third missionary trip (Acts 19:22; 20:4; 2 Cor. 1:1,19).

   K. He becomes Paul's close companion during the apostle's first imprisonment. (See Phil. 1:1; Col. 1:1; Philem. 1:1.)

   L. Like Paul, Timothy also suffers imprisonment. (See Heb. 13:23.)

   M. He performs a ministry in at least five New Testament churches:
      1. Thessalonica (1 Thess. 3:2, 6)
      2. Corinth (1 Cor. 4:17; 16:10; 2 Cor. 1:19)
      3. Philippi (Phil. 2:19-23)
      4. Berea (Acts 17:14)
      5. Ephesus (1 Tim. 1:2)

   N. Timothy may have been a somewhat reserved individual and one who did not always enjoy robust health (1 Tim. 4:12, 14-16).

   O. He was, nevertheless, a man of God (see 1 Tim. 6:11).

   P. This epistle provides the most extended list explaining the needed qualifications for pastors and deacons in the New Testament. (See 3:1-13.)

   Q. It also includes the first of three passages in Paul's writings where he predicts last day conditions. (Compare 1 Tim. 4:1-4 with 2 Tim. 3:1-9; 4:1-4.)

   R. The reason for man's headship over the woman is also given in this epistle. (See 2:9-15.)

S. The book of 1 Timothy is the 16th longest New Testament book and 47th longest biblical book, with six chapters, 113 verses, and 2,269 words. There are quotations or allusions from 11 Old Testament books in 1 Timothy.

T. Great passages would include:
    1. 2:1-6
    2. 3:14-16
    3. 4:11-16
    4. 6:13-16

Overview of the Book of First Timothy

I. Paul and the Family of God
   A. He was an apostle
   B. He was a father
   C. He was a former blasphemer
   D. He became a sinner saved by grace
   E. He thus served as God's trophy
   F. He was a suffering servant
   G. He was, most of all, a preacher
      1. His message—The gospel
      2. His mission field—The Gentiles
      3. His master—The Savior

II. Timothy and the Family of God
   A. Timothy's personal responsibilities
      1. Stay in Ephesus
      2. Maintain a good conscience
      3. Examine yourself
      4. Examine your doctrine
      5. Discipline yourself
      6. Be an example
      7. Develop your gift
      8. Take care of your body
      9. Avoid the love of money
      10. Pursue the good
      11. Be a soldier
      12. Be impartial
   B. Timothy's public responsibilities
      1. Concerning the pulpit in the church
      2. Concerning prayers in the church
      3. Concerning women in the church
      4. Concerning widows in the church
      5. Concerning senior saints in the church
      6. Concerning elders in the church
      7. Concerning the rich in the church
      8. Concerning servants in the church

III. Church Officers and the Family of God
   A. Qualifications for the office of bishop
      1. He must be a male
      2. He must be without reproach
      3. He must be the husband of one wife
      4. He must be temperate

        5. He must be prudent
        6. He must be respectable
        7. He must be given to hospitality
        8. He must be able to teach
        9. He must not be given to wine
        10. He must not be pugnacious
        11. He must be gentle
        12. He must not be contentious
        13. He must be free from the love of money
        14. He must rule his own house well
        15. He must not be a novice or new convert
        16. He must have a good reputation in the unsaved community
    B. Qualifications for the office of a deacon
        1. He must be a man of dignity
        2. He must not be double-tongued
        3. He must not be given to wine
        4. He must be no lover of money
        5. He must possess a pure conscience
        6. He must not be a novice
        7. If married, he must be the husband of a godly wife
        8. He must be the husband of one wife
        9. He must rule his own house well

IV. False Teachers and the Family of God
    A. Their theology
        1. The source of their teaching
        2. The substance of their teaching
    B. Their tactics
        1. Arguing
        2. Stirring up constant friction
    C. Their transgressions
        1. They use the Law in the wrong way
        2. They allow their own conscience to be seared
        3. They use the church for personal gain
        4. They oppose the true faith with false theories of science

V. The Savior and the Family of God
    A. His incarnation
    B. His purpose
    C. His deity
    D. His successful ministry
    E. His suffering and death
    F. His resurrection
    G. His ascension
    H. His mediatorship
    I. His return
    J. His millennial reign

THE BOOK OF FIRST TIMOTHY

Introduction: This epistle is, in essence, a personal letter to the family of God *(Read 1 Tim. 3:14-15)*.

I. Paul and the Family of God
  A. He was an apostle *(Read 1 Tim. 1:1)*
  B. He was a father *(Read 1 Tim. 1:2)*
  C. He was a former blasphemer *(Read 1 Tim. 1:13)*
  D. He became a sinner saved by grace *(Read 1 Tim. 1:14)*

✶ **1:14** Note: Paul lists the three motivating forces in his life:
  ■ Love—His love for Christ constrained him to labor (2 Cor. 5:14).
  ■ Faith—His faith in Christ empowered him to labor (Eph. 1:19).
  ■ Grace—His grace from Christ enabled him to labor (Heb. 12:28). Thus, we are saved by grace (Eph. 2:8-9), that we might serve through grace (Rom. 12:3-6).

  E. He thus served as God's trophy—*"And yet for this reason I found mercy, in order that in me as the foremost Jesus Christ might demonstrate His perfect patience, as an example for those who would believe in Him for eternal life" (1 Tim. 1:16, NASB).*

✶ **1:16** Perhaps no other conversion has proven more profitable in soul-winning than has Paul's. He himself mentioned it often (see Gal. 12; Phil. 3; Acts 22, 26).

  F. He was a suffering servant *(Read 1 Tim. 4:10)*
  G. He was, most of all, a preacher.
    1. His message—The gospel *(Read 1 Tim. 1:11)*
    2. His mission field—The Gentiles *(Read 1 Tim. 2:7)*
    3. His master—The Savior *(Read 1 Tim. 1:12)*

II. Timothy and the Family of God
  A. Timothy's personal responsibilities
    1. Stay in Ephesus—*"As I besought thee to abide still at Ephesus, when I went into Macedonia, that thou mightest charge some that they teach no other doctrine" (1 Tim. 1:3).*
    2. Maintain a good conscience—*"Keeping faith and a good conscience..." (1 Tim. 1:19, NASB).*
    3. Examine yourself—*"Take heed unto thyself" (1 Tim. 4:16).*
    4. Examine your doctrine—*"And unto the doctrine; continue in them: for in doing this thou shalt both save thyself, and them that hear thee" (1 Tim. 4:16).*

✶ **4:16** Here Paul is not referring to the eternal salvation of the believer's soul, but rather the earthly salvation of the believer's service. Thus, self-examination and discipline will save one from being placed by God on the shelf of disservice through sin (1 Cor. 9:27).

    5. Discipline yourself—*"Discipline yourself for the purpose of godliness" (1 Tim. 4:7b, NASB).*

> 6. Be an example—"*Let no man look down on your youthfulness, but rather in speech, conduct, love, faith and purity, show yourself an example of those who believe*" *(1 Tim. 4:12,* NASB*).*
> 7. Develop your gift *(Read 1 Tim. 4:14-15)*

★ **4:15** Totally develop your spiritual gift. What we don't use, we lose (see Heb. 2:1-3). The word "profiting" in 4:15 means "to cut forward, to blaze the way, to make a pioneer advance." A growing pastor means a growing church. A man cannot lead others where he has not been himself.

> 8. Take care of your body *(Read 1 Tim. 5:23)*

★ **5:23**
- This verse cannot be used to support the practice of moderate drinking among believers. The wine here was to be taken for medicinal purposes.
- This verse can be used to support the position that the spiritual gift of healing through individuals may have been phased out even before the completion of the New Testament. Consider:
  - Paul could not heal Timothy.
  - Paul could not heal Trophimus (2 Tim. 4:20).
  - Paul could not heal himself (2 Cor. 12:7-10).

> 9. Avoid the love of money *(Read 1 Tim. 6:10)*
> 10. Pursue the good *(Read 1 Tim. 6:11)*
> 11. Be a soldier *(Read 1 Tim. 6:12-14)*
> 12. Be impartial *(Read 1 Tim. 5:21)*
>   B. Timothy's public responsibilities
>   1. Concerning the pulpit in the church
>   a. What to honor—The Scriptures of God *(Read 1 Tim. 4:6, 11, 13)*

★ **4:13** The minister of God is to proclaim the Word of God as follows:
- He is to provide the information involved; that is, "What does the text say?" "Give attendance to reading."
- He is to provide the interpretation involved; that is, "What does the text mean?" "Give attendance ... to doctrine."
- He is to provide the application involved; that is, "How can this text be applied?" "Give attendance to ... exhortation."

>   b. What to avoid—Human speculations *(Read 1 Tim. 1:4; 6:20)*
>   2. Concerning prayers in the church
>   a. Pray for all *(Read 1 Tim. 2:1-4)*

★ **2:4** Pray for all (2:1). This is to be done because, if the church will not pray, then who else will? We note that kings are at the top of Paul's list. At this time wicked Nero was on the Roman throne.
- Supplications—Asking for one's own needs
- Prayers—Worship and adoration
- Intercessions—Asking for another's needs
- Thanksgiving—Appreciation for past grace and faith for future grace (see Phil. 4:6)

>   b. Pray for all things *(Read 1 Tim. 4:4-5)*
>   3. Concerning women in the church
>   a. Their responsibilities *(Read 1 Tim. 2:9)*
>   b. Their restrictions—"*But I suffer not a woman to teach, nor to usurp authority over the man, but to be in silence*" *(1 Tim. 2:12).* Two factors are involved in the giving of this rule.

> (1) The fact of the original creation—*"For Adam was first formed, then Eve"* (1 Tim. 2:13).
> (2) The fact of the original corruption—*"And Adam was not deceived, but the woman being deceived was in the transgression"* (1 Tim. 2:14).

✱ 2:14
- Do not allow congregational doctrine to be taught by a woman (2:12). Greek scholar Kenneth Wuest points out that here Paul uses the present infinitive tense instead of the aorist tense. Thus the command here should read, "I do not permit a woman to be a teacher." This, of course, does not prohibit her from teaching a ladies' Bible class, Sunday school, etc. But the doctrinal teachers in the family of God are to be men (Acts 13:1; 1 Cor. 12:28-29; Eph. 4:11). Paul now quickly gives Timothy two reasons for this.
  - Because of the original creation—*"For Adam was first formed, then Eve"* (2:13; see also Eph. 5:22; 1 Cor. 11:1-16).
  - Because of the original corruption—*"And Adam was not deceived [apatao, to merely deceive], but the woman being deceived [exapatao, to totally deceive], was in the transgression"* (2:14; see also I Cor. 11:8-9).
  - The Word of God presents a divinely appointed three-fold headship:
    - The headship of Christ over his body (Col. 1:18)
    - The headship of the pastor over his flock (Acts 20:28)
    - The headship of the man over his wife (1 Cor. 11:1 -16; 1 Tim. 2:12)
- The Greek word translated "quietness" in 2:11 and "silent" in 2:12 does not mean total silence, or no talking. It rather means, "settled down," "undisturbed, not unruly," as translated in Acts 22:2 and 2 Thessalonians 3:12. The Greek word meaning "to say nothing" is *sigao*. (See Luke 18:39; 1 Cor. 14:34.)

> c. Their redemption *(Read 1 Tim. 2:15)*

✱ 2:15 I Timothy 2:15 has been the object of much speculation: *"Notwithstanding she shall be saved in childbearing, if they continue in faith and charity and holiness and with sobriety."* There are (at least) three basic interpretations offered to explain this verse.
- That the salvation here refers to spiritual salvation. It is pointed out that the definite article precedes the word "childbearing" and should read "the childbearing," thus referring to the seed of the woman in Genesis 3:15-16. Therefore, according to this view, Paul is saying that, while it was a woman which paved the way for the corruption in Eden, it was also a woman who paved the way for the incarnation at Bethlehem.
- That the "salvation" here is from doctrinal error and warns against women teaching deceptions.
- That they will be kept from the corruption of society by being at home raising children.

> 4. Concerning widows in the church

✱ Duane Liftin writes: "Next Paul offered instruction on how Timothy must deal with the widows in the congregation. Throughout the Old and New Testaments, widows, along with aliens and orphans, are viewed as special objects of God's mercy. As such they are to be taken under the wing of the congregation (cf. Deut. 10:18; 14:29; 24:17-21; Acts 6:1-7; James 1:27). As early as Acts 6 the church had established a charitable outreach to widows. Now about 30 years later the ministry to widows, of whom there were no doubt many, showed signs of being a major burden to the congregation. Paul was therefore eager in this passage to identify those who did not truly need help in order to leave enough for those who did" (*Bible Knowledge Commentary*, New Testament edition, p. 742).

> a. Widows over 60 with no living children (1 Tim. 5:3, 5, 9)—They are to be honored and provided for.
> b. Widows with a family (1 Tim. 5:4,16)—They are to be provided for by their families.
> c. Young widows (1 Tim. 5:6, 11-15)
> (1) The rule—Let them remarry and raise children.

(2) The reason—This will keep them from immorality and idle talk.
5. Concerning senior saints in the church *(Read 1 Tim. 5:1-2)*
6. Concerning elders in the church
   a. To be carefully chosen *(Read 1 Tim. 5:22)*

✱ 5:22

- The exhortation— *"Lay hands suddenly on no man."*
- The explanation—A. Duane Liftin observes: "All people are heading toward judgment, carrying with them either their sins or their good works. For some, their sins or good works go before them and are obvious to all observers. For others their sins or good works trail behind, hidden from view, becoming known only after the individual has passed. Thus Paul emphasized the difficulties inherent in choosing qualified candidates for the ordination. Hasty, superficial assessments, whether positive or negative, are sometimes inaccurate, leading to the enlistment of unqualified men or the overlooking of those whose fine qualities are less obvious. With time, however, a man's true colors will emerge to an astute observer. Thus the perceptive observations of verses 24-25 are designed to underline the warning of verse 22: do not rush to ordain someone" (*Bible Knowledge Commentary*, New Testament edition, p. 745).

   b. To be honored *(Read 1 Tim. 5:17-18)*
   c. To be assumed innocent until proven guilty *(Read 1 Tim. 5:19)*
7. Concerning the rich in the church (1 Tim. 6:6-10, 17-19)
   a. Their faith—It is to be placed in God, and not in gold *(Read 1 Tim. 6:17)*
   b. Their fortune—It is to be shared with others *(Read 1 Tim. 6:18)*
8. Concerning servants (1 Tim. 6:1-2)
   a. Those working for unsaved masters *(Read 1 Tim. 6:1)*
   b. Those working for saved masters *(Read 1 Tim. 6:2)*

LESSON 35

III. Church Officers and the Family of God (1 Tim. 3:1-13)
  A. Qualifications for the office of bishop *(Read 1 Tim. 3:1-7)*

★ **3:1** Bishops (3:1-7; see also Titus 1:5-9) — *"If any man desire the office of a bishop, he desireth a good work"* (3:1). The Greek word for "bishop" is *episkopos* and refers to an overseer. Here, of course, Paul had in mind the office of the pastor. Another name found in the New Testament which may refer to this same position is "elder" (*presbuteros* in the Greek). These two terms, bishop and elder, are often used interchangeably (Acts 20:17-28; Titus 1:5-7). The former term (bishop) speaks of his office responsibility, while the latter term (elder) refers to his spiritual maturity.

  1. He must be a male (1 Tim. 3:1)
  2. He must be without reproach (1 Tim. 3:2)
  3. He must be the husband of one wife (1 Tim. 3:2)

★ Few New Testament statements have been the object of so much speculation as this little phrase in 3:2, *"The husband of one wife."* There are two main interpretations.
  ■ "The prohibition of polygamy" view — According to this theory, Paul is simply saying no church member who had several wives in his home could qualify as a bishop. However, this view has serious problems.
    ● Paul had already forbidden this years ago (1 Cor. 7:2 and Rom. 7:1-3).
    ● The Roman government had outlawed polygamy at this time. There is no evidence that the early church ever had this problem.
    ● This term literally says a "one-woman man" and is found again in 5:9 (though here reversed) where it speaks of a widow as a "one-man woman."
  ■ "The prohibition of divorce" view — According to this theory, a divorced and remarried man is prohibited from occupying the office of the pastorate, regardless of the circumstances which may have surrounded the divorce. It must be kept in mind that Paul in this chapter is not discussing the salvation of a sinner, but the qualifications of an officer.

  4. He must be temperate (1 Tim. 3:2)
  5. He must be prudent (1 Tim. 3:2)
  6. He must be respectable (1 Tim. 3:2)
  7. He must be given to hospitality (1 Tim. 3:2)
  8. He must be able to teach (1 Tim. 3:2)
  9. He must not be given to wine (1 Tim. 3:3)
  10. He must not be pugnacious (1 Tim. 3:3)
  11. He must be gentle (1 Tim. 3:3)
  12. He must not be contentious (1 Tim. 3:3)
  13. He must be free from the love of money (1 Tim. 3:3)
  14. He must rule his own house well *(Read 1 Tim. 3:4-5; 5:8)*
  15. He must not be a novice or new convert *(Read 1 Tim. 3:6)*
  16. He must have a good reputation in the unsaved community (1 Tim. 3:7)
  B. Qualifications for the office of a deacon *(Read 1 Tim. 3:1-3; 8-13)*

★ **3:8** Deacons (3:8-13)—The exact nature and duties of this office are nowhere set forth in any systematic way in the New Testament. It seems almost certain that the office was created to solve the organizational problem of the early church, due in part to its rapid growth (Acts 6:1-8). The Greek word for "deacon" is *diakonos*. (See also Rom. 12:7, here translated "ministry," and Phil. 1:1.)

> 1. He must be a man of dignity (1 Tim. 3:8)
> 2. He must not be double-tongued (1 Tim. 3:8)
> 3. He must not be given to wine (1 Tim. 3:8)
> 4. He must be no lover of money (1 Tim. 3:8)
> 5. He must possess a pure conscience (1 Tim. 3:9)
> 6. He must not be a novice (1 Tim. 3:10)
> 7. If married, he must be the husband of a godly wife (1 Tim. 3:11)
> 8. He must be the husband of one wife (1 Tim. 3:12)
> 9. He must rule his own house well (1 Tim. 3:12)
>
> **IV. False Teachers and the Family of God**
>   A. Their theology
>   1. The source of their teaching *(Read 1 Tim. 4:1)*
>   2. The substance of their teaching *(Read 1 Tim. 4:3)*
>   B. Their tactics
>   1. Arguing *(Read 1 Tim. 4:4, 6-7)*
>   2. Stirring up constant friction—*"He is conceited and understands nothing; but he has a morbid interest in controversial questions and disputes about words, out of which arise envy, strife, abusive language, evil suspicions, and constant friction" (1 Tim. 6:4-5,* NASB*).*
>   C. Their transgressions
>   1. They use the Law in the wrong way *(Read 1 Tim. 1:7-10)*
>   2. They allow their own conscience to be seared *(Read 1 Tim. 4:2)*
>   3. They use the church for personal gain *(Read 1 Tim. 6:5)*
>   4. They oppose the true faith with false theories of science *(Read 1 Tim. 6:20)*
> **V. The Savior and the Family of God**—Paul offers a brief summary of Christ's *work here in this epistle.*
>   A. His incarnation—*"God was manifest in the flesh"* (1 Tim. 3:16b).
>   B. His purpose—*"This is a faithful saying, and worthy of all acceptation, that Christ Jesus came into the world to save sinners; of whom I am chief" (1 Tim. 1:15). "Who is the Saviour of all men" (1 Tim. 4:10).*
>   C. His deity—*"Now unto the King eternal, immortal, invisible, the only wise God, be honour and glory for ever and ever. Amen" (1 Tim. 1:17). "Who only hath immortality, dwelling in the light which no man can approach unto; whom no man hath seen, nor can see: to whom be honour and power everlasting. Amen" (1 Tim. 6:16).*
>   D. His successful ministry—*"And without controversy great is the mystery of godliness: God was manifest in the flesh, justified in the Spirit, seen of angels, preached unto the Gentiles, believed on in the world, received up into glory" (1 Tim. 3:16).*

★ **3:16**

■ *"God was manifest in the flesh"* (3:16; see also John 1:14; Dan. 2:11; Gal. 4:4; Isa. 7:14; 9:6). Note: I Timothy 3:16 is one of the truly great verses in all the Bible, and may be viewed as an amplification of John 3:16. M. F. Unger writes: "It refers to the basic body of divine revelation made known in Scripture and may well have constituted an early Christian hymn."

- *"Preached unto the Gentiles"* (nations). This probably finds its ultimate fulfillment in the words of the Great Commission in Matthew 28:18-20. Note the little phrase, "seen of angels" in 3:16. The earthly ministry of Christ was viewed by both elect and evil angels. (See Luke 2:13; Matt. 4:11; Luke 22:43—elect angels; and Mark 1:23-26; 5:2-13—evil angels.)
- *"Believed on in the world."* In spite of Israel's official rejection of him, our Lord left in his wake a powerful "minority group" of dedicated missionaries, numbering perhaps in the thousands (see 1 Cor. 15:6).

> E. His suffering and death— *"I give thee charge in the sight of God, who quickeneth all things, and before Christ Jesus, who before Pontius Pilate witnessed a good confession" (1 Tim. 6:13)*. *"Who gave himself a ransom for all, to be testified in due time" (1 Tim. 2:6)*.
> F. His resurrection— *"Justified in the Spirit" (1 Tim. 3:16*, a reference to the resurrection; see also Rom. 1:4).
> G. His ascension— *"Received up into glory" (1 Tim. 3:16)*.
> H. His mediatorship— *"For there is one God, and one mediator between God and men, the man Christ Jesus" (1 Tim. 2:5)*.
> I. His return— *"That thou keep this commandment without spot, unrebukeable, until the appearing of our Lord Jesus Christ" (1 Tim. 6:14)*.
> J. His millennial reign— *"Which in his times he shall shew, who is the blessed and only Potentate, the King of kings, and Lord of lords" (1 Tim. 6:15)*.

★ **6:15** There are two significant titles for Jesus in this verse:
- Potentate—This is the Greek word, *dunastes*, which means "the mighty ones of great authority." This title is used but once in describing Jesus.
- King of kings and Lord of lords—This title is used but three times. The other two references are Revelation 17:14 and 19:16.

Introduction to Second Timothy

THE FINAL WORDS OF GOD'S FINEST WITNESS

A. The book of 2 Timothy records these words, as written by Paul.

B. After being released from his first Roman imprisonment (Acts 28), Paul is once again arrested.

C. This arrest may have taken place suddenly in Troas, thus explaining why Paul left there without taking his cloak, parchments, or Old Testament scrolls (2 Tim. 4:13).

D. On July 19, A.D. 64, Rome was burned (probably by Nero) and the Christians were blamed. Christianity then became an illegal religion, and to evangelize was a crime punishable by death.

E. Paul was probably arrested again sometime after July of A.D. 64, and condemned to death.

F. During his second and final imprisonment he wrote 2 Timothy.

G. His second imprisonment was far different from the first.
   1. He was then a political prisoner awaiting trial. He is now a condemned criminal, awaiting death.
   2. Then he lived in his own hired house. Now he huddles in a cold, damp, dark dungeon.
   3. During his first imprisonment he was visited by many. Now he is forsaken by all.

H. This is the most personal letter; in Romans we see Paul the theologian; in 1 Corinthians, Paul the counselor; in 2 Corinthians, Paul the preacher; in Galatians, Paul the defender; in 1 Timothy and Titus, Paul the statesman; but here in 2 Timothy, Paul the man.

I. The letter is rich in personal allusions. Paul mentions 23 men, women, friends, and foes.

J. This epistle is his spiritual swan song, his dying shout of triumph.

K. Paul writes more about last day conditions in this epistle than in any other. (See 3:1-13; 4:1-4.)

L. He also lists (by name) more enemies of the gospel in this epistle. There are Hymenaeus and Philetus (2:17), Jannes and Jambres (3:8), and Alexander the coppersmith (4:14).

M. Dr. J. Vernon McGee writes: "In Second Timothy Paul speaks of the ultimate outcome of gospel preaching. The final fruition will not be the total conversion of mankind, nor will it usher in the Millennium. On the contrary, there will come about an apostasy which will well-nigh blot out 'the faith' from the earth. This is in complete harmony with the startling word of Christ, 'When the Son of man cometh, shall he find faith on the earth?'" *(Second Timothy*, p. 196).

N. At least six analogies depicting the Christian life are given here in this book. The believer is likened to a soldier (2:3), athlete (2:5), farmer (2:6), student (2:15), vessel (2:21), and servant (2:24).

O. Finally, Paul's overall evaluation and summary of his own ministry is seen in his closing words. (See 4:6-8.)

P. The book of 2 Timothy is the 20th longest New Testament book, and 53rd longest biblical book, with four chapters, 83 verses, and 1,703 words. There are quotations or allusions from seven Old Testament books in 2 Timothy.

Q. Great passages would include:
   1. 1:6-10
   2. 1:11-14
   3. 2:1-3

4. 2:11-13
5. 2:15
6. 3:16-17
7. 4:1-5
8. 4:7-8

Overview of the Book of Second Timothy

I. **Paul the Preacher**
   A. The preacher and his student (Timothy)
      1. His concern for Timothy
      2. His confidence in Timothy
   B. The preacher and himself
      1. He reviews his past performance
      2. He retains his permanent hope
      3. He regrets certain actions of some false friends
      4. He rejoices concerning the actions of a true friend
   C. The preacher and his Savior

II. **Paul the Pattern**
   A. A soldier
   B. An athlete
   C. A farmer
   D. A sufferer
      1. The report concerning Paul's sufferings
      2. The reason for Paul's sufferings
      3. The rewards of Paul's sufferings
      4. An instructor
   E. A student
   F. He advises Timothy to study God's Word
      1. He advises Timothy to shun profane words
      2. A vessel
   G. The various vessels
      1. The victorious vessel
      2. A servant

III. **Paul the Prophet**
   A. The symptoms of this "final days disease"
      1. Information concerning this disease
      2. Illustrations of this disease
   B. The solution for this "final days disease"
      1. Continue in the work of God
      2. Continue in the Word of God

IV. **Paul the Pilgrim**
   A. His final charge
      1. Preach the Word of God
      2. Reach your world for God

B. His final warning
C. His final testimony
D. His final commission
   1. Titus is sent to Dalmatia
   2. Tychicus is sent to Ephesus
E. His final farewell
F. His final request
   1. The persons he desires to see
   2. The objects he desires to have
G. His final sorrow
   1. Abused by his foes
   2. Abandoned by his friends
H. His final notes of praise
   1. What God has done for him
   2. What God would do for him

THE BOOK OF SECOND TIMOTHY

I. Paul the Preacher (2 Tim. 1) — *"Whereunto I am appointed a preacher, and an apostle, and a teacher of the Gentiles" (2 Tim. 1:11).*
  A. The preacher and his student (Timothy)
   1. His concern for Timothy
      a. He prayed for him (2 Tim. 1:3)
      b. He knew his tears (2 Tim. 1:4)
   2. His confidence in Timothy
      a. Stir up your gift *(Read 2 Tim. 1:6-7)*

★ **1:6** The Greek word here translated "stir" literally means to rekindle. This is its only reference in the New Testament. Timothy was evidently not making full use of his pastoral gift.

      b. Don't be ashamed:
         (1) Of Christ's message *(Read 2 Tim. 1:8)*
         (2) Of Christ's messenger *(Read 2 Tim. 1:8)*
      c. Hold fast to sound doctrine *(Read 2 Tim. 1:13)*
      d. Remain true to your ministry *(Read 2 Tim. 1:14)*
  B. The preacher and himself
   1. He reviews his past performance—Ministering as:
      a. An apostle (2 Tim. 1:1)
      b. A father (2 Tim. 1:2)
      c. A servant (2 Tim. 1:3)
      d. A prisoner (2 Tim. 1:8)
      e. A preacher (2 Tim. 1:11)
      f. A teacher (2 Tim. 1:11)
      g. A sufferer (2 Tim. 1:12)
   2. He retains his permanent hope *(Read 2 Tim. 1:12)*

★ **1:12** There are two views concerning the use of the word "committed" in this verse.
  ■ Paul was here referring to his salvation, which he had deposited with Christ.
  ■ Paul was here referring to his service, which Christ had deposited with Paul. It may be the apostle had both in mind.

   3. He regrets certain actions of some false friends *(Read 2 Tim. 1:15)*
   4. He rejoices concerning the actions of a true friend *(Read 2 Tim. 1:16-18)*
  C. The preacher and his Savior *(Read 2 Tim. 1:9-10)*
II. Paul the Pattern (2 Tim. 2) — *"And the things that thou hast heard of me among many witnesses, the same commit thou to faithful men, who shall be able to teach others also" (2 Tim. 2:2).* In this chapter Paul likens the work of the ministry to various things.

★ **2:2** The child of God is assigned a threefold duty concerning the Word of God:
- We are to receive it—From others.
- We are to regard it—Within ourselves.
- We are to remit it—To others. To state it in another way: we are to read it, to heed it, and to deed it.

> A. A soldier *(Read 2 Tim. 2:3-4)*
> B. An athlete—*"And also if any one competes as an athlete, he does not win the prize unless he competes according to the rules" (2 Tim. 2:5, NASB).*

★ **2:5** Paul often describes the Christian life in athletic terms.
- A wrestler (Eph. 6:12)
- A fighter (1 Cor. 9:26)
- A runner (1 Cor. 9:24; Heb. 12:1)

> C. A farmer *(Read 2 Tim. 2:6)*
> D. A sufferer (2 Tim. 2:9-13)
>   1. The report concerning Paul's sufferings *(Read 2 Tim. 2:9)*
>   2. The reason for Paul's sufferings *(Read 2 Tim. 2:10)*
>   3. The rewards of Paul's sufferings *(Read 2 Tim. 2:11-13)*

★ **2:13** The word "deny" is mentioned three times in these verses.
- *"If we deny him,"* that is, do not allow him first place in our lives
- *"He also will deny us,"* that is, we will suffer the loss of our rewards at the judgment seat of Christ (see 1 Cor. 3:11-15).
- *"He cannot deny himself,"* that is, his promise of eternal salvation to the elect is secure regardless of their failures (see 2:10, 19).

> E. An instructor *(Read 2 Tim. 2:14)*

★ **2:14** There was apparently a strong (and sinful) tendency in the early church to argue over certain words and concepts found within various false philosophical systems. Note Paul's repeated warnings on this in the pastoral epistles: *"Neither give heed to fables and endless genealogies" (1 Tim. 1.4). "Avoiding profane and vain babblings" (1 Tim. 6:20). "But refuse profane and old wives' fables" (1 Tim. 4:7). "Questions and strifes of words, whereof cometh envy" (1 Tim. 6:4). "But shun profane and vain babblings" (2 Tim. 2:16). "But foolish and unlearned questions avoid" (2 Tim. 2:23). "But avoid foolish questions, and genealogies" (Titus 3:9).*

> F. A student (2 Tim. 2:15-19, 23)
>   1. He advises Timothy to study God's Word *(Read 2 Tim. 2:15)*

★ **2:15** The Greek word translated "rightly dividing" is found only here in the New Testament and literally means, "to cut straight." In light of Paul's former trade he may here have been comparing the art of tentmaking with that of Bible teaching. Careless and crooked cutting of the canvas would weaken the completed tent, thus the importance of each stroke of the knife. Paul's intended lesson here is obvious.

>   2. He advises Timothy to shun profane words *(Read 2 Tim. 2:16-19, 23)*
> G. A vessel
>   1. The various vessels *(Read 2 Tim. 2:20)*

2. The victorious vessel *(Read 2 Tim. 2:21-22)*
 H. A servant *(Read 2 Tim. 2:24-26)*
III. Paul the Prophet (2 Tim. 3)—*"This know also, that in the last days perilous times shall come.... But evil men and seducers shall wax worse and worse, deceiving, and being deceived" (2 Tim. 3:1, 13).*

★ **3:1** The word "perilous" here is translated "exceeding fierce" in Matthew 8:28, describing the maniac of Gadara. Thus, in the last days Satan will attempt to turn this world into his own personal graveyard.

  A. The symptoms of this "final days disease" (2 Tim. 3:1-9)
   1. Information concerning this disease—*"But evil men and seducers shall wax worse and worse, deceiving, and being deceived" (2 Tim. 3:13).*
    a. They will be self-lovers (2 Tim. 3:2).
    b. They will be lovers of money (2 Tim. 3:2).
    c. They will be boastful (2 Tim. 3:2).
    d. They will be arrogant (2 Tim. 3:2).
    e. They will be revilers (2 Tim. 3:2).
    f. They will be disobedient to parents (2 Tim. 3:2).
    g. They will be ungrateful (2 Tim. 3:2).
    h. They will be unholy (2 Tim. 3:2).
    i. They will be unloving (2 Tim. 3:3).

★ Especially to be noted is the little phrase in verse 3, "without natural affection." This phrase is a translation of the Greek word *stergein*, which refers to a special kind of human love. Greek scholar Kenneth Wuest writes: "It is a love that is a natural movement of the soul, something almost like gravitation or some other force of blind nature. It is the love of parents for children and children for parents, of husband for wife and wife for husband, or close relations one for another. It is found in the animal world in the love which the animal has for its offspring. It is a love of obligatoriness, the term being used here not in its moral sense, but in the natural sense. It is a necessity under the circumstances. This kind of love is the binding factor by which any natural or social unit is held together" *(By Paths in the Greek New Testament,* p. 110).

The point of all the above is that Paul predicts that one of the elements prevalent during the final days will be the absence (in some human circles) of even that *stergein* gravitational-type love possessed by the animal kingdom for their young. It would seem in light of this that no more vivid example of Paul's sad prediction can be seen than in the modern abortion movement.

    j. They will be irreconcilable (2 Tim. 3:3).
    k. They will be malicious gossipers (2 Tim. 3:3).
    l. They will be without self-control (2 Tim. 3:3).
    m. They will be brutal (2 Tim. 3:3).
    n. They will be haters of good (2 Tim. 3:3).
    o. They will be treacherous (2 Tim. 3:4).
    p. They will be reckless (2 Tim. 3:4).
    q. They will be conceited (2 Tim. 3:4).
    r. They will be lovers of pleasures rather than lovers of God (2 Tim. 3:4).
    s. They will be holding a form of godliness, although denying its power (2 Tim. 3:5).
   2. Illustrations of this disease *(Read 2 Tim. 3:6-8)*
  B. The solution for this "final days disease" *(Read 2 Tim. 3:10-17)*
   1. Continue in the work of God (2 Tim. 3:10-12)
   2. Continue in the Word of God (2 Tim. 3:14-17)

> a. What it had done for Timothy the young man *(Read 2 Tim. 3:14-15)*
> b. What it would do for Timothy the leader *(Read 2 Tim. 3:16-17)*

✶ **3:17** In this remarkable passage Paul asserts that the Bible is profitable for:
- Doctrine—The Bible may be used as the perfect textbook to present the systematic teachings of the great truths relating to God himself.
- Reproof—The Bible is to be used to convict us of the wrong in our lives.
- Correction—The Bible will then show us the right way.
- Instruction in righteousness—The Bible provides all the necessary details which will allow a Christian to become fully equipped for every good work.

> **IV. Paul the Pilgrim (2 Tim. 4)**—*"The time of my departure is at hand" (2 Tim. 4:6).*
>   A. His final charge (2 Tim. 4:1-2, 5)
>   1. Preach the Word of God *(Read 2 Tim. 4:1-2)*
>   2. Reach your world for God *(Read 2 Tim. 4:5)*
>   B. His final warning *(Read 2 Tim. 4:3-4)*
>   C. His final testimony *(Read 2 Tim. 4:6-7)*

✶ **4:7** The word translated "offered" is a liturgical word and signifies the pouring out of a religious drink offering (Num. 15:1-10). Paul had already regarded his ministry in winning the lost to Christ as an offering to God (Rom. 15:16; Phil. 2:17), and now his approaching death would complete the sacrifice. The word "departure" means "to take down a tent, to break camp, to pull in the anchor." His testimony in verse 7 should be contrasted with God's statement to wicked Belshazzar in Daniel 5:26.

>   D. His final commission (2 Tim. 4:10,12)
>   1. Titus is sent to Dalmatia (2 Tim. 4:10).
>   2. Tychicus is sent to Ephesus (2 Tim. 4:12).
>   E. His final farewell—*"Salute Prisca and Aquila, and the household of Onesiphorus" (2 Tim. 4:19).*
>   F. His final request (2 Tim. 4:9, 11, 13, 21)
>   1. The persons he desires to see (2 Tim. 4:9, 11)
>   a. Timothy—*"Do thy diligence to come shortly unto me" (2 Tim. 4:9)*
>   b. John Mark—*"Only Luke is with me. Take Mark, and bring him with thee: for he is profitable to me for the ministry" (2 Tim. 4:11).*

✶ **4:11** Timothy was to come immediately. He was to bring John Mark with him. Years prior to this Mark had, of course, accompanied Paul and Barnabas on their first missionary trip, but had left the team and gone home. Due to this sign of immaturity, Paul had refused to include him in a second proposed trip. This action then prompted a break between Paul and Barnabas. (See Acts 13:3; 15:36-40.) But since that time Mark had so grown in God's grace that Paul desired to see him before his departure.

>   2. The objects he desires to have (2 Tim. 4:13)
>   a. His cloak
>   b. His books
>   c. His Old Testament scrolls

✶ ■ Timothy was to bring Paul's cloak he had left at Troas (4:13). The great 16th-century Bible translator William Tyndale would later make a similar request while confined to a damp prison cell: "I entreat your lordship, and that by the Lord

Jesus, that if I must remain here for the winter, you would beg the Commissary to be so kind as to send me, from the things of mine which he has, a warmer cap; I feel the cold painfully in my head. Also a warmer cloak to patch my leggings. My overcoat is worn out, my shorts even are worn out. He has a woolen shirt of mine, if he will send it. But most of all I entreat and implore your kindness to do your best with the Commissary to be so good as to send my Hebrew Bible, grammar, and vocabulary, that I may spend my time in that pursuit."

■ He was to bring the parchments—Paul's copies of the Old Testament. This statement is staggering in its implications. Here is a man who conducted the first three missionary trips ever attempted for Christ, who had personally seen the Savior on at least four occasions, who had written approximately half of the New Testament, and who had organized the first 50 or so Christian churches on this earth. Now in his hour of death he requests the Scriptures, for he evidently felt he could still learn from the precious pages. The child of God is in absolutely no danger whatsoever of learning too much about God's Word.

> G. His final sorrow
> 1. Abused by his foes *(Read 2 Tim. 4:14-15)*
> 2. Abandoned by his friends— *"For Demas hath forsaken me, having loved this present world, and is departed unto Thessalonica; Crescens to Galatia, Titus unto Dalmatia" (2 Tim. 4:10). "At my first defense no one supported me, but all deserted me; may it not be counted against them" (2 Tim. 4:16, NASB).*

★ **4:16** Paul thus was the third and final New Testament person to pray for those who had ill-treated him. Note the statements of the first two:
■ The words of Jesus in *Luke 23:34:* *"Then said Jesus, Father, forgive them; for they know not what they do. And they parted his raiment, and cast lots."*
■ The words of Stephen in *Acts 7:59-60:* *"And they stoned Stephen, calling upon God, and saying, Lord Jesus, receive my spirit. And he kneeled down, and cried with a loud voice, Lord, lay not this sin to their charge. And when he had said this, he fell asleep."*

> H. His final notes of praise
> 1. What God has done for him— *"Notwithstanding the Lord stood with me, and strengthened me" (2 Tim. 4:17).*
> 2. What God would do for him
>   a. He would deliver him— *"And the Lord shall deliver me from every evil work, and will preserve me unto his heavenly kingdom: to whom be glory for ever and ever. Amen" (2 Tim. 4:18).*
>   b. He would reward him— *"Henceforth there is laid up for me a crown of righteousness, which the Lord, the righteous judge, shall give me at that day: and not to me only, but unto all them also that love his appearing" (2 Tim. 4:8).*

Introduction to Titus

PAUL'S MESSAGE TO GOD'S MAN IN CRETE

A. The man was Titus and the message was to stay there.

B. Titus, like Timothy, was one of Paul's "preacher boys."

C. Paul had assigned Titus to strengthen a previously established church work on the Isle of Crete. This island, southeast of Greece, was about 150 miles long and 35 miles wide, thus making it the largest of the Mediterranean islands. It was an island of 100 cities, consisting of mountains, but also very fertile valleys. The highest mountain, Mount Ida, was the traditional birthplace of the Greek god Zeus. The Cretans were relatives of the Philistines. They had a notorious reputation of being *"always liars, evil beasts, lazy gluttons" (Titus 1:12,* NASB*)*. This testimony came from one of their own poets and prophets. The origin of the church there is unknown, but may have been started by the same returning Cretans who were present at Pentecost (see Acts 2:11).

D. The epistle to Titus was written about the same time as 1 Timothy, during that period between Paul's first and second Roman imprisonments.

E. The three pastoral epistles may be favorably compared.
  1. In 1 and 2 Timothy Paul stresses doctrine.
  2. In Titus he emphasizes duty.
  3. The child of God is to protect the gospel in 1 Timothy.
  4. He is to proclaim it in 2 Timothy.
  5. He is to practice it in Titus.

F. A summary of the person and ministry of Titus would include:
  1. He was a Gentile (Greek, see Gal. 2:3).
  2. He was probably a convert of Paul (Titus 1:4).
  3. Some believe he may have been the brother of Luke.
  4. Titus first appears in the sacred account when he accompanied Paul and Barnabas to Jerusalem (Gal. 2:1).
  5. He is later sent by Paul to Corinth to straighten out certain disorders in the church there and to initiate an offering for the poor saints at Jerusalem (2 Cor. 8:6,10-11).
  6. He then meets Paul in Macedonia and is sent back to Corinth carrying the epistle of 2 Corinthians to pave the way for Paul's coming and to complete their offering (2 Cor. 2:3,12-13; 7:5-6,13-14; 8:16-17, 23; 12:14,18).
  7. He seems to have accompanied Paul during the third missionary trip.
  8. He is last mentioned in 2 Timothy 4:10, at which time Paul sends him from southern Greece to Dalmatia (Yugoslavia).
  9. Titus may have been the only Gentile to receive a New Testament letter.

G. This epistle marks the last of but two instances where the great theological word "regeneration" is used in the New Testament.
  1. It is found in Matthew 19:28 where it refers to mother nature.

2. It is found in Titus 3:5 where it refers to redeemed sinners.
H. This little epistle contains two of Scripture's greatest passages on the work of Christ and the destiny of believers. (See 2:11-14; 3:4-7.)
I. Titus is the 23rd longest New Testament book, and 61st longest biblical book, with three chapters, 46 verses, and 921 words. There are quotations or allusions from six Old Testament books in Titus.
J. Great passages would include:
   1. 2:11-14
   2. 3:4-7

Overview of the Book of Titus

I. Titus and the Apostle
   A. Paul was God's servant
      1. Serving as an apostle
      2. Serving as a preacher
   B. Titus was Paul's son

II. Titus and the Elders
   A. The nature of their qualifications
      1. They must be above reproach
      2. They must be the husband of one wife
      3. They must have children who believe
      4. They must not be accused of rebellion
      5. They must not be self-willed
      6. They must not be quick-tempered
      7. They must not be addicted to wine
      8. They must not be pugnacious
      9. They must not be lovers of money
      10. They must be hospitable
      11. They must love what is good
      12. They must be sensible
      13. They must be just
      14. They must be devout
      15. They must be self-controlled
      16. They must students of the Word
   B. The necessity for their qualifications
      1. To reprove erring believers
      2. To renounce apostate unbelievers

III. Titus and the Church
   A. Its head, the Savior
      1. The what of his work
      2. The why of his work
   B. Its heirs, the saved
      1. Responsibilities of the sheep
      2. Responsibilities of the undershepherd

IV. Titus and the Future
   A. He is instructed to meet Paul in Nicopolis
   B. He is instructed to help Zenas and Apollos

THE BOOK OF TITUS

I. Titus and the Apostle (Titus 1:1-4)
  A. Paul was God's servant
    1. Serving as an apostle *(Read Titus 1:1-2)*

✶ The God of the Bible is described not only as one who cannot lie, but also as the God who need not lie. The person lying usually does so to get himself out of an unpleasant situation, to avoid punishment, to impress someone, or to obtain something. But the holy, eternal, all-knowing, all-powerful, and all-sufficient God is never confronted by any of these circumstances.

    2. Serving as a preacher *(Read Titus 1:3)*
  B. Titus was Paul's son *(Read Titus 1:4)*
II. Titus and the Elders (Titus 1:5-16) — *"For this cause left I thee in Crete, that thou shouldest set in order the things that are wanting, and ordain elders in every city, as I had appointed thee"* (Titus 1:5).

✶ **1:5** Duane Liftin writes: "As with Timothy in Ephesus (1 Tim. 1:3), Paul had left Titus behind to provide leadership to the fledgling church in Crete. Now the apostle reiterated his previous instructions, both for Titus' sake and for the congregation's sake. The organization of the Cretan church was unfinished due to the brevity of Paul's visit. Thus Titus was to straighten out (lit., "set in order") the situation by appointing elders in every town. Titus was now acting as an apostolic agent (cf. Acts 14:23) in Paul's absence. His authority in the Cretan church was an extension of Paul's own. Such authority ended with the close of the Apostolic Age" (*Bible Knowledge Commentary*, New Testament Volume, p. 762).

  A. The nature of their qualifications
    1. They must be above reproach (Titus 1:6)
    2. They must be the husband of one wife (Titus 1:6)
    3. They must have children who believe (Titus 1:6)
    4. They must not be accused of rebellion (Titus 1:6)
    5. They must not be self-willed (Titus 1:7)

✶ One of the main contrasts between Satan and Christ had to do with the will. Note:
  ■ The self-will of Satan (Isa. 14:12-14; Ezek. 28:11-17)
  ■ The submissive will of Christ (Matt. 26:36-46)

    6. They must not be quick-tempered (Titus 1:7)
    7. They must not be addicted to wine (Titus 1:7)
    8. They must not be pugnacious (Titus 1:7)
    9. They must not be lovers of money (Titus 1:7)
    10. They must be hospitable (Titus 1:8)
    11. They must love what is good (Titus 1:8)
    12. They must be sensible (Titus 1:8)
    13. They must be just (Titus 1:8)
    14. They must be devout (Titus 1:8)
    15. They must be self-controlled (Titus 1:8)

16. They must be students of the Word (Titus 1:9)
  B. The necessity for their qualifications
    1. To reprove erring believers *(Titus 1:9, 13)*.
    2. To renounce apostate unbelievers
      a. Their identity *(Read Titus 1:10, 12)*
      b. Their iniquity *(Read Titus 1:11, 15-16)*

★ **1:16**
- ■ *"Unto the pure, all things are pure."* Paul is here, of course, talking about Mosaic dietary laws, and not morals in general (see Matt. 15:11; Rom. 14:14; Acts 10:15).
- ■ *"They profess that they know God."* The most dangerous (and often most devilish) groups on earth are those who profess but who do not possess the things of God. Paul would warn Timothy of this same group in his final epistle: *"Having a form of godliness, but denying the power thereof"* *(2 Tim. 3:5)*. Our Lord had previously soundly condemned such individuals during his earthly ministry (see Matt. 7:21-23; 23:1-39).

III. Titus and the Church (Titus 2:1-3:11)
  A. Its head, the Savior
    1. The what of his work
      a. His incarnation *(Read Titus 2:11; 3:4)*
      b. His death *(Read Titus 3:5-6)*
      c. His second coming *(Read Titus 1:13)*
    2. The why of his work *(Read Titus 2:12, 14; 3:7)*

★ **3:7** We may observe three aspects in verse 12:
- ■ The selfward aspect—We are to live soberly.
- ■ The manward aspect—We are to live righteously.
- ■ The Godward aspect—We are to live godly.

  B. Its heirs, the saved
    1. Responsibilities of the sheep
      a. The older men *(Read Titus 2:2)*
      b. The older women *(Read Titus 2:3)*
      c. The younger women *(Read Titus 2:4-5)*
      d. The younger men *(Read Titus 2:6)*
      e. Servants *(Read Titus 2:9-10)*
    2. Responsibilities of the undershepherd
      a. To serve as a preacher *(Read Titus 2:1, 15; 3:1-3, 8-9)*
      b. To serve as a pattern *(Read Titus 2:7-8)*
      c. To serve as a purifier *(Read Titus 3:10-11)*

IV. Titus and the Future (Titus 3:12-15)
  A. He is instructed to meet Paul in Nicopolis (Titus 3:12)

★ **3:12** He would be relieved for awhile by Tychicus. Tychicus had already been sent by Paul on various missions to the churches at Ephesus (Eph. 6:21) and Colosse (Col. 4:7). He would later be sent to Ephesus again (see 2 Tim. 4:12). He was then to meet Paul in southern Greece (Nicopolis).

  B. He is instructed to help Zenas and Apollos (Titus 3:13).

LESSON 36
INTRODUCTION TO PHILEMON

THIS IS A LETTER FROM A PRISONER TO A MASTER ABOUT A SLAVE.

A. The book is Philemon (the master); the slave was Onesimus; and the prisoner was Paul.

B. This book, the shortest of all Paul's epistles, is one of the four letters written during his first Roman imprisonment. The other letters are Philippians, Colossians, and Ephesians.

C. It is one of four personal letters to individuals penned by Paul. The others are 1 and 2 Timothy and Titus.

D. Dr. J. Vernon McGee writes: "The Epistles present a different style in revelation. God had used law, history, poetry, prophecy, and the Gospels heretofore, but in the Epistles He adopted a more personal and direct method" *(Through the Bible,* p. 211).

E. The historical background of Philemon is as follows:
   1. Onesimus, a slave owned by Philemon (wealthy Colossian believer and long time friend of Paul) had robbed his master and run away to Rome.
   2. In some wonderful way, Onesimus's path crosses that of Paul, resulting in his glorious conversion to Christ.
   3. Upon hearing his testimony, Paul determines to send him back to Philemon.
   4. To prepare the way (for what could be a very tense meeting), Paul pens this beautiful letter to Philemon. It is a masterpiece of Christian tact and ethics.

F. The letter provides us with one of the finest illustrations of that great theological truth of imputation (the act of reckoning something to another's account) as can be found anywhere in the Bible.

G. This epistle demonstrates that our letter writing can be a ministry for God if we allow it to be so. Some who find it difficult to speak for God may well write for him.

H. It is Paul's only letter where he hints at his age (Philem. 9).

I. Philemon is the 25th longest New Testament book, and 64th longest biblical book, with one chapter, 25 verses, and 445 words.

J. Its great passage is verses 3-6.

Overview of the Book of Philemon

I. **The Appreciation for Praise of Philemon**
    A. Philemon was a friend
        1. To Paul in Rome
        2. To Christians in Colosse
    B. Philemon was a family man

II. **The Appeal and Plea for Onesimus**
    A. The background of this appeal
    B. The basis of this appeal
        1. Forgive him for your sake
        2. Forgive him for his sake
        3. Forgive him for my sake

III. **The Assurance and Pledge of Paul**
    A. His confidence in Philemon
    B. His request to Philemon

THE BOOK OF PHILEMON

I. The Appreciation for Praise of Philemon (Philem. 1-7)
   A. Philemon was a friend.
      1. To Paul in Rome *(Read Philem. 2)*

✷ **v. 1** Although Paul had never been to Colosse, he had in the past met Philemon. We may suppose this wealthy Colossian believer had prayed for and financially invested in the apostle's ministry.

      2. To Christians in Colosse *(Read Philem. 5)*—"*For I have come to have much joy and comfort in your love, because the hearts of the saints have been refreshed through you, brother*" *(Philem. 7, NASB).*

✷ **v. 5** No greater tribute can be paid to a believer than this. Paul speaks of Philemon's love for Jesus (because of who he is), and his faith in Jesus (because of what he is).

✷ **v. 7** Philemon's house was probably a free motel to any and all believers journeying in that area. His life had also touched those saints in the Colosse church.

   B. Philemon was a family man *(Read Philem. 2)*

✷ **v. 2**
- It is believed that Apphia was Philemon's wife and Archippus his son. In his Colossian letter (Col. 4:17) Paul seems to say that Archippus had assumed the role of the pastor there in Colosse when Epaphras (founder of the church) had departed for Rome to visit the imprisoned apostle. At any rate, Philemon seemed to have his family well in hand. He could loudly echo the final words of Joshua: "*Choose you this day whom ye will serve ... but as for me and my house, we will serve the Lord*" (Josh. 24:15).
- Note the phrase, "*the church in thy house.*"

II. The Appeal and Plea for Onesimus (Philem. 8-17)—"*I beseech thee for my son Onesimus, whom I have begotten in my bonds*" *(Philem. 10).*

✷ **v. 10** Onesimus is one of three individuals whom Paul looked upon as his spiritual sons. The other two are:
- Timothy (1 Tim. 1:2; 2 Tim. 1:2)
- Titus (Titus 1:4)

   A. The background of this appeal—Onesimus, Philemon's runaway slave, had been led to Christ in Rome by Paul and was now being sent back to Philemon with a request that he be received as a Christian brother.
   B. The basis of this appeal
      1. Forgive him for your sake *(Read Philem. 11, 15).*

✷ **v. 15** This former dishonest slave had already learned so much in Rome and had proven to be such a help to the apostle. But his spiritual responsibility would demand that he now return and submit himself to Philemon. If he refused to do this, God's blessing upon him would be limited.

> 2. Forgive him for his sake—*"No longer as a slave, but more than a slave, a beloved brother ... in the Lord"* (Philem. 16, NASB).

✱ v. 16 The name Onesimus means "profitable." However, until his conversion, any resemblance between the name and his actions was purely accidental. But now Christ had made all things new. Therefore, if for no other reason (and indeed there were other good reasons), Philemon should restore Onesimus so that he might prove by his actions the meaning of his name.

> 3. Forgive him for my sake *(Read Philem. 9, 17-18)*

✱ v. 18 Paul refers to himself in two ways unique to this epistle:
- "Paul, a prisoner of Jesus Christ" (Philem. 1, 9)
- "Paul, the aged" (Philem. 9)

> **III. The Assurance and Pledge of Paul (Philem. 19-25)**—*"I Paul have written it with mine own hand, I will repay it: albeit I do not say to thee how thou owest unto me even thine own self besides" (Philem. 19).*

✱ v. 19
- Paul has already reminded Philemon concerning his sufferings for Christ in that Roman prison (v. 9). This was in contrast, of course, to the "good life" Philemon was probably enjoying there in Colosse. The intended conclusion thus might be: "If I, Paul, am willing to endure this persecution for Christ, cannot you forgive a fellow saint for Christ?"
- The apostle then gently reminds Philemon that his very conversion experience could be traced back to Paul's ministry.

> A. His confidence in Philemon *(Read Philem. 21)*
> B. His request to Philemon *(Philem. 22)*

Four: GENERAL EPISTLES

A study of the general epistles:

- Hebrews
- James
- I Peter
- II Peter
- I John
- II John
- III John
- Jude

Introduction to Hebrews

WHATEVER HAPPENED TO JESUS? IS HE STILL ALIVE? WHERE IS HE AND WHAT IS HE DOING?

A. He is indeed alive and well. At this very moment he sits at God's right hand to serve as our great High Priest. This, in essence, is what the book of Hebrews is all about. Let us imagine a conversation between a Hindu and a Christian. The Hindu listens intently as the Christian briefly summarizes the earthly ministry of Jesus Christ. At the conclusion of the message, four basic questions might quickly come to his mind.

Question: Why did Jesus have to be born?
Answer: "No man hath seen God at any time; the only begotten Son, which is in the bosom of the Father, he hath declared him" (John 1:18).
Question: Why did Jesus have to die?
Answer: "Who gave himself for our sins, that he might deliver us from this present evil world, according to the will of God and our Father" (Gal. 1:4).
Question: Why did Jesus have to be resurrected?
Answer: "And if Christ be not risen, then is our preaching vain, and your faith is also vain" (1 Cor. 15:14).
Question: Why did Jesus have to ascend?
Answer: The book of Hebrews

B. The book of Hebrews presents the only full discussion in the New Testament of Christ as the believer's High Priest. It answers the question, "Whatever happened to Jesus?"

C. The book of Hebrews has been called the fifth Gospel. The first four describe what Christ once did on earth; while Hebrews describes what he is now doing in heaven.

D. Hebrews 10:11 reveals that the book was written before the destruction of the temple by Titus in A.D. 70.

E. Hebrews may be compared to Romans.
 1. Romans reveals the *necessity* of the Christian faith.
 2. Hebrews reveals the *superiority* of the Christian faith.

F. There are six key words in this book. They are:
 1. Perfect (used 14 times)
 2. Eternal, forever (used 15 times)
 3. Better (used 13 times)
 4. Partakers (used nine times)
 5. Heaven (used 17 times)
 6. Priest, high priest (used 32 times)

G. There are at least 86 direct references to the Old Testament in Hebrews, taken from 100 passages.

H. Hebrews is the only one of the 27 New Testament books whose author is unknown. There are (at least) three suggested authors:
 1. Paul
   a. Because the early church believed he was the author
   b. Because of the characteristic closing of the epistle (13:25; cf. 2 Thess. 3:17-18)

LESSON 36: INTRODUCTION TO HEBREWS

c. Because of the expression *"the just shall live by faith"* — This expression is an Old Testament quote (Hab. 2:4) which is used three times in the New Testament (Rom. 1:17; Gal. 3:11; Heb. 10:38). The argument here is that inasmuch as Paul used the expression the first two times, he probably also used it on the third occasion here in Hebrews.
   d. Because of Peter's statement in 2 Peter 3:15-16 — Here Peter states that Paul had written to the same people he was addressing, the Jews of the dispersion (1 Pet. 1:1; 2 Pet. 3:1). Peter then refers to Paul's letter as Scripture. The book of Hebrews is the only New Testament book which fits this description.
   e. Because it was written from Italy (13:24) by a friend of Timothy (13:23) who was in prison at the time (10:34). This would tie in with Paul's imprisonment as recorded in Acts 28.
  2. Barnabas
   a. Because he was a Levite, and the book of Hebrews seems to have been written by a Levite
   b. Because of the comparison between Acts 4:36 and Hebrews 13:22
  3. Apollos
   a. Because of the eloquent Greek style of Hebrews
   b. Because the Old Testament quotes in Hebrews are taken from the Septuagint, while Paul usually quoted from the Hebrew Old Testament
I. The book provides the most extended biblical record of those conversations between the Father and the Son.
 1. First conversation: Concerning the superiority of Christ over angels (1:5-13).
 2. Second conversation: Concerning Christ's relationship to his people (2:12-13).
 3. Third conversation: Concerning the superior priesthood of Christ (7:17, 21).
 4. Fourth conversation: Concerning the obedience of Christ (10:5-9) Note: These are the first recorded words of Jesus in regard to his earthly mission, apparently uttered as he entered the womb of Mary.

J. It is the only New Testament book to explain the purpose of the Old Testament tabernacle (7-10).

K. It is the first of two New Testament books which refer to the heavenly tabernacle (6:10, 20; 8:1-5; 9:11-12, 23-24). (For the other book, see Rev. 11:19; 5:5.)

L. Hebrews 11 is the greatest chapter on faith in the Bible.

M. This book records the final (of three) New Testament references to that Old Testament quotation, *"The just shall live by faith"* (Hab. 2:4). (They are: Gal. 3:11; Rom. 1:17; Heb. 10:38.)

N. It lists the second (of three) statements concerning the shepherding ministry of Christ.
   1. Jesus said he was the Good Shepherd (John 10:11).
   2. Hebrews says he is the Great Shepherd (Heb. 13:20).
   3. Peter says Christ is the Chief Shepherd (1 Pet. 5:4).

O. Hebrews offers Scripture's greatest analogy between the Old Testament pilgrim and the New Testament pilgrim (3:7-4:16).

P. This epistle also has one of the most controversial passages in the entire Word of God. (See 6:4-6.)

Q. It includes the most extended passage on the subject of divine discipline. (See 12:1-15.)

R. Hebrews 4:12 is probably the Bible's most concise description of itself.

S. It records the third and final instance of the Savior's tears.
   1. John 11:35 (in Bethany)
   2. Luke 19:41 (near Jerusalem)
   3. Hebrews 5:7 (In Gethsemane)

T. It is the only New Testament book referring to Melchizedek (see chapter 7). (Compare with Gen. 14:18-20.)

U. It is the only New Testament book referring to the New Covenant (8:7-13; 10:16-17). (Compare with Jer. 31:31-32.)

V. It mentions by name more Old Testament people than any other New Testament book, a total of 21 individuals.

W. It includes at least eight warnings, writing against:
1. Carelessness (3:1-3)
2. Unbelief (3:12)
3. Immaturity (5:11-14)
4. Overt sin (6:4-6)
5. Inconsistency (10:25)
6. Fear (10:38)
7. Discouragement (12:3-5)
8. Bitterness (12:15)

X. Hebrews is the ninth longest New Testament book, and 31st longest biblical book, with 13 chapters, 303 verses, and 6,913 words. There are quotations or allusions from 21 Old Testament books in Hebrews.

Y. Great passages would include:
1. 2:5-18
2. 4:9-16
3. 6:17-20
4. 9:24-28
5. 10:12-14
6. 10:19-20
7. 10:35-39
8. 11:1-2
9. 11:32-40
10. 12:1-2
11. 13:20-21

Overview of the Book of Hebrews

I. Christ, the Superior Person
  A. He is better than the prophets
    1. Because of the Father's declaration to him
    2. Because of the Father's description of him
  B. He is better than the angels
    1. Because of his reputation
    2. Because of his rank
    3. Because of his relationship
    4. Because of his righteousness
    5. Because of his reign
    6. Because of his reliability
    7. Because of his redemptive ministry
  C. He is better than Moses
    1. Moses was but a servant in the Father's house
    2. Moses was not able to provide a rest for his people
    3. Christ is the unique Son in the Father's house
    4. Only Christ is able to provide a rest for his people
  D. He is better than Joshua
  E. He is better than Aaron
    1. Christ possessed perfectly that which Aaron had in part
    2. Christ possessed perfectly that which Aaron lacked completely

II. Maturity, the Superior Purpose
  A. The appeal for spiritual maturity
    1. Be faithful in dividing the Word of God
    2. Be faithful in doing the work of God
  B. The anchor for spiritual maturity
    1. The promise of the Father
    2. The priesthood of the Savior

III. Melchizedek, the Superior Priesthood
  A. It offers a better source — From Aaron to Melchizedek
    1. It is a royal priesthood
    2. It is a timeless priesthood
    3. It is an authoritative priesthood
    4. It is an independent priesthood
    5. It is an everlasting priesthood
    6. It is a perfecting priesthood
    7. It is a guaranteed priesthood
    8. It is a continuous priesthood

       9. It is a permanent priesthood
    10. It is a holy priesthood
    11. It is an all-sufficient priesthood
    12. It is a divine priesthood
  B. It offers a better script — From the Old Covenant to the New Covenant
    1. The Old Covenant
    2. The New Covenant
  C. It offers a better sanctuary — From the earthly to the heavenly
    1. The earthly tabernacle
    2. The heavenly tabernacle
  D. It offers a better sacrifice — From animal lambs to God's Lamb
    1. The Shepherd and his sacrifice
    2. The sheep and their Savior

IV. Faith, the Superior Principle
  A. The people of faith
    1. Who they were
    2. What they did
    3. What they endured
    4. Why they endured
  B. The pattern of faith
    1. Perform the work of God
    2. Ponder the discipline of God
    3. Prepare for the kingdom of God
  C. The performance of faith
    1. What the Savior has done
    2. What the saints are to do

THE BOOK OF HEBREWS

> **I. Christ, the Superior Person (Heb. 1:1-5:10)**
>   A. He is better than the prophets (Heb. 1:1-3).
>   1. Because of the Father's declaration to him *(Read Heb. 1:1-2)*

★ **1:1** The phrase *"at sundry times and in divers manners,"* is literally, "by various means and in various ways." We know God spoke to human beings, but how did he speak? A careful examination of the Bible reveals at least nine different modes of communication. These are:
- Through angels (Dan. 9:21-27; Luke 1:11-20, 26-37)
- Through a loud voice (Gen. 3:9-19; 6:13-21; 12:1-3)
- Through a still, small voice (1 Kings 19:11-12)
- Through nature (Psa. 19:1-3; Rom. 1:18-20)
- Through an animal (Num. 22:28)
- Through dreams (Gen. 28:12; Matt. 1:20; 2:13)
- Through visions (Gen. 46:2; Isa. 6:1-8)
- Through Christophanies—A Christophany is an Old Testament, pre-Bethlehem appearance of Christ (Gen. 32:24-30; Exod. 3:2; Judg. 6:11).
- Through the earthly body of Christ (Heb. 1:1-2)

>   2. Because of the Father's description of him *(Read Heb. 1:2b-3)*
>   a. He is the creator of all things.
>   b. He is the upholder of all things.
>   c. He is the heir of all things.
>   d. He is the redeemer of all things.
>   B. He is better than the angels (Heb. 1:4-2:18).
>   1. Because of his reputation (Heb. 1:4)—*"Having become as much better than the angels, as He has inherited a more excellent name than they" (Heb. 1:4,* NASB).
>   2. Because of his rank *(Read Heb. 1:9, 13)*

★ **1:6** John Bunyan once wrote: "If Jesus be not God, then heaven will be filled with idolaters."

>   3. Because of his relationship *(Read Heb. 1:5)*
>   4. Because of his righteousness—*"A sceptre of righteousness is the sceptre of thy kingdom"* (Heb. 1:8b).
>   5. Because of his reign—*"But unto the Son he saith, Thy throne, O God, is for ever and ever"* (Heb. 1:8a).

★ **1:8a** This verse, a quotation of Psalm 45:6, provides one of Scripture's strongest declarations of Christ's deity, for here we read of the Father calling the Son God.

>   6. Because of his reliability *(Read Heb. 1:10-12)*
>   7. Because of his redemptive ministry (Heb. 2:1-18)
>   a. Redemption: The warning involved *(Read Heb. 2:1-3a)*

✱ **2:3a**
- There is no answer to this question, of course, because there is no escape.
- Hebrews contains five key warnings. This is the first. Here is the argument. If Israel in Old Testament times was punished for disobeying the word of angels, how much greater would be punishment for disobeying God's Word as spoken by his own Son. (Gen. 19; Deut. 33:2; Psa. 68:17; Acts 7:53; Gal. 3:19; cf. Luke 4:18-21; 19:10; Matt. 16.21; 20:28.)

> b. Redemption: The witness involved *(Read Heb. 2:3b-4)*

✱ **2:3b-4** God did indeed confirm his message through both Christ and his followers by signs and wonders.
- Christ (John 2:23; 3:2)
- His followers
  - Peter and the apostles (Acts 2:43; 4:30; 5:12)
  - Stephen (Acts 6:8)
  - Philip (Acts 8:6, 13)
  - Paul (Acts 14:3; 15:12; Rom. 15:19; 2 Cor. 12:12)

> c. Redemption: The works involved
> (1) Christ came to recapture our lost destiny (Heb. 2:5-9).
> (a) This destiny reviewed *(Read Heb. 2:5-8)*

✱ **2:8a**
- God placed all things under man during the Creator's first recorded words to his creatures (Adam and Eve) *(Read Gen. 1:28)*.
- Author Ray C. Stedman writes the following: "The writer insists that when David says 'all things', he means all things, everything. For he adds, Now in putting everything in subjection to him, he left nothing outside his control. Here is man's intended destiny, his authorized dominion. Man was made to be king over all God's universe. Surely this passage includes far more than the earth. It envisions the created universe of God as far as man has ever been able to discover it, in all the illimitable reaches of space and whatever lies beyond that. All this is to be put under man's dominion. It is a vast and tremendous vision.

  "But man's authority was derived authority. Man himself was to be subject to the God who indwelt him. He was to be the means by which the invisible God became visible to His creatures. He was to be the manifestation of God's own life which dwelt in the royal residence of his human spirit. As long as man was subject to the dominion of God within him, he would be able to exercise dominion over all the universe around. Only when man accepted dominion could he exercise dominion.

  "The writer further points out that man was made lower than the angels for a limited time to learn what the exercise of that dominion meant. He was given a limited domain: this earth, this tiny planet whirling its way through the great galaxy to which we belong, amid all the billions of galaxies of space! And he was also given a limited physical body so that within that limited area man should learn the principles by which his dominion could be exercised throughout the universe. This limitation is described as being lower than the angels" (*What More Can God Say?* p. 20).

> (b) This destiny revoked— *"But now we see not yet all things put under him"* (Heb. 2:8c).

✱ **2:8b** Man's lofty position was revoked as described by the saddest verse in Scripture *(Read Gen. 3:6)*.
Stedman continues: "But the passage goes on to describe man's present state of futility. As it is we do not yet see everything in subjection to him. There is the whole story of human history in a nutshell. How visibly true this is: we do not yet see everything in subjection to him. Man attempts to exercise his dominion but he no longer can do so adequately. He has never forgotten the position God gave him, for throughout the history of the race there is a continual restatement of the dreams of man for dominion over the earth and the universe. This is why we cannot keep off the highest mountain. We have to get up there, though we have not lost a thing up there and we know when we get there we will only see what the bear saw: the other side of the mountain. But

we have to be there. We have to explore the depths of the sea. We have to get out into space. Why? Because it is there.

"Man consistently manifests a remarkable racial memory, a vestigial recollection of what God told him to do. The trouble is that when he tries to accomplish this now he creates a highly explosive and dangerous situation, for his ability to exercise dominion is no longer there. Things get out of balance. This is why we are confronted with an increasingly serious situation in our day when our attempt to control insects by pesticides and other poisons creates an imbalance that threatens serious results. The history of man is one of continually precipitating a crisis by attempting to exercise dominion.

"If we go back into recorded history to the earliest writings of men, the most ancient of history, we find that men were wrestling with the same moral problems then that we are wrestling with today. We have made wonderful advances in technology, but have made absolutely zero progress when it comes to moral relationships. Somewhere man has lost his relationship with God. The fall of man is the only adequate explanation of this. Since then the universe is stamped with futility. Everything man does is a dead-end to a successful conclusion. Even in the individual life this is true. How many have realized the dreams and ideals they began with? Who can say, 'I have done all that I wanted to do; I have been all that I wanted to be'? Paul in Romans puts it, 'The creation was subjected to futility' (Rom. 8:20)" (*What More Can God Say?* p. 21).

> (c) This destiny revived *(Read Heb. 2:9)*

★ **2:9**
- But the writer of Hebrews says, "We see Jesus!" This is our one hope. With the eye of faith we see Jesus already crowned and reigning over the universe, the man Jesus fulfilling our own lost destiny.
- By way of summary, consider these three tremendous truths described in Hebrews 2:5-9.
    - In regard to the past—The revealing. *"But ... |we see| thou hast put all things ... under his feet."* This may well have included everything from animals to angels, and from the grass of the fields, to the galaxies of the skies.
    - In regard to the present—The revoking. *"But we see not ... all things ... under him."* Apart from the new birth, human beings cannot subdue their own sinful nature, let alone their environment.
    - In regard to the future—The realizing. *"But we see Jesus!"* In a nutshell, one of the reasons Jesus left heaven's glory 20 centuries ago was to guarantee redeemed humanity of his original destiny, namely, to help rule the universe. This glorious truth is proclaimed no less than five times in the New Testament. (See 2 Tim. 2:12; Rev. 5:10; 20:4, 6; 22:5.)

> (2) Christ came to restore our lost fellowship (Heb. 2: 10-18).
>   (a) His suffering ministry *(Read Heb. 2:10)*
>   (b) His sanctifying ministry *(Read Heb. 2:11)*
>   (c) His singing ministry *(Read Heb. 2:12)*

★ **2:12** This passage (Heb. 2:11-17) is the final of only two New Testament passages where believers are referred to as the brothers (and sisters) of Christ. (See also Rom. 8:29.) This precious relationship is predicted in Psalm 22:22 and Isaiah 8:18. Thus, as a child of God, Jesus is not only my Creator (John 1:3), my Redeemer (Rev. 5:9), and my Shepherd (John 10:11), but also my elder Brother.

> (d) His suppressing ministry *(Read Heb. 2:14-15)*
> (e) His sympathizing ministry
>   1) He understands our nature *(Read Heb. 2:16)*
>   2) He understands our need *(Read Heb. 2:17-18)*

C. He is better than Moses (Heb. 3:1-4, 7, 9-16).
  1. Moses was but a servant in the Father's house *(Read Heb. 3:5)*
  2. Moses was not able to provide a rest for his people.
     a. Israel's sin *(Read Heb. 3:7-10)*
     b. Israel's sentence *(Read Heb. 3:11, 16-19)*

> 3. Christ is the unique Son in the Father's house *(Read Heb. 3:3, 6)*
> 4. Only Christ is able to provide a rest for his people.
>   a. An illustration of this rest—Creation *(Read Heb. 4:5-6)*
>   b. The exhortation concerning this rest *(Read Heb. 4:12-15 and 4:1, 9-11)*.

✶ 4:11

- Concerning the phrase, "Let us"—This chapter (Heb. 4) records the first of 13 "Let us" admonitions to be found in Hebrews. Note:
  - *"Let us therefore fear" (4:1).*
  - *"Let us labour therefore to enter into that rest" (4:11).*
  - *"Let us hold fast our profession" (4:14).*
  - *"Let us therefore come boldly unto the throne of grace" (4:16).*
  - *"Let us go on unto perfection" (6:1).*
  - *"Let us draw near with a true heart in full assurance of faith" (10:22).*
  - *"Let us hold fast the profession of our faith without wavering" (10:23).*
  - *"Let us consider one another to provoke unto love and to good works" (10:24).*
  - *"Let us lay aside every weight" (12:1).*
  - *"Let us run with patience the race that is set before us" (12:1).*
  - *"Let us have grace" (12:28).*
  - *"Let us go forth therefore unto him without the camp" (13:13).*
  - *"Let us offer the sacrifice of praise to God continually" (13:15).*
- Concerning the word "rest"
  - The word "rest" as found in Hebrews 3 and 4 is a very important concept, being used no less than nine times (see 3:11, 18; 4:1, 3, 5, 8-11).
  - In essence, there are three facts concerning this rest:
    - ✦ The sin of unbelief once kept Israel from entering God's rest (3:11, 18; 4:11).
    - ✦ The sin of unbelief will keep the believer from entering God's rest (4:1).
    - ✦ Faith will assure us of entering God's rest (4:9-10).
  - Here it should be stated that this is the rest of sanctification and not that of salvation. For example, Moses died a saved man (Heb. 11:24-29), but because of one tragic act of unbelief (Num. 20:7-12), he was prevented from entering the Promised Land.
  - Some have claimed, however, that the rest here is the rest of salvation, based on Hebrews 4:2: *"For unto us was the gospel preached, as well as unto them: but the word preached did not profit them, not being mixed with faith in them that heard it."*

    To be sure, the word gospel does mean "good news." Zane Hodges writes: "But this good news does not always refer to the plan of salvation from sin. In some circles the word 'gospel' has acquired a sense too technical and narrow to do justice to the writer's ideas here. What was preached to the Israelites of old was, quite clearly, God's offer of rest. This, of course, was 'good news' for them just as it is for people now, but it is not exactly what is meant today by 'gospel.' The Greek verb used, *euangelizomai*, was fully capable of having a nontechnical sense in the New Testament (cf. its use in Luke 1:19; 1 Thess. 3:6), but naturally the writer here did not sharply distinguish the 'good news' about rest, which his readers had heard, from the 'good news' to which the term 'gospel' is more usually applied (cf. 1 Cor. 15:1-4). But as the whole context shows, his concern was with the good news about a future rest for God's people (cf. Heb. 4:10), not with the fundamental facts Paul spoke of in I Corinthians 15" (*Bible Knowledge Commentary*, New Testament Volume, p. 788).
  - We have now, listed for us, three great biblical rests:
    - ✦ The rest of creation (4:4)
    - ✦ The rest of salvation (4:10)
    - ✦ The rest of consecration (4:11)

> c. The appropriation of this rest—How is it obtained? Answer: Through obedience to the Word of God *(Read Heb. 4:2, 12-13)*.

✶ **4:13** These verses give us one of nine symbols for the Word of God as found in the Bible itself. These symbols are:
- A mirror (James 1:23-25)
- A seed (James 1:18; 1 Pet. 1:23)
- Water (Eph. 5:25-27)
- A lamp (Psa. 119:105; Prov. 6:23; 2 Pet. 1:19)
- Precious metals
  - Gold (Psa. 19:10; 119:127)
  - Silver (Psa. 12:6)
- Nourishing food
  - Milk (1 Pet. 2:2)
  - Meat (Heb. 5:12-14)
  - Bread (John 6:51)
  - Honey (Psa. 19:10)
- A hammer (Jer. 23:29)
- A fire (Jer. 20:9)
- A sword (Heb. 4:12; Eph. 6:17)

> d. The location of this rest—Where can it be found? *(Read Heb. 4:14-16)*

✶ **4:16** Luther, Zwingli, and Calvin nailed to the masthead of their movement three great principles taken from Hebrews:
- No sacrifice but Calvary
- No priest but Christ
- No confessional but the throne of grace

> D. He is better than Joshua (Heb. 4:8)—*"For if Joshua had given them rest, He would not have spoken of another day after that"* *(Heb. 4:8, NASB)*.
> E. He is better than Aaron (Heb. 5:1-10).
>   1. Christ possessed perfectly that which Aaron had in part.
>   a. Like Aaron, he was taken from among men *(Read Heb. 5:1)*
>   b. Like Aaron, he offered up a sacrifice—*"That he may offer both gifts and sacrifices for sins"* (Heb. 5:1). He is obligated to offer sacrifices for sins, "as for the people" (Heb. 5:3, personal paraphrase).
>   c. Like Aaron, he possessed compassion *(Read Heb. 5:2)*

✶ **5:2a** While upon this earth, our Lord showed great compassion:
- Upon the sick multitudes (Matt. 14:14)
- Upon the shepherdless multitudes (Matt. 9:36)
- Upon the hungry multitudes (Matt. 15:32)
- Upon a widow (Luke 7:13)
- Upon a leper (Mark 1:41)
- Upon a father (Mark 9:22-23)
- Upon a demoniac (Mark 5:19)

> d. Like Aaron, he experienced the infirmities of the flesh *(Read Heb. 5:2)*

✵ **5:2b** Jesus took upon himself at Bethlehem all the sinless infirmities associated with humanity.
- He possessed flesh and blood (Heb. 2:14).
- He grew (Luke 2:40).
- He asked questions (Luke 2:46).
- He was tempted (Matt. 4:1).
- He hungered (Matt. 4:2).
- He thirsted (John 4:7).
- He became weary (John 4:6).
- He slept (Matt. 8:24).
- He wept (John 11:35).
- He experienced joy (Heb. 12:2; Luke 10:21).
- He was troubled (John 12:27).
- He suffered (1 Pet. 4:1).
- He bled (John 19:34).
- He died (Matt. 27:50).

> e. Like Aaron, he was chosen by God *(Read Heb. 5:4)*
> f. Like Aaron, he prayed *(Read Heb. 5:7)*
> g. Like Aaron, he learned obedience— *"Though he were a Son, yet learned he obedience"* (Heb. 5:8).
> h. Like Aaron, he suffered— *"By the things which he suffered"* (Heb. 5:8).

✵ **5:8b** Zane Hodges observes: "In a real sense not fully comprehensible, the Incarnation gave the already infinitely wise and perfect Son of God the experiential acquisition of knowledge about the human condition. Suffering thus became a reality that He tasted and from it He can sympathize deeply with His followers. (The Greek has an interesting play on words in the verbs He learned [*emathen*] and He suffered [*epathen*])" (*Bible Knowledge Commentary*, p. 792).

> 2. Christ possessed perfectly that which Aaron lacked completely.
>   a. Unlike Aaron, he offered no sacrifice for his own self (Heb. 5:3).
>   b. Unlike Aaron, he is God's Son— *"Thou art my Son, today have I begotten thee"* (Heb. 5:5).
>   c. Unlike Aaron, he is God's eternal High Priest— *"Thou art a priest forever"* (Heb. 5:6).
>   d. Unlike Aaron, he is a priest like Melchizedek *(Read Heb. 5:10)*.
>   e. Unlike Aaron, he became the source of eternal salvation *(Read Heb. 5:9)*.
> **II. Maturity, the Superior Purpose (Heb. 5:11-6:20)**— *"Therefore leaving the elementary teaching about the Christ, let us press on to maturity"* (Heb. 6:1, NASB).
>   A. The appeal for spiritual maturity (Heb. 5:11-6:12)
>   1. Be faithful in dividing the Word of God *(Read Heb. 5:11-14)*

✵ **5:14** Author Ray Stedman writes: "I read of a principal in a high school who had an administrative post to fill. He promoted one of his teachers with ten years of teaching experience to the job. When the announcement was made, another teacher in this school came to him terribly upset. She said, 'Why did you put that teacher in this position? He has only had ten years of experience and I've had twenty-five years, yet you passed me over in favor of him.' And the principal said, 'I'm sorry; you're wrong. You haven't had twenty-five years of experience. You have had one year's experience twenty-five times'" (*What More Can God Say?*)

The reason for this uncertainty and immaturity is explained in 5:13-14; cf. I Corinthians 3:1-2; 1 Peter 2:1-2. See also Joshua 5:12, where we are told that the manna ceased after Israel entered the Promised Land.

LESSON 37

> 2. Be faithful in doing the work of God.
> a. The futility of dead works—*"Therefore let us leave the elementary teachings about Christ and go on to maturity, not laying again the foundation of repentance from acts that lead to death, and of faith in God, instruction about baptisms, the laying on of hands, the resurrection of the dead, and eternal judgment.... It is impossible for those who have once been enlightened, who have tasted the heavenly gift, who have shared in the Holy Spirit, who have tasted the goodness of the word of God and the powers of the coming age, if they fall away, to be brought back to repentance, because to their loss they are crucifying the Son of God all over again and subjecting him to public disgrace. Land that drinks in the rain often falling on it and that produces a crop useful to those by whom it is farmed receives the blessing of God. But land that produces thorns and thistles is worthless and is in danger of being cursed. In the end it will be burned"* (Heb. 6:1-2, 4-8, NIV).

★ **6:8**
- Perhaps no other single biblical passage has been the subject of more speculation and interpretation than these words in Hebrews 6:4-6. Various theories hold that these verses describe one of the following kinds of people.
  - Saved people who lose their salvation through some horrible sin—Of course, if this were true, then the same passage also teaches that they could never be saved again.
  - Professed believers who have only "tasted" the things of God and never really "swallowed" them—However, this is entirely unsupportable, for the same Greek word is used also in Hebrews 2:9 concerning Jesus who, "by the grace of God should taste death for every man."
  - Jewish professed believers living while the temple was still standing—*The Scofield Bible* presents this view: "Hebrews 6:4-8 presents the case of Jewish professed believers who halt short of faith in Christ after advancing to the very threshold of salvation, even 'going along with' the Holy Spirit in His work of enlightenment and conviction (John 16:8-10). It is not said that they had faith. This supposed person is like the spies at Kadesh-barnea (Deut. 1:19-26) who saw the land and had the very fruit of it in their hands, and yet turned back" (p. 1,295).
  - A hypothetical case of what could not happen—"If one could 'fall away' (v. 6), it would be impossible to renew him again to repentance; for, in such an instance, it would be necessary for Christ to be crucified a second time. Obviously, this will not occur (Heb. 10:12, 14); thus to fall away is impossible" (*The New Scofield Bible*, p. 1,315).
  - Backsliders who are in danger of committing the sin unto death (see I Cor. 11:30; Acts 5:1-11; 1 John 5:16-17)—None of these views is without its problems.
- It should be noted (v. 8) that here it is not the field which is destroyed, but the fruit. (See also I Cor. 3:15; John 15:6; Heb. 10:30.)

> b. The fruits of dedicated works *(Read Heb. 6:9-12)*

★ **6:12** Thus, while good works will not save a sinner from hell, they will spare a saint from judgment. (See I Cor. 11:31.)

> B. The anchor for spiritual maturity (Heb. 6:13-20)
> 1. The promise of the Father—*"When God made his promise to Abraham, since there was no one greater for him to swear by, he swore by himself, saying, 'I will surely bless you and give you many descendants.' And so, after waiting patiently, Abraham received what was promised. Men swear by someone greater than themselves, and the oath confirms what is said and puts an end to all argument. Because God wanted to make the unchanging*

nature of his purpose very clear to the heirs of what was promised, he confirmed it with an oath. God did this so that, by two unchangeable things in which it is impossible for God to lie, we who have fled to take hold of the hope offered to us may be greatly encouraged" (Heb. 6:13-18, NIV).
   2. The priesthood of the Savior *(Read Heb. 6:19-20)*

✶ **6:20** Jesus is described here as our forerunner. This word has been associated with a small boat called a forerunner. In the ancient world large ocean vessels often experienced difficulty when approaching the shallow Greek harbors. To counteract this, a small forerunner boat would often be sent out to help secure the vessel's anchor within the harbor itself. Dr. Kenneth Wuest writes: "The anchor of the believer is, therefore, fastened within the veil of the Holy of Holies of heaven. We have some rich figures here. This present life is the sea; the soul ... of the believer, as a tempest-tossed ship, is held by the anchor within the veil, fastened by faith to the blessed reality within the veil" (*Hebrews in the Greek New Testament*, p. 125).

III. Melchizedek, the Superior Priesthood (Heb. 7:1-10:39)
   A. It offers a better source—From Aaron to Melchizedek (Heb. 7).
      1. It is a royal priesthood *(Read Heb. 7:1-2)*

✶ **7:2** Who was this mysterious Melchizedek who appeared in the time of Abraham (Gen. 14:18-20) and is later spoken of in the Psalms (Psa. 110)? The following theories have been advocated concerning his identity:
- That he was Shem, one of Noah's three sons
- That he was a godly priest-king over the city of Salem (thought to be a reference to Jerusalem, and thus the first mention of the Holy City in the Bible)
- That he was Christ himself—This theory is based on Hebrews 7:3 which says of Melchizedek: *"Without father, without mother, without descent, having neither beginning of days, nor end of life."* This does not necessarily mean that Melchizedek was actually Christ (although he may have been), but that inasmuch as we have no record of his birth or death he does become a type of Christ, not only in his office, but also in his origin.
- That he was a heavenly creature—Zane Hodges suggests: "If this is correct, Melchizedek may have been an angelic being who reigned for a time at Salem (i.e., Jerusalem). If so, the statement that he was 'without beginning of days' would not mean that he was eternal, but simply that he had a pretemporal origin. Nor would this concept of Melchizedek as an angel elevate him to the same level as God's Son, since the author painstakingly asserted the Son's superiority to the angels (1:5-14). There is indeed evidence that, at Qumran, Melchizedek was regarded as an angelic personage" (*Bible Knowledge Commentary*, p. 798).

      2. It is a timeless priesthood *(Read Heb. 7:3)*
      3. It is an authoritative priesthood (Heb. 7:4-10).
         a. Fact: Abraham tithed to Melchizedek.
         b. Fact: Abraham was the ancestor of Levi, founder of the Levitical priesthood.
         c. Conclusion: The yet unborn Levi tithed to Melchizedek while he was still in the loins of Abraham.
         d. Conclusion: The Melchizedek priesthood is therefore greater than the Levitical priesthood, for it received tithes from it. *"And without all contradiction the less is blessed of the better"* (Heb. 7:7).
      4. It is an independent priesthood (Heb. 7:11-15).
         a. Independent of the Law *(Read Heb. 7:11-12)*
         b. Independent of the tribe of Levi *(Read Heb. 7:13-14)*

✶ **7:14** Christ was given an independent priesthood. Melchizedek was ordained by an oath from God and not by the tribe of Levi. In the Old Testament no one could serve as a priest unless he was descended from Aaron (Ezra 2:61-62). However, neither Melchizedek nor Christ came from this tribe.

> 5. It is an everlasting priesthood *(Read Heb. 7:16-17)*
> 6. It is a perfecting priesthood (Heb. 7:19, 25)
>   a. The fact of this perfection *(Read Heb. 7:19)*
>   b. The extent of this perfection *(Read Heb. 7:25)*

★ **7:25** This verse is usually applied to the salvation of the lost (from "the uttermost to the uttermost"), but in its context it refers to the preservation of the saved. Thus, Christ died down here on Calvary to bring us salvation, and now lives up there in glory to keep us saved. (See also Rom. 8:34; Rev. 1:18.)

> 7. It is a guaranteed priesthood *(Heb. 7:20-22)*
> 8. It is a continuous priesthood (Heb. 7:23)—"*And the former priests, on the one hand, existed in greater numbers, because they were prevented by death from continuing*" *(Heb. 7:23, NASB)*.
> 9. It is a permanent priesthood (Heb. 7:24)—"*But He, on the other hand, because He abides forever, holds His priesthood permanently*" *(Heb. 7:24, NASB)*.
> 10. It is a holy priesthood *(Read Heb. 7:26)*

★ **7:26** This is in contrast to the Levitical priesthood, whose representatives often allowed corruption and idolatry to control their lives (see Exod. 32:1-6, 21-25; 1 Sam. 2:12-17; 8:1-3).

> 11. It is an all-sufficient priesthood *(Read Heb. 7:27)*

★ **7:27** Author Ray Stedman writes: "As a priest, Jesus Christ could find no unblemished sacrifice that He could offer except Himself, so He offered Himself as a sacrifice; there was found no other priest worthy of offering such a sacrifice, so Christ became both Priest and Victim" (*What More Can God Say?* p. 115).

This dual arrangement can be seen by listening to his seven final sentences while on the cross. The first three demonstrate his priestly ministry while the final four speak of his sacrificial role.

- His priestly ministry:
    - "*Father, forgive them; for they know not what they do*" *(Luke 23:34)*.
    - "*Verily, I say unto thee, today shalt thou be with me in paradise*" *(Luke 23:43)*.
    - "*Woman, behold thy son! ... Behold thy mother!*" *(John 19:26-27)*.
- His sacrificial ministry
    - "*My God, my God, why hast thou forsaken me?*" *(Matt. 27:46)*.
    - "*I thirst*" *(John 19:28)*.
    - "*It is finished*" *(John 19:30)*.
    - "*Father, into thy hands I commend my spirit*" *(Luke 23:46)*.

> 12. It is a divine priesthood *(Read Heb. 7:28)*
>   B. It offers a better script—From the Old Covenant to the New Covenant (Heb. 8).

★ The Old Testament Hebrew word for "covenant" was *berit*, meaning "to cut or divide." (See Gen. 15:10; Jer. 34:18-19.) This cutting was in reference to the cutting of sacrificial animals. Between these bloody pieces of flesh the two parties of the *berit* would walk. However, in the Genesis 15 account, God put Abraham to sleep and walked through alone, thus signifying that particular *berit* to be unconditional. This ceremony was also known as a blood covenant. This Old Testament concept is brought out in the New Testament by the Greek word *diatheke*. A *diatheke* is a treaty between two parties, but binding only on one, according to the terms fixed by the others. This important word appears no less than 22 times in the book of Hebrews. It is always translated by the English words "covenant" and/or "testament." (See also Luke 22:20; 1 Cor. 11:25; 2 Cor. 3:6.) Another

Greek word, *suntheke*, although it is the regular term employed for a treaty, is used but four times and always in a bad light (see John 9:22; Luke 22:5; Acts 23:20; 24:9). Thus, a covenant (*berit* in the Old Testament Hebrew; *diatheke* in the New Testament Greek) is a promise or agreement between God and man. It may be a conditional or an unconditional agreement. In Hebrews 8, the author refers to both a conditional agreement (the Old Covenant), and an unconditional agreement (the New Covenant).

> 1. The Old Covenant
>   a. Mediated by Moses *(Read Heb. 8:5)*
>   b. Conditional (Heb. 8:7-9)
>   (1) The terms—Obedience by Israel
>   (2) The tragedy—Disobedience by Israel *(Read Heb. 8:9)*
>   c. Condemning—*"For finding fault with them"* (Heb. 8:8)
>   d. Written on dead stones (Exod. 32:15)

★ **8:9** Thus, to summarize the Old Covenant:
- It was mediated by Moses (Exod. 19; John 1:17; Gal. 3:19).
- It was conditional (see Deut. 28).
- It could not produce the necessary righteousness (8:8).
- It was written on dead stones (Exod. 32:15).

> 2. The New Covenant
>   a. Mediated by Christ *(Read Heb. 8:1-4)*
>   b. Unconditional *(Read Heb. 8:6)*
>   c. Justifying *(Read Heb. 8:12)*
>   d. Written on living hearts (Heb. 8:10-11)
>   (1) Producing a special relationship with God *(Read Heb. 8:10)*
>   (2) Producing a special revelation from God *(Read Heb. 8:11)*

★ **8:11** Thus, to summarize the New Covenant:
- The features involved
  - It is mediated by Christ (Heb. 9:15; John 1:17), but originally given by God to Jeremiah the prophet (see Jer. 31:31-34).
  - It is unconditional (8:9).
  - It can produce the necessary righteousness (8:11).
  - It is written on living hearts (8:10).
- The theories involved—There are at least four theories concerning the recipients of this New Covenant. These are:
  - The church has replaced Israel as the participant in the New Covenant. This is totally refuted by Paul in Romans 9-11.
  - The New Covenant is with the nation Israel only. However, this seems to be out of context with Hebrews 8.
  - There are two new covenants in this chapter. One refers to Israel, and the other to the church.
  - There is but one New Covenant which will be fulfilled eschatologically with Israel, but participated in soteriologically by the church today. Of these four views it would seem that while the third is possible, the fourth is probable.

> C. It offers a better sanctuary—From the earthly to the heavenly (Heb. 9).
>   1. The earthly tabernacle
>   a. It was of this world *(Read Heb. 9:1)*
>   b. Its work was external in nature *(Read Heb. 9:10)*
>   c. It was temporary *(Read Heb. 9:8)*
>   d. It was a shadow of the real *(Read Heb. 9:9)*

> e. It was inaccessible *(Read Heb. 9:7)*
> f. It was made by human hands *(Read Heb. 9:24)*
> g. It featured animal blood *(Read Heb. 9:13)*
> h. It had daily sacrifice *(Read Heb. 9:6, 25)*
> i. It was serviced by sinful priests (Heb. 9:7)
> j. It could not purge sin (Heb. 9:9)
> k. It had no abiding hope (Heb. 9:10)
> 2. The heavenly tabernacle
> a. It was of heaven *(Read Heb. 9:23)*
> b. Its work was internal in nature (Heb. 9:9)
> c. It was permanent *(Read Heb. 9:12)*
> d. It was the real thing (Heb. 9:24)
> e. It was accessible to all *(Read Heb. 4:16; 10:19)*
> f. It was made by God himself (Heb. 9:24)
> g. It featured the blood of Christ (Heb. 9:12)
> h. It had but one sacrifice (Heb. 9:12)
> i. It was serviced by the Holy Spirit *(Read Heb. 9:14)*
> j. It was able to purge sin (Heb. 9:12)
> k. It has an abiding hope.
> (1) Because of Christ's past work—*"So Christ was once offered to bear the sins of many" (Heb. 9:28a)*.
> (2) Because of Christ's present work—*"For Christ is ... entered ... into heaven itself, now to appear in the presence of God for us" (Heb. 9:24)*
> (3) Because of Christ's future work—*"And unto them that look for him shall he appear the second time without sin unto salvation" (Heb. 9:28b)*.

★ **9:28b** At this point the author of Hebrews has described for us the full sevenfold ministry of our Lord.
- His incarnation (1:2; 2:16-17)
- His ministration (5:7-9)
- His crucifixion (6:6; 7:27; 2:9)
- His resurrection (13:20)
- His ascension (4:4; 6:20)
- His intercession (7:25; 8:1; 9:12, 24)
- His revelation (9:28)

> D. It offers a better sacrifice—From animal lambs to God's Lamb (Heb. 10)
> 1. The Shepherd and his sacrifice (Heb. 10:1-18)—Jesus, the sovereign Shepherd, is pictured as the sacrificial Lamb.
> a. The need for his sacrifice *(Read Heb. 10:1, 4)*

★ **10:4** These sacrifices could (for awhile) cover sin; but these sacrifices could not cleanse it. (See also 10:6, 11; Isa.1:11; Jer. 6:20; Hos. 6:6; Amos 5:21-22.)

> b. The obedience in his sacrifice *(Read Heb. 10:5-9)*

★ **10:7** These may be considered as our Lord's first recorded words in reference to his earthly ministry, uttered perhaps as he left the ivory palaces of glory to join himself to that tiny mass of human flesh within Mary's womb.

> c. The results from his sacrifice (Heb. 10:10-14)
>   (1) His followers have been forever sanctified *(Read Heb. 10:10, 14)*
>   (2) His Father has been forever satisfied *(Read Heb. 10:11-13)*
> d. The witness to his sacrifice *(Read Heb. 10:15-18)*
>
> 2. The sheep and their Savior (Heb. 10:19-39)
>   a. Concerning supplication—Be bold. *(Read Heb. 10:19)*
>   b. Concerning past sins—Be assured. *(Read Heb. 10:22)*
>   c. Concerning service—Be steadfast. *(Read Heb. 10:13, 25)*

✶ **10:25** The "day" here may be a reference to the predicted destruction of Jerusalem (Matt. 24:1-2), or the coming of the Lord. The context strongly suggests the second meaning (see Heb. 10:37).

> d. Concerning other saints—Be helpful. *(Read Heb. 10:24)*
> e. Concerning sacrilege—Be careful. *(Read Heb. 10:26, 30-31)*

✶ **10:31** Do these fearful verses refer to saved or unsaved people? While one cannot be absolutely dogmatic here, it would seem from the phrase in verse 30, "The Lord shall judge his people," that the author had believers in mind. If this is correct, then the sin unto death may be intended here. Thus (if that is true), this passage can be tied into Hebrews 6:4-6. (See also I Pet. 4:17.)

> f. Concerning suffering—Be mindful. *(Read Heb. 10:32, 34)*
> g. Concerning the second coming—Be watchful. *(Read Heb. 10:35-37)*
> h. Concerning spirituality—Be faithful. *(Read Heb. 10:38-39)*

✶ **10:39** This marks the third and final New Testament quotation of that phrase found in the Old Testament, *"The just shall live by faith" (Hab. 2:4).* The first two references are Romans 1:17; Galatians 3:11.

> **IV. Faith, the Superior Principle (Heb. 11:1-13:25)**

✶ The author of Hebrews has just ended chapter 10 with a summary statement concerning the believer and his great High Priest. The statement is: *"Now the just shall live by faith" (10:38).*

Having come this far in the epistle, some of the readers might be wondering: Exactly what is this faith like? Has anyone really lived like this before? The author now answers these questions. This chapter has been called the divine Hall of Fame and the Westminster Abbey of Scripture.

> A. The people of faith (Heb.11) *(Read Heb. 11:1-3, 6)*

✶ **11:6** Various attempts have been made to define the word "faith." Here are but a few:
- Faith is the confident assurance of things hoped for, the proof of things not seen (11:1, loosely paraphrased).
- "Faith enables the believing soul to treat the future as present, and the invisible as seen" (J. Oswald Sanders). According to verse 3, faith is vital if we are to go beyond the very first verse in Genesis 1. (See also 11:6.)
- Faith is trust in the unseen, but not the unknown. (See also 11:27.)
- "Faith is the title-deed of things hoped for" (Moulton and Milligan).

> 1. Who they were
>   a. Abel (Heb. 11:4)

✸ **11:4** Abel was the second baby to be born in history and the first martyr (Gen. 4:2, 8).

> b. Enoch (Heb. 11:5)

✸ **11:5** Enoch was the first of two human beings who left this earth without dying (Gen. 5:24). Elijah was the other person (2 Kings 2:11).

> c. Noah (Heb. 11:7)

✸ **11:7**
- By faith Enoch was removed before the great flood and becomes a type of the Christian who will be taken out before the coming great tribulation.
- By faith Noah was preserved during the great flood and becomes a type of Israel, who will be protected during the great tribulation.

> d. Abraham (Heb. 11:8-10, 17-19)

✸ **11:8** It has been observed that by faith Abraham obeyed God when he did not know where (11:8-10); when he did not know how (11:11-12); when he did not know when (11:13-16); and when he did not know why (11:17-19).

> e. Sarah (Heb. 11:11-12)
> f. Isaac (Heb. 11:20)

✸ **11:21**
- Isaac predicted the future of Jacob (Gen. 27:26-40).
- Jacob predicted the future for both his 12 sons and two grandsons of Joseph (Gen. 48-49).

> g. Jacob (Heb. 11:21)
> h. Joseph (Heb. 11:22)
> i. Moses' parents (Heb. 11:23)
> j. Moses (Heb. 11:24-29)
> k. Joshua (Heb. 11:30)
> l. Rahab (Heb. 11:31)
> m. Gideon (Heb. 11:32)
> n. Barak (Heb. 11:32)
> o. Samson (Heb. 11:32)
> p. Jephtah (Heb. 11:32)
> q. David (Heb. 11:32)
> r. Samuel (Heb. 11:32)
> 2. What they did
>   a. Offered proper sacrifices *(Read Heb. 11:4)*
>   b. Left the earth without dying *(Read Heb. 11:5)*
>   c. Survived the great flood *(Read Heb. 11:7)*
>   d. Inherited a land *(Read Heb. 11:8)*
>   e. Bore children in their old age *(Read Heb. 11:11)*
>   f. Predicted the future *(Read Heb. 11:20-21)*

> g. Defied kings *(Read Heb. 11:23)*
> h. Forsook the pleasures of sin *(Read Heb. 11:24-26)*
> i. Left Egypt *(Read Heb. 11:27)*
> j. Kept the Passover *(Read Heb 11:28)*
> k. Crossed the Red Sea *(Read Heb. 11:29)*
> l. Shouted down a city *(Read Heb. 11:30)*
> m. Subdued kingdoms *(Read Heb. 11:33)*
> n. Performed acts of righteousness (Heb. 11:33)
> o. Obtained promises (Heb. 11:33)
> p. Shut the mouths of lions (Heb. 11:33)

✴ Faith accomplished this for at least three Old Testament individuals:
- Samson (Judg. 14:5-6)
- David (1 Sam. 17:34-37)
- Daniel (Dan. 6:22)

> q. Quenched the power of fire *(Read Heb. 11:34)*
> r. Escaped the edge of the sword (Heb. 11:34)
> s. Saw their weakness turned into strength (Heb. 11:34)
> t. Put foreign armies to flight (Heb. 11:34)

✴ A number of Old Testament men won battles without using a single sword or arrow.
- Joshua (Josh. 6:20)
- Gideon (Judg. 7:20-21)
- Samuel (1 Sam. 7:9-12)
- Elijah (2 Kings 1:1-12)
- Elisha (2 Kings 6:15-18)
- Asa (2 Chron. 14:9-13)
- Jehoshaphat (2 Chron. 20:1-32)
- Hezekiah (2 Kings 19:35)

> u. Saw their dead raised *(Read Heb. 11:35)*

✴ Two Old Testament mothers experienced this:
- The widow of Zarephath (1 Kings 17:17-24)
- The woman at Shunem (2 Kings 4:30-37)

> 3. What they endured
> a. Terrible torture (Heb. 11:35)
> b. Ridicule *(Read Heb. 11:36)*
> c. Beatings (Heb. 11:36)
> d. Imprisonment (Heb. 11:36)
> e. Stoning *(Read Heb. 11:37)*
> f. Being cut in half (Heb. 11:37)

✴ There is a tradition that wicked Judean king Manasseh ordered the prophet Isaiah to be sawn assunder.

> g. Severe temptation (Heb. 11:37)
>
> h. Extreme poverty *(Read Heb. 11:37-38)*
>
> 4. Why they endured *(Read Heb. 11:10, 13-16, 39)*
>
> B. The pattern of faith (Heb. 12)
>
> 1. Perform the work of God (Heb. 12:1-3).
>
> a. The patience involved *(Read Heb. 12:1)*

★ **12:1** Many believe Paul to be the author of Hebrews.

- This amazing apostle was many things. He was a missionary, a soul winner, a pastor, a great theologian, a tentmaker. But in his spare time he also seemed to be a sports lover. Often in his writings, Paul uses sports as an analogy to get his point across. For example:
  - Wrestling—*"For we wrestle not against flesh and blood, but against principalities, against powers, against the rulers of the darkness of this world, against spiritual wickedness in high places"* (Eph. 6:12).
  - Boxing—*"I have fought a good fight"* (2 Tim. 4:7). *"So fight I, not as one that beateth the air"* (1 Cor. 9:26).
  - Racing—*"Know ye not that they which run in a race run all, but one receiveth the prize? So run that ye may obtain ... I therefore so run"* (1 Cor. 9:24, 26). Here in Hebrews 12, Paul chooses the third analogy—that of a foot race.
- At least four phrases in this verse merit special attention:
  - *"So great a cloud of witnesses"*
    - ✦ Great—We often feel (wrongly so) that we are all alone, as Elijah once did (1 Kings 19:10, 14,18).
    - ✦ Cloud—This underlines the word "great." The Greek here is not *nephele*, which refers to a detached and sharply outlined cloud, but *nephos*, speaking of a huge mass of clouds, covering the entire visible space of the heavens.
    - ✦ Witnesses—Who are these witnesses? They are not angels, for the Greek word is *marturos*, referring to one who has both seen, heard, and performed something, usually while suffering. It speaks of a well-qualified expert. The context strongly suggests that these witnesses are the faith heroes mentioned in chapter 11.
  - *"Let us lay aside every weight"*—Here the word is *onkos* and refers to a bulk or mass. The concern of the Greek runner was not simply whether something was immoral or moral, but rather how it would affect his race. Thus, the enemy of the best is often not the worst, but the good.
  - *"And the sin which doth so easily beset us"*—The word "beset" means "to surround, to cleverly encircle, to ambush." It speaks of a loosely fitting robe. Paul may have had in mind the sin of unbelief here, but it also refers to any sin the believer allows to upset him.
  - *"Let us run with patience the race that is set before us"*—Note the implications of this statement.
    - ✦ Every believer has been entered in this race by God himself. It is not just for pastors and missionaries. Note: The usual word for race (*dromos*) is not used here, but rather the Greek word *agon*, from which we get our English word "agony." This is a serious race.
    - ✦ The pace of each runner is set by God.
    - ✦ The object of the race is to please God and win rewards. Its goal is not heaven.
    - ✦ Every runner is expected to win.

> b. The person involved *(Read Heb. 12:2-3)*

★ **12:2-3**

- *"Looking unto Jesus"* (12:2)—The phrase here speaks of a steadfast, intent, and continuous gaze. How easy it is to get our eyes off him and look to the left or right. Perhaps to our left we see another runner behind us. It may be that a runner is far ahead of us to the right. This then can produce pride (as we view the left runner) and envy (as we view the runner on the right). Both are sin and cause us to slow down. We are instead to keep looking at Jesus.
  - If you would be disappointed, look to others.

- If you would be discouraged, look to yourself.
- If you would be delighted, look at Jesus.

■ *"The author and finisher of our faith" (12:2)*—Christ is both Founder and Finisher of the Christian faith. Confucius, Buddha, and Mohammed founded three worldwide religious movements, but death finished Confucius, Buddha, and Mohammed.

■ *"For the joy that was set before him endured the cross" (12:2)*—The nature of this joy is explained in *Jude 24*: "Now unto him [Jesus] that is able to keep you from falling, and to present you faultless before the presence of his glory with exceeding joy" (see also John 17:6-12, 26).

■ *"Despising the shame, and is set down at the right hand ... of God" (12:2*; see Phil. 2:5-11).

■ *"For consider him" (12:3)*—Time and again we are driven back to the Gospel accounts by the writers of the epistles.

> 2. Ponder the discipline of God (Heb. 12:4-11).

✶ If rightly understood and accepted, the discipline of God upon his children can prove to be a very fruitful experience indeed.

> a. The reasons for discipline *(Read Heb. 12:6-8)*

✶ **12:8**
- The word "chasten" here refers to that instruction in right behavior. The word "scourge" speaks of that correction in wrong behavior.
- Thus, divine chastisement upon a sinning Christian does not imply condemnation, but rather confirmation, demonstrating that we belong to God.

> b. The reaction to discipline
> (1) We can despise it (underreact to it)— *"My son, despise not thou the chastening of the Lord"* (Heb. 12:5).
> (2) We can faint under it (overreact to it)— *"Nor faint when thou art rebuked of him"* (Heb. 12:5).
> (3) We can be exercised by it *(Read Heb. 12:9-10)*.

✶ **12:10** The real question is not simply how many mistakes a Christian makes, but how much he learns through those mistakes. The Psalms speak concerning this: *"Blessed is the man whom thou chastenest, O LORD, and teachest him out of thy law"* (94:12). *"Before I was afflicted I went astray: but now have I kept thy word"* (119:67). *"It is good for me that I have been afflicted: that I might learn thy statutes"* (119:71). *"I know, O LORD, that thy judgments are right and that thou in faithfulness hast afflicted me"* (119:75).

> c. The results of discipline *(Read Heb. 12:11)*
> 3. Prepare for the kingdom of God (Heb. 12)
> a. Straighten up *(Read Heb. 12:12-14)*

✶ **12:14** Homer Kent writes: "If one's feet are lame, special care must be taken that the path on which they walk has no dangerous obstacles. Spiritually speaking, the one whose faith is weak must not venture into areas where his spiritual strength is insufficient. Otherwise the. ... lame believer may aggravate his lameness into a dislocation of the limbs" (*Epistle to the Hebrews*, p. 265).

> b. Measure up (Heb. 12:15-17).
> (1) The attitude involved *(Read Heb. 12:15)*
> (2) The apostate involved *(Read Heb. 12:16-17)*

★ **12:17**
- The birthright here had to do with the spiritual responsibility of the eldest son in continuing the family faith. Esau, being both irreverent and immoral, had no desire whatsoever in this matter (Gen. 25:27-34).
- The blessing here had to do with receiving a double portion of the family wealth plus a prophetical prayer from the father asking God to protect and prosper the son. This, of course, Esau very much desired (Gen. 27).

> c. Look up (Heb. 12:18-24).
> (1) From—Mount Sinai, the old life under the Law *(Read Heb. 12:18-21)*
> (2) To—Mount Zion, the new life under grace *(Read Heb. 12:22-24)*
> d. Become wise *(Read Heb. 12:25-27)*
> e. Cheer up *(Read Heb. 12:28-29)*
> C. The performance of faith (Heb. 13)
> 1. What the Savior has done *(Read Heb. 13:8)*
> a. He died to save us *(Read Heb. 13:12)*
> b. He lives to sanctify us *(Read Heb. 13:20-21)*
> 2. What the saints are to do
> a. We are to display charity *(Read Heb. 13:1-2)*

★ **13:2** At least two Old Testament individuals come to mind here:
- Abraham (Gen. 18:1-8)
- Lot (Gen. 19:1-3)

> b. We are to display compassion *(Read Heb. 13:3)*
> c. We are to display chastity *(Read Heb. 13:4)*
> d. We are to display contentment *(Read Heb. 13:5)*
> e. We are to display courage *(Read Heb. 13:6)*
> f. We are to display consideration—This consideration and respect is to be directed toward our spiritual leaders.
> (1) Their divine appointment *(Read Heb. 13:7)*
> (2) Their divine accountability *(Read Heb. 13:17)*
> g. We are to display consistency *(Read Heb. 13:9)*
> h. We are to display commitment *(Read Heb. 13:13-14)*
> i. We are to display consecration *(Read Heb. 13:15-16)*

★ **13:16** In addition to offering up a sacrifice of praise, the believer is commanded to offer up the sacrifice of his own body (Rom. 12:1), and that of good works (Heb. 13:16).

LESSON 38

INTRODUCTION TO JAMES

THIS NEW TESTAMENT BOOK IS THE PROVERBS OF THE NEW TESTAMENT.

A. The book of James aptly fits this description.
B. His epistle is perhaps the earliest in the New Testament, dated around A.D. 45. The synagogue is mentioned as the place of meeting, rather than the church (see 2:2). It was thus written when the church was still in the circle of Judaism.
C. It is the most Jewish book in the New Testament. M. F. Unger writes: "If the several passages referring to Christ were eliminated, the whole epistle would be as proper in the canon of the Old Testament as it is in the New Testament. In fact, the epistle could be described as an interpretation of the Old Testament law and the Sermon on the Mount in the light of the Gospel of Christ" *(Unger's Bible Handbook, p. 783)*.
D. It may be considered the Proverbs of the New Testament.
E. The Greek language of James is of the highest quality.
F. There are only four Old Testament direct quotes, but at least 53 Old Testament references in the epistle of James.
G. It is the only New Testament book specifically addressed to the 12 tribes (1:1).
H. James gives God's present-day plan for healing (5:13-18).
I. James was the oldest half brother of Jesus (Mark 6:3; Matt. 13:55). He was the full brother of Jude, who wrote the book of Jude.
J. James was an unbeliever prior to the resurrection (John 7:3-10).
K. James then appeared in the Upper Room awaiting Pentecost (Acts 1:13).
L. He became the first pastor of the Jerusalem church (Acts 12:17; 15:13; Gal. 2:1, 9-10, 12). "He was known as an unusually good man, and was surnamed 'the Just' by his countrymen. It is said that he spent so much time on his knees in prayer that they became hard and callused like a camel's knees. He is thought to have been married" (1 Cor. 9:5). *(Halley's Bible Handbook, p. 657)*.
M. Like Jude, James does not "pull his rank" by pointing out the physical relationship between himself and Christ. He simply refers to himself as *"a servant of God and of the Lord Jesus Christ"* (1:1).
N. James, like Jesus, loved to use Old Testament characters and the realm of nature as illustrations. Note:
   1. Old Testament characters
      a. Abraham (2:21)
      b. Isaac (2:21)
      c. Rahab (2:25)
      d. Job (5:11)
      e. Elijah (5:17)

2. Realm of nature
   a. Wind-tossed waves of the sea (1:6)
   b. Withering grass and fading flowers (1:10-11)
   c. Fire (3:5)
   d. Fountains of water (3:11)
   e. Figs and olives (3:12)
   f. Sowing and harvesting (3:18)
   g. Early and latter rains (5:7)
   h. Drought (5:17)

O. Some have imagined a contradiction between James and Paul. Martin Luther believed this, and referred to the book as "a right strawy epistle"! James wrote: *"Ye see, then, that by works a man is justified, and not by faith only" (2:24)*. Paul wrote: *"For by grace are ye saved through faith; and that not of yourselves; it is the gift of God: not of works, lest any man should boast" (Eph. 2:8-9)*. Luther and others were, of course, wrong on this conclusion. There is no contradiction here. Note:
   1. Paul speaks of justification before God.
   2. James describes justification before people.
   3. We are justified by faith, says Paul.
   4. We are justified for works, says James.
   5. Paul is interested in the root of justification.
   6. James is concerned about the fruit of justification.
   7. It was John Calvin who said: "Faith alone saves, but the faith that saves is not alone."
   8. Furthermore, on occasion Paul stresses works (1 Tim. 6:18; Titus 3:8; Eph. 2:10), while James emphasizes faith (James 2:5).

P. James met Paul during his (Paul's) first trip to Jerusalem after his Damascus Road conversion (Gal. 1:18-19).

Q. He also conferred with Paul during the apostle's last trip to Jerusalem (Acts 21:18-25).

R. Tradition says that shortly before Jerusalem was destroyed, when many Jews were accepting Christ, Annas the high priest assembled the Sanhedrin and commanded James publicly to renounce Christ as Israel's Messiah. Upon his refusal, he was thrown from the pinnacle of the temple and stoned to death as he lay dying from the fall.

S. The most extended discussion on the human tongue is found in James 3.

T. James is the 15th longest New Testament book, and 46th longest biblical book, with five chapters, 108 verses, and 2,309 words. There are quotations or allusions from 17 Old Testament books in James.

U. Great passages would include:
   1. 1:2-8
   2. 1:12-27
   3. 4:6-10
   4. 4:13-15
   5. 5:8-11
   6. 5:16-20

Overview of the Book of James

I. Suffering makes a Mature Person
   A. The background of sufferings
      1. God's purpose is to purify and strengthen us. He wants to make us better.
      2. Satan's purpose is to pervert and weaken us. He wants to make us bitter.
   B. The purpose of suffering
      1. It produces endurance down here
      2. It promises rewards up there
   C. The response to suffering
      1. Positive
      2. Negative

II. Scripture study makes a Mature Person
   A. Its author
   B. Its accomplishments
   C. Its admonitions
      1. Our talk is to be pure
      2. Our walk is to be pure
   D. Its analogy
   E. Its assurance

III. Sincerity makes a Mature Person
   A. Commands against partiality
      1. An earthly example
      2. A heavenly example
   B. Consequences of partiality
      1. To be guilty of the Law
      2. To be judged by the Law

IV. Christian Service makes a Mature Person
   A. The problem—Some have imagined a contradiction between James and Paul
      1. Paul's words
      2. James' words
   B. The particulars
      1. Paul speaks about vertical justification before God
      2. James speaks about horizontal justification before other people
   C. The pattern
      1. Two examples of head faith only
      2. Two examples of head and heart faith

V. Sound speech makes a Mature Person

    A. Importance of the tongue
    B. Illustrations of the tongue
        1. How it can control
        2. How it can consume
    C. Iniquity of the tongue
        1. It can destroy our witness for God
        2. It can defile our walk with God
    D. Incorrigibility of the tongue
    E. Inconsistency of the tongue
        1. The contradiction
        2. The conclusion
    F. Instructions for the tongue
        1. Seek and speak the wisdom of God
        2. Refuse and renounce the slander of Satan

VI. Submission to God makes a Mature Person
    A. What we escape when we do this
        1. The flesh
        2. The world
        3. The devil
    B. What we enjoy when we do this
        1. God's grace
        2. God's guarantee
        3. God's guidance

VII. Simplicity in life makes a Mature Person
    A. The consternation of the selfish rich
    B. The corruption of the selfish rich
    C. The cruelty of the selfish rich
    D. The condemnation of the selfish rich

VIII. Steadfastness makes a Mature Person
    A. A past example—Job and his trials
    B. A present example—A farmer and his crops
    C. A future example—The Savior and his return

IX. Supplication makes a Mature Person
    A. The season of prayer—When should one pray?
        1. In times of trouble
        2. In times of triumph
    B. The reasons for prayer—Why should one pray?
        1. Prayer can alleviate the infirm
        2. Prayer can accomplish the impossible

X. Soul Winning makes a Mature Person

THE BOOK OF JAMES

"James, a servant of God and of the Lord Jesus Christ, to the twelve tribes which are scattered abroad, greeting. My brethren, count it all joy when ye fall into divers temptations; knowing this, that the trying of your faith worketh patience. But let patience have her perfect work, that ye may be perfect and entire, wanting nothing" (James 1:1-4). The word "perfect" (a reference to maturity) is found many times in James. Thus the term "maturity" will be used in outlining this book.

> I. Suffering Makes a Mature Person (James 1:1-15).
>   A. The background of sufferings—Both God and Satan are usually involved in the sufferings of a Christian.
>   1. God's purpose is to purify and strengthen us. He wants to make us better. *"My brethren, count it all joy when ye fall into divers temptations" (James 1:2). "Blessed is the man that endureth temptation" (James 1:12).*

✱ **1:1-5** To summarize these verses:
- The facets of temptation—The word "temptation" carries with it a twofold meaning.
  - First meaning-To test in a good sense with the goal of confirming one in matters of righteousness. (See Gen. 22:1; Deut. 8:2-3; Exod. 20:20.)
  - Second meaning-To test in a bad sense with the goal of corrupting one in matters of righteousness. (See Gen. 3:1-6; Matt. 4:1.)
- The facts about temptations (according to James 1:2)
  - They are often sudden— *"When ye fall" (1:2).*
  - They are certain—James says when ye fall, not, if ye fall.
  - They are sorted— *"Into divers |various| temptations."* These are financial, physical, spiritual, mental, and social trials.

>   2. Satan's purpose is to pervert and weaken us—He wants to make us bitter *(Read James 1:13-15)*.
> B. The purpose of suffering
>   1. It produces endurance down here *(Read James 1:3-4)*
>   2. It promises rewards up there *(Read James 1:12)*
> C. The response to suffering
>   1. Positive
>   a. We are to praise God for it (James 1:2).
>   b. We are to pray while in it *(Read James 1:5)*
>   2. Negative
>   a. We are not to become as tossed waves *(Read James 1:6-8)*
>   b. We are not to become as wilted flowers *(Read James 1:9-11)*

II. Scripture Study Makes a Mature Person (James 1:16-25).
  A. Its author *(Read James 1:17)*
  B. Its accomplishments *(Read James 1:18)*
  C. Its admonitions (James 1:19-22)
    1. Our talk is to be pure *(Read James 1:19)*
    2. Our walk is to be pure *(Read James 1:21-22, 27)*
  D. Its analogy *(Read James 1:23-24)*
  E. Its assurance *(Read James 1:25)*

LESSON 38: THE BOOK OF JAMES

III. Sincerity Makes a Mature Person (James 2:1-13).
A. Commands against partiality *(Read James 2:1-8)*

✱ **2:8** This "royal law" was given in Leviticus 19:18 and reaffirmed by Jesus in Matthew 22:36-40. It is considered royal or regal because it was decreed by the King of kings and functions as the Law of laws. Note its features: *"Jesus said unto him, Thou shalt love the Lord thy God with all thy heart, and with all thy soul, and with all thy mind. This is the first and great commandment. And the second is like unto it, Thou shalt love thy neighbor as thyself. On these two commandments hang all the law and the prophets"* (Matt. 22:37-40).
- The first part of the royal law (loving one's God) is vertical and fulfills laws 1-4 in the Ten Commandments (Exod. 20:3-11).
- The second part of the royal law (loving one's neighbor) is horizontal and fulfills laws 5-10 in the Ten Commandments (Exod. 20:12-17).

    1. An earthly example *(Read James 2:2-4)*
    2. A heavenly example *(Read James 2:5)*
B. Consequences of partiality (James 2:9-13)
    1. To be guilty of the Law *(Read James 2:9-11)*
    2. To be judged by the Law *(Read James 2:12-13)*

IV. Christian Service Makes a Mature Person (James 2:14-26).
A. The problem—Some have imagined a contradiction between James and Paul. Note:
    1. Paul's words *(Read Eph. 2:8-9)*
    2. James's words *(Read James 2:14, 24)*
B. The particulars
    1. Paul speaks about vertical justification before God.
    2. James speaks about horizontal justification before other people.

✱ These verses are not meant to be saving texts, but sign texts. The proof of the pudding is still in the eating. The only test of a man's salvation is through his works. A silent believer may indeed be considered a saint before God, but he remains a sinner before man until he walks the walk and talks the talk of Christian service.

C. The pattern
    1. Two examples of head faith only
        a. Concerning the destitute *(Read James 2:15-16)*
        b. Concerning the devil *(Read James 2:19)*
    2. Two examples of head and heart faith
        a. Abraham *(Read James 2:21-23)*

✱ **2:23** The chronology of Abraham's life is important to note here. He was justified before God at the age of 85 (Gen. 15:6; 16:16). He was justified before humanity at the age of (approximately) 137 (Gen. 22:1-14; 23:1).

        b. Rahab *(Read James 2:25)*

✱ **2:25** Rahab's salvation is recorded in Joshua 2:1-14, and the service in 2:15-16. Dr. Charles Ryrie writes: "Unproductive faith cannot save, because it is not genuine faith. Faith and works are like a two-coupon ticket to heaven. The coupon of works is not good for passage, and the coupon of faith is not valid if detached from works" (*Ryrie Study Bible*, p. 421).

D. The principle *(Read James 2:17-18, 20, 26)*

★ **2:26** In a nutshell:
- ■ We are saved not by good works, but rather for good works. (See Eph. 2:8-10.)
- ■ Workless faith is worthless faith.
- ■ Faith is the basis of one's salvation, while works become the barometer of that salvation.

> **V. Sound Speech Makes a Mature Person (James 3:1-18; 1:26-27).**
>   A. Importance of the tongue *(Read James 3:2)*

★ **3:2** Taken in proper context, this is one of the most profound and far-reaching statements in the entire Bible. It has been suggested that the body is the congregation and the tongue is its teacher.

> B. Illustrations of the tongue
>   1. How it can control
>   a. It is as a bridle to a horse *(Read James 3:3)*
>   b. It is as a rudder to a ship *(Read James 3:4)*
>   2. How it can consume *(Read James 3:5)*
> C. Iniquity of the tongue (James 3:5-6:1:26)
>   1. It can destroy our witness for God *(Read James 1:26)*
>   2. It can defile our walk with God *(Read James 3:6)*
> D. Incorrigibility of the tongue *(Read James 3:7-8)*
> E. Inconsistency of the tongue (James 3:9-12)
>   1. The contradiction *(Read James 3:9-10)*

★ **3:10** An Egyptian king named Amasis once sent a sacrifice to his god and requested the priest to send back the best and worst part of the animal. The priest sent back the tongue, which organ, said he, represented both demands. It has been said that the Christian should so live that he would not hesitate to sell his talking parrot to the town gossip.

>   2. The conclusion *(Read James 3:11-12; 5:12)*.
> F. Instructions for the tongue
>   1. Seek and speak the wisdom of God *(Read James 3:13, 17-18)*
>   2. Refuse and renounce the slander of Satan *(Read James 3:14-16)*
> **VI. Submission to God Makes a Mature Person (James 4:1-17)**
>   A. What we escape when we do this
>   1. The flesh *(Read James 4:1-3, 11-12, 16-17)*

★ **4:3**
- ■ Concerning spiritual things—They had not received because they had not asked (example, the gift of wisdom; see 1:5).
- ■ Concerning sinful things—They had not received even though they had asked.

>   2. The world *(Read James 4:4-5)*
>   3. The devil *(Read James 4:7)*
>   B. What we enjoy when we do this
>   1. God's grace *(Read James 4:6)*

★ **4:6** There are numerous biblical examples of God rejecting the haughty but receiving the humble.
- ■ Cain and Abel (Gen. 4:1-7)

LESSON 38: THE BOOK OF JAMES

- Jacob and Esau (Rom. 9:13)
- Moses and Korah (Num.12:3; 16:1-4)
- Barak and Sisera (Judges 4-5)
- David and Saul (1 Sam. 24:9-22; 26:17-25)
- Nehemiah and Sanballat (Neh. 6:1-14)
- Daniel and Nebuchadnezzar (Dan. 4)
- Daniel and Belshazzar (Dan. 5)
- Mordecai and Haman (book of Esther)
- Amos and Amaziah (Amos 7)
- The Pharisee and the publican (Luke 18:9-14)
- Diotrephes and Demetrius (3 John 1:9-12)

> 2. God's guarantee
>   a. Of his presence *(Read James 4:8)*
>   b. Of his promotion *(Read James 4:10)*

✶ 4:10 The classic Old Testament example of this statement can be seen in the life of Joseph, whom God promoted from being a prisoner in Egypt, to being prime minister over Egypt. (See Gen. 39-41.)

> 3. God's guidance *(Read James 4:13-15)*
> **VII. Simplicity in Life Makes a Mature Person (James 5:1-6)**—Here James contrasts this virtue by referring to the selfish rich.
>   A. The consternation of the selfish rich *(Read James 5:1)*
>   B. The corruption of the selfish rich *(Read James 5:2, 5)*
>   C. The cruelty of the selfish rich *(Read James 5:4, 6)*
>   D. The condemnation of the selfish rich *(Read James 5:3)*
> **VIII. Steadfastness Makes a Mature Person (James 5:7-11)**
>   A. A past example—Job and his trials *(Read James 5:10-11)*

✶ 5:11
- The misery job received from Satan is recorded in Job 1-2.
- The mercy Job received from God is recorded in Job 42:7-17.

> B. A present example—A farmer and his crops *(Read James 5:7)*
> C. A future example—The Savior and his return *(Read James 5:8-9)*
> **IX. Supplication Makes a Mature Person (James 5:12-18)**
>   A. The season of prayer—When should one pray?
>   1. In times of trouble—*"Is any among you afflicted?" (James 5:13). "Is any sick among you?" (James 5:14)*
>   2. In times of triumph—*"Is any merry? let him sing psalms." (James 5:13)*
>   B. The reasons for prayer—Why should one pray?
>   1. Prayer can alleviate the infirm *(Read James 5:14-16)*

✶ 5:16 These verses have been the object of much speculation.
- What is meant by the anointing of a sick person with oil?
  - Negative
    - This is not a reference to extreme unction, a Roman Catholic practice which prepares a dying person for death. The practice in these verses is to restore the sick, not to bury them.

- ✦ This does not give sanction to faith healers. We note instead that several elders of the church are to be involved here.
- ● Positive
  - ✦ The men involved—*"The elders of the church" (5:14)*. As we have already stated, these were the spiritual leaders of the church.
  - ✦ The medicine involved—*"Anointing him with oil" (5:14)*. The Greek word here is a reference to olive oil, used as a common medicinal remedy in the ancient East (see Isa. 1:6; Luke 10:34). In his book *The Game of Life*, author Roy Roberts gives the following helpful words as taken from professor James E. Rosscup:

    "In brief, oil did have therapeutic value in ancient times as well as today, but it is best to understand it here as a symbol of God's miraculous work in healing. That it had good medicinal effects is clear. It possessed soothing and curative value for animals, like sheep (Psa. 23:5), and men (Isa. 1:6). The good Samaritan in Christ's parable applied oil to the wounds of the man he helped (Luke 19:34). But, it is not the meaning of James for various reasons. Though it was therapeutic in some cases, it would not be a cure in all sicknesses in general. Further, James does not say in v. 15 that the oil will cure the sick or even that the oil plus the prayer will make him well. Specifically, he does say that 'the prayer of faith shall save the sick,' and makes no claim for the oil. It is not the oil, but the Lord who 'shall raise him up.' It is more adequate to say that the anointing is for the purpose of symbolizing tangibly the setting apart of the man to the miraculous healing work of God. It would be an aid to his faith by prompting a sense of expectancy. Christ Himself applied saliva to men at times evidently to symbolize, by physical contact, the healing that God would effect (Mark 7:33; 8:23). There is Old Testament support for the idea that the anointing could signify the setting apart of the man to God for His will and operation. There are numerous applications of oil, not to cure but to set disciples, they 'anointed with oil many that were sick, and healed them'" (Mark 6:13) (*The Game of Life*, pp. 171-172).

- ■ Will all sick people be automatically healed by this action? To rephrase the question: Is it ever God's will for believers to experience prolonged illness? It is sometimes not God's will to heal sick Christians. Suffering, if rightly understood and endured by the believer, can bring about the glory of God. (See Exod. 4:11; 1 Tim. 5:23; 2 Tim. 4:20; 2 Cor. 12:1-10; John 9:1-3.) Sometimes, of course, sickness is penalty for sin (see John 5:14).
- ■ What is involved in the confession of 5:16? James says we are to confess our faults one to another. As we have already noted, there are times when unconfessed sin does bring suffering. James may have reference to this very thing here at this point. If a sick believer had wronged another Christian in the church, he was now encouraged to confess this, that God might be able to bless him both spiritually and physically. James then says: "The effectual fervent prayer of a righteous man availeth much" (5:16). The "righteous man" spoken of here may refer either to the elder who prays for the sick believer, or the believer himself who, having been restored to fellowship through confession, can now pray effectively. James mentions Elijah as an Old Testament example of effective prayer (5:17; cf. I Kings 17-18).

> 2. Prayer can accomplish the impossible *(Read James 5:17-18)*
> **X. Soul Winning Makes a Mature Person** *(Read James 5:19-20)*

LESSON 39

INTRODUCTION TO FIRST PETER

SOME SOUND ADVICE TO SOME SUFFERING SAINTS

This is what 1 Peter is all about.

    A. Of the original 12 apostles, three were chosen to write inspired New Testament books or epistles. The three are Matthew, John, and Peter.

    B. This epistle is the final fulfillment of a twofold commission given to Peter by Christ. Both were issued at the Sea of Galilee.

        1. The first part—"Catch fish" (Luke 5:10). This Peter did, through the spoken word at Pentecost (Acts 2:14).

        2. The second part—"Feed sheep" (John 21:15-17). This Peter does, through the written word at Babylon (1 Pet. 2:2; 5:13).

    C. Peter's name appears 210 times in the New Testament. Paul's name is found 162 times. The names of the remaining 11 apostles combined appear 142 times.

    D. Peter has been called "the apostle of hope" (see 1:3, 13, 21; 3:15). Paul could thus be classified as the apostle of faith, and John the apostle of love.

    E. A key word in this epistle is "suffering." It, or its equivalent is used 16 times. Six times it speaks of Christ's suffering and ten times that of believers. Another important word is "grace," which appears eight times.

    F. The letter was probably written at the end of his life. It is thought that after this epistle he was arrested and tried. Between his trial and execution he wrote 2 Peter (2 Pet. 1:13-21).

    G. It must have been written around A.D. 64 on the eve of the outbreak of persecution by Nero. Nero died in A.D. 68.

    H. In 5:13 he identifies the place of writing as Babylon. There are two main theories concerning the location of Babylon.

        1. It is literal Babylon on the Euphrates River—This would seem to be the natural interpretation of the passage. Furthermore, the list of countries in 1 Peter 1:1 is from East to West, which suggests that the writer was in the East at the time of writing. J. Vernon McGee writes: "There was at this time a large colony of Jews in ancient Babylon who had fled Rome due to severe persecution under Claudius and at the time of writing bloody Nero was on the throne" *(Through the Bible*, p. 256).

            In addition to this, the descendants of those Jews taken captive by Nebuchadnezzar were still living in and around Babylon.

        2. It is Rome—Charles Ryrie writes: "The place of the writing was Babylon (5:13), a symbolic name for Rome much used by writers who wished to avoid trouble with Roman authorities.... Peter was in Rome during the last decade of his life and wrote this epistle about A.D. 63, just before the outbreak of Nero's persecution in 64. Peter was martyred about 67" *(The Ryrie Study Bible*, p. 425). Furthermore, it

is argued that Peter states Mark (5:13) was with him at the time the epistle was written. However, just prior to this, Paul had written Timothy to bring Mark to Rome with him (2 Tim. 4:11).

I. The church apparently was affected by worldliness in the pews (2:11) and materialism in the pulpit (5:1-3).

J. Because of its many passages on suffering (1:6-7; 4:12-19; 5:10) this epistle can be looked upon as the Job of the New Testament.

K. Chapter 3 can be considered the marriage chapter (vv. 1-12) because of the advice Peter gives to both husbands and wives.

L. In a remarkable passage (3:18-22) Peter explains the activities of Christ during that time between his death and resurrection.

M. The book of 1 Peter provides the final of three descriptive phrases concerning the shepherding ministry of Christ.
   1. Jesus said he was the Good Shepherd (John 10:11).
   2. Hebrews said he is the Great Shepherd (Heb. 13:20).
   3. Peter says he is the Chief Shepherd (1 Pet. 5:4).

N. Satan is referred to as a roaring lion in this epistle (5:8).

O. Peter has much to say about the Word of God. He says it is incorruptible (1:23), eternal (1:25), and is, to the believer, as wholesome milk (2:2).

P. Peter develops the doctrine of Christ in a remarkable way in this short epistle. He discusses:
   1. The incarnation of Christ (1:20)
   2. The names for Christ
      a. A spotless Lamb (1:19)
      b. The chief Cornerstone—His relationship to the Scriptures (2:6)
      c. The precious Stone—His relationship to believers (2:7)
      d. The stumbling Stone—His relationship to unbelievers (2:8)
      e. The Bishop of our souls (2:25)
      f. The Chief Shepherd (5:4)
   3. His sinless life (1:19; 2:22)
   4. His suffering and death (1:11; 2:23-24; 3:18; 4:1, 13; 5:1)
   5. His resurrection (3:21-22)
   6. His ascension (3:22)
   7. His presence at God's right hand (3:22)
   8. His second coming (1:13, 17; 4:13; 5:1, 4)

Q. He also offers a number of titles which describe believers. Perhaps in no other New Testament book are so many given. We are referred to as:
   1. Obedient children (1:14)
   2. Newborn babes (2:2)
   3. Living stones (2:5)
   4. A holy priesthood (2:9)
   5. A royal priesthood (2:9)
   6. A holy nation (2:9)
   7. A peculiar people (2:9)
   8. Strangers and pilgrims (2:11)

     9. Christians (4:16)
    10. The righteous (4:18)
    11. The elect of God (1:2)
    12. The people of God (2:10)
    13. The oracles of God (4:11)
    14. The flock of God (5:2)

R. This epistle recounts the last of three instances where believers are called Christians.
   1. Acts 11:26 (as used by the unbelievers at Antioch)
   2. Acts 26:28 (as used by King Agrippa)
   3. 1 Peter 4:16 (as used by Peter)

S. The book of 1 Peter can be compared to Colossians.
   1. For its size, Colossians has more to say about the Person of Christ than any other New Testament book.
   2. For its size, 1 Peter has more to say about the work of Christ than any other New Testament book.

T. This epistle contains the final of three New Testament passages commanding believers to be good citizens.
   1. Romans 13:1-7
   2. 1 Timothy 2:1-4
   3. 1 Peter 2:13-17

U. Peter and John are the only two New Testament authors to refer to Christ as a Lamb (John 1:29, 36; Rev. 5:6; 1 Pet. 1:19).

V. A careful reading of 1 Peter and Ephesians shows more than 100 parallels in teaching and wording.

W. Peter was also familiar with the book of Romans, and perhaps other epistles from Paul (see 2 Pet. 3:15-16).

X. It is generally considered that the Gospel of Mark reflects the teaching of Peter. Young John Mark had, no doubt, often heard Peter speak and preach.

Y. The book of 1 Peter is the 14th longest New Testament book, and 45th longest biblical book, with five chapters, 105 verses, and 2,483 words. There are quotations or allusions from 15 Old Testament books in 1 Peter.

Z. Great passages would include:
   1. 1:3-12
   2. 1:18-25
   3. 2:1-10
   4. 2:21-25
   5. 4:12-19
   6. 5:1-11

Overview of the Book of First Peter

I. **The Salvation of the Believer**
   A. The facts concerning our salvation
      1. The source of our salvation—The entire Trinity
      2. The blessing of our salvation
      3. The guarantee of our salvation
      4. The trials in our salvation
      5. The Old Testament prophets and our salvation
      6. The holy angels and our salvation
      7. The desired response in light of our salvation
      8. The awesome cost of our salvation
      9. The vehicle of our salvation
   B. The fellowship involved concerning our salvation
      1. We are members of the same family
      2. We are stones in the same building
      3. We have been joined to the same cornerstone
      4. We are ministers in the same priesthood
      5. We are citizens of the same nation
      6. We are pilgrims on the same journey

II. **The Submission of the Believer**
   A. Peter's exhortation for submission
      1. Our responsibilities to the unsaved
      2. Our responsibilities to civil authorities
      3. Our responsibilities to our employers
      4. Our responsibilities in the home
   B. Peter's example of submission
      1. The sinless Savior
      2. The silent Savior
      3. The sacrificial Savior
      4. The shepherd Savior

III. **The Suffering of the Believer**
   A. Suffering justifies the sinner
      1. Christ's ministry on the cross
      2. Christ's ministry under the earth
      3. Christ's ministry in the heavens
   B. Suffering purifies the saint
      1. Concerning the godly believer
      2. Concerning the carnal believer
   C. Suffering anticipates the second coming

    D. Suffering verifies the separated life
    E. Suffering multiplies future rewards
    F. Suffering unifies the local church
    G. Suffering glorifies the Lord

IV. The Service of the Believer
    A. Serving as a shepherd
        1. The responsibilities
        2. The rewards
    B. Serving as a servant
        1. Subject yourselves to the saints
        2. Submit yourselves to the Savior
    C. Serving as a soldier
        1. The predator
        2. The plan
        3. The purpose

THE BOOK OF FIRST PETER

> **I. The Salvation of the Believer**
>   A. The facts concerning our salvation
>   1. The source of our salvation—The entire Trinity
>   a. Elected by the Father— *"Elect according to the foreknowledge of God the Father" (1 Pet. 1:2)*

✶ 1:2a We are not told the basis of this election, it should be noted. However, God's selection is based squarely upon foreknowledge. Note: *"For whom he did foreknow, he also did predestinate" (Rom. 8:29)*. It should be quickly noted, though, that both man's responsibility (John 3:16; Rom. 10:13; Rev. 22:17) and God's sovereignty (Eph. 1:4-5) are clearly taught in the Bible.

In one single statement, our Lord combined both doctrines of election and free will. Note his words: *"All that the Father giveth me shall come to me* [this is election]*; and him that cometh to me I will in no wise cast out* [this is free will]*" (John 6:37)*.

>   b. Redeemed by the Son— *"And sprinkling of the blood of Jesus Christ" (1 Pet. 1:2)*.

✶ 1:2c Richard DeHaan writes: "The basis for this statement is found in the Old Testament ceremonial system. In certain of the rituals, the blood of the sacrificial animals was sprinkled in special areas. This sprinkling had three different meanings:
- First, it signified cleansing—The person who had been cured of leprosy, for example, went before the priest, and blood was sprinkled to indicate that he was now free from the disease and clean (Lev. 14:1-7).
- Second, this act was used to symbolize the ratification of a covenant between God and man. Whenever Jehovah and His people entered into a covenant, it was sealed by the sprinkling of the blood of a sacrificial animal (see Exod. 24:3-8).
- Third, the application of blood designated certain articles of the tabernacle or temple as set apart for worship. From that point on, the vessel was used exclusively for the service of the Lord (see Exod. 29:20-22)" (*Good News for Bad Times*, p. 15).

>   c. Sanctified by the Spirit— *"Through sanctification of the Spirit" (1 Pet. 1:2)*.
>   2. The blessing of our salvation (1 Pet. 1:3-4)
>   a. A living hope *(Read 1 Pet. 1:3)*

✶ 1:3 In light of all this, the triune God is to be blessed by the believer (v. 3). The Greek word for "blessed" is *eulogetos*, meaning "to speak well of." From this we get our word eulogize. Thus, the child of God is to speak well of the triune God. By doing this we "bless" God. Note his reaction to this. *"Then they that feared the Lord spake often one to another; and the Lord hearkened, and heard it, and a book of remembrance was written before him for them that feared the Lord, and that thought upon his name" (Mal. 3:16)*.

In this epistle Peter mentions three living things:
- A living hope (1:3)
- A living word (1:23)
- A living stone (2:4)

>   b. A lasting hope *(Read 1 Pet. 1:4)*

✶ 1:4
- This inheritance is perfect (incorruptible).
- This inheritance is pure (undefiled).

- This inheritance is permanent (it "fadeth not away").

> 3. The guarantee of our salvation *(Read 1 Pet. 1:5)*
> 4. The trials in our salvation (1 Pet. 1:6-9)
>   a. The necessity of these trials *(Read 1 Pet. 1:6)*
>   b. The reasons for these trials
>   (1) They strengthen our faith in Christ *(Read 1 Pet. 1:7)*

★ **1:7** Peter speaks of how precious is the trial of our faith. In this epistle he also refers to precious blood (1:19), a cornerstone, (2:4, 6-7), and a humble spirit (3:4). All these, says Peter, are precious. In his second epistle he adds two more: "precious faith" (1:1) and "precious promises" (1:4).

Dr. Kenneth Wuest writes the following concerning verse 7: "Peter tells us that this approval of our faith is much more precious than the approval of gold, even though that gold be approved through firetesting.... The picture here is of an ancient goldsmith who puts his crude gold ore in a crucible, subjects it to intense heat, and thus liquifies the mass. The impurities rise to the surface and are skimmed off. When the metal-worker is able to see the reflection of his face clearly mirrored in the surface of the liquid, he takes it off the fire, for he knows that the contents are pure gold."

"So it is with God and His child. He puts us in the crucible of Christian suffering, in which process sin is gradually put out of our lives, our faith is purified from the slag of unbelief that somehow mingles with it so often, and the result is the reflection of the face of Jesus Christ in the character of the Christian. This, above all, God the Father desires to see. Christlikeness is God's ideal for His child. Christian suffering is one of the most potent means to that end" (*First Peter in the Greek New Testament*, p. 27).

> (2) They strengthen our love for Christ *(Read 1 Pet. 1:8)*
> 5. The Old Testament prophets and our salvation (1 Pet. 1:10-12)
>   a. Their scrutiny *(Read 1 Pet. 1:10)*

★ **1:10**
- The Old Testament prophets (like Isaiah) did not always understand their inspired prophecies about the Messiah.
- When they sought to know, they were told the predictions would be understood only at a later date (New Testament times). Our Lord once referred to this during his earthly ministry while speaking to his disciples. *"For verily I say unto you, that many prophets and righteous men have desired to see those things which ye see, and have not seen them; and to hear those things which ye hear, and have not heard them"* (Matt. 13:17). (See also Dan. 12:8-13.)

> b. Their source—*"The Spirit of Christ, which was in them ... testified beforehand"* (1 Pet. 1:11).
> c. Their summary (1 Pet. 1:11-12)
>   (1) They predicted the nature of his first coming—*"The sufferings of Christ"* (1 Pet. 1:11). (See Isa. 53.)
>   (2) They predicted the nature of his second coming—*"And the glory that should follow"* (1 Pet. 1:11). (See Isa. 9, 11.)

★ All Bible prophecy concerning the Lord Jesus Christ is summarized in this little sentence: *"The sufferings of Christ, and the glory that should follow."* Here Peter connects Christ's first coming (the sufferings) with his second coming (the glory). This, in a nutshell, is a panorama of the purpose, plan, and program of Almighty God. Note this beautiful outline as we trace it through the Word of God:
- The sufferings—A Baby, wrapped in swaddling clothes (Luke 2:12). The glory—A King, clothed in majestic apparel (Psa. 93:1).
- The sufferings—He was the wearied traveler (John. 4:6). The glory—He will be the untiring God (Isa. 40:28-29).
- The sufferings—He had nowhere to lay his head (Luke 9:58). The glory—He will become heir to all things (Heb. 1:2).
- The sufferings—He was rejected by Israel (John 1:11). The glory—He will be accepted by all the nations (Isa. 9:6).

- The sufferings—Wicked people took up stones to throw at him (John 8:59). The glory—Wicked people will cry for stones to fall upon them to hide them from him (Rev. 6:16).
- The sufferings—A lowly Savior, acquainted with grief (Isa. 53:3). The glory—The mighty God, anointed with the oil of gladness (Heb. 1:9).
- The sufferings—He was clothed with a scarlet robe in mockery (Luke 23:11). The glory—He will be clothed with a vesture dipped in the blood of his enemies (Rev. 19:13).
- The sufferings—He was smitten with a reed (Matt. 27:30). The glory—He will rule the nations with a rod of iron (Rev. 19:15).
- The sufferings—Wicked soldiers bowed their knees and mocked (Mark 15:19). The glory—Every knee shall bow and acknowledge him (Phil. 2:10).
- The sufferings—He wore the crown of thorns (John 19:5). The glory—He will wear the crown of gold (Rev. 14:14).
- The sufferings—His hands were pierced with nails (John 20:25). The glory—His hands will carry a sharp sickle (Rev. 14:14).
- The sufferings—His feet were pierced with nails (Psa. 22:16). The glory—His feet will stand on the Mount of Olives (Zech. 14:4).
- The sufferings—He had no form or comeliness (Isa. 53:2). The glory—He will be beautiful (Psa. 27:4).
- The sufferings—He delivered up his spirit (John 19:30). The glory—He is alive forevermore (Rev. 1:18).
- The sufferings—He was laid in the tomb (Matt. 27:59-60). The glory—He will sit on his throne (Heb. 8:1). Note: Peter refers to the sufferings and glory theme again in 4:13 and 5:1. But on these occasions he includes the believer. In other words, to share in Christ's pain is to share in Christ's reign.

> 6. The holy angels and our salvation— *"Which things the angels desire to look into" (1 Pet. 1:12).*

★ **1:12** One of the accomplishments of our salvation is to serve as an object lesson to heaven's elect angels. They do not experience our redemption but they are intensely interested in observing it. The following passages clearly bring this out: *"Then I Daniel looked and behold, there stood other two [angels], the one on this side of the bank of the river, and the other on that side of the bank of the river. And one said ... How long shall it be to the end of these wonders?" (Dan. 12:5-6).* *"For I think that God hath set forth us the apostles last, as it were appointed to death: for we are made a spectacle unto the world, and to angels, and to men" (1 Cor. 4:9).* *"To the intent that now unto the principalities and powers in the heavenly places might be known by the church the manifold wisdom of God" (Eph. 3:10).*

> 7. The desired response in light of our salvation (1 Pet. 1:13-17)
>   a. God desires our determination *(Read 1 Pet. 1:13)*

★ **1:13** Gird up the loins of your mind. Peter will repeat this in his second epistle: *"This second epistle, beloved, I now write unto you: in both which I stir up your pure minds by way of remembrance" (2 Pet. 3:1).* This girding calls to mind a patriarch of the Old Testament who wore a long flowing robe. Around that robe he had a big belt called a girdle. When the time came that he had to move swiftly, he pulled the robe up and lapped it over the belt. He girded up his loins and was ready for action.

>   b. God desires our repudiation *(Read 1 Pet. 1:14)*
>   c. God desires our sanctification *(Read 1 Pet. 1:15-16)*
> 8. The awesome cost of our salvation (1 Pet. 1:18-22)
>   a. The price involved *(Read 1 Pet. 1:18-19)*
>   b. The planning involved *(Read 1 Pet. 1:20)*
> 9. The vehicle of our salvation *(Read 1 Pet. 1:23-25)*
> B. The fellowship involved concerning our salvation (1 Pet. 1:1-11)
>   1. We are members of the same family.
>   a. We have experienced the same birth (1 Pet. 1:23).
>   b. We partake of the same food *(Read 1 Pet. 2:2)*

★ **2:2**
- The word "desire" speaks of an intense yearning. David has this desire for God's Word. *"The judgments of the Lord are true and righteous altogether. More to be desired are they than gold, yea, than much fine gold, sweeter also than honey and the honeycomb" (Psa. 19:9-10).*

    The nation Israel had shown no desire for the Word of God in the Old Testament. Thus, when the Son of God appeared they viewed him in the same manner. *"And when we shall see him, there is no beauty that we should desire him" (Isa. 53:2).*
- The word "sincere" is literally "unadulterated"—That is, nothing mixed with it. See Revelation 14:10 concerning a similar passage dealing with God's unadulterated wrath during the tribulation.

> 2. We are stones in the same building— *"You also, as lively stones, are built up a spiritual house" (1 Pet. 2:5a).*
> 3. We have been joined to the same cornerstone *(Read 1 Pet. 2:6)*
>   a. To believers, this is a security stone.
>   b. To unbelievers, this is a stumbling stone *(Read 1 Pet. 2:8)*

★ **2:8** The word "rock" or "stone" appears five times and the word "precious" is found three times in 1 Peter 2:3-8. Note the various usages of this Redeemer-like rock as described in the Bible.
- He is the smitten Rock to all who will drink (Exod. 17:6; 1 Cor. 10:4; John 4:13-14; 7:37-39).
- He is the precious Stone to all who have drunk (1 Pet. 2:3, 7).
- He is the chief Cornerstone to the church (Eph. 2:20).
- He is the stumbling Stone to the Jews at his first coming (Rom. 9:32-33; 1 Cor. 1:23).
- He is the Headstone of the corner to the Jews at his second coming (Zech. 4:7).
- He is the smiting Stone cut without hands to Gentile world powers at his second coming (Dan. 2:34).
- He is the crushing Stone of judgment to all unbelievers (Matt. 21:44). Peter says (2:4) this great Stone was "disallowed" by Israel. This word means "to put to a test and then repudiate." After examining Christ for 34 years, Israel rejected him. He simply was not what they were looking for in a Messiah.

    Note, furthermore, the apostle's statement in 2:6: *"Wherefore also it is contained in the scripture, Behold, I lay in Sion a chief cornerstone."* Certainly here is the fulfillment of Christ's promise in Matthew 16:16, 18. Peter was not that foundation; Christ was. Finally (see 2:5), all believers are *"lively stones, built up [into] a spiritual house, an holy priesthood, to offer up spiritual sacrifices, acceptable to God by Jesus Christ."* (See also Rev. 1:6.)

> 4. We are ministers in the same priesthood— *"An holy priesthood, to offer up spiritual sacrifices, acceptable to God by Jesus Christ" (1 Pet. 2:5b). "But ye are a chosen generation, a royal priesthood" (1 Pet. 2:9a).*
> 5. We are citizens of the same nation— *"An holy nation, a peculiar people" (1 Pet. 2:9b).*

★ **2:9b**
- Old Testament Israel had a priesthood, but the church is a priesthood. *The New Scofield Bible* (p. 1,334) offers the following summary of the priesthood.
    - "Until the Law was given, the head of each family was the family priest (Gen. 8:20; 26:25; 31:54).
    - "When the Law was proposed, the promise to perfect obedience was that Israel should be unto God 'a kingdom of priests' (Exod. 19:6); but Israel violated the Law, and God shut up the priestly office to the Aaronic family, appointing the tribe of Levi to minister to Israel, thus constituting the typical priesthood. (Compare Exod.13:2 and 19:6 with Num. 8:16. See also Exod. 28:1.)
    - "In the church age, all Christians are unconditionally constituted 'a kingdom of priests' (v. 9; Rev. 1:6), the distinction which Israel failed to achieve by works.
    - "The priesthood of the Christian is, therefore, a birthright, just as every descendant of Aaron was born to the priesthood (Heb. 5:1).

- "The chief privilege of a priest is access to God. Under the Law the high priest only could enter 'the holiest of all,' and that but once a year (Heb. 9:7). But when Christ died, the veil, a type of Christ's human body (Heb. 10:20), was rent, so that now believers—priests, equally with Christ the High Priest—have access to God in the holiest (Heb. 10:19-22).
- "The High Priest is corporeally there (Heb. 4:14-16; 9:24; 10:19-22)."
- In the exercise of his office, the New Testament believer-priest is:
  - A sacrificer who offers a four-fold sacrifice:
    - His own living body (Rom. 12:1; Phil. 2:17; 2 Tim. 4:6; James 1:27; 1 John 3:16)
    - Praise to God, "the fruit of our lips giving thanks to his name," to be offered continually (Heb. 13:15; cf. Exod. 25:22: "I will commune with thee from above the mercy seat").
    - His substance (Rom. 12:13; Gal. 6:6, 10; Titus 3:14; Heb. 13:2, 16; 3 John 5-8)
    - His service, i.e., "to do good" (Heb. 13:16)
  - An Intercessor (Col. 4:12; 1 Tim. 2:1)

> 6. We are pilgrims on the same journey *(Read 1 Pet. 2:11)*
>
> **II. The Submission of the Believer (1 Pet. 2:12-3:12)**
>   A. Peter's exhortation for submission
>   1. Our responsibilities to the unsaved (1 Pet. 2:12)—*"Be careful how you behave among your unsaved neighbors; for then, even if they are suspicious of you and talk against you, they will end up praising God for your good works when Christ returns" (1 Pet. 2:12, TLB).*
>   2. Our responsibilities to civil authorities *(Read 1 Pet. 2:13-17)*
>   3. Our responsibilities to our employers *(Read 1 Pet. 2:18-20)*
>   4. Our responsibilities in the home (1 Pet. 3:1-12)
>   a. The wife (1 Pet. 3:1-6)
>   (1) Her attitude—*"In the same way, you wives, be submissive to your own husbands so that even if any of them are disobedient to the word they may be won without a word by the behavior of their wives" (1 Pet. 3:1, NASB).*
>   (2) Her apparel *(Read 1 Pet. 3:3-4)*

✷ 3:4 It should be quickly noted that this verse does not forbid a Christian woman to visit a beauty shop or a jewelry store. Those who would insist it does have a problem here, for Peter also refers to the wearing of clothes. What the passage does teach is that believing women are not to dress in a gaudy manner. History tells us the Roman women of that day went to ridiculous lengths in the adornment of the hair. The hair was arranged layer upon layer and interlaced with golden combs and nets. After the styling ordeal was completed many would stay up all night lest they spoil their coiffures for the next day's festivities. This godless external display had already been soundly condemned by the prophet Isaiah centuries ago (Isa. 3:16-26).

> (3) Her example *(Read 1 Pet. 3:5-6)*
>   b. The husband *(Read 1 Pet. 3:7)*

✷ 3:7 Here the Christian husband is to do two things in regard to his wife:
- He is to *"dwell with [her] according to knowledge."* That is, he must have an intelligent recognition of the marriage relationship. He simply must understand that:
  - His wife is a weaker vessel. This weakness is limited to the physical realm, however. She is not weaker intellectually or spiritually.
  - His wife is his fellow-heir. She shares the same spiritual equality before God as he does. Thus, the arrogant husband who lightly dismisses his wife to "the kitchen and the bedroom," insults not only her, but God himself.
- He is to give *"honour unto the wife."* That is, he is to assign her a special place in his heart. If these principles are not followed, then every prayer coming from that household will be hindered.

> c. The entire family *(1 Pet. 3:8-12)*
> B. Peter's example of submission *(Read 1 Pet. 2:21-25)*

★ "The word 'leaving' is literally 'leaving behind.' When Peter used the Greek word here translated 'example,' he went back to his boyhood days for an illustration. The word means literally 'writing under.' It was used of words given children to copy, both as a writing exercise and as a means of impressing a moral. Sometimes it was used with reference to the act of tracing over written letters ... just as a child slowly, with painstaking effort and close application, follows the shape of the letters of his teacher and thus learns to write, so saints should, with like painstaking effort and by close application, endeavor to be like the Lord Jesus in their own personal lives" (Kenneth Wuest, *First Peter in the Greek New Testament*, p. 67).

> 1. The sinless Savior *(Read 1 Pet. 2:22)*
> 2. The silent Savior *(Read 1 Pet. 2:23)*
> 3. The sacrificial Savior *(Read 1 Pet. 2:24)*

★ **2:24** Note especially Peter's statement, "by whose stripes ye were healed" (2:24). Is there physical healing in the atonement? According to Matthew 8:16-17, this was indeed predicted by Isaiah (53:4) and was fulfilled during the earthly ministry of Christ. But in I Peter chapter 2 the apostle definitely links up Christ's stripes to the healing of our souls and not our bodies.

Kenneth Wuest writes: "The word 'stripes' in the Greek presents a picture of our Lord's lacerated back after the scourging He endured at the hands of the Roman soldiers. The Romans used a scourge of cords or thongs to which latter were attached pieces of lead or brass, on small, sharp-pointed bones. Criminals condemned to crucifixion were ordinarily scourged before being executed. The victim was stripped to the waist and bound in a stooping position, with the hands behind the back, to a post or pillar. The suffering under the lash was intense. The body was frightfully lacerated. The Christian martyrs at Smyrna about A.D. 155 were so torn by the scourges that their veins were laid bare, and the inner muscles and sinews and even the intestines were exposed.... Peter remembered the body of our Lord after the scourging, the flesh so dreadfully mangled that the disfigured form appeared in his eyes as one single bruise" (*First Peter in the Greek New Testament*, p. 69).

> 4. The shepherd Savior *(Read 1 Pet. 2:25)*
>
> **III. The Suffering of the Believer (1 Pet. 3:13-4:19)**
> A. Suffering justifies the sinner.
> 1. Christ's ministry on the cross *(Read 1 Pet. 3:18)*
> 2. Christ's ministry under the earth *(Read 1 Pet. 3:19-20)*

★ **3:20** Richard DeHaan observes: "Just who were these spirits? Your answer determines your interpretation of this perplexing passage, and dictates the answer to a second question, 'What message was preached?' The word 'preached' means 'to herald' or 'to proclaim,' and can refer either to communicating the Gospel or giving an announcement. Four main views are held regarding the identification of these 'spirits in prison.'

- They were the souls of the people to whom Christ preached by the Holy Spirit through Noah during the 120 years the ark was being built. Many good scholars hold this view, but it is not without problems. The word of God seldom calls human beings 'spirits.' This term seems to be reserved for supernatural and nonhuman beings.
- The 'spirits in prison' were the mongrel offspring of a union between fallen angels (the 'sons of God' of Genesis 6:1-2) and women. Those who take this position contend that when Jesus died, He descended immediately into hades and announced to these imprisoned spirits that He had paid the price for sin. Objections to this view are that the purpose for this declaration is not given, and that one must accept the theory that fallen angels were actually able to live in the marriage relationship with human women and produce offspring.
- These spirits were wicked angels of Noah's day who engaged in some kind of monstrous evil, but who probably did not actually marry women. The people who hold this view consider the 'sons of God' of Genesis 6 to befallen angels who entered into or possessed the bodies of violent men. These men in turn fathered children with even more lawless traits. The term *nephilum*, translated 'giants' in Genesis 6:4, thus would denote men who 'fall upon' or attack others rather than

'fallen ones' or 'giants.' Scholars who give this explanation of the 'spirits in prison' see the sinning angels of Genesis as the same ones to whom Peter referred as 'delivered... into chains of darkness' (2 Pet. 2:4). They say the purpose of Christ's entrance into hades was to tell this special group of wicked angels that their doom was certain. He had paid the price for sin and would soon demonstrate that He was indeed their Master by rising from the dead. This interpretation is possible only for those who feel that the 'sons of God' of Genesis 6 were fallen angels, and that they possessed men's bodies and personalities for the purpose of leading the human race away from God.

- The 'spirits in prison' are wicked beings and Old Testament believers. Those who hold this view say that Christ descended into hades between His death and resurrection to make an announcement to all wicked spirits, and to release the Old Testament saints being kept there in a special compartment. Paul declares that Jesus 'descended first into the lower parts of the earth' and 'led captivity captive' (Eph. 4:8-10). Some Bible scholars see a dual purpose for our Lord's descent into hades. They say He first announced to fallen angels that He had conquered sin and paid its penalty. Then, contending that the believers of the ages before Calvary were not fully forgiven until Christ had presented His sacrifice, they maintain that He went to them immediately after His death to take them to heaven. This view can be held only if one is convicted that the 'compartment' theory of hades is biblical, and that Old Testament saints were not permitted to enter heaven until Jesus had died on the cross" (*Good News for Bad Times*, pp. 103-104).

> 3. Christ's ministry in the heavens *(Read 1 Pet. 3:22)*
> B. Suffering purifies the saint.
>   1. Concerning the godly believer
>   a. It gives him scriptural maturity *(Read 1 Pet. 4:1, 14, 19)*
>   b. It gives him scriptural answers *(Read 1 Pet. 3:15-17)*
>   2. Concerning the carnal believer
>   a. It is meant to bring about repentance for the sinfulness of the flesh *(Read 1 Pet. 4:15)*
>   b. It is meant to bring about respect for the holiness of God *(Read 1 Pet. 4:17-18)*

★ **4:18** Peter here refers to judgment beginning at the house of God. He may have been thinking of Ananias and Sapphira (see Acts 5:1-11).

> C. Suffering anticipates the second coming *(Read 1 Pet. 4:7)*
> D. Suffering verifies the separated life *(Read 1 Pet. 4:3-5)*
> E. Suffering multiplies future rewards *(Read 1 Pet. 4:12-13)*

★ **4:13** Note the phrase "the fiery trial" in 4:12. This is the second time Peter speaks of our faith being tried by fire (see 1:7). The intended meaning here can be metaphorical or historical, referring to the actual burning of believers by Nero in Rome.

> F. Suffering unifies the local church *(Read 1 Pet. 4:8-10)*
> G. Suffering glorifies the Lord *(Read 1 Pet. 4:11, 16)*. "For even hereunto were ye called" (2:21a).

★ **4:16** Note: Peter refers to a believer as a Christian. This title is used but two other times in the entire Bible (Acts 11:26 and 26:28). What Peter is saying in these verses is that suffering glorifies the Savior if one suffers as a Christian, that is, for his faith. But if he suffers as an evildoer, the Lord is not glorified. We are to suffer because of our position, and not our disposition.

★ **2:21a** This call to suffer here is the final of seven divine calls from God to the believer, proceeding from the very counsels of eternity past itself. Here are these "Seven Sovereign Summons:"
- The call to salvation (Rom. 8:30)
- The call to sanctification (1 Thess. 5:23-24)
- The call to service (1 Cor. 1:26-27)
- The call to separation (2 Cor. 6:17-18)
- The call to sonship (1 John 3:1)

- The call to subjection
  - Children to their parents (Eph. 6:1)
  - Wives to their husbands (Eph. 5:22)
  - Employees to their employers (1 Pet. 2:18)
  - Citizens to their country (1 Pet. 2:13-14)
  - Believers to God (Rom. 12:1-2)
- The call to suffering (Phil. 1:29; 1 Pet. 2:21)

IV. The Service of the Believer (1 Pet. 5:1-14)
  A. Serving as a shepherd (1 Pet. 5:1-4)
    1. The responsibilities *(Read 1 Pet. 5:1-3)*
    2. The rewards *(Read 1 Pet. 5:4)*

✶ 5:4 This is one of at least five possible rewards a believer may earn. These are:
- The incorruptible crown—Given to those who master the old nature (1 Cor. 9:25-27)
- The crown of rejoicing—Given to soul winners (Prov. 11:30; 1 Thess. 2:19-20; Dan. 12:3)
- The crown of life—Given to those who successfully endure temptation (James 1:12; Rev. 2:10)
- The crown of righteousness—Given to those who especially love the doctrine of the Rapture (2 Tim. 4:8)
- The crown of glory—Given to faithful preachers and teachers (1 Pet. 5:2-4; 2 Tim. 4:1-2; Acts 20:26-28) It has been suggested that these "crowns" will actually be talents and abilities with which to glorify Christ. Thus, the greater the reward, the greater the ability.

  B. Serving as a servant (1 Pet. 5:5-7)
    1. Subject yourselves to the saints *(Read 1 Pet. 5:5)*
    2. Submit yourselves to the Savior *(Read 1 Pet. 5:6-7)*

✶ 5:7 *"Humble yourselves ... that he may exalt you."* Our Lord both declared and demonstrated this principle.
- The declaration *(Read Luke 14:11)*
- The demonstration *(Read Phil. 2:5-11)*

  C. Serving as a soldier (1 Pet. 5:8-11)
    1. The predator *(Read 1 Pet. 5:8)*
    2. The plan *(Read 1 Pet. 5:9)*
    3. The purpose *(Read 1 Pet. 5:10-11)*

✶ 5:10 Especially to be noted are the words *"the God of all grace."* This is the story of the Christian life. The believer is to go from grace to grace. (See John 1:16.) James says, *"He giveth more grace"* (James 4:6). The Scriptures speak of:
- Saving grace (Eph. 2:8-9)
- Serving grace (1 Cor. 15:9-10)
- Sanctifying grace (Rom. 5:17; 6:17)
- Sacrificing grace (2 Cor. 8:1-9)
- Singing grace (Col. 3:16)
- Speaking grace (Col. 4:6)
- Strengthening grace (2 Tim. 2:1)
- Suffering grace (1 Pet. 5:10; 2 Cor. 12:9) In closing, Peter refers to Silvanus, *"a faithful brother"* (5:12). He was the messenger of this epistle and Peter's secretary. Silvanus is the lengthened form of Silas and doubtless this was the same individual who was Paul's traveling companion. (See Acts 15:40; 2 Cor. 1:19; 1 Thess. 1:1; 2 Thess. 1:1.)

LESSON 40

INTRODUCTION TO SECOND PETER

THE FINAL WORDS OF A FORMER FISHERMAN

A. The book of 2 Peter contains Simon Peter's last words.
B. This epistle contains the only interconnective reference from one apostolic epistle to another. In other words, Peter refers to Paul's writing (3:15-16).
C. It is very similar to the book of Jude. Out of 25 verses in Jude, no less than 19 are reiterated in some fashion in 2 Peter.
D. The theme of 1 Peter is suffering, while that of 2 Peter is full knowledge. It appears some 16 times with cognate words.
E. The book of 2 Peter may be compared to 2 Timothy, in matters of both authorship and content. For example:
  1. One (Paul) was the official messenger to the Gentiles, while the other (Peter) was God's spokesman to the Jews (Gal. 2:7-8).
  2. Both played important roles in the Jerusalem Council (Acts 15).
  3. Both healed a lame man (Acts 3:1-8; 14:8-12).
  4. Both dealt with satanic pretenders.
      a. Peter confronted Simon the sorcerer at Samaria (Acts 8: 9-24).
      b. Paul confronted Bar-jesus the sorcerer at Salamis on the Isle of Cyprus (Acts 13:5-11).
  5. Both were released from prison miraculously.
      a. God sent an angel to free Peter (Acts 12:5-10).
      b. God sent an earthquake to free Paul (Acts 16:25-29).
  6. Both raised the dead.
      a. Peter raised Dorcas from the dead (Acts 9:40).
      b. Paul raised Eutychus from the dead (Acts 20:12).
  7. Both received heavenly visions to minister to the lost.
      a. Peter saw his vision at Joppa (Acts 10:9-23).
      b. Paul saw his vision at Troas (Acts 16:8-10).
  8. Both authored New Testament books.
      a. Peter wrote two epistles.
      b. Paul wrote 13 (and possibly 14) epistles
  9. Both wrote key passages on the subjects of biblical inspiration (2 Pet. 1:19-21; 2 Tim. 3:16-17)
  10. Both knew they would die as martyrs for Christ.
      a. Peter's testimony— *"Yea, I think it meet, as long as I am in this tabernacle, to stir you up by putting you in remembrance; knowing that shortly I must put off this my tabernacle, even as our Lord Jesus Christ hath shewed me"* (2 Pet. 1:13-14).
      b. Paul's testimony— *"For I am now ready to be offered, and the time of my departure is at hand. I have fought a good fight, I have finished my course, I have kept the faith"* (2 Tim. 4:6-7).

F. The book of 2 Peter is the only biblical book which discusses God's sovereign dealings with the former, present, and future worlds.
   1. The former world—Destroyed by the great flood (3:4-6)
   2. The present world—To be destroyed by a great fire (3:7-12)
   3. The future world—To be created in righteousness (3:13-14)

G. This epistle is the only New Testament book after the four Gospels to mention Christ's transfiguration (1:16-18).

H. The book of 2 Peter is the 21st longest New Testament book, and 55th longest biblical book, with three chapters, 61 verses, and 1559 words. There are quotations or allusions from six Old Testament books in 2 Peter.

I. Great passages would include:
   1. 1:4-8
   2. 3:1-2
   3. 3:13-14

Overview of the Book of Second Peter

I. The Proclamation of the Power of God

II. The Application of the Promises of God
    A. The what of these promises
    B. The why of these promises
        1. To apply them leads to fruitfulness
        2. To avoid them leads to blindness

III. The Examination of the Calling of God

IV. The Revelation to the Apostle of God

V. The Transfiguration of the Son of God
    A. The glorious sight
    B. The glorious sound

VI. The Inspiration of the Word of God
    A. Its importance
    B. Its interpretation
    C. Its impartation

VII. The Deviation of the Enemies
    A. The identity of these enemies
        1. In former days
        2. In the latter days
    B. The iniquity of these enemies
        1. Inventors of heresies
        2. Christ deniers
        3. Sensuous flesh indulgers
        4. Truth maligners
        5. Greedy materialists
        6. Exploiters
        7. Despisers of all authority
        8. Self-willed
        9. Unreasoning brute animals
        10. Ignorant revilers
        11. Committed to the playboy philosophy
        12. Cancers within the Christian community
        13. Eaten with lust
        14. Totally forsaking the right way

15. Empty clouds
16. Waterless wells
17. Arrogant rabble rousers
18. Blind captives attempting to lead other blind captives
19. Cold-blooded apostates
20. Filthy hogs and dogs
21. Scoffers of the second coming
22. Closed-minded fools

VIII. The Condemnation of the Former World of God

IX. The Annihilation of the Present World of God
  A. The coming calamity
    1. The certainty involved
    2. The compassion involved
    3. The chronology involved
  B. The current challenge

X. The New Creation of the Future World of God
  A. The anticipation of this new world
  B. The preparation for this new world
    1. Maintain a proper relationship to the Scriptures
    2. Maintain a proper relationship to the Savior

THE BOOK OF SECOND PETER

> I. The Proclamation of the Power of God *(Read 2 Pet. 1:1-3)*
> II. The Application of the Promises of God *(Read 2 Pet. 1:4)*

✱ **1:4** Henrietta Mears writes concerning 1:3-4: "Look at a criminal condemned to be hanged. Suppose a messenger comes to him and says: 'The governor has taken your case into consideration, and I have brought you a purse of a thousand dollars.' The criminal will say, 'What good will it do me? I am to be hanged tomorrow.' 'Well, I have another message. He has considered your case and sent you the deed to a million-dollar estate.' The condemned man despairingly shakes his head and says, 'What can I do with that? I must be hanged tomorrow.' But the messenger goes on. 'Stop! I have another offer to make. I have brought you the governor's own inauguration robe for you to wear with special favor.' The condemned man bursts into tears, as he says, 'Do you intend to mock me? How would I appear ascending the steps of the gallows, wearing the governor's own robe?' Then the messenger says, 'Wait, I have one more message. The governor has sent you a pardon. What do you say to that?' The poor man looks at him and says he doesn't believe it. But the messenger hands the pardon, signed by the governor, with the official stamp upon it. Then the man leaps for joy, while tears of gratitude run down his face. Then the messenger says, 'I am not through yet. I have brought you the pardon, the purse of gold, the deed, and the royal robe which are yours in addition.' These are the 'all things' God has given us in Christ, His Son. With these, nothing can defeat the young Christian. The way I can escape the awful sins in this world every day and all the day is by partaking of His nature and letting Him live through me. Lay hold of the great and precious promises: that by these ye might be partakers of the divine nature" (*What the Bible Is All About*, pp. 622-633).

> A. The *what* of these promises *(Read 2 Pet. 1:5-7)*

✱ **1:7** By encouraging his readers to supply themselves with these Christian virtues, Peter literally fulfilled Jesus' two-fold command to him.
- The command before the resurrection— *"And the Lord said, Simon, Simon, behold, Satan hath desired to have you, that he may sift you as wheat: but I have prayed for thee, that thy faith fail not: and when thou art converted, strengthen thy brethren" (Luke 22:31-32).*
- The command after the resurrection— *"Feed my lambs.... Feed my sheep" (John 21:15-16).*

> B. The *why* of these promises (2 Pet. 1:8-9)
>   1. To apply them leads to fruitfulness *(Read 2 Pet. 1:8)*
>   2. To avoid them leads to blindness *(Read 2 Pet. 1:9)*
> III. The Examination of the Calling of God *(Read 2 Pet. 1:10-12)*

✱ **1:10** Peter is saying here that we are to possess that necessary confidence concerning both our salvation from God, and our service for God. No child of God is effective if he has doubts concerning either of these.

> IV. The Revelation to the Apostle of God *(Read 2 Pet. 1:13-15)*

✱ **1:14** Peter knew of his approaching death (John 21:18), as did Moses (Deut. 4:22; 31:14), and Paul (2 Tim. 4:6). He speaks of his death as *"my decease"* (1:15). The word here is actually "my exodus," and is also used to describe the death of Jesus (Luke 9:31).

V. The Transfiguration of the Son of God (2 Pet. 1:16-18)
   A. The glorious sight *(Read 2 Pet. 1:16)*
   B. The glorious sound *(Read 2 Pet. 1:17-18)*

VI. The Inspiration of the Word of God (2 Pet. 1:19-21)
   A. Its importance *(Read 2 Pet. 1:19)*

★ **1:19** It should be noted that Peter had just described the mighty transfiguration, but now declares that the written Word (the Scriptures) become a surer confirmation for the believer than even Peter's eyewitness account on that mountain. This of course does not contradict Christian experience, but it does say that Christian experience should be confirmed by the Word of God. Note Peter's beautiful description of Christ here: *"Until the day dawn, and the day star arise in your hearts."* To the church, he is the day star (see Rev. 22:16), but to Israel, he becomes the Sun of righteousness (Mal. 4:2).

   B. Its interpretation— *"Knowing this first, that no prophecy of the scripture is of any private interpretation"* (2 Pet. 1:20).

★ **1:20** This teaches that no single verse in the Bible should be interpreted in and of itself, apart from the remaining 31,172 verses. For example:
- Proxy baptism is not taught in 1 Corinthians 15:29 (whatever else it may teach), for no other verse in the Bible confirms this.
- Baptismal regeneration cannot be concluded from Acts 2:38, for many other verses clearly refute it. It is still true that a text taken out of context is a pretext.

   C. Its impartation *(Read 2 Pet. 1:21)*

★ **1:21** Here we are told that the authors of the Bible were carried along by the Spirit of God as (it may be said) a sailboat is carried along by the wind. They did not go into a coma or trance, but were fully aware of what was happening (see also 2 Tim. 3:16; Luke 1:70; Acts 3:18). One final thought here. The same Holy Spirit who originally gave the Word now desires to teach it both to and through God's people today. (See 1 Cor. 2:9-16; John 14:26; 16:13-14.)

VII. The Deviation of the Enemies of God *(Read 2 Pet. 2:1-3:4)*

★ Kenneth Gangel writes: "When the Edict of Milan was passed in A.D. 313 the church was then free to move into the world, legally and openly propagating its doctrines. But at the same time, the world also began to move into the church, diluting its message for the next 1,200 years until the Reformation broke forth on the scene. But it is obvious from 2 Peter chapter 2 that the world was already in the church well before the time of Constantine. Believers in all ages must be constantly on guard against its attack" (*The Bible Knowledge Commentary*, p. 869).

   A. The identity of these enemies
      1. In former days
         a. Wicked angels *(Read 2 Pet. 2:4)*

★ **2:4** All angels who sided in with Lucifer during his great revolt (Isa. 14:12-15; Ezek. 28:11-19; Rev. 12:3-4) will, of course, along with Satan, someday be judged by God. However, it is believed by many that in this passage Peter has in mind a special group of fallen angels who added to their original iniquity by the sin described in Genesis 6:1-5. As a result, these evil spirits are already *"delivered ... into chains* [literally, pits] *of darkness, to be reserved* [kept, confined] *unto judgment"* (see also Jude 6).

         b. Those living in Noah's day (2 Pet. 2:5)
           (1) The godless *(Read 2 Pet. 2:5)*

> (2) The godly *(Read 2 Pet. 2:5)*
> c. Those living in Lot's day (2 Pet. 2:6-9)
> (1) The godless *(Read 2 Pet. 2:6)*
> (2) The godly *(Read 2 Pet. 2:7-9)*

✶ 2:9
- In these verses we are given some additional facts about Lot not recorded in the Genesis 19 account:
  - Facts about his salvation—He is referred to as just and righteous. It would have been difficult to deduce this at times from the Old Testament account, *"Nevertheless, the foundation of God standeth sure, having this seal, the Lord knoweth them that are his"* (2 Tim. 2:19).
  - Facts about his soul—We are told that he *"vexed his righteous soul from day to day with their unlawful deeds"* (2:8). Also note the phrase, *"And delivered just Lot, vexed with the filthy conversation* [conduct] *of the wicked"* (2:7). The verb "vexed" is found twice in these verses. Each comes from a different Greek word. In 2:7 the word is *kataphoneo*, which means "to wear down with toil, to exhaust with labor, to oppress." The second word is *basanizo*, meaning "to torture, to torment." Thus, through compromise, Lot subjected his righteous soul to exhausting labor and cruel torment.
  - Facts about his Savior—*"The Lord knoweth how to deliver the godly out of temptation"* (2:9; see Gen. 19:15, 17, 22; Psa. 34:15, 17, 19; 1 Cor. 10:13). During his earthly ministry our Lord used the historical account of both Noah and Lot to illustrate those conditions which will prevail just prior to the final judgment. (See Luke 17:26-30.)
- In passing it may be said here that Lot is a type of the church, which will be taken out prior to judgment, while Noah is a foreshadow of Israel, which nation will be preserved during judgment.

> d. False prophets *(2 Pet. 2:1, 15-16)*

✶ 2:16
- This is the first of three New Testament passages which speak of the Old Testament false prophet Balaam. He is condemned in all three passages.
  - The way of Balaam (2 Pet. 2:15)
  - The error of Balaam (Jude 11)
  - The doctrine of Balaam (Rev. 2:14)
- Balaam's ass is the second of two brute creatures recorded as speaking in the Old Testament.
  - A serpent, as used by the devil (Gen. 3:1-4)
  - An ass, as used by the Lord (Num. 22:28-30)

> 2. In the latter days
> a. False teachers (2 Pet. 2:1)
> b. Scoffers *(Read 2 Pet. 3:3)*
> B. The iniquity of these enemies
> 1. Inventors of heresies (2 Pet. 2:1)

✶ They bring in destructive heresies. These heresies are introduced along with and alongside the truth. A tiny portion of deadly poison placed in a gallon of wholesome milk is far more dangerous than a bottle of marked poison, for the fatal milk is often unrecognized until it is too late.

> 2. Christ deniers (2 Pet. 2:1)
> 3. Sensuous flesh indulgers (2 Pet. 2:2, 10, 14)
> 4. Truth maligners (2 Pet. 2:2)

LESSON 40: THE BOOK OF SECOND PETER

★ They speak evil of the way of truth. In doing this they gather to themselves many disciples. *"And many shall follow their pernicious* [lustful] *ways."* False followers will go after false teachers. The passage in 1 Corinthians 11:19 explains why God permits the cults of the day. *"For there must also be factions among you, in order that those who are approved may have become evident among you"* (1 Cor. 11:19, NASB).

> 5. Greedy materialists (2 Pet. 2:3)
> 6. Exploiters (2 Pet. 2:3)

★ They will exploit (if possible) the very elect of God. *"And through covetousness shall they with feigned words make merchandise of you" (2:3)*. The phrase translated "feigned works" is *plastos* in the Greek. We get our word "plastic" from this. Peter is saying that their work may be stretched or shortened to fit any and all theological systems. However, the heretics will be punished, for *"their damnation slumbereth not"* (see also Deut. 32:35).

> 7. Despisers of all authority (2 Pet. 2:10)
> 8. Self-willed (2 Pet. 2:10)
> 9. Unreasoning brute animals (2 Pet. 2:12)
> 10. Ignorant revilers (2 Pet. 2:12)
> 11. Committed to the playboy philosophy (2 Pet. 2:13)
> 12. Cancers within the Christian community (2 Pet. 2:13)

★ They pretend to have roots in historic Christianity— *"Sporting* [revealing] *themselves with their own deceivings while they feast with you."* This is thought to have referred to that love feast held in the early church before the Lord's Supper (1 Cor. 11:17-34).

> 13. Eaten with lust (2 Pet. 2:14)
> 14. Totally forsaking the right way (2 Pet. 2:15)
> 15. Empty clouds (2 Pet. 2:17)

★ They are empty *"clouds that are carried with a tempest; to whom the mist of darkness is reserved for ever"* (2:17). Dr. Kenneth Wuest writes: "Tempest is *lailaps* in the Greek, referring to a whirlwind, a tempestuous wind, a squall, violent wind. It is never a single gust, nor a steadily blowing wind, however violent, but a storm breaking from black thunder clouds in furious gusts ... throwing everything topsy-turvy" (*In These Last Days*, p. 59).

> 16. Waterless wells (2 Pet. 2:17)
> 17. Arrogant rabble rousers (2 Pet. 2:18)
> 18. Blind captives attempting to lead other blind captives (2 Pet. 2:19)

★ *"While they promise them liberty, they themselves are the servants of corruption."* On at least two occasions our Lord referred to this characteristic while he was on earth. *"Let them alone; they be blind leaders of the blind. And if the blind lead the blind, both shall fall into the ditch"* (Matt. 15:14). *"Woe unto you, scribes and Pharisees, hypocrites! For ye compass sea and land to make one proselyte, and when he is made, ye make him twofold more the child of hell than yourselves"* (Matt. 23:15).

> 19. Cold-blooded apostates (2 Pet. 2:21)

★ Their *"latter end is worse with them than the beginning"* (2:20). One of our Lord's most frightening accounts on demonic activity vividly illustrates the 23rd characteristic of the enemies of the faith. He said: *"When the unclean spirit is gone out of a man, he walketh through dry places, seeking rest, and findeth none. Then he saith, I will return into my house from whence I came out; and when he is come, he findeth it empty, swept, and garnished. Then goeth he, and taketh with himself seven other spirits more wicked than himself, and they enter in and dwell there: and the last state of that man is worse than the first. Even so shall it be also unto this wicked generation"* (Matt. 12:43-45). Here is a case of reformation without regeneration. Peter then concludes: *"For it had been better for them [false teachers] not to have known the way of righteousness, than, after they have known it, to turn from the holy commandment delivered unto them"* (2:21). Again it should be observed that Christ had previously spoken concerning this subject. *"And that servant, which knew his lord's will, and prepared not himself, neither did according to his will, shall be beaten with many stripes. But he that knew not, and did commit things worthy of stripes, shall be beaten with few stripes. For unto whomsoever much is given, of him shall be much required: and to whom men have committed much, of him they will ask the more"* (Luke 12:47-48).

> 20. Filthy hogs and dogs (2 Pet. 2:22)

✶ *"The dog is turned to his own vomit again; and, the sow that was washed [in the Greek tense it is literally the sow that washed itself] to her wallowing in the mire."* Is Peter teaching here that a Christian can lose his salvation? He is not. See his statements on eternal security in 1 Peter 1:3-5. Nowhere in the Bible does God call a believer a hog or a dog. These are false teachers.

> 21. Scoffers of the second coming (2 Pet. 3:3-4)
> 22. Closed-minded fools (2 Pet. 3:5)

✶ They utterly and eternally close their minds to those truths revealed in both God's world and in his Word. *"For this they willingly are ignorant of"* (3:5). An agnostic is therefore not a person who says "I can't believe," but rather, "I won't believe." They are without excuse. (See Rom. 1:18-20.)

> **VIII. The Condemnation of the Former World of God (2 Pet. 3:5-6)**— *"But they deliberately forget that long ago by God's word the heavens existed and the earth was formed out of water and by water. By these waters also the world of that time was deluged and destroyed"* (2 Pet. 3:5-6, NIV).

✶ **3:6** The phrase, *"The earth was formed out of the water and by the water,"* may be a reference to the statement in Genesis 1:7: *"And God made the firmament [space], and divided the waters which were under the firmament from the waters which were above the firmament."* A number of Bible students have advocated a canopy theory which teaches that prior to the great flood much of the ocean's present water volume was suspended in the upper atmosphere in the form of invisible water vapor. Thus, as early as the second day of creation, God had already prepared for the watery judgment he would employ in Noah's day. These atmospheric oceans then came pouring down as recorded in Genesis 7:11. The word "overflowed" in the Greek is *katakluzo*, from whence our English word "cataclysm" comes.

> **IX. The Annihilation of the Present World of God (2 Pet. 3: 7-12)**
>   A. The coming calamity (2 Pet. 3:7-10)
>   1. The certainty involved *(Read 2 Pet. 3:7-8)*

✶ **3:8**
  ■ Some have attempted to twist this passage to say:
    ● That the "days" in Genesis 1 are not six literal 24-hour days, as indicated by the phrase, *"one day is with the Lord as a thousand years."*
    ● That the "years" in Revelation 20 are not 1,000 literal years, as indicated by the phrase, *"a thousand years [is] as one day."*

- Both assumptions are false, however. Peter is simply saying God is not conditioned by time. He both created it and controls it. We measure time against time. He measures time against eternity. In essence, a single day in his sight is no shorter than a thousand years, nor is a thousand years longer than a single day.

> 2. The compassion involved *(Read 2 Pet. 3:9)*
> 3. The chronology involved *(Read 2 Pet. 3:10)*

✱ **3:10** Dr. Henry Morris writes: "Question: 'Will the world eventually be destroyed in a nuclear holocaust?' Answer: The over forty generation still remembers the awful destruction in Hiroshima, when the first atomic bomb was unveiled and the world entered the nuclear age. Bible-believing Christians recall how they thought immediately of the great prophecy in 2 Peter 3:10. Yes, the earth will eventually undergo a cataclysmic destruction, which may well consist of actual atomic disintegration. The Greek word translated 'elements' in the above passage actually means the basic subdivisions of matter, corresponding quite closely to the modern scientific concept of the chemical elements. The word translated 'melt' means 'break apart.' The phrase 'pass away' does not mean 'be annihilated' but, rather 'pass out of sight.' The 'heavens' are not the stars, but the 'sky' or 'air.' Finally, 'great noise' and 'fervent heat' are intrinsically associated with atomic explosions.

"Peter's prophecy may well describe, therefore, a final cataclysm when the earth itself, with its atmosphere, will experience a vast nuclear chain reaction and perish in a tremendous atomic holocaust. Although it is conceivable that man's activities may lead to this final conflagration, it seems likely that God Himself will bring it about.

"The very existence of such a remarkable prophecy in the Bible is evidence of inspiration. The scientific discovery that matter can be converted into energy is one of the greatest triumphs of twentieth-century science, and yet this plain forecast of atomic disintegration into 'fervent heat' has been in the Bible for 1900 years" *(The Bible Has the Answer*, p. 344).

> B. The current challenge *(Read 2 Pet. 3:11-12)*
>
> **X. The New Creation of the Future World of God (2 Pet. 3:13-18)**
>   A. The anticipation of this new world *(Read 2 Pet. 3:13-14)*
>   B. The preparation for this new world
>   1. Maintain a proper relationship to the Scriptures *(Read 2 Pet. 3:15-17)*

✱ **3:17** Peter's statement about Paul here brings out four facts:
- He and Paul apparently continued to be good friends, following their confrontation in Antioch (see Gal. 2:11-14). This is indicated by the phrase *"our beloved brother Paul."*
- Peter attested to the divine inspiration of Paul's writings.
- Peter stated some of Paul's writings were *"hard to be understood."*
- Peter realized that (even back then) some of the cults and false religious systems of the day were twisting and perverting Paul's writings as they continue to do in modern times.

> 2. Maintain a proper relationship to the Savior *(Read 2 Pet. 3:18)*

LESSON 41
INTRODUCTION TO FIRST JOHN

INTIMATE INSIGHTS ON THE FATHER, FELLOWSHIP, AND THE FAMILY OF GOD

A. John the apostle writes his first epistle to develop this wonderful theme.
B. It has more to say about the Father than does any other epistle. He is referred to 12 times.
C. The *New Scofield Bible* suggests: "It [1 John] is a family letter from the Father to His 'little children' who are in the world. With the possible exception of the Song of Solomon, it is the most intimate of the inspired writings. The sin of a Christian is treated as a child's offense against his Father, and is dealt with as a family matter (1:9; 2:1)" (p. 1,342).
D. The word *love* is found 37 times, more often in this epistle than in any other Old or New Testament book, with the single exception of the Psalms.
E. The Spirit of God directed John the apostle to pen five of the New Testament books. Apart from Paul, no other author would write as many books in the New Testament as he did. His five books are: The Gospel of John, the three epistles of John, and the Revelation. The following distinction between these books is offered:
  1. Gospel of John
     a. Speaks of salvation
     b. The past
     c. Christ the Prophet
     d. The cross
  2. Epistles of John
     a. Speak of sanctification
     b. The present
     c. Christ the Priest
     d. The *koinonia* (fellowship)
  3. Revelation of John
     a. Speaks of glorification
     b. The future
     c. Christ the King
     d. The crown
F. A comparison can be made between John's Gospel account and the epistle of 1 John.
  1. John begins his Gospel account by proving the *deity* of Christ (John 1:1).
  2. John begins his epistle by proving the *humanity* of Christ (1 John 1:1-3).
  3. John ends his Gospel account with the following words: "But these are written, that ye might believe that Jesus is the Christ, the Son of God; and that believing ye might have life through his name" (John 20:31).
  4. John ends his epistle with the following words: *"These things have I written unto you that believe on the name of the Son of God; that ye may know that ye have eternal life, and that ye may believe on the name of the Son of God" (1 John 5:13).*

G. In the Gospel, John describes believers as sheep in God's fold; in the epistle as members in his family; and in the Revelation as priests in his kingdom (John 10; 1 John 2; Rev. 1).

H. It is believed by some that John directed his epistles to the same readers who would later receive the book of Revelation—that is, the seven churches in Asia Minor.

I. This epistle describes several great contrasts. In it John speaks of light versus darkness, love versus hatred, Christ versus Antichrist, belief versus unbelief, and truth versus error.

J. It is the first of but two biblical books referring to the coming world dictator, the Antichrist (see 1 John 2:18, 22; 4:3; 2 John 7).

K. It is the only biblical book containing the phrase, *"sin unto death"* (5:16), describing what had already taken place in Acts 5:1-11 and 1 Corinthians 11:29-30.

L. It is the only biblical book classifying sin and temptation into three categories (2:15-17).

M. It has more to say about a Christian's sin and confession than any other biblical book for its size.

N. The book of 1 John is the 13th longest New Testament book, and 44th longest biblical book with five chapters, 105 verses, and 2,523 words. There are quotations or allusions from seven Old Testament books in the first epistle of John.

O. Great passages would include:
   1. 1:5-9
   2. 2:1-2
   3. 2:15-17
   4. 3:1-3
   5. 3:18-23
   6. 4:7-10
   7. 5:11-15

OVERVIEW OF THE BOOK OF FIRST JOHN

This epistle is outlined with the word "fellowship" in mind

I. The Source of this Fellowship
    A. The incarnation of Jesus Christ
        1. The reality of his incarnation
        2. The reason for his incarnation
    B. The atonement of Jesus Christ
        1. The divine extent
        2. The divine example

II. The Goal of this Fellowship
    A. That we might know more about the Father
        1. He is light
        2. He is love
        3. He is life
        4. He is righteous
        5. He is all-knowing
        6. He is invisible
    B. That we might allow the Father's love to be perfected in us
    C. That we might love the family of God
    D. That we might experience the fullness of joy
    E. That we might receive assurance
        1. Concerning our salvation
        2. Concerning our supplications

III. The Requirements for this Fellowship
    A. Help my brother
    B. Abide in Christ
    C. Keep his commandments
        1. The old commandment
        2. The new commandment
    D. Recognize my sin
    E. Confess my sin
    F. Walk in the light

IV. The Tests of this Fellowship
    A. Do I conduct my life down here in view of the Rapture?
    B. Do I continually dwell in sin?
    C. Do I hate my spiritual brother?
    D. Do I desire to help my brother?

E. Do I really love my brother?
   F. Do I really love God?
   G. Do I enjoy a rapport with other servants of God?
   H. Am I plagued with constant fear?
   I. Can I recognize false doctrine when it comes my way?
   J. Am I straight on the deity of Christ?
   K. Am I straight on the work of Christ?
   L. Do I have the witness of the Spirit?

V. The Maintenance of this Fellowship
   A. Accomplished through the occupation of the Son of God
      1. He serves as our advocate
      2. He serves as our atoning sacrifice
   B. Accomplished through the habitation of the Spirit of God
   C. Accomplished through the cooperation of the saint of God

VI. The Family Members in this Fellowship
   A. Little children (new converts)
   B. Young men (those saved for awhile)
   C. Fathers (those mature in the faith)

VII. The Enemies of this Fellowship
   A. The evil systems in this world
      1. The divisions
      2. The destruction
   B. The evil seducers in this world
      1. Their appearance
      2. Their apostasy
   C. The evil spirits in this world
      1. The fruit of these spirits
      2. The root of these spirits

VIII. The Witnesses to this Fellowship
   A. The witnesses in heaven
   B. The witnesses on earth

IX. The Separation from This Fellowship

X. The Encouragements for This Fellowship
   A. The promise of eternal life
   B. The promise of a new body
   C. A life without fear
   D. Confidence at the Rapture
   E. Boldness at the judgment

THE BOOK OF FIRST JOHN

"That which we have seen and heard declare we unto you, that ye also may have fellowship with us: and truly our fellowship is with the Father, and with his Son Jesus Christ" (1 John 1:3). This epistle is outlined with the word "fellowship" in mind.

> **I. The Source of This Fellowship**
>   A. The incarnation of Jesus Christ (1 John 1:1-2; 3:5, 8)
>   1. The reality of his incarnation *(Read 1 John 1:1-2)*

✱ **1:2** The Apostle John was well qualified to give witness concerning the validity of the incarnation. For over three action-packed and life-changing years he listened to the Savior's sermons, learned from his parables, and marveled at his miracles. John, along with Peter and James, enjoyed a special relationship with Jesus.
- They alone witnessed the transfiguration (Matt. 17:1-2).
- They alone were present at the raising of Jairus's daughter (Luke 8:51-56).
- They alone were taken to a special place in the Garden of Gethsemane (Matt. 26:36-38).
- John leaned on the bosom of Christ during the Last Supper (John 13:23).
- John witnessed the trial of Jesus before the Jewish high priest (John 18:15-16).
- John was the only apostle present at the crucifixion (John 19:26-27).
- John and Peter were the first two apostles at the empty tomb (John 20:1-8).

> 2. The reason for his incarnation *(Read 1 John 3:5, 8)*

✱ **3:8** It must be understood that Jesus did not come to preach the gospel. He came rather that there might be a gospel to be preached.

> B. The atonement of Jesus Christ (1 John 2:2; 3:16; 4: 9-10, 14)
>   1. The divine extent—For whom did Christ die? *(Read 1 John 2:2)*

✱ **2:2** The word "propitiation" is from the Greek *hilasmos* and is found four times in the New Testament (Rom. 3:25; Heb. 9:5; 1 John 2:2; 4:10). Its literal meaning is "mercy seat" (as translated in Heb. 9:5). In the Old Testament, once yearly, the high priest made atonement for Israel by sprinkling the blood of a sacrificial animal upon the lid of the Ark of the Covenant, also known as the mercy seat (Lev. 16:13-19). Thus, the theological meaning of "propitiation" is to render favorable, to satisfy, to appease. In a nutshell, John is saying here in 2:2 that the sacrifice of Christ is looked upon as our mercy seat whereby God's holiness is satisfied by the blood of his Son. Note also this propitiation is sufficient not only for the nation Israel (as was the case in the Old Testament) but for the entire world.

> 2. The divine example—Why did Christ die? *(Read 1 John 3:16; 4:9-10,14)*
> **II. The Goal of This Fellowship**
>   A. That we might know more about the Father
>   1. He is light *(Read 1 John 1:5)*
>   2. He is love *(Read 1 John 4:8,16; 3:16)*
>   3. He is life *(Read 1 John 5:11-12)*

4. He is righteous *(Read 1 John 3:7)*
5. He is all-knowing *(Read 1 John 3:20)*

✱ **3:20** There are two difficult phrases used by John, the first in this verse and the second in the next:
- *"If our heart condemn us"* (3:20).
- *"If our heart condemn us not"* (3:21). The first phrase may result from an oversensitive conscience, revealing how frail we really are. If so, a classic illustration here can be seen in the answer given by a distraught father of a demon-possessed son when asked by Christ if he had faith for the healing of his son. *"And straightway the father of the child cried out, and said with tears, Lord, I believe; help thou mine unbelief"* (Mark 9:24).

The second phrase would thus become a reality when one realizes that God knows all about us and yet still loves us. *"Like as a father pitieth his children, so the LORD pitieth them that fear him. For he knoweth our frame; he remembereth that we are dust"* (Psa. 103:13-14).

"Watch and pray, that ye enter not into temptation: the spirit indeed is willing, but the flesh is weak" (Matt. 26:41).

      6. He is invisible— *"No man hath seen God at any time"* (1 John 4:12a).
  B. That we might allow the Father's love to be perfected in us *(Read 1 John 2:5)*
  C. That we might love the family of God— *"If we love one another, God dwelleth in us, and his love is perfected in us"* (1 John 4:12b).
  D. That we might experience the fullness of joy *(Read 1 John 1:4)*
  E. That we might receive assurance
      1. Concerning our salvation *(Read 1 John 5:13)*
      2. Concerning our supplications *(Read 1 John 3:22; 5:14-15)*

III. The Requirements for This Fellowship
  A. Help my brother *(Read 1 John 3:17)*
  B. Abide in Christ *(Read 1 John 2:28)*
  C. Keep his commandments *(Read 1 John 2:3-8; 5:2-3)*
      1. The old commandment *(Read 1 John 2:7)*. The old commandment was to love others as you love yourself (Lev. 19:34; Deut. 10:19).
      2. The new commandment— *"Again, a new commandment I write unto you, which thing is true in him and in you: because the darkness is past, and the true light now shineth"* (1 John 2:8).
  D. Recognize my sin *(Read 1 John 1:8)*

✱ **1:8** Those who hold to sinless perfection make claim to something that neither John nor Paul would make claim to (see Phil. 3:12-14).

  E. Confess my sin *(Read 1 John 1:9)*

✱ **1:9** The word "confess" here is the Greek word *homologeo*, which means "to agree with." Thus, when the Holy Spirit points out a sin in our life we are immediately to agree with him. While the blood of Christ will cleanse us from every sin, it will not cleanse us of even one excuse.

  F. Walk in the light *(Read 1 John 1:7)*

IV. The Tests of This Fellowship—A quick quiz to determine our fellowship
  A. Do I conduct my life down here in view of the Rapture? *(Read 1 John 3:3)*
  B. Do I continually dwell in sin? *(Read 1 John 2:29; 3:6, 9-10; 5:4-5, 18)*

★ **5:18** These verses, of course, do not teach sinless perfection. The Greek verbs are all in the present tense, referring to the constant practice of sin. Thus, while we may not be sinless, John nevertheless states that we should sin less.

> C. Do I hate my spiritual brother? *(1 John 4:20)*
> D. Do I desire to help my brother? *(1 John 3:17-18)*
> E. Do I really love my brother? *(1 John 2:10; 3:12, 14-15; 4:7, 21)*

★ **4:21** The word "love" is mentioned no less than eight times in these few verses. What is real Christian love? Consider these suggested definitions:
- Christian love is unselfish concern for the welfare of another.
- Christian love is the act of one person seeking the highest good for another person. Thus, acting upon these definitions, we can love those individuals we may not even like.

> F. Do I really love God? *(1 John 5:2)*
> G. Do I enjoy a rapport with other servants of God? *(1 John 4:6)*
> H. Am I plagued with constant fear? *(1 John 4:18)*
> I. Can I recognize false doctrine when it comes my way? *(1 John 4:1-3)*

★ **4:3** The title "Antichrist" is found but four times in the Bible, all employed by John the apostle (1 John 2:18, 22; 4:3; 2 John 1:7). According to John:
- The Antichrist will appear during the last days (2:18; 4:3).
- He has, however, many prototypes throughout history (2:18; 4:3).
- The Antichrist denies the deity of Christ (2:22).
- The Antichrist denies the humanity of Christ (4:3; 2 John 7).

> J. Am I straight on the deity of Christ? *(1 John 4:15)*
> K. Am I straight on the work of Christ? *(1 John 3:5, 8; 3:13, 20)*
> L. Do I have the witness of the Spirit? *(1 John 3:24; 4:13; 5:9-10)*
>
> **V. The Maintenance of This Fellowship**
>   A. Accomplished through the occupation of the Son of God
>   1. He serves as our advocate *(Read 1 John 2:1)*

★ **2:1** The word "advocate" here is the Greek word *parakletos*, meaning "to call alongside of." The *New Scofield Bible* defines this office as follows: "Advocacy is that work of Jesus Christ for sinning believers which He carries on with the Father, whereby, because of the eternal efficacy of Christ's sacrifice, He restores them to fellowship" (p. 1,343).

>   2. He serves as our atoning sacrifice *(Read 1 John 2:2)*

★ **2:2** As brought out before in this study, the root Greek word here translated "propitiation" is rendered "mercy seat" in Hebrews 9:5. The mercy seat was a part of that sacred Ark of the Covenant which rested in the holy of holies. Upon this golden mercy seat, every day of atonement, was sprinkled the blood of an animal (Lev. 16:14). This meant that the righteous sentence of the Law had been executed, changing a judgment seat into a mercy seat (Heb. 9:11-15). It signified that humanity had thus been reconciled to God. The work of Christ thus served as a propitiation, whereby God's righteousness was forever satisfied. (See also 4:10.)

>   B. Accomplished through the habitation of the Spirit of God *(Read 1 John 2:20, 27)*

LESSON 41: THE BOOK OF FIRST JOHN

★ **2:27** This verse does not, of course, deny the office of a human teacher (see Eph. 4:11-12). What it does say is that we are to test any system of teaching by the Word of God.

> C. Accomplished through the cooperation of the saint of God *(Read 1 John 1:8-9)*
> **VI. The Family Members in This Fellowship** *(Read 1 John 3:1)*
>   A. Little children (new converts) *(Read 1 John 2:12, 13b)*
>   B. Young men (those saved for awhile) *(Read 1 John 2:13-14)*
>   C. Fathers (those mature in the faith) *(Read 1 John 2:13)*
> **VII. The Enemies of This Fellowship** *(Read 1 John 2:15; 5:19)*

★ **5:19** A definition of this world—In the Bible there are several kinds of worlds.
- The physical world (Acts 17:24)
- The human world (John 3:16)
- The evil world (1 John 5:19; John 12:31; 15:18)—Obviously John had this third "world" in mind here. A believer lives on the first world, is a member of the second, but must avoid the third.

> A. The evil systems in this world
>   1. The divisions (1 John 2:16)
>   a. The lust of the flesh
>   b. The lust of the eyes
>   c. The pride of life

★ As John penned these words his thoughts may well have gone back to a beautiful garden and a terrible wilderness where two individuals were subjected to these satanic temptations by the devil himself.
- Eve and the beautiful garden (Gen. 3:6)
  - *"The woman saw that the tree was good for food"*—The lust of the flesh.
  - *"And that it was pleasant to the eyes"*—The lust of the eyes.
  - *"And a tree ... to make one wise"*—The pride of life.
- Christ and the terrible wilderness (Matt. 4:3, 8, 6)
  - *"Command that these stones be made bread" (4:3)*—The lust of the flesh.
  - *"He [Satan] sheweth him [Jesus] all the kingdoms of the world" (4:8)*—The lust of the eyes.
  - *"Cast thyself down [from the pinnacle of the temple] ...for he shall give his angels charge concerning thee" (4:6)*—The pride of life.

> 2. The destruction *(Read 1 John 2:17)*
> B. The evil seducers in this world *(Read 1 John 2:26)*
>   1. Their appearance *(Read 1 John 2:18)*
>   2. Their apostasy *(Read 1 John 2:19)*

★ **2:19** The actions of the following individuals serve to illustrate John's words here:
- Cain (Gen. 4:1-8; 1 John 3:10-12)
- Korah (Num. 16:1-3)
- Achan (Josh. 7:20)
- Saul (1 Sam. 28:3-20)
- Ahithophel (2 Sam. 15:31)
- Judas (Matt. 26:14-16)
- Demas (2 Tim. 4:10)

C. The evil spirits in this world
      1. The fruit of these spirits *(Read 1 John 2:22; 4:1-2)*.
      2. The root of these spirits *(Read 1 John 4:3)*.

VIII. The Witnesses to This Fellowship (1 John 5:6-8)
   A. The witnesses in heaven *(Read 1 John 5:7)*
   B. The witnesses on earth *(Read 1 John 5:8)*

★ **5:8** These verses are not among the easiest to interpret. Let us begin by observing that the last part of verse 7 is not listed in most ancient manuscripts. Thus, the first part of the verse should read, "Because there are three that bear record." This apparently refers to the three witnesses already mentioned in verse 6 and amplified in verse 8. What are these witnesses?
- The identity of the witnesses:
  - The water
  - The blood
  - The Spirit
- The interpretation of the witnesses—There are at least four theories here.
  - The baptism and death of Christ
  - The water and blood that flowed from his side
  - A symbolic reference to purification and redemption
  - A symbolic reference to the ordinances of baptism and the Lord's Supper-Most conservative theologians prefer the first of these, the baptism and death of Christ (Matt. 3:13-17; Heb. 9:12).
- The implications of these witnesses—A two-fold witness is all that is necessary (Deut. 19:15; Matt. 18:16; John 8:17), but God has given us three.

IX. The Separation from This Fellowship—Sin causes a break in our fellowship with God. *"If anyone sees his brother committing a sin not leading to death, he shall ask and God will for him give life to those who commit sin not leading to death. There is a sin leading to death; I do not say that he should make request for this. All unrighteousness is sin, and there is a sin not leading to death"* (1 John 5:16-17, NASB).

★ **5:17** "There is a sin unto death" (5:16). The Bible teaches that my union with Christ is so strong that nothing can break it; but my communion with him is so fragile that the slightest sin shatters it. M. F. Unger writes: "Prayer and the Problem of Serious Sin, 16-17. It is possible for a true believer to fall into sin, 16a. If and when this happens, a fellow believer is to pray for him, 16b. As a result God will give the sinning Christian preservation of physical life (not eternal life, for this life is eternal and unforfeitable). However, this intercession is effective only in the case of sin not unto physical death, 16c. 'There is a sin unto death,' 16d. This is persistent, willful sinning in a believer in which 'the flesh is destroyed' (physical death) so 'that the spirit might be saved' (1 Cor. 5:1-5; Acts 5:1-11; 1 Cor. 11:30). Both Saul and Samson are types of this very severe chastening in the Old Testament. This sin is not to be prayed for because it involved the execution of an immutable law of God unaltered by prayer, 16e. Sin has different degrees of seriousness, 16. 'All unrighteousness is sin, but there is a sin which is not unto [physical] death' (involving lesser chastisements, cf. 1 Cor. 11:30)" (*Unger's Bible Handbook*, p. 829).

X. The Encouragements for This Fellowship
   A. The promise of eternal life *(Read 1 John 2:25)*
   B. The promise of a new body *(Read 1 John 3:2)*
   C. A life without fear *(Read 1 John 3:19, 21; 4:18)*
   D. Confidence at the Rapture *(Read 1 John 2:28)*
   E. Boldness at the judgment *(Read 1 John 4:17)*

Introduction to Second John

THE EPISTLE FROM AN ELDER TO AN ELECT LADY

   A. This is John's second epistle. It is the only book in the Bible addressed to a woman. It holds the same place in John's writing that Philemon holds in Paul's epistles.
   B. John does not mention his own name or the name of this woman. This may have been to prevent persecution from the Roman authorities of the time, who viewed Christianity as an unlawful religion.
   C. The book of 2 John is the 26th longest New Testament book and 65th longest biblical book, with one chapter, 13 verses, and 303 words. There are quotations or allusions to one Old Testament book in 2 John.
   D. Its great passage is found in verses 7-8.

Overview of the Book of Second John

It is the only book in the Bible addressed to a woman.

I. She is commended by the Apostle

II. She is commanded by the Apostle
    A. That she walk in love
    B. That she walk in truth

III. She is cautioned by the Apostle
    A. Look out for Satan
        1. The deception of his ministers
        2. The rejection of his ministers
    B. Look out for self

IV. She is comforted by the Apostle

THE BOOK OF SECOND JOHN

I. She Is Commended by the Apostle *(Read 2 John 1-4)*

✶ **v. 4** Here it perhaps should be noted that some Bible students believe the "elect lady" of this epistle was actually a local church. If this is the case, then the children here are church members. However, it is the view of this author that it is written to an actual woman and these are her children.

II. She Is Commanded by the Apostle
    A. That she walk in love *(Read 2 John 5)*
    B. That she walk in truth *(Read 2 John 6)*

✶ **v. 6** In verses 5 and 6 John exhorts to walk in love and truth. How important it is not to separate these two. To practice truth without love leads to legalism. To employ love without truth leads to liberalism. Paul likewise combines these two: *"But, speaking the truth in love, may grow up into him in all things, which is the head, even Christ"* (Eph. 4:15).

III. She Is Cautioned by the Apostle
    A. Look out for Satan
        1. The deception of his ministers *(Read 2 John 7)*
        2. The rejection of his ministers
            a. What the elect lady was to do *(Read 2 John 10)*

✶ **v. 10** Perhaps this lady was extending hospitality to all those who claimed to be Christians, though some were heretics.

            b. Why she was to do it *(Read 2 John 11)*

✶ **v. 11** This may have been one of the reasons why Paul denounced a demon-possessed girl in Philippi in spite of the fact that she attempted to identify with his message *(Read Acts 16:17-18)*.

    B. Look out for self *(Read 2 John 8)*

✶ **v. 8** John wanted this beloved lady to receive a full reward for faithful service at the judgment seat of Christ (see 1 Cor. 3:5-17).

IV. She Is Comforted by the Apostle *(Read 2 John 12)*

Introduction to Third John

AN EPISTLE FROM AN ELDER CONCERNING: AN EXHORTER, AN EGOTIST, AND AN EXAMPLE

A. The epistle is 3 John. The elder is John. The exhorter is Gaius; the egotist, Diotrephes; and the example, Demetrius.

J. Vernon McGee says: "This is a letter similar to John's second epistle, in that it is personal in character, and it carries the same theme of truth. However, this letter deals with principalities. In his second epistle, John says that truth is worth standing for; and in the third epistle that truth is worth working for!" *(Third John, p. 291)*.

B. In his second epistle John dealt with the problem of welcoming deceivers (which should not have been done); in this epistle he discusses the error of not receiving believers (which should have been done).

C. This is the shortest book in the Bible.

D. Both 2 and 3 John end in similar fashion.
   1. In 2 John— *"Having many things to write unto you, I would not write with paper and ink: but I trust to come unto you, and speak face to face, that our joy may be full"* (2 John 12).
   2. In 3 John— *"I had many things to write, but I will not with ink and pen write unto thee: but I trust I shall shortly see thee, and we shall speak face to face. Peace be to thee. Our friends salute thee. Greet the friends by name"* (3 John 13-14).

E. This epistle gives an excellent (though brief) glimpse of church life at the close of the first century.

F. The book of 3 John is the smallest biblical book, with one chapter, 14 verses, and 299 words. There are quotations or allusions from one Old Testament book in 3 John.

G. Its great passage is verse 11.

OVERVIEW OF THE BOOK OF THIRD JOHN

I. **The Prosperity of Gaius the Exhorter**
    A. John's prayer for him
    B. John's praise of him
        1. His faithfulness to the message of God
        2. His helpfulness to the messengers of God

II. **The Pride of Diotrephes the Egotist**
    A. He attempted to occupy the leading place
    B. He refused to receive the Apostle John
    C. He had slandered the apostles
    D. He had refused to entertain missionaries
    E. He attempted to excommunicate believers
    F. He was not of God

III. **The Praise of Demetrius, the Example**

THE BOOK OF THIRD JOHN

> **I. The Prosperity of Gaius the Exhorter (3 John 1-8)**
> A. John's prayer for him *(Read 3 John 1-2, 13-14)*

✶ **v. 14** Note the phrase in verse 2, *"that thou mayest prosper and be in health."* One of America's most famous faith healers during the latter part of the 20th century, by his own testimony, had based his entire healing ministry squarely upon this little verse, claiming he found in it God's will for every believer to enjoy continual health and considerable wealth. Even the most casual reading of John's letter here, however, would totally reject this bizarre interpretation. The Greek word here translated "prosper" is *euodoumai*, meaning "to have a good journey."

> B. John's praise of him
>   1. His faithfulness to the message of God *(Read 3 John 3-4)*
>   2. His helpfulness to the messengers of God *(Read 3 John 5-8)*

✶ **v. 8** Note two phrases here in verse 6:
- *"Which have borne witness of thy charity before the church."* John seems to be saying here that his church had heard of Gaius's love for both the Savior and the saints. At this time John may have been pastor of the church at Ephesus. If so, the quality of Gaius's love was sadly absent among the apostles congregation (see Rev. 2.4).
- *"Bring forward on their journey after a godly sort."* John here instructs Gaius and his church to perform a two-fold ministry for visiting Christian workers.
  - Provide for them while they were there.
  - Anticipate their needs when they leave, that is, send them away with an offering.

> **II. The Pride of Diotrephes the Egotist (3 John 9-11)**
> A. He attempted to occupy the leading place (3 John 9).
> B. He refused to receive the Apostle John (3 John 9).
> C. He had slandered the apostles (3 John 10).
> D. He had refused to entertain missionaries (3 John 10).
> E. He attempted to excommunicate believers (3 John 10).
> F. He was not of God (3 John 11).

✶ **v. 11.** J Vernon McGee summarizes the actions of both Gaius and Diotrephes: "The missionaries of the early church were itinerants. They went from place to place. Since the local inn was a wretched and dirty place, and there were no Holiday Inns or Howard Johnson Motels, these missionaries were entertained in the homes of believers. Gaius opened his home, for which John congratulates him. Diotrephes opposed this practice, and John censors him for it. His 'hang-up' was that he loved to have recognition and attention, and be the center of attraction. He had to rule or ruin. There is generally one like him in every church who wants to control the church and the preacher. He tried to be the first pope. He was Diotrephes, the dictator" (*Through the Bible*, p. 292.)

> **III. The Praise of Demetrius, the Example** *(Read 3 John 12)*

✱ **v. 12** After issuing a sixfold condemnation of Diotrephes, John now gives a three-fold commendation of Demetrius.
- A public commendation—*"A good report of all men"*
- A scriptural commendation—*"Of the truth itself"*
- A personal commendation—*"We also bear record."*

LESSON 42

INTRODUCTION TO JUDE

THE ARROGANT APOSTATE, DESCRIBED AND DENOUNCED

A. Such is the message of the book of Jude.

B. Jude was the brother of James (author of the book of James and first pastor of the Jerusalem church in Acts 15) and half brother of Jesus (see Mark 6:3).

C. Along with his brothers, Jude did not believe in the ministry of Jesus until after the resurrection (John 7:3-8). But sometime between the resurrection and ascension both men were gloriously saved. They were present (along with their mother Mary) in the Upper Room just prior to Pentecost (Acts 1:13).

D. Jude was apparently married and was accompanied by his wife as he performed missionary work (1 Cor. 9:5).

E. "The beginning of the age of the Church is described in the Acts of the Apostles. The end of the Church Age is set forth in the Epistle of Jude, which might well be called the Acts of the Apostates. Jude is the only book in all God's Word entirely devoted to the great apostasy which is to come upon Christendom before the Lord Jesus Christ returns" (Dr. S. Maxwell Coder, *Jude, the Acts of the Apostates*, pp. 3-4).

F. Jude can be compared to 2 Peter.
   1. Both epistles give the marks of false teachers.
      a. See 2 Peter 2:1-3, 10-22.
      b. See Jude 4, 10-19.
   2. Peter placed the ministry of false teachers in the future (2:1), whereas Jude saw them as already present (v. 4).
   3. Both epistles refer to fallen angels (2 Pet. 2:4; Jude 6).
   4. Both mention Sodom and Gomorrah (2 Pet. 2:6; Jude 7).
   5. Both use Balaam as an example of apostasy (2 Pet. 2:15-16; Jude 11).
   6. Both liken apostasy to waterless clouds (2 Pet. 2:17; Jude 12)

G. Jude has been called the Judges of the New Testament.

H. Jude refers to two noncanonical books. These are:
   1. The Assumption of Moses (Jude 9)
   2. The book of Enoch (Jude 14-15) — Paul had previously also done this. (See Acts 17:28; Titus 1:12.)

I. "Jude was intending to write an epistle regarding 'our common salvation' (v. 3), when the Spirit detoured him to write concerning the apostasy. It is a graphic and striking description of the apostasy. What was a little cloud the size of a man's hand in Jude's day is, in our day, a storm of hurricane proportions — because we are in the apostasy of which he foretold. It is a question now of how much worse it can become before genuine believers are taken out by the Rapture" (J. Vernon McGee *Through the Bible*, p. 293).

J. It is the first of two New Testament books referring to Michael the archangel. Both deal with his encounter with Satan (Jude 9; Rev. 12:7).

K. The book of Jude is the only New Testament book to provide for us a sample of the kind of preaching pre-flood sinners once heard. (See Jude 14-15.)

L. Jude concludes his epistle with one of the New Testament's greatest doxologies. (See Jude 24-25.)

M. The epistle of Jude is the 24th longest New Testament book, and 63rd longest biblical book, with one chapter, 25 verses, and 613 words. There are quotations or allusions from eight Old Testament books in Jude.

N. Great passages would include:
   1. Jude 3
   2. Jude 20-23

Overview of the Book of Jude

I. **The Problem of Apostasy**
    A. Jude's commendation
    B. Jude's compulsion
    C. Jude's concern

II. **The Description of Apostasy**
    A. Apostates are ungodly
    B. Twisters of God's grace
    C. Christ deniers
    D. Sensuous
    E. Flesh defilers
    F. Despisers of authority
    G. Ignorant critics
    H. Unreasoning animals
    I. Immoral fault-finders
    J. Arrogant to the core
    K. Lying flatterers for personal gain
    L. Divisive
    M. Worldly minded
    N. Devoid of the Spirit

III. **Historical Example and Causes of Apostasy**
    A. The nation Israel, caused by unbelief
    B. The fallen angels, caused by disloyalty
    C. The citizens of Sodom and Gomorrah, caused by sexual perversion
    D. The devil, caused by pride and self-will
    E. Cain, caused by religious perversion
    F. Balaam, caused by greed for money
    G. Korah, caused by rejection of divine authority

IV. **The Metaphors of Apostasy**
    A. Hidden rocks
    B. Waterless clouds
    C. Dead autumn trees
    D. Wandering stars

V. **The Judgment upon Apostasy**
    A. The messenger
    B. The message

VI. The Safeguards against Apostasy
- A. The believer and himself
    1. He is to build on the Word of God
    2. He is to pray with the Spirit of God
    3. He is to keep in the love of God
    4. He is to look for the return of God
    5. He is to testify to the glory of God
- B. The believer and the lost
    1. Concerning those in great doubt
    2. Concerning those who are in great danger
    3. Concerning those who are in great depravity
- C. The believer and the Lord
    1. What he does for us now
    2. What he will do for us later

THE BOOK OF JUDE

I. The Problem of Apostasy (Jude 1-4)
   A. Jude's commendation *(Read Jude 1-2)*

★ v. 2
- We note that neither Jude nor James, half brothers of Jesus, ever attempted in their epistles to "pull rank" by reminding their readers of that fact (see Matt. 13:55). In fact, to the contrary, both brothers refer to themselves as servants of Jesus Christ. (See James 1:1; Jude 1.)
- The phrase "preserved in Jesus Christ" should be translated "kept for Jesus Christ." It is used of Peter's and Paul's imprisonments in Acts 12:5 and 25:4, 21. (See also 1 Pet. 1:4.) Even before Jude warns about the terrible apostasy which had already settled down upon the world of his day and would grow progressively worse, he reassures the believers that they are kept for Christ. Here he supplies us with the inspired answer to the prayer of Christ: *"Holy Father, keep through thine own name those whom thou hast given me" (John 17:11)*. (See also 1 Thess. 5:23.)
- Jude continues with: *"Mercy unto you, and peace, and love, be multiplied" (v. 2)*. S. Maxwell Coder writes: "There is an upward look in the word mercy, an inward look in the word peace, and an outward look in the word love. These three related us properly to God, to our own inner being, and to our brethren around us. When they are multiplied, and only then, will we be able to cope with the great apostasy" (*Jude, the Acts of the Apostates*, p. 13).

   B. Jude's compulsion *(Read Jude 3)*

★ v. 3
- The meaning of the word needful is "to bear down upon, to compress." God literally pressured Jude to write this (see also 1 Cor. 9:16).
- He said we are to contend, but not be contentious. For the latter, see Titus 3:9. To contend involves both defense and offense. An excellent Old Testament example of this is found in Nehemiah 4:17-18. Note also what we are to contend for. It is the faith, that is, the entire Word of God. Furthermore, this faith (in the Greek language) was once for all delivered unto the saints. John would later warn all not to add to or take from this faith (see Rev. 22:18-19).

   C. Jude's concern— *"For there are certain men crept in unawares" (Jude 4)*.

★ v. 4 The word "unawares" is literally "having settled down alongside." (See also 2 Pet. 2:1.)

II. The Description of Apostasy

★ In no less than 14 terse and terrible terms, Jude describes the filthy fruit of apostasy. Before listing these, let us define what an apostate really is. S. Maxwell Coder writes: "An apostate has received light, but not life. He may have received, in some degree, the written Word; but he has not received the living Word, the Son of God." (See also 2 Thess. 2:10; Acts 8:13-23.) (*Jude, the Acts of the Apostates*, p. 21.)

   A. Apostates are ungodly (Jude 4).
   B. Twisters of God's grace (Jude 4)

C. Christ deniers (Jude 4)

D. Sensuous (Jude 8)

E. Flesh defilers (Jude 8)

F. Despisers of authority (Jude 8)

G. Ignorant critics (Jude 10)

H. Unreasoning animals (Jude 10)

I. Immoral fault-finders (Jude 16)

J. Arrogant to the core (Jude 16)

K. Lying flatterers for personal gain (Jude 16)

L. Divisive (Jude 19)

M. Worldly minded (Jude 19)

N. Devoid of the Spirit (Jude 19)

III. Historical Example and Causes of Apostasy. (See also Num. 14:22-23; Psa. 106:6-33; Heb. 3:8-19.)

A. The nation Israel, caused by unbelief *(Read Jude 5)*

★ **v. 5**
- Question: When and where did this take place? It began at Kadesh-barnea shortly after Israel had left Egypt for Palestine. Here at Kadesh they were influenced by the "mixed multitude" (an unsaved group of Egyptians and non-Hebrews) who had left Egypt with them, causing them to rebel against God's Word.
- Question: Does this mean that all the children of Israel became apostates, and, upon dying, went into eternal hell? It does not, for God never sends his people to hell. (See Exod. 3:7; 5:1; Deut. 33:29.) What it does mean is that it is tragically possible for even believers to become ensnared into the trap of apostasy and suffer for it without actually becoming apostates themselves. (See also 1 Cor. 10:1-12; Heb. 3:12, 18-19; 4:1.) The word *apollumi*, translated "destroyed" in this verse, is used elsewhere as "physical death" (Luke 15:17).

B. The fallen angels, caused by disloyalty. (See also Gen. 6:1-4; 1 Pet. 3:18-20; 2 Pet. 2:4; Rev. 12:3-4.)

C. The citizens of Sodom and Gomorrah, caused by sexual perversion. (See Gen. 13:13; 18:20-21; 19:4-13; 2 Pet. 2:6.) *(Read Jude 7)*

★ **v. 7** Some of the most depraved sexual perverts of ancient times lived in Sodom. God destroyed this cesspool of sin in Genesis 19. Let us now go back to the wicked angels of verse 6, for a similarity may exist between their sin and that of Sodom. Here we must consider two things:
- The fact of their sin—The Scriptures are explicit that there exist two kinds of fallen angels, the unchained and those chained. The unchained at present have access to high places and to the bodies of the unsaved (Eph. 6:12; Luke 8:27; Mark 1:23). These unchained angels will, of course, someday be judged by God. Their one main sin was that of following Satan in his foul rebellion against God (1 Cor. 6:3; Isa. 14:12-17; Ezek. 28:12-19). The chained are at present already incarcerated, as stated by both Peter (2 Pet. 2:4) and Jude. It was apparently to this place that certain unchained fallen angels on two separate occasions begged Christ not to send them "before their time" (Mark 1:24; Luke 8:31; Matt. 8:28).
- The nature of their sin. It is believed that the sin which led to this premature punishment of a limited number of fallen angels can be directly linked to Genesis 6. It will be remembered that in this chapter we read of the "sons of God" marrying the "daughters of men." Many believe this to be a reference to fallen angels (sons of God) actually mating with earthly women (daughters of men). Dr. Kenneth Wuest, Greek scholar, brings out the fact that the words in Jude "in like manner" are an adverbial accusative, referring back to the phrase "giving themselves over to fornication." In other words, the comparison is made between the sin of Sodom and the sin of the angels. What was the sin of Sodom? The answer, of course, was the sexual perversion. Wuest writes: "The word 'strange' is the translation of the Greek word *heteras* which means 'another of a different kind.' In committing this sin of fornication, the angels transgressed the limits

of their own kind, and invaded the realm of another order of being. The sin of Sodom was the transgressing of the male beyond the limitations imposed by God" (*Word Studies in First Peter*, p.103).
- One final thought concerning this passage and this subject. Jude is admonishing his readers to remember three well-known Old Testament examples of apostasy. These were:
  - The historical example of Israel's unbelief
  - The historical example of those angels who kept not their first estate
  - The historical example of Sodom's destruction
- Concerning the first example, the minds of Jude's readers would immediately go back to Numbers 14, the account of Israel's great rebellion at Kadesh-barnea. As they read the third example, they would at once remember the frightful passage recorded in Genesis 19, the fiery destruction of Sodom on the plains. But what other chapter would come to mind concerning the second historical example if Genesis 6 is ruled out? Note: At this point we have described for us representatives of each of the three great classes of God's creatures mentioned in Scripture:
  - Saved people
  - Angels
  - Unsaved people

> D. The devil, caused by pride and self-will. (See Isa. 14:12-15; Ezek. 28:11-19) *(Read Jude 9)*

★ **v. 9** In this passage Satan is indirectly brought in as an apostate.
- The source of this statement—It appears to have been quoted from a first-century book entitled *The Assumption of Moses*. A copy of this was found in 1861. This, of course, does not mean that the entire book was inspired simply because Jude takes one little part from it. Paul quoted from Titus 1:12. He also mentions the name of two of the magicians in Egypt, although their names are not mentioned in the Old Testament (2 Tim. 3:8). James also tells us that Elijah's prayer caused a three-and-a-half-year drought, a fact not recorded in the Old Testament account (James 5:17 cf. 1 Kings 17:1; 18:1).
- The theology of this statement—Why did Satan desire Moses' body? The Assumption of Moses gives two reasons why Moses should not have a decent burial.
  - Because Moses had formerly murdered an Egyptian.
  - Because he (Satan) was king of death and had a right to all dead bodies. Two other reasons have been offered by church theologians to explain this, both of which seem more reasonable than the above two.
  - Because Satan wanted the body to be found by Israel and worshiped as a sacred relic—We do know that the nation would later worship the serpent of brass he had once made (2 Kings 18:4).
  - Because Satan desired to keep Moses from appearing with Elijah on the Mount of Transfiguration (Matt. 17).
- The hero of this statement In Deuteronomy 34:5-6 we read, *"So Moses, the servant of the Lord, died there in the land of Moab, according to the word of the Lord. And he buried him in a valley in the land of Moab ... but no man knoweth of his sepulchre unto this day."* Apparently the "he" in this verse is reference to the archangel Michael, the hero of this statement. He is mentioned three times in the Old Testament (Dan. 10:13, 21; 12:1), and again in the New Testament, in addition to the reference in Jude (Rev. 12:7-9).

> E. Cain, caused by religious perversion (see Gen. 4:1-8; 1 John 3:12)—*"Woe unto them! for they have gone in the way of Cain" (Jude 11).*

★ **v. 11a** The way (apostasy) of Cain is described in Genesis 4:1-7. He brought a bloodless sacrifice to God. That is the way of the apostate liberals of our day. They look to culture instead of Calvary. (See 1 John 3:11-12.)

> F. Balaam, caused by greed for money (see Num. 22:15-17)—*"And ran greedily after the error of Balaam for reward" (Jude 11).*

LESSON 42: THE BOOK OF JUDE

✱ **v. 11b** Balaam was a money-grabbing false prophet mentioned in Numbers 22-25. Thus the error of Balaam was making merchandise of the gospel ministry. Many modern apostates do this.

> G. Korah, caused by rejection of divine authority (see Num. 16:1-3) — *"And perished in the gainsaying of Core"* (Jude 11).

✱ **v. 11c** In Numbers 16, Korah (Core) led a rebellion against Moses, the official spokesman for God. For this great sin he was sent down into the pit, the earth opening up its bowels and swallowing him. Present-day apostates speak evil against pastors, missionaries, Bible teachers, and other God-appointed men.

> **IV. The Metaphors of Apostasy (Jude 12-13)**

✱ "The more minutely we examine this great epistle, the most impressive becomes its delineation of the doctrine of apostasy. Jude has now covered the whole creation, from angels to men and brute beasts. There yet remains the realm of nature, and in five flashing inspired word-pictures he brings before us the earth, the air, the trees, the sea, and the starry heavens, to complete the panorama needed to provide the church with a magnificent final summary of conditions as they are to be in Christendom just before the scenes of Revelation are unveiled" (*Jude, the Acts of the Apostates*, p. 75).

> A. Hidden rocks — *"These men are those who are hidden reefs in your love-feasts when they feast with you without fear, caring for themselves"* (Jude 12, NASB). This describes the unseen dangers of apostasy.

✱ **v. 12a** We note that these rocks are hidden in the Christian love feasts, a reference to the Lord's table in the early days of the church. How are we to understand this? Paul explains it in 1 Corinthians 11:17-30. The first-century church had a full meal in connection with the Holy Communion. But some of these apostates (or perhaps believers influenced by apostasy) had joined themselves to these gatherings. As a result, some practiced gluttony and drunkenness, while others were actually going hungry. Divine judgment had taken many in death due to this.

> B. Waterless clouds — *"Clouds they are without water, carried about of winds"* (Jude 12). This describes the false claims of apostasy.

✱ **v. 12b** See also Proverbs 25:14. These clouds are said to be carried along by the winds. Doubtless the "winds" here are demonic activity. Apostates are the captives of Satan. For a refreshing contrast, see 2 Peter 1:21.

> C. Dead autumn trees — *"Autumn trees without fruit, doubly dead, uprooted"* (Jude 12, NASB). This describes the wasted efforts of apostasy.

✱ **v. 12c** The Greek phrase here is literally "late autumn trees," suggesting the fact that the great apostasy is to come as the autumn of the Church Age is waning and the winter of judgment is nigh. (See also Matt. 13:30; 15:30; Prov. 2:22.)

> A. Wandering stars — *"Wandering stars, to whom is reserved the blackness of darkness forever"* (Jude 13). This describes the aimless purpose of apostasy.

✱ **v. 13a** This is perhaps both the most descriptive and horrifying characteristic of apostasy. A quote from S. Maxwell Coder is appropriate here: "By way of contrast, true believers enjoy a lifelong love feast. They are borne along by the Holy Spirit, unmoved by winds of false doctrine. After a life of fruitfulness, they go home to be with Christ, in glory and honor. Forever afterward they dwell in light unutterable. Instead of being lifeless, dangerous rocks, they are living stones (1 Pet. 2:5).

Rather than waterless clouds they are sources of living water (John 7:38). Far from being dead trees, they are called 'trees of righteousness, the planting of the LORD' (Isa. 61:3). In contrast with raging waves, their peace is like a river and their righteousness as the waves of the sea (Isa. 48:18). Whereas wandering stars have reserved for them the blackness of darkness forever, true believers shall shine as the stars forever and ever" (Dan. 12:3) (*Jude, the Acts of the Apostates*, pp. 82-83).

> **V. The Judgment upon Apostasy (Jude 14-15)**
>   A. The messenger— *"And Enoch also, the seventh from Adam, prophesied of these, saying"* (Jude 14).
>   B. The message— *"Behold, the Lord cometh with ten thousands of his saints, to execute judgment upon all, and to convince all that are ungodly among them of all their ungodly deeds which they have ungodly committed, and all of their hard speeches which ungodly sinners have spoken against him"* (Jude 14-15).

✱ **v. 15**
  ■ The source of this statement— Around 100 B.C., a noncanonical book entitled *The Book of Enoch* was written. It contained 108 chapters. In 1773 a copy of this work was discovered. The Apostle Jude was inspired by God to take the words which are found here in verses 14-15 from this book.
  ■ The speaker of this statement—The book, of course, was not written by Enoch, but the statement here was apparently taken from his text. Both Enoch and Noah were fearless preachers of prophecy and righteousness. (See also 2 Pet. 2:5.) The amazing faith of this pre-flood prophet may be seen in that he predicted the second coming of Christ centuries before our Lord came the first time. Enoch thus predicts his coming in Genesis, while John proclaims it in Revelation (see Rev. 19:11-14). Both men refer to the same event.
    ● He comes with his saints (Col. 3:4; 1 Thess. 3:13).
    ● He comes to judge (Heb. 9:26-28; 2 Pet. 3:7).

> **VI. The Safeguards against Apostasy (Jude 20-25)**
>   A. The believer and himself
>   1. He is to build on the Word of God— *"But ye, beloved, building up yourselves on your most holy faith"* (Jude 20).
>   2. He is to pray with the Spirit of God— *"Praying in the Holy Ghost"* (Jude 20).
>   3. He is to keep in the love of God— *"Keep yourselves in the love of God"* (Jude 21).

✱ **v. 21a** In verse 1 Jude tells us we are kept for Jesus, but here he says we are to keep in God's love. How is this done? While the believer cannot escape the boundary of God's love (Psa. 139:7-12), he can withdraw himself from the full blessings of this love (John 15:9).

>   4. He is to look for the return of God— *"Looking for the mercy of our Lord Jesus Christ unto eternal life"* (Jude 21).
>   5. He is to testify to the glory of God— *"To the only wise God our Saviour, be glory and majesty, dominion and power, both now and ever. Amen"* (Jude 25).
>   B. The believer and the lost
>   1. Concerning those in great doubt— *"And have mercy on some, who are doubting"* (Jude 22, NASB).
>   2. Concerning those who are in great danger— *"Save others, snatching them out of the fire"* (Jude 23, NASB).
>   3. Concerning those who are in great depravity— *"And on some have mercy with fear, hating even the garment polluted by the flesh"* (Jude 23, NASB).

✱ **v. 23** S. Maxwell Coder writes: "In a brief manual for personal work, three groups of people are set before us:
  ■ Those who need compassionate tenderness, because sincere doubts trouble them.
  ■ Those requiring urgent boldness if they are to be snatched from an eternity of fiery judgment.

- Those who must be dealt with in cautious compassion lest the soul winner himself be contaminated by their sins" (*Jude, the Acts of the Apostates*, p. 113.)

C. The believer and the Lord
  1. What he does for us now— *"Now unto him that is able to keep you from falling" (Jude 24)*.
  2. What he will do for us later— *"And to present you faultless before the presence of his glory with exceeding joy" (Jude 24)*.

Five: PROPHECY

A study of the things to come:

➤ Revelation

LESSON 43
INTRODUCTION TO REVELATION

THE STORY HAS A HAPPY ENDING—THE BRIDEGROOM AND THE BRIDE ARE MARRIED AND LIVE HAPPILY IN A BEAUTIFUL CITY FOREVER.

  A. Revelation is the only prophetical book in the New Testament (in contrast to 17 books in the Old Testament).
  B. Revelation is the only book in all the Bible that begins by promising a special blessing on those who study it, and ends by promising a special curse on those who add to or take away from it.
  C. It was written by the Apostle John, who had already written four other New Testament books. They are: the Gospel of John, 1 John, 2 John, 3 John. The author had previously reached farther back into eternity than any other Bible writer (see John 1:1-3). In Revelation he reaches farther on into eternity than any other writer (see Rev. 21-22).
  D. Revelation may be compared to the book of *Daniel*.
    1. Concerning the indestructible Jewish nation (Dan. 3, 6; cf. Rev. 12).
    2. Concerning the ministry of the Antichrist (Dan. 3:1-7; 7:7-8, 24-25; 8:9-12, 23-25; 9:27; 11:36-45; cf. Rev. 13).
    3. Concerning the length of the tribulation (Dan. 9:24-27; cf. Rev. 11:2; 12:6,14; 13:5). Note, however, that Daniel was a sealed book (Dan. 12:9), whereas Revelation is not (Rev. 22:10).
  E. Revelation may be compared to the book of *Genesis*.
    1. In Genesis we read: *"In the beginning God created the heaven and the earth" (1:1)*. In Revelation we read: *"I saw a new heaven and a new earth" (21:1)*.
    2. In Genesis we see described the *first Adam* with his wife Eve in the Garden of Eden, reigning over the earth (1:27-28). In Revelation we see described the *last Adam* with his wife, the church, in the City of God, reigning over all the universe (21:9).
    3. In Genesis we are told: *"And the gathering together of the waters called he Seas" (1:10)*. In Revelation we are told: *"and there was no more sea" (21:1)*.
    4. In Genesis God created the sun and moon, the day and the night (1:5-16). In Revelation *"There shall be no night there" (22:5)*. *"And the city had no need of the sun, neither of the moon, to shine in it: for the glory of God did lighten it, and the Lamb is the light thereof" (21:23)*.
    5. In Genesis the Tree of Life is denied to sinful humans (3:22). In Revelation the Tree of Life *"yielded her fruit every month: and the leaves of the tree were for the healing of the nations" (22:2)*.
    6. In Genesis people hear God say: *"Cursed is the ground for thy sake" (3:17)*. In Revelation people will hear God say: *"And there shall be no more curse" (22:3)*.
    7. In Genesis Satan appears to torment human beings (3:1). In Revelation Satan disappears, himself to be tormented forever (20:10).
    8. In Genesis the old earth was punished through a flood (7:12). In Revelation the new earth shall be purified through a fire (2 Pet. 3:6-12; Rev. 21:1).
    9. In Genesis man's early home was beside a river (2:10). In Revelation our eternal home will be beside a river—*"And he shewed me a pure river of water of life, clear as crystal, proceeding out of the throne of God and of the Lamb" (22:1)*.

10. In Genesis the patriarch Abraham weeps for Sarah (23:2). In Revelation the children of Abraham will have God himself wipe away all tears from their eyes (21:4).
11. In Genesis God destroys an earthly city, wicked Sodom, from the sands (chapter 19). In Revelation, God presents a heavenly city, New Jerusalem, from the skies (21:1).
12. Genesis ends with a believer in Egypt, lying in a coffin (50:1-3). Revelation ends with all believers in eternity, reigning forever (22:5).

F. J. Vernon McGee writes: "This book is like a great union station where the great trunk lines of prophecy come in from other portions of Scripture. Revelation does not originate, but consummates. It is imperative to a right understanding of the book to be able to trace each great subject of prophecy from the first reference to the terminal" *(Reveling Through Revelation,* p. 4).

G. Some of the great subjects of prophecy that find their consummation here are:
1. The Lord Jesus Christ (Gen. 3:15; cf. Rev. 1:13; 12:5)
2. The church (Matt. 16:18; cf. Rev. 19:7-9)
3. The resurrection of saints (Dan. 12:2-3; 1 Thess. 4:13-18; 1 Cor. 15:51-52; Rev. 20:4-6)
4. The great tribulation (Deut. 4:30-31; Isa. 24; cf. Rev. 6-18)
5. Satan (Isa. 14:12-15; Ezek. 28:11-19; cf. Rev. 20:1-10)
6. The man of sin (2 Thess. 2:1-12; cf. Rev. 19:19-21)
7. False religion (Gen. 11:1-9; Matt. 13; cf. Rev. 17)
8. The times of the Gentiles (Dan. 2:37; Luke 21:23; cf. Rev. 18)
9. The second coming of Christ (Jude 14-15; cf. Rev. 19:11-16)

H. There are at least four main interpretations to this last book in the Bible:
1. It is pure fiction—This is the view of the agnostics.
2. It is allegorical—This says no part of the book may be taken literally. It is simply a symbolic account of the agelong struggle between good and evil. This is the view of most liberals.
3. It is historical—Here two kinds of history are in mind.
    a. Past history—This is often called the preterist theory. "Preterist" is from a Latin word that means "past."
    b. Continuous history—This interpretative viewpoint states that in Revelation there is a panorama of the history of the church from the days of John to the end of the age. It holds that the book has been in the process of being fulfilled throughout the whole Christian era.
4. It is prophetical—This view sees those events from chapter 4 onward as yet to be fulfilled. This view alone does justice to the book. Revelation, like all other books in the Bible, is to be taken in the plain, normal sense of the words. To do otherwise is to dishonor Christ, the divine Author. Dr. David L. Cooper once suggested: "When the plain sense of Scripture makes common sense, seek no other sense."

I. This book lists more titles for the Savior than does any other book in the Bible. Note but some of them:
1. Jesus Christ (1:1)
2. The faithful witness (1:5)
3. The first begotten of the dead (1:5)
4. The Prince of kings of the earth (1:5)
5. The Alpha and Omega (1:8)
6. The first and the last (1:8)
7. The Son of man (1:13)
8. The Son of God (2:18)
9. The keeper of David's keys (3:7)
10. The keeper of the keys of hell and death (1:18)
11. The Lion of the tribe of Judah (5:5)
12. The Root of David (5:5)

13. The slain Lamb (5:6)
14. The angry Lamb (6:16-17)
15. The tender Lamb (7:17)
16. Our Lord (11:8)
17. The man child (12:5)
18. The King of saints (15:3)
19. The faithful and true (19:11)
20. The Word of God (19:13)
21. The King of kings (19:16)
22. The Lord of lords (19:16)
23. The beginning and the end (22:13)
24. The bright and morning Star (22:16)

J. The numbers seven and 12 are predominant in the book of Revelation.
   1. The number seven
      a. Seven spirits (1:4)
      b. Seven stars (1:16)
      c. Seven lamps (4:5)
      d. Seven seals (5:1)
      e. Seven horns (5:6)
      f. Seven eyes (5:6)
      g. Seven angels (8:2)
      h. Seven trumpets (8:2)
      i. Seven thunders (10:3)
      j. Seven heads (12:3)
      k. Seven crowns (12:3)
      l. Seven plagues (15:1)
      m. Seven vials (17:1)
      n. Seven mountains (17:9)
      o. Seven kings (17:10)
   2. The number 12
      a. 12,000 from each of the 12 tribes (7:4-8)
      b. A crown of 12 stars (12:1)
      c. 12 gates (21:12)
      d. 12 angels (21:12)
      e. 12 foundations (21:14)
      f. 12,000 furlongs (21:16)

K. In essence, the book of Revelation contains:
   1. The last of three New Testament passages describing Balaam, the false prophet of the Old Testament (see Num. 22-25)—*Peter* speaks of the way of Balaam (2 Pet. 2:15). *Jude* speaks of the error of Balaam (Jude 11); *Revelation* speaks of the doctrine of Balaam (Rev. 2:14).
   2. The most detailed description of the ascended Christ in the Bible (1:9-20)
   3. The last words of Christ to his churches (Rev. 2-3)
   4. The most vivid description of heaven in all Scripture (Rev. 4-5; 21-22)
   5. The only description of four specialized angelic creatures (4:6-8)
   6. The most detailed account of heaven's activities (Rev. 4-5; 8:1-5; 11:19; 15:1-8; 19:1-10)
   7. The greatest prayer meeting of the unsaved in history (6:15-17)
   8. History's most severe judgments (chapters 6, 8, 10, 16)

9. The only New Testament listing of Israel's 12 tribes (7:4-8)
10. The world's greatest revival (7:9-17)
11. The only description of demons in the Bible (chapter 9)
12. The most descriptive account of the age-old battle between Satan and Israel (chapter 12)
13. The only biblical book to describe both the Antichrist and his false prophet (chapter 13)
14. The only biblical book to record the preaching of angels (14:6-7)
15. Scripture's most frightening descriptions of hell (14:10-11)
16. The most vivid account of Armageddon and the second coming (14:14-20; 16:16-21; 19:11-21)
17. The world's greatest earthquake and hailstorm (16:18-21)
18. The only biblical book to distinguish between the two Babylons:
    a. Religious Babylon is described in chapter 17.
    b. Political Babylon is described in chapter 18.
19. The only biblical book that gives the actual duration of the millennium (20:5)
20. The most detailed description of the great white throne judgment (20:11-15)
21. The most Old Testament quotations and allusions of any New Testament book
22. The last of three attempts by Satan to consolidate his religious system around a project:
    a. First attempt—A tower in Shinar (Gen. 11)
    b. Second attempt—A statue in Babylon (Dan. 3)
    c. Final attempt—A statue in the temple (Rev. 13)
23. It is the second of two biblical books offering a description of the Father (Dan. 7:9-10; Rev. 4:2-3).
24. It is the only biblical book to use that greatest of all praise words, Alleluia. (See 19:1,3-4,6.)
25. It is the only biblical book given almost in its entirety by vision form.
26. It is the only biblical book written from a small island (1:9).

L. The book of Revelation is the sixth longest New Testament book, and 24th longest biblical book, with 22 chapters, 404 verses, and 12,000 words. There are quotations or allusions from 32 Old Testament books in Revelation.

M. Great passages would include:
1. 1:5-8
2. 2:2-5
3. 3:2-3
4. 3:8-12
5. 3:20-21
6. 4:8-11
7. 5:9-13
8. 7:13-17
9. 11:15-18
10. 12:10-11
11. 15:3-4
12. 19:6-9
13. 19:11-16
14. 20:11-15
15. 21:1-4
16. 21:23-27
17. 22:1-4
18. 22:12-14
19. 22:16-17

OVERVIEW OF THE BOOK OF REVELATION

Part One: The Witnesses of the Lamb Instructed (Rev. 1-3)

   I. **The Servant of God**
      A. The source of the message
      B. The recorder of the message
      C. The nature of the message
      D. The promise of the message
      E. The recipients of the message
      F. The greetings in the message
         1. From the Father
         2. From the seven Spirits
         3. From the Son
      G. The theme of the message—Jesus Christ
         1. Who he is
         2. What he has done
         3. What he shall do
      H. The authority behind the message
      I. The place of the message
      J. The day of the message

  II. **The Son of God**
      A. The designation
      B. The description
      C. The devastation
      D. The declaration
      E. The dictation
      F. The delineation

 III. **The Churches of God**
      A. The church at Ephesus
         1. The counselor (what Jesus says about himself)
         2. The commendation (the good things he says about the church)
         3. The condemnation (the bad things he says about the church)
         4. The counsel (his advice to the church)
         5. The challenge (his encouragement to the church)
      B. The church at Smyrna
         1. The counselor
         2. The commendation
         3. The condemnation

    4. The counsel
    5. The challenge
  C. The church at Pergamos
    1. The counselor
    2. The commendation
    3. The condemnation
    4. The counsel
    5. The challenge
  D. The church at Thyatira
    1. The counselor
    2. The commendation
    3. The condemnation
    4. The counsel
    5. The challenge
  E. The church at Sardis
    1. The counselor
    2. The commendation
    3. The condemnation
    4. The counsel
    5. The challenge
  F. The church at Philadelphia
    1. The counselor
    2. The commendation
    3. The condemnation—None given
    4. The counsel
    5. The challenge
  G. The church at Laodicea
    1. The counselor
    2. The commendation—None given
    3. The condemnation
    4. The counsel
    5. The challenge

Part Two: The Worship of the Lamb Invited (Rev. 4-5)

 I. The Creation Hymn of Worship
  A. The place
  B. The persons
    1. The Father
    2. The 24 elders
    3. The seven spirits of God
    4. The four living creatures
  C. The praise
    1. The singers
    2. The song

II. The Redemption Hymn of Worship
  A. The proclamation
  B. The investigation
  C. The lamentation
  D. The manifestation
   1. The Lion of Judah
   2. The Lamb of Jehovah
  E. The adoration
   1. The song
   2. The singers

Part Three: The Wrath of the Lamb Invoked (Rev. 6-19)

I. He pours out the Seven Seal Judgments
  A. First Seal
  B. Second Seal
  C. Third Seal
  D. Fourth Seal
  E. Fifth Seal
   1. The altar for the saints
   2. The anger of the saints
   3. The answer to the saints
  F. Sixth Seal
   1. The destruction of earth's surface
   2. The darkening of earth's skies
   3. The despair of earth's sinners
  G. Interlude
   1. On earth
   2. In heaven
  H. Seventh Seal
   1. The silence before the trumpets
   2. The sounding of the trumpets
      a. First trumpet
      b. Second trumpet
      c. Third trumpet
      d. Fourth trumpet
      e. Fifth trumpet
      f. Sixth Trumpet
      g. Interlude
      h. Seventh trumpet

II. He allows the Devil to reign on earth
  A. The devil and Israel
   1. Satan's former hatred for the Jews

        2. The future hatred for the Jews
    B. The devil and the world
        1. His false son, the Antichrist
        2. His unholy spirit, the false prophet

III. He pours out the Seven Vial Judgments
    A. Those events preceding the vial judgments
        1. The song of the witnesses of God
        2. The messages of the angels of God
        3. The assurance of the Spirit of God
        4. The reaping of the harvest of God
        5. The praise of the victors of God
        6. The events in the temple of God
    B. Those events accompanying the vial judgments
        1. First vial judgment
        2. Second vial judgment
        3. Third vial judgment
        4. Fourth vial judgment
        5. Fifth vial judgment
        6. Sixth vial judgment
        7. Seventh vial judgment

IV. He destroys the world's religious systems
    A. The history of this harlot
        1. Depraved with the fifth of hell
        2. Decked with the wealth of the world
        3. Drunken with the blood of saints
    B. The future of this harlot
        1. To be teamed up (at first) with the Antichrist
        2. To be torn up (at last) by the Antichrist

V. He destroys the world's political and economic systems
    A. The designation of the city
    B. The denunciation of the city
    C. The degeneration of this city
        1. Godless materialism
        2. Arrogance and pride
        3. Immorality
        4. Demonism and false religions
        5. Drug peddling
        6. Slavery
        7. Blood shedding
    D. The devastation of the city
        1. The source of its destruction
        2. The means of its destruction
        3. The reaction to its destruction

   VI. He defeats his enemies at Armageddon
      A. The celebration in heaven
         1. Praising God for his wrath upon a cruel whore
         2. Praising God for his wedding to a chaste wife
      B. The confrontation on earth
         1. The appearance of heaven's King
         2. The attire of heaven's King
         3. The armies of heaven's King
         4. The action of heaven's King

Part Four: The Reign of the Lamb Instituted (Rev. 20)

   I. The Great Chain
      A. The prisoner
      B. The prison

   II. The Great Reign
      A. The resurrection of the just
      B. The rule of the just

   III. The Great Revolt
      A. The adversary
      B. The arrogance
      C. The attack
      D. The abyss

   IV. The Great Throne
      A. The Judge
      B. The judged
      C. The judgment

PART FIVE: THE WIFE OF THE LAMB INTRODUCED (REV. 21-22)

   I. Her Habitation—The Fabulous City
      A. Its purity
      B. Its wall
      C. Its gates
      D. Its size and shape
      E. Its foundation
      F. Its street
      G. Its light source
      H. Its river
      I. Its Tree of Life

    J. Its relationship to the earth
    K. Its worship center
    L. Its activities—What will we do in heaven?
        1. Learning about Christ
        2. Working for Christ
        3. Reigning with Christ

II. Her husband, the Faithful Spouse
    A. The blessings of the wife
        1. The comfort from Christ
        2. The character of Christ
        3. The counsel of Christ
        4. The concern of Christ
    B. The blunders of the writer
        1. First occasion
        2. Second occasion

THE BOOK OF REVELATION

PART ONE: The Witnesses of the Lamb Instructed (Rev. 1-3)

> I. **The Servant of God (Rev. 1:1-10)**—A heavenly message was revealed to a man on a lonely island some 20 centuries ago.
>   A. The source of the message *(Read Rev. 1:1)*
>   B. The recorder of the message *(Read Rev. 1:1b-2)*
>   C. The nature of the message *(Read Rev. 1:1)*
>   D. The promise of the message *(Read Rev. 1:3)*

✱ **1:3**
- This is the first of seven beatitudes in Revelation. See also:
  - *Revelation 14:13*—"Blessed are the dead which die in the Lord."
  - *Revelation 16:15*—"Blessed is he that watcheth."
  - *Revelation 19:9*—"Blessed are they which are called unto the marriage supper of the Lamb."
  - *Revelation 20:6*—"Blessed ... is he that hath part in the first resurrection."
  - *Revelation 22:7*—"Blessed is he that keepeth the sayings ... of this book."
  - *Revelation 22:14*—"Blessed are they that do his commandments."
- Note the phrase, "for the time is at hand." Here the word is not *chronos* (regular word for clock-time) but *kairos*, referring to a fixed season. This "fixed season" is that described by Daniel in 9:24-27. Someday a group of Jews will be able to rightly conclude by comparing both Daniel and Revelation, that this "fixed, determined season" is indeed at their very doorsteps.
- In addition to this, God is desirous to *"shew unto his servants things which must shortly be done"* (22:6b)—as God records time. See 2 Peter 3:9; Romans 16:20 (1:1). The word "shortly" can also mean rapidly. Note the following verses which reveal God's desire to lift back the curtain of the future for his saints.
  - *"Surely the Lord GOD will do nothing but he revealeth his secret unto his servants"* (Amos 3:7).
  - *"But there is a God in heaven that revealeth secrets"* (Dan. 2:28).
  - *"I thank thee, O Father, Lord of heaven and earth, because thou hast hid these things from the wise and prudent, and hast revealed them unto babes"* (Matt. 11:25).
  - *"Unto you it is given to know the mysteries of the kingdom of God"* (Luke 8:10).

> E. The recipients of the message—*"To the seven churches which are in Asia"* (Rev. 1:4)
> F. The greetings in the message
>   1. From the Father—*"Grace be unto you, and peace, from him which is, and which was, and which is to come"* (Rev. 1:4).
>   2. From the seven Spirits (or, sevenfold spirit, a possible reference to the Holy Spirit and his perfection)—(Rev. 1:4).
>   3. From the Son—*"And from Jesus Christ"* (Rev. 1:5)
> G. The theme of the message—Jesus Christ.
>   1. Who he is—*"Who is the faithful witness, and the first begotten of the dead, and the prince of the kings of the earth"* (Rev. 1:5a).
>   2. What he has done—*"Unto him that loved us, and washed us from our sins in his own blood, and hath made us kings and priests unto God and his Father; to him be glory and dominion for ever and ever. Amen"* (Rev. 1:5b-6).

> 3. What he shall do *(Read Rev. 1:7)*
> H. The authority behind the message *(Read Rev. 1:8)*
> I. The place of the message *(Read Rev. 1:9)*

✷ 1:9
- John now explains why he was on this isle. He was exiled there from about A.D. 86 to 96. Patmos was a rugged, volcanic island off the coast of Asia Minor. It was about ten miles long and six miles wide. He was probably put there by the Roman Emperor Domitian. Domitian was the brother of Titus (who destroyed the city of Jerusalem). Thus, God allowed one pagan to destroy his earthly city, but would use his brother to allow the heavenly new Jerusalem to first be described to humans. Marvelous and mysterious indeed are the workings of grace.
- John speaks of being in tribulation. There were at least four reasons why Rome persecuted Christians:
  - For political purposes—The Christian took no part in the pantheon (worship of many gods). In fact, Christians were regarded as atheists, for they worshiped no visible God.
  - For economic purposes—No money or sacrifices were forthcoming from believers to Roman idols.
  - For "moral" purposes—Christians were often looked upon as cannibals, for did they not secretly "eat the flesh and drink the blood" of their religious founder?
  - For scapegoat purposes—Nero attempted to blame various state problems upon the Christians living in Rome.

> J. The day of the message *(Read Rev. 1:10)*

✷ 1:10
- The time involved—"The Lord's day." This was probably on a Sunday (see Matt. 28:1; Acts 20:7; 1 Cor. 16:1-2).
- The trumpet involved—The trumpet call is heard many more times in this book (see 4:1; 8:2, 7-8, 10, 12; 9:1, 13; 11:15).

> **II. The Son of God (Rev. 1:11-20)**
> A. The designation *(Read Rev. 1:11)*
> B. The description *(Read Rev. 1:12-16)*

✷ 1:16 This is the only detailed description of the ascended Christ in the entire New Testament.

> C. The devastation *(Read Rev. 1:17)*

✷ 1:17 The effect of this dazzling sight upon John was nothing less than paralyzing. John had once walked with Christ for three years. He had witnessed his miracles and heard his sermons. He had leaned upon his breast in the Upper Room and watched him die on the cross. Finally he had rejoiced in his resurrection and viewed his ascension. But that had all happened some 60 years before. Now, he sees the resplendent Redeemer in all his blinding brightness and drops at his feet as though dead. John became struck as by the sun. But John's loving Lord quickly performed that tender task the apostle had so often seen him do. He reached out and touched the one in need. Compare Revelation 1:17 with the following Gospel accounts:
- *Matthew 8:14-15*—"And when Jesus was come into Peter's house, he saw his wife's mother laid, and sick of a fever. And he touched her hand, and the fever left her."
- *Matthew 9:27-30a*—"Two blind men followed him saying and crying, Thou Son of David, have mercy on us ... then touched he their eyes ... and their eyes were opened."
- *Matthew 17:7*—"And Jesus came and touched them [Peter, James, and John, who became terrified after watching his transfiguration on a mountain] and said, Arise, and be not afraid."
- *John 9:6*—"He spat on the ground and he anointed the eyes of the blind man."
- *Luke 5:12-13*—"And it came to pass when he was in a certain city, behold a man full of leprosy: who seeing Jesus fell on his face and besought him saying, Lord, if thou wilt, thou canst make me clean. And he put forth his hand and touched him."

- *Luke 7:14* — "And he came and touched the bier [of the widow's dead son in Nain] ... and said, Young man, I say unto thee, arise."
- *Luke 22:51* — "And he touched his ear [of one of his enemies whom Peter had wounded in the garden] and healed him."

D. The declaration *(Read Rev. 1:18)*

✱ 1:18

- Jesus assures John that "I am alive!" The real symbol of Christianity is not the cross, but the empty tomb. History relates the account of Julian the apostate, a nephew of the Roman Caesar Constantine. Julian was reared in a Christian home. But in his youth he renounced his faith and embraced paganism. When he became Emperor in A.D. 361, he sought to blot out Christianity. In the days of his cruel reign, one of his cronies said to a humble Christian, "And your Jesus—what is your carpenter of Nazareth doing now?" The Spirit filled believer quietly replied, "He is building a coffin for your emperor!" In 363, after he had reigned but two years, Julian died on the battlefield, facing a Persian army. One of the most famous incidents of history then followed. As they carried the Emperor off the field and as he lay dying, he lifted up his dimming eyes to heaven, and with a gasp, cried out, "O Galilean, thou hast conquered at last!"
- Jesus furthermore assures John that, *"I have the keys of hell and of death."* There are five keys mentioned in the New Testament and our Lord carries them all. The other four are:
  - The keys of the kingdom (Matt. 16:19)
  - The key of knowledge (Luke 11:52)
  - The key of the throne of David (Rev. 3:7)
  - The key to the bottomless pit (Rev. 9:1; 20:1)

E. The dictation *(Read Rev. 1:19)*

✱ 1:19

- This is the first of at least 11 instances where John is commanded to write down something.
  - He was to write concerning the seven churches in Asia Minor (2:1, 8, 12, 18; 3:1,7,14).
  - He was to write concerning the martyred dead (14:13).
  - He was to write concerning the marriage supper of the Lamb (19:9).
  - He was to write concerning the New Jerusalem (21:5).
- On one occasion, however, he was commanded not to write down what he had seen and heard (see 10:4).

F. The delineation *(Read Rev. 1:20)*

✱ 1:20

- The seven stars were the angels of the seven churches. J. Vernon McGee writes: "Angels can be either human or divine — the word here is messenger. It could refer to a member of the angelic host of heaven; it could refer to a ruler or teacher of the congregation. Personally, I think that it refers to the local pastors. It is good to hear a pastor being called an angel — sometimes we are called other things!" (*Reveling Through Revelation*, p. 1.)
- The seven lampstands were seven specific churches. Upon hearing this, John could understand why he saw Christ dressed the way he was. He is now appearing as our great High Priest. The golden lampstands speak of his present work in heaven in maintaining the lights. Aaron lighted the lamps in the tabernacle, put them out with snuffers, filled them with oil, and trimmed the wicks. Christ now does this with his present lights, which are the local churches.

III. The Churches of God (Rev. 2-3)

✶ At the time Revelation was written (around A.D. 95-100) there may have existed well over 100 separate and independent local churches in the world. Paul had, of course, personally planted dozens of churches by himself. Other apostles would doubtless have done the same thing. But out of the many, Christ chose seven representative churches and addressed himself to these. It has been suggested that the listing of these seven appears in the sacred record to accomplish at least the following purposes:
- The contemporary purpose—That Christ had a direct message to seven literal churches existing at that time.
- The composite purpose—That these messages are meant to be applied by all churches existing in all ages.
- The chronological purpose—That the characteristics of these churches serve as a prophetical preview of the seven great periods in Christendom from Pentecost to the Rapture. A suggested outline of this predictive panorama may be seen as follows:
  - Ephesus (A.D. 30-300)—Name means "desirable": The Apostolic church
  - Smyrna (100-313)—Name means "myrrh": The martyr church
  - Pergamos (314-590)—Name means "marriage": The compromising church
  - Thyatira (590-1517)—Name means "continual sacrifice": The Roman Catholic church
  - Sardis (1517-1700)—Name means "remnant": The Reformation church
  - Philadelphia (1700-1900)—Name means "brotherly love": The revival church
  - Laodicea (1900-Rapture)—Name means "people's rights": The worldly church In Revelation 2-3, the Savior speaks his mind to his churches. It is therefore in these chapters (and not in Matt. 28 or Acts 1) that the final words of Christ to the church are recorded.

A. The church at Ephesus (Rev. 2:1-7).

✶ J. Vernon McGee describes Ephesus for us: "Ephesus was the chief city of the province of Asia. It was called 'the Vanity Fair of Asia.' It was both the religious and commercial center of that entire area which influenced both east and west-Europe and Asia. The temple of Diana was there, which was one of the seven wonders of the ancient world, being the largest Greek temple ever constructed (418 feet by 240 feet). There were over 100 external columns about 56 feet in height, of which 36 were hand-carved. It was built over a marsh on an artificial foundation of skins and charcoal so that it was not affected by earthquakes. The doors were of cypress wood; columns and walls were of Parian marble; the staircase was carved out of one vine from Cyprus. The temple served as the bank of Asia and was the depository of vast sums of money. It was an art gallery displaying the masterpieces.... Behind a purple curtain was the lewd and crude image of Diana, the goddess of fertility. She was many-breasted, carried a club in one hand and a trident in the other" (*Reveling Through Revelation*, p. 19). Ephesus was a large city with a population of 225,000 and possessed a huge harbor.

1. The counselor (what Jesus says about himself) *(Read Rev. 2:1)*
2. The commendation (the good things he says about the church) *(Read Rev. 2:2-3, 6)*

✶ **2:6**
- Our Lord begins by making a statement that will be repeated to every one of the seven churches. The statement is, *"I know thy works"* (2:2, 9, 13, 19; 3:1, 8, 15).
- According to the Savior:
  - Ephesus was an evangelistic church.
  - It was a patient church (unlike the Christians Peter wrote to; see 2 Pet. 1:6).
  - It was a separated church (unlike the Corinthian church; cf. 1 Cor. 5).
  - It was an orthodox church.
  - It was a persecuted but persistent church (unlike the Christians in the book of Hebrews; see Heb. 12:1-15).
  - It was a democratic church—*"Thou hatest the deeds of the Nicolaitanes, which I also hate"* (2:6). The word "Nicolaitanes" comes from two Greek words, *nikao*, meaning "to conquer," and *laos*, meaning "people." Many

believe John was speaking here to the growing distinction between clergy and laity. Thus: This church was zealous, long-suffering, orthodox, separated, and reliable.

> 3. The condemnation (the bad things he says about the church) *(Read Rev. 2:4)*

✶ **2:4**
- It is tragically possible to be so busy working for Christ that one neglects Christ. God did not create Adam to evangelize the world with the gospel, or to build the largest Sunday school in Eden (as important as these may be), but to fellowship with his Creator.
- The spiritual temperature of the church had apparently cooled drastically since Paul had written his epistle to them, observing their *"faith in the Lord Jesus, and love unto all the saints" (Eph. 1:15)*. (See also Eph. 3:14-19.)

> 4. The counsel (his advice to the church) *(Read Rev. 2:5)*

✶ **2:5**
- In essence, the church was to do three things:
  - Remember—Their heads were to be given over to Christ.
  - Repent—Their hearts were to be given over to Christ.
  - Repeat—Their hands were to be given over to Christ. Unless this was done, fearful results would transpire. "I will come unto thee quickly, and will remove thy candlestick out of his place" (2:5).
- The child of God need never pray the words of Psalm 51:11, *"Cast me not away from thy presence, and take not thy holy spirit from me."* However, every Bible-believing local church should often repeat these words. There is absolutely no eternal security for any local church presented in the Bible. A believer can never fall from grace, but his church can. History records the sad fact that Christ did indeed later remove the lampstand of the church in Ephesus. It has been gone for centuries, smothered by the Muslims. There is today no local church within miles of Ephesus.

> 5. The challenge (his encouragement to the church) (Rev. 2:7)

✶ **2:7** This tree, once given to Adam, disappears after his sin (Gen. 3:24). Here (Rev. 2:7) it is mentioned again for the first time. (See also Rev. 22:2, 14.) The definition and method of overcoming is given in 1 John 5:4-5.

> B. The church at Smyrna (Rev. 2:8-11)

✶ Facts about the city of Smyrna:
- It was some 40 miles north of Ephesus.
- It was a splendid city of rare beauty on a fine bay.
- It was on a direct trade route from India and Persia to Rome.
- It was celebrated for its schools of science and medicine, for its handsome buildings and wide paved streets.
- The temple of Bacchus, god of wine, was there.
- Many apostate Jews lived here.
- It was the traditional birthplace of Homer.

> 1. The counselor *(Read Rev. 2:8)*
> 2. The commendation *(Read Rev. 2:9)*

✶ 2:9
- They had suffered poverty for Christ (but God saw them as rich). Many believers doubtless belonged to the various city labor guilds of that day prior to their conversion. But because of their newfound faith they apparently had lost the right to guilds. Many may have gone bankrupt. (See also Matt. 6:20; 2 Cor. 6:10.)
- They had suffered persecution for Christ (but God promised them a reward). Dr. Charles Ryrie writes: "The instigators of the persecution were apostate Jews who were in reality instruments of Satan. At the martyrdom of Polycarp (disciple of John the Apostle) in 158, these Jews eagerly assisted by gathering on the Sabbath wood and faggots for the fire in which he was burned." (See also Rom. 2:28-29; John 8:44; Rev. 3:9.) (Revelation, p. 23).

> 3. The condemnation (none given)
> 4. The counsel *(Read Rev. 2:10)*

✶ 2:10
- Jesus warns his church that they would have "tribulation ten days" (2:10). He may have referred to an actual ten-day period of fearful bloodletting. Or he might have meant the ten intensive periods of persecution by ten Roman Emperors. It has been estimated that at least five million saints were martyred during this period. This would be over 100 million, in proportion to today's world population.
- These ten Roman persecution periods are:
  - Nero (64-68)—Killed Peter and Paul.
  - Domitian (81-90)—Thought Christianity was atheistic. Killed thousands of believers. Banished John to Patmos.
  - Trajan (98-117)—Was the first to pass laws against Christianity. Burned Ignatius at the stake.
  - Pius (137-161)—Killed Polycarp, disciple of John.
  - Marcus Aurelius (161-180)—Thought Christianity an absurd superstition. Beheaded the great writer and defender of the faith, Justin Martyr.
  - Severus (193-211)—Killed Origen's father.
  - Thracian (235-238)—Brutal barbarian; commanded all Christian leaders to die.
  - Decius (249-251)—Determined to exterminate Christianity.
  - Valerian (253-260)—Killed Cyprian, Bishop of Carthage.
  - Diocletian (284-305)—Last and most severe persecution. For ten years believers were hunted in caves and forests. They were burned, thrown to wild beasts, and put to death by every torture cruelty could devise. But Diocletian's own wife and daughter accepted Christ.

> 5. The challenge *(Read Rev. 2:11)*
> C. The church at Pergamos (Rev. 2:12-17)

✶ Facts about the city of Pergamos:
- It was the political capital city of Asia, some 75 miles north of Ephesus.
- It boasted one of the finest libraries of antiquity which contained some 200,000 volumes. This library was later given by Mark Antony to Cleopatra.
- It was in this city that parchment was first used.

> 1. The counselor *(Read Rev. 2:12)*
> 2. The commendation *(Read Rev. 2:13)*

✶ 2:13
- They had kept the faith, even though living in the very city Satan had chosen as his temporary headquarters. For centuries the devil had carried on his empire from Babylon. (See Gen. 11:1-9; Dan. 5.) But when that nation fell he apparently

transferred it (at least for awhile) to Pergamos. The city worshiped, among other objects, a living serpent. Satan will later move his capital back to Babylon (Rev. 17-18).
- Many in Pergamos had been martyred for their faith. One is mentioned here, Antipas by name. His name never appears in any other historical record. But God knew all about this anonymous humble believer who lived and died for Christ some 20 centuries ago. (See John 10:3; 2 Tim. 2:19.)

> 3. The condemnation
>   a. The church was tolerating the doctrine of Balaam *(Read Rev. 2:14)*

✱ **2:14** Some were practicing the doctrine of Balaam. Balaam was a false Old Testament prophet who attempted to put a curse on the nation Israel (Num. 22:1-25:9). The New Testament refers to his doctrine, his error and his way.
- His way (2 Pet. 2:15) — His way was his covetousness. Balaam's services could be readily bought.
- His error (Jude 11) — He wrongly supposed a holy God would be forced to curse sinful Israel.
- His doctrine (Rev. 2:14) — He concluded that if you can't curse them, then you can corrupt them through immorality and idolatry. Some were practicing the doctrine of the Nicolaitanes (2:15). This philosophy had already been condemned by Christ in the church at Ephesus (2:6). However, we see that what was once deeds in the first church had now become hardened into doctrine.

> b. The church was tolerating the doctrine of the Nicolaitanes *(Read Rev. 2:15)*
> 4. The counsel *(Read Rev. 2:16)*
> 5. The challenge *(Read Rev. 2:17)*

✱ **2:17** Charles Ryrie writes: "The meaning of the white stone with the new name written is derived from either one or both of two customs of the day. The first was that of judges who determined a verdict by placing in an urn a white and black pebble. If the white one came out it meant acquittal; thus the white stone would mean the assurance that there is no condemnation to those who are in Christ Jesus. The other custom was the wearing of amulets, a good luck charm worn around the neck. If this is the reference, then the stone is the Lord's way of reminding the people that they had Him and needed no other thing" (*Revelation*, p. 25).

> D. The church at Thyatira (Rev. 2:18-29)

✱ Facts about the city of Thyatira:
- It was 35 miles southeast of Pergamos.
- The city may have been founded by Alexander the Great around 300 B.C.
- It was a union city, and headquarters for the trade guilds, such as tanners, potters, weavers, dyers, and robemakers.
- Lydia, the first convert of Paul in Europe (Acts 16:14), was a native of this city. Today it has a population of 25,000.

> 1. The counselor *(Read Rev. 2:18)*
> 2. The commendation *(Read Rev. 2:19)*
> 3. The condemnation *(Read Rev. 2:20)*

✱ **2:20** God's main objection to this church centered on the fact that they were allowing the ministry of a false prophetess aptly named Jezebel.
- Her Old Testament counterpart — This Jezebel was the pagan murderous wife of King Ahab (1 Kings 16:28-19:21; 21:1-29; 2 Kings 9:22-37).
- Her sin in the church

- She was teaching men, which was forbidden (see 1 Tim. 2:12-14).
- She was teaching immorality and idolatry.

> 4. The counsel *(Read Rev. 2:24-25)*
> 5. The challenge *(Read Rev. 2:26-28)*
> E. The church at Sardis (Rev. 3:1-6)

★ Facts about the city of Sardis:
- It was 30 miles south of Thyatira and the capital of Lydia.
- The city was thought to be impregnable, but Cyrus the Great captured it by following a secret path up the cliff.
- Coins were first minted here.
- It was noted for its great wealth, the chief of which was its flourishing carpet industry.

> 1. The counselor *(Read Rev. 3:1)*
> 2. The commendation *(Read Rev. 3:4)*

★ **3:4** God always has his remnant in every church and church age (see 1 Kings 19:10, 18; Rom. 11:5).

> 3. The condemnation *(Read Rev. 3:1)*

★ **3:1** J. Vernon McGee observes: "This is a picture of Protestantism. The great truths which were recovered in the Reformation have been surrendered by a compromising church. Although the great denominations and churches still repeat by rote the creeds of the church; in mind, heart and life they have repudiated them. Imposing programs, elaborate rituals, and multiplication of organizations have been substituted for the Word of God and real spiritual life. There is activity, but no actions, motion without movement, promotion without progress, and program without power. Although the outward form remains, the living creature has vacated the shell" (*Reveling Through Revelation*, p. 28). The word to Sardis proves that the Reformation was not a restoration to the New Testament ideal church.

> 4. The counsel *(Read Rev. 3:3)*
> 5. The challenge *(Read Rev. 3:5)*

★ **3:5** Here the challenge is twofold to the overcomers:
- His name would remain in the Book of Life. Often this book is referred to in both Old and New Testament (Exod. 32:32; Dan. 12:1; Psa. 69:28; Luke 10:20; Phil. 4:3; Heb. 12:23; Rev. 3:5; 13:8; 17:8; 20:12, 15; 21:27; 22:19). Whatever else may be involved here, these verses do not teach that a saved person can ever be lost. In fact, quite the opposite, for many prove one cannot be lost because each saved person's name is written in this book. (See especially Dan. 12:1; Luke 10:20; Rev. 13:8; 17:8; 21:27.)
- His name would be confessed by Jesus before the Father (Luke 12:8-9).

LESSON 44

> F. The church at Philadelphia (Rev. 3:7-13)

✶ Facts about the city of Philadelphia:
- It was built as a center of Greek culture around 200 B.C.
- It is located some 30 miles southeast of Sardis.
- Philadelphia was celebrated for its excellent wine.
- The city had a large Jewish population.
- It was destroyed by an earthquake in A.D. 17, but soon rebuilt by Tiberius Caesar.

> 1. The counselor *(Read Rev. 3:7)*

✶ **3:7** J. Vernon McGee writes the following concerning Christ's description here: "Christ reminds them that He is holy—holy at His birth (Luke 1:35), holy at His death (Acts 2:27), and holy in His present priestly office (Heb. 7:26). He is likewise true (John 1:9; 14:6; 15:1). 'True' means genuine with an added note of perfection and completeness. Moses did not give the true bread. See John 6:32-35. He also has the Key of David (see Isa. 22:22). This is different from the keys of hades and death (1:18). This speaks of His regal claims as the Ruler of this universe (Luke 1:32). He will sit on the throne of David in the Millennium, but today He is sovereign" (*Reveling Through Revelation*, p. 31).

> 2. The commendation *(Read Rev. 3:8)*

✶ **3:8** This is the first of four special doors in Revelation. These are:
- The door of service (3:8). (See also Acts 14:27; 1 Cor. 16:9; 2 Cor. 2:12; Col. 4:3.)
- The door of the human heart (Rev. 3:20)
- The door of Rapture (4:1)
- The door of the second coming (19:11)

> 3. The condemnation—None given
> 4. The counsel *(Read Rev. 3:11)*
> 5. The challenge
>   a. To be given power *(Read Rev. 3:9)*

✶ **3:9** *"The synagogue of Satan"*—Both Jesus and Paul had previously spoken out concerning this group. (See John 8:44; Matt. 23:1-35; 1 Thess. 2:14-16.)

>   b. To be given protection *(Read Rev. 3:10)*
>   c. To be given privilege *(Read Rev. 3:12)*

✶ **3:12** This is the first mention in the Scriptures of that shining city in the stars, our ultimate and eternal home, the New Jerusalem. (See also 21:2.)

> G. The church at Laodicea (Rev. 3:14-22)

✱ Facts about the city of Laodicea: "These seven churches lie within a great arc beginning with Ephesus, swinging upward and eastward through Smyrna and Pergamum and back down to Laodicea. Thus, this last city is about ninety miles due east of Ephesus and about forty-five miles southeast of Philadelphia. The name of the town means 'judgment of the people" (*Reveling Through Revelation*, p. 31).
- This city was founded by Antiochus II and named after his wife. It was a very common name for women.
- It was a banking center and possessed immense wealth.
- It was graced with resplendent temples and theaters.
- An excellent and well-known medical school was built there.
- The city was famous for its eye salve called cellyrium.
- It was noted for the manufacture of rich garments of black glossy wool. Several mineral streams were located nearby.

1. The counselor *(Read Rev. 3:14)*

✱ 3:14 We now move from the best of the seven churches, Philadelphia, to the worst, Laodicea. While nothing bad was said about the former, nothing good is said about this one. John Phillips writes: "He introduces Himself to Laodicea as 'the beginning of the creation of God,' or as the margin of the American Standard version puts it, 'the origin of the creation of God.' He it was who flung the stars into space, plowed out the basins of the sea, reared against the skyline of the world the mighty Himalayan range. Not a blade of grass grows without His permission nor a speck of dust moves. He is the origin of the creation of God, the all-controlling one of the dynamic Christ" (*Exploring Revelation*, p. 89).

2. The commendation (none given)
3. The condemnation
   a. The indictment of the Lord *(Read Rev. 3:15-16)*

✱ 3:16 The word "spue" or "spew" is the Greek *emeo*, meaning "to vomit." Charles Ryrie writes: "Near Laodicea were hot mineral springs whose water could be drunk only if very hot. When lukewarm it became nauseating" (*Exploring Revelation*, p. 31). According to Christ's words here, he apparently has more respect for fiery hot fanaticism or icy cold formalism than for lifeless and lame lukewarmness.

   b. The ignorance of the Laodiceans *(Read Rev. 3:17)*
4. The counsel *(Read Rev. 3:18-19)*
5. The challenge *(Read Rev. 3:20-21)*

✱ 3:21 J. Vernon McGee writes: "His invitation is to the evening meal, the last call for dinner. It is an invitation to come to Him before the night of the Great Tribulation" (*Reveling Through Revelation*, p. 36). Millions of Christians have doubtless viewed Holman Hunt's famous picture of Christ as the Light of the World. Here the artist has depicted Jesus wearing a crown of thorns and standing outside a door which represents the human heart. This painting now hangs in Saint Paul's Cathedral in London. Phillips writes: "When it was first displayed, critics came to comment on the work. One of them turned to the painter and said, 'Mr. Hunt, you have painted a masterpiece, but you have made one very serious mistake. You have painted a door without a handle.' 'That is no mistake,' replied the artist. 'The handle is on the inside'" (*Exploring Revelation*, p. 93).

Dr. John Walvoord aptly summarizes the Savior's words to his people here in Revelation 2-3. "The letters to the seven churches are a remarkably complete treatment of problems that face the church today. The recurring dangers of losing their first love (2:4), of being afraid of suffering (2:10), doctrinal defection (2:14-15), moral departure (2:20), spiritual deadness (3:1-2), not holding fast (v. 11), and lukewarmness (vv. 15-16) are just as prevalent today as they were in first century churches. Because these letters come from Christ personally, they take on significance as God's final word of exhortation to the church down through the centuries. The final appeal is to all individuals who will hear. People in churches today would do well to listen" (*Bible Knowledge Commentary*, New Testament Volume, p. 942).

PART TWO: The Worship of the Lamb Invited (Rev. 4-5)

This section is in reality the story of two songs of praise.

> **I. The Creation Hymn of Worship (Rev. 4)**
> A. The place *(Read Rev. 4:1)*

★ **4:1** John begins this new section with the words "after this" (4:1). The Greek phrase is *meta tauta*, "after these things." What things? The context would suggest that he refers to the Rapture which occurs between chapters 3 and 4. The *meta tauta* phrase both opens and closes this verse in the original language. The church has been referred to some 19 times in the first three chapters. It now completely drops from the pages of the book until the end of the tribulation in Revelation 19. The only godly group Satan can find to torment during the tribulation is the nation Israel. Only two conclusions may be reached from these facts.
- The church has been wiped out, through persecution by Satan. This concept is, of course, totally unscriptural (see Matt. 16:18).
- The church has been taken out, through the Rapture, by Christ. Various New Testament passages would strongly support this (see 1 Cor. 15:51; 1 Thess. 4:16). Now John:
  - Sees a door (John 10:9)
  - Hears a trumpet (1 Thess. 4:16)

> B. The persons
> 1. The Father *(Read Rev. 4:2-3)*

★ **4:3** John now becomes the second of two recorded human beings who are allowed a glimpse of that dazzling kingdom in the sky called heaven. (For the other, see 2 Cor.12:2-4.) He sees the glory of the Father upon the throne (4:2-3). Revelation is a throne book, the word being used 45 times, as compared with only 15 other occurrences of the word in the entire New Testament. John could distinguish no form or give no description of the awesome One upon this throne, save to say, *"He that sat was to look upon like a jasper and a sardine stone"* (4:3). Here the jasper, a white stone, and the sardine, a fiery red stone, may refer to God's two basic characteristics, his glory and his grace. These were also the first and last stones among the 12 that the Old Testament high priest bore upon his breastplate. These stones represented the 12 tribes of Israel, arranged according to the births of the 12 sons of Jacob (Exod. 28). Reuben was the first tribe, which name meant "Behold a son"; and Benjamin was the last, meaning "Son of my right hand." This may be God's way of reminding all creatures throughout all eternity of:
- The incarnation of Christ (his humanity) via the jasper stone, Reuben ("Behold a son").
- The exaltation of Christ (his deity) via the sardine stone, Benjamin ("Son of my right hand").

> 2. The 24 elders *(Read Rev. 4:4)*

★ **4:4**
- He sees 24 elders with golden crowns (4:4). These 24 may consist of a special representative body of both Old Testament and New Testament saints (1 Chron. 24:3-5, 18; Luke 1:5-9; Rev. 21:12-14). The Greek tells us they are all wearing *stephanos* crowns (martyr crowns) rather than *diadems* (monarch crowns). Thus they must be human beings rather than angels. John saw these thrones being set up—not "cast down," as Daniel saw them (see Dan. 7:9). They were empty in Daniel's day. John sees them occupied now.
- He hears lightnings and thunderings, which means that the awful storm of the great tribulation is about to unleash its fury (4:5). In the Old Testament at Mount Sinai, God thundered when he gave his Law. Now he does the same when he prepares to judge people for breaking that Law.

> 3. The seven spirits of God *(Read Rev. 4:5)*

✱ **4:5** He sees *"seven lamps of fire burning before the throne, which are the seven spirits of God" (4:5).* Several suggestions have been offered to explain this verse:
- It refers to the earthly ministry of Christ as prophesied in Isaiah 11:1-3.
- It refers to the sevenfold ministry of the Holy Spirit (restraining, convicting, regenerating, sealing, baptizing, indwelling, filling).
- It refers to the seven angels of judgment later spoken of in Revelation 8:1-6.

> 4. The four living creatures
>   a. The description of these creatures *(Read Rev. 4:6-7)*

✱ **4:7**
- He sees a crystal sea of glass (Rev. 4:6). Dr. Donald Barnhouse has written concerning this sea: "Before the throne there was a glassy sea, like crystal. The concordance immediately takes us to the temple built by Solomon after the model of the tabernacle. 'And he made a molten sea, ten cubits from one brim to the other; it was round all about and his height was five cubits' (1 Kings 7:23). This great basin, fifteen feet in diameter, was supported on the backs of twelve oxen of brass, facing outward. Here the priests came for their cleansing. Each time before they entered the holy place they stopped for the cleansing ceremony. But thank God the laver will be turned to crystal. The day will come when none of the saints will ever need confession. One of the greatest joys in the anticipation of Heaven is that the laver is of crystal. I shall never have to go to the Heavenly Father again to tell Him I have sinned. I shall never have to meet that gaze of Christ that caused Peter to go out and weep bitterly. The laver is of crystal only because I and all the saints of the ages will have been made like unto the Lord Jesus Christ" *(Revelation, an Expository Commentary,* p. 94).
- He sees and hears the testimony of four special angelic creatures (4:6-8). The Greek for "wild beast" is *therion*. But here the word used is *zoa* (root word for zoology), meaning "living creatures." Who are these four living creatures? J. Vernon McGee writes: "These creatures, of the highest intelligence, are in God's presence. They resemble the Cherubim of Ezekiel 1:5-10; 10:20 and the seraphim of Isaiah 6:2-3. Are they a new order of creatures in heaven that have not been revealed before in Scripture?" *(Reveling Through Revelation,* p. 43). What is their purpose? Perhaps to remind all creatures throughout all eternity of the blessed earthly and heavenly ministry of Christ. This is suggested by their appearance:
  - The first was like a lion. He communicates the office of Christ as King as seen in the Gospel of Matthew.
  - The second was like a calf. He communicates the office of Christ as a servant as seen in the Gospel of Mark.
  - The third was like a man. He communicates the humanity of Christ as seen in the Gospel of Luke.
  - The fourth was like an eagle. He communicates the deity of Christ as seen in the Gospel of John.

>   b. The duties of these creatures *(Read Rev. 4:8)*
> C. The praise
>   1. The singers *(Read Rev. 4:9-10)*
>   2. The song *(Read Rev. 4:11)*

✱ **4:11** It may be said that everything God has ever done, is doing, or will do, can be placed in one of two basic categories, his work in creation (Gen. 1-2), and his work in redemption (Gen. 3-Rev. 22). Throughout eternity these two works will be celebrated in song by the redeemed. Here is the first glorious hymn, thanking God for his work in creation. For the second song, see Revelation 5:9.

> **II. The Redemption Hymn of Worship (Rev. 5)**
>   A. The proclamation *(Read Rev. 5:1-2)*

✱ **5:2** What is this book (actually a rolled-up scroll), sealed so securely with seven seals? Whatever it contained, the scroll was extremely important, for history informs us that under Roman law all legal documents pertaining to life and death were to be sealed seven times. A number of theologians believe that this is actually the legal title deed to the earth. Thus the angel's proclamation was, in effect, "Who is worthy to reclaim the earth's title deed? Who is able to pour out the seven-sealed judgment to purify this planet, and to usher in the long-awaited golden-age millennium?" Who indeed was worthy? (See also Jer. 32:6-16.)

> B. The investigation *(Read Rev. 5:3)*

✷ **5:3** Let us follow the angel as he begins his three-fold search.
- The search in heaven—Was there any among the redeemed worthy to claim the earth's title deed? There was not.
  - Adam originally possessed this title deed (Gen. 1:28-29), but was cheated out of it by the devil (Gen. 3:1-19).
  - Noah, the hero of the flood, subsequently became the drunkard of the vineyard, thus disqualifying himself (Gen. 6-9).
  - Abraham, the father of Israel, backslid and went to Egypt temporarily (Gen. 12).
  - David, the man after God's own heart (1 Sam. 16:7), later broke God's heart through lust and murder (2 Sam. 11).
  - John the Baptist, the forerunner of Christ, in a moment of weakness doubted that same Messiah (Matt. 11:3).
  - Peter, the "rock," denied his Lord in the hour of need (Matt. 26:70).
  - Paul, perhaps the greatest Christian who ever lived, compromised his testimony (Acts 21).
- The search on earth—Who could accomplish in the sinful environment of earth what no man could achieve even in the sinless environment of heaven? Preachers and priests might minister on the earth, and kings rule over sections of it, but claim it they could not.
- The search under the earth (in Hades). If no saint or angel could purify this earth, then certainly no sinner or demon would, even if this were possible.

> C. The lamentation *(Read Rev. 5:4)*

✷ **5:4** Why did John weep? Perhaps because (among other reasons) he realized that the ultimate resurrection and glorification of his own body was directly connected with the removal of the curse placed upon this earth. (See Rom. 8:17-23.) This passage marks the final instance of a believer weeping. Sorrow, sufferings, and death have combined to carve out an ocean of human tears since Adam's tragic rebellion against God.

> D. The manifestation
>   1. The Lion of Judah *(Read Rev. 5:5)*
>   2. The Lamb of Jehovah
>   a. His appearance *(Read Rev. 5:6)*

✷ **5:6** "John turned to behold a Lion. But instead of a shaggy mane and gaping jaws and dreadful teeth, he saw a Lamb! Was there ever a more dramatic moment in the history of the universe? The Lion was none other than the Lamb!" (*Exploring Revelation*, p. 106). Who is this heavenly Hero who so boldly removes the scroll from the Father's right hand? We need not speculate for one second about his identity, for he is the Lord Jesus Christ himself. The proof is overwhelming.
- He has the characteristics of a lamb. Our Lord is referred to as a lamb 29 times in the New Testament. In all but one instance (1 Pet. 1:19) it is the Apostle John who employs this title. Furthermore,
  - It is a pet lamb. There are two words for "lamb" in the Greek New Testament. One is *amnos* (a lamb in general) and the other is *arnion* (a special household pet lamb). Here in Revelation 5:6 the second Greek word is used. (For a related Old Testament passage, see 2 Sam. 12:1-4.)
  - It is a slain lamb. Here the Greek word for slain is *sphatto*, and refers to a violent death of some sort. The same word is found in the following passage: "We should love one another. Not as Cain, who was of that wicked one, and slew his brother" (1 John 3:11-12). The word *sphatto* is found only seven times in the New Testament, and four of these usages refer to the death of Christ (Rev. 5:6, 9, 12; 13:8).

- It is an all-powerful lamb. The lamb is pictured as possessing seven horns, which in biblical symbolic language refers to power and authority.
- It is an all-knowing lamb. The lamb is pictured as possessing seven eyes, referring to perfect knowledge and wisdom.
■ He has the characteristics of a lion. John calls him "The Lion of the tribe of Judah, the Root of David"; and so he is. Three key Bible chapters explain this title.
  - In Genesis 49, the dying Jacob predicted that Judah, his fourth son, would be like a lion, and that the later kings of Israel, including Christ himself, would come from his tribe (Gen. 49:8-10).
  - In 2 Samuel 7, God told David (who was of the tribe of Judah) that his kingdom would be eternal and that his household would rule forever (2 Sam. 7:8-17).
  - In Luke 1, the angel Gabriel explained to Mary (who was of the house of David) that her virgin-born son would inherit all the Old Testament promises as found in Genesis 49 and 2 Samuel 7 (Luke 1:30-33). Thus John sees Christ as a Lamb, since he once came to redeem his people. This was his past work. John also sees him as a lion, for he shall come again to reign over his people. This will be his future work. The source of his claim to the earth's scepter is therefore related to his slain Lamb characteristics while the strength of his claim is due to his mighty Lion characteristics.

> b. His action *(Read Rev. 5:7)*
> E. The adoration
> 1. The song *(Read Rev. 5:9-10, 12)*

✶ 5:12
- ■ "*And they sung a new song.*" This is the second hymn of praise, thanking God for his work in redemption.
- ■ "*Worthy is the Lamb.*" The Bible can be aptly summarized by three lamb-centered statements:
  - The statement of Isaac—"*Where is the lamb?*" (Gen. 22:7).
  - The statement of John—"*Behold, the lamb!*" (John 1:29).
  - The statement of the redeemed—"*Worthy is the lamb!*" (Rev. 5:12).

> 2. The singers *(Read Rev. 5:11, 13-14)*

✶ 5:14 Two aspects of this celestial choir can be noted:
- ■ Its diversity—Both angels and humans will participate. Inasmuch as angels had previously been allowed to be present at the creation of the world (Job 38:1, 4, 7) and its redemption (Luke 2:8-14), it is only appropriate that they be permitted to join in this celebration.
- ■ Its universality—We note every creature, saved and unsaved alike, will give honor to the Lamb. This of course in no way suggests that all will be saved. A similar passage is found in *Philippians 2:5-11:* "*Let this mind be in you, which was also in Christ Jesus: who, being in the form of God, thought it not robbery to be equal with God: but made himself of no reputation, and took upon him the form of a servant, and was made in the likeness of men: and being found in fashion as a man, he humbled himself, and became obedient unto death, even the death of the cross. Wherefore God also hath highly exalted him, and given him a name which is above every name: that at the name of Jesus every knee should bow, of things in heaven, and things in earth, and things under the earth; and that every tongue should confess that Jesus Christ is Lord, to the glory of God the Father.*" What these verses are saying is that no creature has a choice concerning whether he or she will acknowledge the glory of Christ, but only how that acknowledgment will be made. He will either be recognized as one's Savior and Lord of all on earth, or as one's judge and Lord of all throughout eternity.

PART THREE: The Wrath of the Lamb Invoked (Rev. 6-19)

> **I. He Pours Out the Seven Seal Judgments (Rev. 6-11)**

✴ "For two breathtaking, soul-inspiring chapters, we have been in heaven. The scroll has changed hands, and the right to judge and rule the world has been placed upon Jesus. Now we must come down from the mount and out of the ivory palaces. Down here, on the rebel planet of earth, the tempo is increasing, passions are rising. Evil men and seducers are waxing worse and worse. Disobedience to parents has grown up into brawling maturity, defying all authority. Men have become inventors of evil things, and their fearful inventions have become Frankenstein monsters, threatening to destroy the globe. The time has come for God to intervene in human affairs, so judgment is given to the Son" (*Exploring Revelation*, p. 110). At the beginning of chapter 4, John took us up from earth to heaven by means of the rapture of Christ. Here in chapter 6 we abruptly return to earth to view the wrath of Christ. The wrath of Jesus is invoked along the following six avenues (in these chapters):

- He pours out the seven seal judgments (6-11).
- He allows the devil and the Antichrist to reign on earth (12-13).
- He pours out the seven vial (bowl) judgments (14-16).
- He destroys the world's religious systems (17).
- He destroys the world's political and economic systems (18).
- He defeats his enemies at Armageddon (19).

   A. First seal *(Read Rev. 6:1-2)*

✴ **6:2** This is doubtless a symbolic picture of the Antichrist as he subdues to himself the ten nations of the revived Roman Empire. This may be thought of as the "cold war" period. We note that he carries no arrow, which may indicate conquest by diplomacy rather than a shooting war.

   B. Second seal *(Read Rev. 6:3-4)*

✴ **6:4** The uneasy peace which the rider on the white horse brings to earth is temporary and counterfeit. The Antichrist promises peace, but only God can actually produce it. As Isaiah would write, *"But the wicked are like the troubled sea, when it cannot rest, whose waters cast up mire and dirt. There is no peace, saith my God, to the wicked"* (Isa. 57:20-21). Now open and bloody hostility breaks out among some of the nations.

   C. Third seal *(Read Rev. 6:5-6)*

✴ **6:6** Dr. Charles Ryrie observes: "The third judgment brings famine to the world. The black horse forebodes death, and the pair of balances bespeaks a careful rationing of food. Normally, a 'penny' (a Roman denarius, a day's wages in Palestine in Jesus' day, Matt. 20:2) would buy eight measures of wheat or twenty-four of barley. Under these famine conditions the same wage will buy only one measure of wheat or three of barley. In other words, there will be one-eighth of the normal supply of food. The phrase 'see thou hurt not the oil and the wine' is an ironic twist in this terrible situation. Apparently luxury food items will not be in short supply, but of course most people will not be able to afford them. This situation will only serve to taunt the populace in their impoverished state" (*Revelation*, pp. 45-46).

   D. Fourth seal *(Read Rev. 6:7-8)*

✴ **6:8**
- The identity of these riders—John calls them "Death" and "Hell," apparently referring to physical and spiritual death. Thus the devil will destroy the bodies and damn the souls of multitudes of unbelievers during this third-seal plague.
- The damage done by these riders—One fourth of all humanity perishes during this plague. It is estimated that during the Second World War one out of 40 persons lost their lives, but this seal judgment alone will claim one out of four persons—nearly one billion human beings. We note the phrase, "with the beasts of the earth." Here John Phillips has

written: "The beasts are closely linked with the pestilence, and this might be a clue. The most destructive creature on earth as far as mankind is concerned, is not the lion or the bear, but the rat. The rat is clever, adaptable, and destructive. If ninety-five percent of the rat population is exterminated in a given area, the rat population will replace itself within a year. It has killed more people than all the wars in history, and makes its home wherever man is found. Rats carry as many as thirty-five diseases. Their fleas carry bubonic plague, which killed a third of the population of Europe in the fourteenth century. Their fleas also carry typhus, which in four centuries has killed an estimated two hundred million people. Beasts, in this passage, are linked not only with pestilence, but with famine. Rats menace human food supplies, which they both devour and contaminate, especially in the more underdeveloped countries which can least afford to suffer loss" (*Exploring Revelation*, p. 116).

> E. Fifth seal (Rev. 6:9-11)
>   1. The altar for the saints *(Read Rev. 6:9)*
>   2. The anger of the saints *(Read Rev. 6:10)*
>   3. The answer to the saints *(Read Rev. 6:11)*

✶ **6:11** Here is religious persecution as never before. These three verses are loaded with theological implications.
  ■ They refute the false doctrine of soul sleep.
  ■ They correct the error of one general resurrection. It is evident that these martyred souls did not receive their glorified bodies at the Rapture, as did the church-age saints. Therefore it can be concluded that these are Old Testament saints who will experience the glorious bodily resurrection after the tribulation (see Rev. 20:4-6).
  ■ They suggest the possibilities of an intermediate body. (See also 2 Cor. 5:1-3.) Dr. John Walvoord writes: "These martyred dead here pictured have not been raised from the dead and have not received their resurrection bodies. Yet it is declared that they are given robes. The fact that they are given robes would almost demand that they have a body of some sort. A robe could not hang upon an immaterial soul or spirit. It is not the kind of body that Christians now have, that is, the body of earth; nor is it the resurrection body of flesh and bones of which Christ spoke after His own resurrection. It is a temporary body suited for their presence in heaven but replaced in turn by their everlasting resurrection body given at the time of Christ's return" (*The Revelation of Jesus Christ*, p. 134).

> F. Sixth seal (Rev. 6:12-17)
>   1. The destruction of earth's surface—*"There was a great earthquake"* (Rev. 6:12). *"And every mountain and island were moved out of their places"* (Rev. 6:14).
>   2. The darkening of earth's skies *(Read Rev. 6:12-14)*

✶ **6:14** As it can be seen, this fearful judgment ushers in:
  ■ The greatest earthquake in history—There have, of course, been hundreds of severe earthquakes in human history.
    ● The earliest recorded was in July of 365 in the Middle East.
    ● The most destructive was in January of 1556 in China. Nearly one million lost their lives. Note: At the end of the tribulation there will be an earthquake even worse than the one occurring here at the time of the sixth seal. (See Rev. 16:18.)
  ■ The greatest cosmic disturbances in history—These may be a result of nuclear war. Hal Lindsey writes: "Do you know what happens in a nuclear explosion? The atmosphere rolls back on itself! It's this tremendous rush of air back into the vacuum that causes much of the destruction of a nuclear explosion. John's words in this verse are a perfect picture of an all-out nuclear exchange. When this happens, John continues, every mountain and island will be jarred from its present position. The whole world will be literally shaken apart!" (*There's a New World Coming*, p. 110).
  ■ The greatest prayer meeting in history—But they prayed for the wrong thing. The only object to protect the sinner from the wrath of the Lamb is the righteousness of the Lamb.

>   3. The despair of earth's sinners
>   a. The classification of these sinners *(Read Rev. 6:15)*
>   b. The consternation of these sinners *(Read Rev. 6:16-17)*
> G. Interlude (Rev. 7:1-17)
>   1. On earth—The sealing of the servants of God (Rev. 7:1-8) *(Read Rev. 7:1)*
>   a. The sealers *(Read Rev. 7:2-3)*
>   b. The sealed *(Read Rev. 7:4)*

✱ **7:4** This passage does not mean that God will save only Jews during the tribulation, for in Revelation 7:9-17, the Bible declares that a great multitude from every nation will be saved. What this chapter does teach, however, is that God will send out 144,000 "Hebrew Billy Sundays" to evangelize the world. This will be a massive number indeed, especially when we consider that there are less than 35,000 missionaries of all persuasions in the world today. Our Lord doubtless had the ministry of the 144,000 in mind when He said, *"And this gospel of the kingdom shall be preached unto all nations; and then shall the end come"* (Matt. 24:14). Judah heads up this list, and not Reuben, the firstborn. Both Dan and Ephraim are missing. Both tribes were guilty of going into idolatry (Judg. 18; 1 Kings 11:26; Hosea 4). The tribes of Levi and Manasseh here take their place. However, both are listed in Ezekiel's millennial temple (Ezek. 48), so they simply forfeit their chance to preach during the tribulation. Some have concluded on the basis of Genesis 49:17 and Jeremiah 8:16 that the Antichrist will come from the tribe of Dan.

>   2. In heaven—The singing of the servants of God (Rev. 7:9-17) *(Read Rev. 7:9, 13-14)*
>   a. Their song *(Read Rev. 7:10)*
>   b. Their support *(Read Rev. 7:11-12)*
>   c. Their service *(Read Rev. 7:15)*
>   d. Their Savior *(Read Rev. 7:17)*
> H. Seventh seal (Rev. 8-11)—The seventh seal actually consists of seven trumpets.
>   1. The silence before the trumpets *(Read Rev. 8:1-5)*

✱ **8:5** This marks the only occasion in recorded history that heaven is silent. There is not the slightest sound or movement.
- The purpose of the silence—During the sixth seal, mankind seemed to weaken for the first time during the tribulation. A merciful and patient God now awaits further repentance, but all to no avail. God takes no pleasure in the death of the wicked (Ezek. 33:11).
- The duration of the silence—It lasted for 30 minutes. The number 30 in the Bible is often associated with mourning. Israel mourned for 30 days over the death of both Aaron (Num. 20:29) and Moses (Deut. 34:8).

>   2. The sounding of the trumpets *(Read Rev. 8:6)*
>   a. First trumpet *(Read Rev. 8:7)*

✱ **8:7** It has been observed that plant life was the first to be created, and it is the first to be destroyed (Gen. 1:11-12).

>   b. Second trumpet *(Read Rev. 8:8-9)*

✱ **8:9** Dr. Herman A. Hoyt writes: "Here we read of a great mountain burning with fire. This may refer to a meteoric mass from the sky falling headlong into the sea, perhaps the Mediterranean Sea. The result is to turn a third part of the sea a blood-red color and bring about the death of a third part of the life in the sea. Death may be caused by the chemical reaction in the water, such as radioactivity following atomic explosion. The third part of ships may be destroyed by the violence of the waters produced by the falling of the mass" (*Revelation*, p. 49).

LESSON 44: THE BOOK OF REVELATION – PART 2

> c. Third trumpet *(Read Rev. 8:10-11)*

✸ **8:11** This star could refer to a meteor containing stifling and bitter gases, which fall on the Alps or some other freshwater source. During the second trumpet a third of the salt water was contaminated. Now a third of earth's fresh water suffers a similar fate. Many species of wormwood grow in Palestine. All species have a strong, bitter taste.

> d. Fourth trumpet (Rev. 8:12-13)
> (1) The fearful darkening *(Read Rev. 8:12)*

✸ **8:12**
- Our Lord may have had this trumpet judgment in mind when he spoke the following words: *"And except those days should be shortened, there should no flesh be saved; but for the elect's sake those days shall be shortened"* (Matt. 24:22). "And there shall be signs in the sun, and in the moon, and in the stars" (Luke 21:25).
- The Old Testament prophecy of Amos is also significant here: *"And it shall come to pass in that day, saith the Lord God, that I will cause the sun to go down at noon, and I will darken the earth in the clear day"* (Amos 8:9).
- It was on the fourth day that God created the sun, moon, and stars (Gen. 1:14-16). They were to be for *"signs, and for seasons, and for days, and years."* After the flood, God promised not to alter this divine arrangement (Gen. 8:22). But in the tribulation, during the fourth trumpet, earth's very light will be limited by judgment.

> (2) The future destruction *(Read Rev. 8:13)*

✸ **8:13** The word "angel" here should be translated "eagle." An eagle is sometimes pictured as God's method of judgment (Deut. 28:49; Hosea 8:1). Thus, even the brute creation will be used by God during the tribulation. This marks the last of three occasions on which a creature speaks in the Bible. (For the other two, see Gen. 3:1-5—a serpent; and Num. 22:28-30—an ass.)

> e. Fifth trumpet (Rev. 9:1-12)—This trumpet unleashes the first hellish invasion of demons upon the earth.

✸ The ninth chapter of Revelation, which contains both fifth and sixth trumpet judgments, may be the most revealing section in all the Bible concerning the subject of demonology. Prior to this, God has already made it known that there are two kinds of unfallen angels. These are the Cherubim (Gen. 3:24; Exod. 25:18-22; Ezek. 10:1-20), and the Seraphim (Isa. 6:1-8). Here he may be describing for us the two kinds of fallen angels.

> (1) Their location *(Read Rev. 9:1-2)*

✸ **9:2**
- Literally, the phrase "bottomless pit" is "shaft of the abyss." The word "shaft" here indicates that there is an entrance from the surface of the earth to the heart of our planet. In this chapter we learn for the first time of a place called the bottomless pit. God mentions it no less than seven times in the book of Revelation (9:1-2, 11; 11:7; 17:8; 20:1-3).
- Some have identified these with the sons of God in Genesis 6:1-2. Here the theory is that these demons attempted sexual relations with women, resulting in immediate confinement in the bottomless pit. We do know that some demons are already chained and others at present have access to the bodies of people.
  - Unchained demons (Luke 4:34; Matt. 8:29; Luke 8:27-31).
  - Chained demons (Jude 6-7; 2 Pet. 2:4; 1 Pet. 3:18-20). Thus another name for this bottomless pit may be the *tartarus* mentioned in the Greek text of 2 Peter 2:4. Here Satan will be confined during the millennium (Rev. 20:3).

> (2) Their leader *(Read Rev. 9:11)*

✷ **9:11** This "fallen star" mentioned in 9:1 seems to be Satan himself. (See also Isa. 14:12; Luke 10:18; 2 Cor. 11:14.) Prior to this time, Christ has held the key to the pit (Rev. 1:18), but now he allows the devil to use it for a specific purpose.

> (3) Their torment *(Read Rev. 9:3-4, 5b)*

✷ **9:5** The pain from the sting of a scorpion, though not generally fatal, is perhaps the most intense that any animal can inflict upon the human body. The insect itself is the most malignant that lives, and its poison is in kind.

> (4) Their duration *(Read Rev. 9:5-6)*

✷ **9:6** Charles Ryrie writes: "Horrible as the torment will be, God will place certain limitations on the activity of these demons. They will be limited as to what they may strike and as to how far they may go and as to how long they may do what they will do. They will not attack the vegetation of the earth (as common locusts do); they may only attack certain men, that is, those who have not the seal of God in their foreheads (the 144,000; cf. 7:3). The wicked will persecute God's servants, the 144,000; but in turn they will be tormented by this plague which God allows. The demon-locusts will also be limited in that they may not kill men, just torment them. Further, the duration of this plague will be five months. The effect of this torment is to drive men to suicide, but they will not be able to die. Although men will prefer death to the agony of living, death will not be possible. Bodies will not sink and drown; poisons and pills will have no effect; and somehow even bullets and knives will not do their intended job" (*Revelation*, p. 62).

> (5) Their description *(Read Rev. 9:7-10)*
> f. Sixth trumpet (Rev. 9:13-21) — This trumpet unleashed the second hellish invasion of demons upon the earth.
> (1) Their four leaders *(Read Rev. 9:13-14)*

✷ **9:14**
- *"Loose the four angels"* — These may function to Satan as the four living creatures do to God (see Rev. 4:6-8).
- *"The great river Euphrates"* — This is where evil began on earth (Zech. 5:8-11; Gen. 3), where false religion began (Gen. 4:3; 10:9-10; 11:4), and where it will come to its end (Rev. 17-18).

> (2) Their mission *(Read Rev. 9:15)*

✷ **9:15** One third of humanity is killed through fire, smoke, and brimstone. One fourth had already been slain by the fourth seal (6:8). This would be approximately one billion. Now one third is killed, meaning another billion die. This invasion is therefore the opposite of the fifth trumpet judgment during which no man was able to die.

> (3) Their number *(Read Rev. 9:16)*

✷ **9:16** By normal standards, this mighty army would occupy a territory one mile wide and 87 miles long.

> (4) Their description *(Read Rev. 9:17)*
> (5) Their torment *(Read Rev. 9:19)*
> (6) Their effect *(Read Rev. 9:20-21)*

✷ **9:21** At this point over one half of the world's population has been wiped out. And what is the response of the survivors? Total unrepentance and intensified rebellion. That very year the F.B.I. reports will probably show a thousand percent increase in murder, drug-related crimes (the word "sorceries" is the Greek *pharmakeion*, from which we get our "pharmacy." It is the Greek word for drugs), sex, felonies, and robbery.

LESSON 44: THE BOOK OF REVELATION – PART 2

> g. Interlude (Rev. 10:1-11:14)—Seven events occur between the sixth and seventh trumpets.
> > (1) The message of the angel of God (Rev. 10:1-7)
> > > (a) The vision *(Read Rev. 10:1-2)*

✱ **10:2**
- *"Another mighty angel"*—This angel may well be Michael the Archangel (see Dan. 12:1). He is probably the same angel referred to in 5:2; 7:2; 8:3; and 18:2.
- *"A little book"*—This is probably the seven-sealed book mentioned in Revelation 5:1.

> > > (b) The voice *(Read Rev. 10:3)*
> > > (c) The veto *(Read Rev. 10:4)*

✱ **10:4** This passage contains the only sealed part of the book of Revelation.

> > > (d) The vow *(Read Rev. 10:5-6)*
> > > (e) The victory *(Read Rev. 10:7)*
> > (2) The mission of the apostle of God *(Read Rev. 10:8-11)*
> > (3) The measuring of the temple of God *(Read Rev. 11:1-2)*

✱ **11:2** Here John is put to work with a nine foot ruler (see Ezek. 40:5), measuring the tribulation temple. He is also to record the identity of its worshipers. God is always interested in those who worship him. However, the outer court was to be left out, *"for it is given unto the Gentiles: and the holy city shall they tread underfoot forty and two months"* (11:2).

> > (4) The ministry of the witnesses of God (Rev. 11:3-6)
> > > (a) The duration involved in their ministry *(Read Rev. 11:3-4)*
> > > (b) The devastation caused by their ministry *(Read Rev. 11:5-6)*

✱ **11:6** Who are these witnesses?
- Some hold that they are Elijah and Enoch—Hebrews 9:27 states that all men are appointed to die, and since these two men did not experience physical death, they will be sent back to witness and eventually to die a martyr's death.
- Some hold that they are Elijah and Moses.
  - Elijah—Because of Malachi 4:5-6, which predicts that God will send Elijah during that great and dreadful day of the Lord. (See also Matt. 17:11.) Because Elijah appeared with Moses on the Mount of Transfiguration to talk with Jesus (Matt. 17:3). Because Elijah's Old Testament ministry of preventing rain for some three years will be repeated by one of the witnesses during the tribulation (1 Kings 17:1; cf. Rev. 11:6).
  - Moses—Because of Jude 9, where we are informed that after the death of Moses, Satan attempted to acquire his dead body, so that God would not be able to use him against the Antichrist during the tribulation. Because Moses' Old Testament ministry of turning water into blood will be repeated by one of the witnesses during the tribulation (Exod. 7:19; cf. Rev. 11:6). Because Moses appeared with Elijah on the Mount of Transfiguration (Matt. 17:3).

> > (5) The martyrdom of the witnesses of God (Rev. 11:7-10)
> > > (a) The person involved *(Read Rev. 11:7)*

✱ **11:7** The Antichrist is finally allowed to kill them. The word "beast" is first mentioned here in 11:7. There are 35 other references to him in Revelation. It should also be noted that he could not kill the witnesses until "they shall have finished their testimony." Satan cannot touch one hair on the head of the most humble saint until God gives him specific permission (see Job. 1:12; 2:6). These two, like Paul, finished their testimonies (2 Tim. 4:7). Contrast this with Belshazzar's sad death (Dan. 5:26-30).

> (b) The place involved *(Read Rev. 11:8)*

✶ **11:8** Their bodies will be on display in Jerusalem (11:8). It is called Sodom because of its immorality, and Egypt because of its worldliness.

> (c) The perversion involved *(Read Rev. 11:9-10)*
> (6) The metamorphosis of the witnesses of God (Rev. 11:11-12)
>   (a) From death to life *(Read Rev. 11:11)*
>   (b) From earth to heaven *(Read Rev. 11:12)*
> (7) The manifestation of the judgment of God *(Read Rev. 11:13)*
> h. Seventh trumpet (Rev. 11:15-19)
>   (1) The proclamation *(Read Rev. 11:15)*
>   (2) The adoration *(Read Rev. 11:16-17)*
>   (3) The vindication *(Read Rev. 11:18-19)*

✶ **11:19** Note the phrase, *"And the temple of God was opened in heaven."* It would appear that an actual tabernacle exists in heaven from this and other verses. (See Isa. 6:1-8; Exod. 25:9, 20; Heb. 8.-2,5; 9:24; Rev. 14:15, 17; 15:5-6, 8; 16:1,17.)

LESSON 45

II. He Allows the Devil to Reign on Earth (Rev. 12-13)
   A. The devil and Israel (Rev. 12)
      1. Satan's former hatred for the Jews (Rev. 12:1-5)
         a. His sin in the beginning when he attempted to steal God's throne—*"And there appeared another wonder in heaven; and behold a great red dragon, having seven heads and ten horns, and seven crowns upon his heads" (Rev. 12:3). "And his tail* [influence] *swept away a third of the stars* [angels] *of heaven, and threw them to the earth" (Rev. 12:4, NASB).*

✱ **12:4a** There is no question concerning the identity of this vicious creature. He is given at least five titles and subtitles in Revelation 12 alone.
- The great red dragon (12:3)—Great, because of his vast power (see Matt. 4:8-9); red, because he was the first murderer (see John 8:44); dragon, because of his viciousness (see 2 Cor. 6:15).
- The old serpent (12:9)—Old, which takes us back to the Garden of Eden (Gen. 3); serpent, which reminds us of the first body he used (Gen. 3).
- The devil (12:9)—One who slanders (see 12:10; also Job 1-2; Zech. 3:1-7; Luke 22:31)
- Satan (12:9)—The adversary (see 1 Pet. 5:8).
- The deceiver of the world (12:9)—Note: He not only deceives men, but angels as well. In 12:4 we are told that his tail "drew [literally, 'pulled down; or 'to drag'; see Acts 14:19 where the same word is used] the third part of the stars of heaven." This is apparently a reference to the number of angels Satan persuaded to join him in his original revolt against God (Isa. 14:12-15; Ezek. 28:11-19).

         b. Satan's sin at Bethlehem, when he attempted to slaughter God's Son *(Read Rev. 12:4)*
         c. Israel's rise—Israel began with Jacob's 12 sons *(Read Rev. 12:1)*

✱ **12:1** Here is the first of four symbolic women in Revelation:
- A suffering woman—Israel (Rev. 12)
- A bloody harlot—The world's religious system (Rev. 17)
- An arrogant queen—The world's economic system (Rev. 18)
- A pure bride—The true church (Rev. 19)

         d. Israel's prize—Israel gave birth to her Messiah *(Read Rev. 12:2)*

✱ **12:2** We note that she cries aloud in her agony. Dr. Herman A. Hoyt writes: "The activity of the woman from the time of Abraham to the birth of Christ is described in verse 2. The present tense of the verses provides a dramatic setting. The woman is continuously with child. She is continually crying ... in the pain of travail. She is continuously experiencing labor to be delivered.... Herein, then, are pictured the experiences of Israel as a nation from the moment she was brought into existence with the call of Abraham until the day Christ was born in Bethlehem. The entire message of the Old Testament from Genesis to Malachi describes what is here set forth in one verse" (*Revelation*, p. 61).

      2. His future hatred for the Jews (Rev. 12:6-17)
         a. His defeat in heaven—Satan is cast out of the very heavenlies during the tribulation *(Read Rev. 12:7-9)*

> (1) Heaven's reaction to his defeat *(Read Rev. 12:10-11)*
> (2) Satan's reaction to his defeat *(Read Rev. 12:12)*
> b. His depravity on earth—Satan now instigates an all-out attempt to destroy Israel.
> (1) The devil's persecution *(Read Rev. 12:13, 15, 17)*

✷ 12:17 This marks the last and most severe anti-Semitic movement in history. A. W. Kac writes: "Next to the survival of the Jews, the most baffling historical phenomenon is the hatred which he has repeatedly encountered among the nations of the earth. This hostility to the Jews, which goes under the name of antisemitism, is as old as Jewish existence. It is endemic; i.e., like many contagious diseases it is always with us to some degree. But under certain circumstances it assumes epidemic proportions and characteristics. It is prevalent wherever Jews reside in sufficiently large numbers to make their neighbors aware of their presence. 'The growth of antisemitism,' Chaim Weizman declares, 'is proportionate to the number of Jews per square kilometre. We carry the germs of antisemitism in our knapsack on our backs'" (*Rebirth of the State of Israel*, p. 306).

Throughout their long history, Satan has made every attempt to exterminate Israel. This he has done by resorting to:
- Enslaving (Exod. 2)
- Drowning (Exod. 14)
- Starving (Exod. 16)
- Tempting (Exod. 32: Num. 14)
- Cursing (Num. 23)
- Capturing (2 Kings 17-24)
- Swallowing (Jonah 2)
- Burning (Dan. 3)
- Devouring (Dan. 6)
- Hanging (Esther 3)

Of course, to all this could be added the gas ovens of Adolph Hitler. But the most vicious attack is yet to come.

> (2) The Lord's protection *(Read Rev. 12:6, 14, 16)*

✷ 12:16 According to Zechariah 13:9 it would seem that at least one third of Israel will remain true to God and be allowed by him to escape into a special hiding place for the duration of the tribulation. We shall now consider the location of this hiding place. While it is not actually specified in Scripture, many Bible students believe that this place will be Petra. This is based on the following three passages:
- Zechariah 14:5: *"And ye shall flee to the valley of the mountains, for the valley of the mountains shall reach unto Azal; yea, ye shall flee ... and the Lord my God shall come, and all the saints with thee."* (The "Azal" mentioned here is thought to be connected with Petra.)
- Isaiah 63:1: *"Who is this that cometh from Edom, with dyed garments from Bozrah?"* The first few verses of Isaiah 63 deal with the second coming of Christ. He comes to Edom (of which Petra is the capital) and Bozrah (a city in Edom) for some reason, many believe to receive his Hebrew remnant who are hiding there.
- Daniel 11:41: *"He shall enter also into the glorious land, and many countries shall be overthrown; but these shall escape out of his hand, even Edom."* Thus for some reason the land of Edom will not be allowed to fall into the hands of the Antichrist. It is assumed by some that the reason is to protect the remnant. Many years ago the noted Bible scholar W. E. Blackstone, on the basis of these verses, hid thousands of copies of the New Testament in and around the caves and rocks of Petra. He felt that someday the terrified survivors of the Antichrist's bloodbath will welcome the opportunity to read God's Word, preferring it even over the Dow-Jones stock average and the *Wall Street Journal*. Petra has been called "the rainbow city," and once had 267,000 inhabitants. It was a large market center at the junction of a great caravan route. The city is inaccessible except through the gorge or canyon in the mountains, which is wide enough for only two horses abreast. The perpendicular walls of the gorge are from 400 to 700 feet high and are brilliant in splendor, displaying every

color of the rainbow. The old buildings, cut from the solid rock of the mountain, still stand. A clear spring bubbles over rose-red rocks. Wild figs grow on the banks. Everything awaits Israel.

> B. The devil and the world (Rev. 13)
>   1. His false son, the Antichrist (Rev. 13:1-10)
>   a. The description of the Antichrist *(Rev. 13:1-2)*

✱ **13:2a**
- The frightful and vicious individual described by John here is given various names and titles in the Scriptures. He is called:
  - The Antichrist
  - The man of sin (2 Thess. 2:8)
  - The son of perdition (2 Thess. 2:8)
  - The wicked one (2 Thess. 2:8)
  - The willful king (Dan. 11:36)
  - The beast—This title is found 36 times in the book of Revelation.
  - The little horn (Dan. 7:8)
  - The seven heads and ten horns may be a political reference to the Antichrist's rise to power. Many believe he will proceed from a ten-dictatorship confederation which will come into existence during the tribulation. These dictators are referred to as "ten horns" in Daniel 7:7; Revelation 12:3; 13:1; 17:7, 12. In his rise to power he will defeat three of these dictators (Dan. 7:8, 24). This ten-horned confederation is the revived Roman Empire. This is derived from the fact that the most important prophetic details concerning the old Roman Empire in Daniel 2:40-44 are still unfulfilled.
- Both Daniel and John write concerning the Antichrist's personal characteristics:
  - He will be an intellectual genius (Dan. 8:23).
  - He will be an oratorical genius (Dan. 11:36).
  - He will be a political genius (Rev. 17:11-12).
  - He will be a commercial genius (Rev. 13:16-17; Dan. 11:43).
  - He will be a military genius (Rev. 6:2; 13:2).
  - He will be a religious genius (Rev. 13:8; 2 Thess. 2:4).

>   b. The authority of the Antichrist *(Read Rev. 13:2)*

✱ **13:2b**
- He begins by controlling the Western power bloc (Rev. 17:12).
- He makes a seven-year covenant with Israel but breaks it after three and a half years (Dan. 9:27). There is ample scriptural evidence to show that the Antichrist will allow (and perhaps even encourage) the building of the temple and the rendering of its sacrifices during the tribulation. (See Dan. 9:27; Matt. 24:15; 2 Thess. 2:4; Rev. 13:14-15; 11:2.)
- He gains absolute control over the Middle East after the Russian invasion (Ezek. 38-39).
- He attempts to destroy all of Israel (Rev. 12).
- He destroys the false religious system, so that he may rule unhindered (Rev. 17:16-17).
- He thereupon sets himself up as God (Dan. 11:36; 2 Thess. 2:4-11; Rev. 13:5).
- He briefly rules over all nations (Psa. 2; Dan. 11:36; Rev. 13:16).
- He is utterly crushed by the Lord Jesus Christ at the battle of Armageddon (Rev. 19).
- He is the first creature to be thrown into the lake of fire (Rev. 19:20).

>   c. The possible resurrection of the Antichrist *(Read Rev. 13:3)*
>   d. The worship of the Antichrist *(Read Rev. 13:4, 8)*

LESSON 45: THE BOOK OF REVELATION – PART 3

> e. The power of the Antichrist
>   (1) Its scope *(Read Rev. 13:7)*
>   (2) Its duration *(Read Rev. 13:5b)*
> f. The blasphemy of the Antichrist *(Rev. 13:5a, 6)*
> 2. His unholy spirit, the false prophet (Rev. 13:11-18)
>   a. His militancy *(Rev. 13:11-12)*

★ 13:12 Who is this second beast of Revelation 13 who is also called on three later occasions "the false prophet" (Rev. 16:13; 19:20; 20:10)? Some believe he will be a Jew (while the Antichrist will be a Gentile), and that he will head up the apostate church.

> b. His mission *(Read Rev. 13:12)*
> c. His miracles
>   (1) The deception *(Read Rev. 13:13)*
>   (2) The deceived *(Read Rev. 13:14)*
> d. His mark
>   (1) The nature of this mark *(Read Rev. 13:15-17)*
>   (2) The number of this mark *(Read Rev. 13:18)*

★ 13:18 To understand this passage requires some basic information concerning the world 2,000 years ago. When the Apostle John wrote these words an identification system known as Gematria was widely practiced. Under this arrangement, the Greek, Latin, and Hebrew alphabetical letters also represented a specific number. We do not have this system in the English alphabet, but if we did, the letter A might stand for the number six, B for 12, C for 18, etc. Of course, all those speaking the language where this practice is observed would have to agree upon the numerical equivalent of each letter. With this in mind, what John is saying here is that the total number of the name used by the Antichrist during the tribulation will equal 666. The figure will then become all important in matters of buying, selling, etc. What does this mean? It seems to suggest that at the beginning of the tribulation the world will adopt some sort of letter-numbering system.

> **III. He Pours Out the Seven Vial Judgments (Rev. 14-16)**
>   A. Those events preceding the vial judgments (Rev. 14-15)
>   1. The song of the witnesses of God *(Read Rev. 14:1-5)*

★ 14:3 This group is the same as mentioned in chapter 7. There they are redeemed. Here they are raptured. And note-not one is missing. J. Vernon McGee writes: "It is clear from Chapter 13 that this is the darkest day and the most horrible hour in history. It is truly hell's holiday. Every thoughtful mind must inevitably ask the question— How did God's people fare during this period? Could they make it through to the end with overwhelming odds against them? The Shepherd who began with 144,000 sheep is now identified with them as a Lamb with 144,000. He did not lose one" (*Reveling Through Revelation*, p. 21).

>   2. The messages of the angels of God (Rev. 14:6-12)
>   a. First message *(Read Rev. 14:7)*
>   b. Second message *(Read Rev. 14:8)*
>   c. Third message
>   (1) Concerning the people who were worshiping the beast *(Read Rev. 14:9)*
>   (2) Concerning the punishment for worshipping the beast *(Read Rev. 14:10-11)*

★ 14:11 Here is the last hellfire-and-brimstone message that will ever be preached to the unsaved, and it is delivered not by a Jonathan Edwards or a Billy Sunday, but by an angel. Apparently no one responds to the invitation. Here God will pour out his undiluted wrath, something he has done once before upon Christ at Calvary. How tragic that Christ once drank this same cup for the very unrepentant sinners who are now forced to drink it again.

> 3. The assurance of the Spirit of God *(Read Rev. 14:13)*

★ **14:13** It has been rightly observed that this world is the only heaven the unsaved will ever know, and the only hell the saved will ever experience.

> 4. The reaping of the harvest of God (Rev. 14:14-20)
>   a. The Judge (the Lord Jesus Christ, assisted by the angels) *(Read Rev. 14:14)*
>   b. The judged *(Read Rev. 14:16,19-20)*

★ **14:20** This is the first of three references in Revelation to the Battle of Armageddon. It is mentioned again in 16:13-16 and 19:17-19. An overview of this battle is given under the final reference.

> 5. The praise of the victors of God *(Read Rev. 15:1-4)*

★ **15:4** There are two songs mentioned here, the song of Moses and the song of the Lamb. Note the contrast between the two: The song of Moses was sung beside the Red Sea (Exod. 15); the song of the Lamb will be sung beside the crystal sea. The song of Moses was sung over Egypt; the song of the Lamb will be sung over Babylon. The song of Moses described how God brought his people out; the song of the Lamb will describe how God brings his people in. The song of Moses was Scripture's first song; the song of the Lamb will be Scripture's last song.

> 6. The events in the temple of God (Rev. 15:5-8)
>   a. The guardians of the temple *(Read Rev. 15:5-7)*
>   b. The glory in the temple *(Read Rev. 15:8)*
> B. Those events accompanying the vial judgments (Rev. 16) *(Read Rev. 15:1; 16:1)*
>   1. First vial judgment *(Read Rev. 16:2)*
>   2. Second vial judgment *(Read Rev. 16:3)*
>   3. Third vial judgment (Rev. 16:4-7)
>   a. The action *(Read Rev. 16:4)*
>   b. The reaction *(Read Rev. 16:5-6)*

★ **16:6** Two significant things may be noted in these verses:
- This third vial judgment is, among other things, an answer to the cry of the martyrs under the altar at the beginning of the tribulation. Their prayer at that time was, *"How long, O Lord, holy and true, dost thou not judge and avenge our blood on them that dwell on the earth?"* (Rev. 6:10).
- These verses indicate that God has assigned a special angel as superintendent on earth's waterworks. When we compare this with Revelation 7:1, where we are told that four other angels control the world's winds, we realize that even during the hellishness of the tribulation, this world is still controlled by God.

> 4. Fourth vial judgment (Rev. 16:8-9)
>   a. The action *(Read Rev. 16:8)*
>   b. The reaction *(Read Rev. 16:9)*

★ **16:9** Perhaps the two most illuminating passages in Scripture about man's total depravity can be found in Revelation 9:20-21 and 16:9. Both sections deal with the world's attitude toward God during the tribulation. What do these verses prove? They prove that in spite of horrible wars, of terrible famines, of darkened skies, of raging fires, of bloody seas, of stinging locusts, of demonic persecutions, of mighty earthquakes, of falling stars, and of cancerous sores, sinful mankind still will not repent.

> 5. Fifth vial judgment (Rev. 16:10-11)
>   a. The action *(Read Rev. 16:10)*
>   b. The reaction *(Read Rev. 16:11)*

✶ **16:11** This plague, poured out upon *"the seat of the beast"* (literally, his "throne"), will apparently concentrate itself upon the ten nations of the revived Roman Empire. Again we read those tragic words *"and repented not of their deeds."*

> 6. Sixth vial judgment (Rev. 16:12-16)
>   a. The what of this judgment *(Read Rev. 16:12)*

✶ **16:12** Here the God of heaven employs psychological warfare upon his enemies, conditioning them to gather themselves together in the near future at Armageddon. The Euphrates River is 1,800 miles long and in some places 3,600 feet wide. It is 30 feet deep. This river has been the dividing line between western and eastern civilization since the dawn of history. It served as the eastern border of the Old Roman Empire. Thus, the Euphrates becomes both the cradle and grave of man's civilization. Here the first godless city (Enoch, built by Cain; see Gen. 4:16-17) went up, and here the last rebellious city will be constructed (Babylon, built by the Antichrist; see Rev. 18).

> b. The who of this judgment *(Read Rev. 16:13)*
> c. The why of this judgment *(Read Rev. 16:14, 16)*
> d. The warning of this judgment *(Read Rev. 16:15)*
> 7. Seventh vial judgment (Rev. 16:17-21) *(Read Rev. 16:17)*
>   a. History's greatest earthquake *(Read Rev. 16:18-20)*
>   b. History's greatest hailstorm *(Read Rev. 16:21)*

✶ **16:21** The seventh and final vial judgment brings about two frightening events:
- The world's greatest earthquake takes place. The intensity of an earthquake is measured on an instrument called a Richter scale. The greatest magnitude ever recorded so far has been 8.9. The greatest loss of life due to an earthquake occurred on January 23, 1556, in Shensi Province, China, and killed some 830,000 people. However, that earthquake will be but a mild tremor compared to the tribulation earthquake, which, we are told, will level all the great cities of the world.
- The world's greatest shower of hailstones comes crashing down on mankind. These gigantic icy chunks will weigh up to 125 pounds apiece.

> **IV. He Destroys the World's Religious Systems (Rev. 17)**

✶ This brutal, bloody, and blasphemous harlot is none other than the universal false church, the wicked wife of Satan. God had no sooner begun his blessed work in preparing for himself a people than the devil did likewise. In fact, the first baby to be born on this earth later became Satan's original convert. (See Gen. 4:8; 1 John 3:12.) We shall now consider the historical and future activities of this perverted prostitute.

> A. The history of this harlot (Rev. 17:1-6) *(Read Rev. 17:1, 3)*
>   1. Depraved with the filth of hell *(Read Rev. 17:2, 5)*
>   2. Decked with the wealth of the world *(Read Rev. 17:4)*
>   3. Drunken with the blood of saints *(Read Rev. 17:6)*

★ 17:6
- Satan's church began officially at the Tower of Babel in Genesis 11:1-9, nearly 24 centuries B.C. Here, in the fertile plain of Shinar, probably very close to the original Garden of Eden, the first spade of dirt was turned for the purpose of devil-worship.
- The first full-time minister of Satan was Nimrod, Noah's wicked and apostate grandson (Gen. 10:8-10).
- Secular history and tradition tell us that Nimrod married a woman who was as evil and demonic as himself. Her name was Semerimus. Knowing God's promise of a future Savior (Gen. 3:15), Semerimus brazenly claimed that Tammuz, her first son, fulfilled this prophecy.
- Semerimus thereupon instituted a religious system which made both her and her son the objects of divine worship. She herself became the first high priestess. Thus began the mother-child cult which later spread all over the world. The city of Babylon was the seat of Satan worship until it fell, in 539 B.C., to the Persians.
  - From Babylon it spread to Phoenicia under the name of Ashteroth and Tammuz.
  - From Phoenicia it traveled to Pergamos in Asia Minor. This is the reason for John's admonition to the church at Pergamos in the book of Revelation: *"I know thy works, and where thou dwellest, even where Satan's seat is"* (Rev. 2:13).
  - In Egypt the mother-child cult was known as Isia and Horus.
  - In Greece it became Aphrodite and Eros.
  - In Rome this pair was worshiped as Venus and Cupid.
  - In China it became known as Mother Shing Moo and her child. Dr. J. Dwight Pentecost writes: "Several years ago I visited an archaeological museum in Mexico City. A recent find had just been put on display which Mexican archaeologists had authenticated as belonging to the period about 200 years before Christ. The object was the center of religious worship among some of the early Indians in Mexico. To my amazement, it was an image of a mother with a child in her arms. This Babylonian religion spread abroad to become the religion of the world" (*Prophecy for Today*, p. 133).
- What was the teaching of Semerimus' satanic church?
  - That Semerimus herself was the way to God—She actually adopted the title "Queen of Heaven."
  - That she alone could administer salvation to the sinner through various sacraments, such as the sprinkling of holy water.
  - That her son Tammuz was tragically slain by a wild boar during a hunting trip.
  - That he was, however, resurrected from the dead 40 days later. Thus, each year afterward, the temple virgins of this cult would enter a 40-day fast as a memorial to Tammuz's death and resurrection.
  - After the 40-day fast, a joyful feast called Ishtar took place. At this feast colored eggs were exchanged and eaten as a symbol of the resurrection. An evergreen tree was displayed and a yule log was burned. Finally, hot cakes marked with the letter "T" (to remind everybody of Tammuz) were baked and eaten.
- About 2000 B.C., God called Abraham away from all this (see Josh. 24:2-3) and led him into the Promised Land. But by the ninth century B.C., Israel had returned to this devil-worship under the influence of wicked Jezebel (1 Kings 16:30-33). At this time the cult was worshiped under the name of Baal.
- Both Ezekiel and Jeremiah warned against this hellish thing. *"Then he brought me to the door of the gate of the Lord's house which was toward the north; and behold, there sat women weeping for Tammuz"* (Ezek. 8:14). *"The children gather wood, and the fathers kindle the fire, and the women knead their dough, to make cakes to the queen of heaven ... to burn incense to the queen of heaven, and to pour out drink offerings unto her"* (Jer. 7:18; 44:25).
- By the time of Christ, this cult had so influenced Roman life that the Caesars were not only crowned as emperors of Rome, but also bore the title Pontifex Maximus, meaning "high priest." They were high priests of the Babylonian satanic church.

> B. The future of this harlot (Rev. 17:7-18)
> 1. To be teamed up (at first) with the Antichrist (Rev. 17:7-9) *(Read Rev. 17:7)*—It is thought that both the religious system (the mystery Babylon, v. 5), and the political system (the 10 kings of v. 12) join up with the Antichrist (the beast of vv. 7-8, 11-13) at the beginning of the tribulation *(Read Rev. 17:13)*.
> 2. To be torn up (at last) by the Antichrist *(Read Rev. 17:15-17)*

✷ **17:17** In essence, the false church lends all her evil strength to elevate the Antichrist during the first part of the tribulation. For awhile she flourishes, luxuriating in surpassing wealth and opulence. But suddenly things change drastically. The Antichrist suddenly turns on her. The probable reason for all this is that after she has put the Antichrist into power, the harlot then attempts to control him. History gives us many examples of various religious systems attempting to control kings and rulers. But the Antichrist won't bow. He will turn on her, destroy her buildings, burn her "holy" books, and murder her priests. One of the most ironical turn of events in all history will be the destruction of the false church. For this evil organization will meet its doom not at the hands of Gabriel, or the Father, or the Son, or the Spirit, but the Antichrist.

V. He Destroys the World's Political and Economic Systems (Rev. 18).

✷ Dr. J. Vernon McGee writes: "In chapters 17 and 18 two Babylons are brought before us. The Babylon of chapter 17 is ecclesiastical. The Babylon of chapter 18 is economic. The first is religious the apostate church. The second is political and commercial. The apostate church is hated by the kings of the earth (Rev. 17:16); the commercial center is loved by the kings of the earth (Rev. 18:9). The apostate church is destoyed by the kings of the earth; political Babylon is destroyed by the judgment of God (verses 5, 8). Obviously, mystery Babylon is destroyed first-in the midst of the Great Tribulation; while commercial Babylon is destroyed at the Second Coming of Christ. These two Babylons are not one and the same city" (*Reveling Through Revelation*, p. 58). It is possible that a literal city will become the headquarters for both of these systems, probably built by the Antichrist himself. *"What city is like unto this great city!" (Rev. 18:18).*

✷ **18:18** Charles Ryrie writes: "Whether the city will be rebuilt once again on the Euphrates is a matter of debate. Nevertheless, the name is used for more than a city in these chapters (17-18); it also stands for a system. This is much the same as the way Americans speak of Wall Street or Madison Avenue. They are actual streets, but they also stand for the financial or advertising enterprises" (*Revelation*, p. 100).

> A. The designation of the city *(Read Rev. 18:10)*—A literal interpretation of this chapter would say ancient Babylon will be rebuilt by the Antichrist during the tribulation and become his headquarters.
> B. The denunciation of the city *(Read Rev. 18:1-2, 5, 21)*
> C. The degeneration of this city
>   1. Godless materialism—*"Cargoes of gold and silver and precious stones and pearls and fine linen and purple and silk and scarlet, and every kind of citron wood and every article of ivory and every article made from very costly wood and bronze and iron and marble, and cinnamon and spice and incense and perfume and frankincense and wine and olive oil and fine flour and wheat and cattle and sheep, and cargoes of horses and chariots" (Rev. 18:12-13, NASB).*
>   2. Arrogance and pride *(Read Rev. 18:7)*
>   3. Immorality *(Read Rev. 18:3)*
>   4. Demonism and false religions *(Read Rev. 18:2)*
>   5. Drug peddling—*"For by thy sorceries were all nations deceived" (Rev. 18:23b)*
>   6. Slavery—*"And slaves, and souls of men" (Rev. 18:13b)*
>   7. Blood shedding *(Read Rev. 18:24)*
> D. The devastation of the city
>   1. The source of its destruction—God himself. *"For strong is the Lord God who judgeth her" (Rev. 18:8b). "For God hath avenged ... her" (Rev. 18:20b).*
>   2. The means of its destruction—Possibly by nuclear energy. This is suggested because of the quickness and nature of the destruction *(Read Rev. 18:8-10, 17, 19).*
>   3. The reaction to its destruction
>   a. Despair on earth *(Read Rev. 18:11, 19)*
>   b. Delight in heaven *(Read Rev. 18:20)*

VI. He Defeats His Enemies at Armageddon (Rev. 19).
   A. The celebration in heaven (Rev. 19:1-10)
      1. Praising God for his wrath upon a cruel whore *(Read Rev. 19:1-5)*
      2. Praising God for his wedding to a chaste wife *(Read Rev. 19:6-10)*

✱ **19:9** There are three events in the tribulation which cause all of heaven to rejoice.
   ■ When Satan is cast out (Rev. 12:12)
   ■ When Babylon is destroyed (Rev. 18:20)
   ■ When the Lamb is married to the church (Rev. 19:7) This glorious event is celebrated by the usage of heaven's greatest praise word. That word is *Alleluia* (Halleluja)! Nowhere else in the New Testament can it be found. The Holy Spirit has reserved it for this occasion. (In the Old Testament it appears some 24 times in the Psalms.) Heaven now celebrates the Lamb's victory over the harlot, and his marriage to the bride. We are told that *"to her was granted that she should be arrayed in fine linen, clean and white: for the fine linen is the righteousness of saints"* (19:8).

   B. The confrontation on earth (Rev. 19:11-21)
      1. The appearance of heaven's King *(Read Rev. 19:11)*
      2. The attire of heaven's King *(Read Rev. 19:12-13, 16)*
      3. The armies of heaven's King *(Read Rev. 19:14)*
      4. The action of heaven's King
         a. Armageddon—The victory over Satan's horseman *(Read Rev. 19:15, 17-18, 21)*

✱ **19:21** Dr. Herman A. Hoyt aptly describes Armageddon: "The staggering dimensions of this conflict can scarcely be conceived by man. The battlefield will stretch from Megiddo on the north (Zech. 12:11; Rev. 16:16) to Edom on the south (Isa. 34:5-6; 63:1), a distance of sixteen hundred furlongs-approximately two hundred miles. It will reach from the Mediterranean Sea on the west to the hills of Moab on the east, a distance of almost one hundred miles. It will include the Valley of Jehoshaphat (Joel 3:2, 12) and the Plains of Esdraelon. At the center of the entire area will be the city of Jerusalem (Zech. 14:1-2). Into this area the multiplied millions of men, doubtless approaching 400 million, will be crowded for the final holocaust of humanity. The kings with their armies will come from the north and the south, from the east and from the west.... In the most dramatic sense this will be the 'Valley of decision' for humanity (Joel 3:14) and the great winepress into which will be poured the fierceness of the wrath of Almighty God (Rev. 19:15)" (*The End of Times*, p. 163).

         b. Gehenna—The victory over Satan's henchman *(Read Rev. 19:19-20)*

PART FOUR: The Reign of the Lamb Instituted (Rev. 20)

   I. The Great Chain (Rev. 20:1-3)
      A. The prisoner *(Read Rev. 20:1-2)*
      B. The prison *(Read Rev. 20:3)*
   II. The Great Reign
      A. The resurrection of the just *(Read Rev. 20:5-6)*
      B. The rule of the just *(Read Rev. 20:4)*
   III. The Great Revolt
      A. The adversary *(Read Rev. 20:7)*
      B. The arrogance *(Read Rev. 20:8)*

✱ **20:8** Dr. J. Dwight Pentecost quotes F. C. Jennings, who writes: "Has human nature changed, at least apart from sovereign grace? Is the carnal mind at last at friendship with God? Have a thousand years of absolute power and absolute benevolence, both in unchecked activity, done away with all war forever and forever? These questions must be marked by a practical test. Let Satan be loosed once more from his prison. Let him range once more earth's smiling fields that he knew of old. He saw them last soaked with blood and flooded with tears, the evidence and accompaniments of his own reign; he sees them now 'laughing with abundance'... But as he pursues his way further from Jerusalem, the center of this blessedness, these tokens become fainter, until, in the far off 'corner of the earth', they cease altogether, for he finds myriads who have instinctively shrunk from close contact with that holy center, and are not unprepared once more to be deceived" (*Things to Come*, p. 549).

   C. The attack *(Read Rev. 20:9)*
   D. The abyss *(Read Rev. 20:10)*
IV. The Great Throne (Rev. 20:11-15)
   A. The Judge *(Read Rev. 20:11)*
   B. The judged *(Read Rev. 20:12-13)*
   C. The judgment *(Read Rev. 20:14-15)*

PART FIVE: The Wife of the Lamb Introduced (Rev. 21-22)

"And there came unto me one of the seven angels which had the seven vials full of the seven last plagues, and talked with me, saying, Come hither, I will shew thee the bride, the Lamb's wife" (Rev. 21:9).

   I. Her Habitation—The Fabulous City (Rev. 21:1-22:5) *(Read Rev. 21:1-4, 10-11, 18)*
   A. Its purity *(Read Rev. 21:8, 27)*
   B. Its wall *(Read Rev. 21:12, 14, 17-18)*
   C. Its gates *(Read Rev. 21:12-13, 21, 25)*
   D. Its size and shape *(Read Rev. 21:15-16)*

✱ **21:16** According to our present-day measurements, this city would be roughly 1,500 miles long, wide, and high. If placed in America, it would reach from New York City to Denver, Colorado, and from Canada to Florida.

   E. Its foundation—Twelve foundations *(Read Rev. 21:19)*
   F. Its street *(Read Rev. 21:21)*
   G. Its light source *(Read Rev. 21:23; 22:5)*
   H. Its river *(Read Rev. 22:1)*
   I. Its Tree of Life *(Read Rev. 22:2)*
   J. Its relationship to the earth *(Read Rev. 21:24, 26)*
   K. Its worship center *(Read Rev. 21:22)*
   L. Its activities—What will we do in heaven?
      1. Learning about Christ— *"And they shall see his face; and his name shall be in their foreheads"* (Rev. 22:4).
      2. Working for Christ— *"And his servants shall serve him"* (Rev. 22:3).
      3. Reigning with Christ— *"And they shall reign for ever and ever"* (Rev. 22:5).
II. Her Husband, the Faithful Spouse (Rev. 22:6-21)
   A. The blessings of the wife
      1. The comfort from Christ
         a. He promises to return *(Read Rev. 22:12)*
         b. He promises to reward *(Read Rev. 22:12, 14)*

2. The character of Christ *(Read Rev. 22:13,16)*
3. The counsel of Christ *(Read Rev. 22:10)*
4. The concern of Christ
    a. His concern about the water of life *(Read Rev. 22:17)*
    b. His concern about the Word of Life
        (1) That we not add to it *(Read Rev. 22:18)*
        (2) That we not take from it *(Read Rev. 22:19)*
B. The blunders of the writer—John the apostle is so enthralled by these glorious sights and sounds he has been writing about that on two occasions he attempts to worship the attending angel. Each time he is rebuked.
    1. First occasion *(Read Rev. 19:10)*
    2. Second occasion *(Read Rev. 22:8-9)*

CPSIA information can be obtained at www.ICGtesting.com
Printed in the USA
BVOW06s0415111013

333434BV00002B/3/P